THE CUSTODIANS

"Beyond Abduction"

By
Dolores Cannon

For permission, or serialization, condensation, adaptations, or for our catalog of other publications, write to Ozark Mountain Publishing, Inc., P.O. Box 754, Huntsville, AR 72740 Attn.: Permission Department.

Library of Congress Cataloging-in-Publication Data
Cannon, Dolores 1931 - 2014
The Custodians by Dolores Cannon
     Investigations through hypnotherapy of suspected alien abduction cases. Twelve years of UFO extraterrestrial research dating from 1986 to 1998 conducted by Dolores Cannon.

1. UFOs. 2. Extraterrestrials. 3. Hypnosis.
I. Cannon, Dolores, 1931-2014 II. UFO/Extraterrestrials III. Title

Library of Congress Catalog Card Number: 98 - 068365
ISBN: 1-886940-04-8

Cover Design: Victoria Cooper Art
Book Set in: Times New Roman
Book Design: Nancy Vernon
Published By

OZARK
MOUNTAIN
PUBLISHING

P.O. Box 754
Huntsville, AR 72740
WWW.OZARKMT.COM
Printed in the United States of America

TWO ROADS

DIVERGE IN A WOOD,

AND I . . .

I TOOK THE ONE

LESS TRAVELED BY

AND THAT

HAS MADE ALL THE

DIFFERENCE.

ROBERT FROST (1875-1963)

Books by Dolores Cannon

Conversations with Nostradamus, Volume I
Conversations with Nostradamus, Volume II
Conversations with Nostradamus, Volume III
Jesus and the Essenes
They Walked with Jesus
Between Death and Life
(Formerly titled Conversations with a Spirit)
A Soul Remembers Hiroshima
Keepers of the Garden
The Legend of Starcrash
Legacy from the Stars
The Convoluted Universe 1, 2, 3, 4, 5
Five Lives Remembered
The Three Waves of Volunteers and the New Earth
The Search for Hidden Sacred Knowledge
A Very Special Friend
Horns of the Goddess

For more information about any of the above titles, or other titles in
our catalog, write or visit our web site.

Ozark Mountain Publishing, Inc.
PO Box 754
Huntsville, AR 72740

WWW.OZARKMT.COM

Wholesale Inquiries Welcome

Table of Contents

SECTION

ONE

The Custodians

CHAPTER 1
A CHANGE OF DIRECTION

When I first began to work in regressive hypnosis and past-life therapy in 1979 I never imagined the unusual places and situations that road would take me. Over the ensuing years it has taken me into some strange byways. I have had some incredible adventures, met some fascinating people from the shadow land of the past and retrieved valuable information that was thought to have been lost forever. It was brought to the light of day by the incredible practice of regressive hypnosis techniques. My time was devoted exclusively to exploring the past, and writing books about my discoveries. My insatiable curiosity, my ravenous desire for research, and the craving for knowledge swept me up and carried me along on a constant search. I was not concerned with hypnosis as applied to present day situations, unless it could be used to solve a person's problems in life. Problems which arose from phobias or health problems caused by the effects of a past life, or karmic connections that carried over and were affecting present day family relationships. I only used the standard form of hypnosis, which deals with the understanding and control of habits (smoking and overeating, etc.) if it was incorporated with past life regression. The technique I developed automatically put the subject into a past life situation. Thus, I did not concentrate on their present life.

All of this changed when I was inadvertently introduced to the phenomenon of UFO abduction experiences. My adventures took a totally different and unexpected direction. Doors opened and I was allowed glimpses of a world that others thought should be left shrouded in the murky darkness of the unknown. Some say it is better not to probe into things that our human mind is probably incapable of understanding. But if knowledge and understanding are there I knew I would have to search and ask my inexhaustible questions. Any new avenue of research always presents a challenge to me, and it is a challenge that I cannot ignore. But my entry into *this* field of research deviated from my normal course and would require altering my technique and adapting to new circumstances.

I have always had an interest in UFOs, so-called "flying saucers." I have read much of the literature dealing with the phenomenon, and was most impressed by the Betty and Barney Hill case when it was first introduced in the 1960's (*The Interrupted Journey*). This was the first so-called "abduction" case. There were many things in that report that convinced me that the Hills had a true experience. For example, the apparent telepathic communication and the non-hostile intent of the aliens seemed to me perfectly plausible. I also read what the critics had to say about the strange events in our skies that would not quietly disappear. After weighing the pros and the cons I was privately convinced there was something real occurring that could not be explained by the rational, logical thinking of the skeptics. Maybe the entire subject was never intended to be logical and simply explained. Maybe the aliens' tactics were intended to do the very thing they ended up doing: making man wonder and consider the impossible.

Even as a teenager in the late 1940s and early 1950s when the first "flying saucer" accounts were made public, and were met generally by public ridicule, I kept thinking there might be something to it. Over the years I maintained a passive interest by reading and keeping up on the latest developments. But I never once thought I would be taking an active part in the research, and end up communicating directly with aliens from another sphere of existence. Maybe my years of work in the bizarre had carefully prepared me for the eventual encounter, because when it happened I was not astonished, disbelieving or frightened. I was curious. This has become my trademark, "curiosity," and it was to serve me well when it came to extracting information.

I was introduced to the area of UFO research and investigation in May 1985. My friend, Mildred Higgins, invited me to attend a State meeting with members of MUFON (Mutual UFO Network), to be held at her home in Fayetteville, Arkansas. Mildred was Assistant Director for the state of Arkansas. She knew about my interest in the strange and unusual, and thought I might like to meet some of the investigators and other interested people. Even though it was not in my field of hypnotic past life regression I thought it would be interesting to ask questions about some of the UFO cases I had read about.

At the meeting I learned that MUFON is the largest and most respected of UFO investigative organizations and has members worldwide. Since I suspected most of the people at the meeting would be scientifically oriented, I thought it best not to mention my work. It was still considered by many to be in the realm of the absurd, and I take my research too seriously to open myself up to ridicule. At that time my work was carried on in private and few knew what I was exploring.

Walt Andrus, the international director of MUFON, was present, and I found him to be a talkative and demonstrative man who seemingly had the facts of any UFO case filed in his memory for instant recall. I was impressed by his knowledge of the cases, many of which he had personally investigated.

Another man, who was to have a profound effect upon my future connection with UFOs, was not impressive upon first meeting. Lucius Farish was so quiet the average person would not have noticed him. He listened intently and seemed to be absorbing information like a sponge. I now know that he learns more this way than by being in the center stage. He publishes the monthly "UFO News clipping Service," and has all the latest UFO information from all over the world instantly at his fingertips.

Before this meeting was over I had become more comfortable with the people there, and disclosed that I was a hypnotist working in the realm of past-life research. I expected them to dismiss me, because this was definitely not what would be considered a "scientific" approach. But to my surprise Walt said hypnosis could be a valuable tool, and any tool that helped to disclose information would surely be welcomed.

After the meeting I set up communication with Lucius Farish. He was supportive of my work and did not ridicule, as I had feared. A year passed before my first encounter with the realm of UFO hypnotic research. About the time this happened Whitley Strieber's book *Communion* burst upon the scene. Budd Hopkin's book *Missing Time* had been out for a while, but I was too involved with my own work to read either of these. By coincidence, in May 1986, my agent gave me a copy of Strieber's book and suggested that I read it, since it contained accounts of hypnotic regression concerning UFOs. At the same time Lucius (or Lou, as he is known to friends) called to tell me there would be another annual meeting at the Higgin's house in Fayetteville. He had been contacted by a woman who thought she had been abducted by aliens and wanted to have a hypnotic regression. He wanted to know if I would conduct it. Although I had no experience in this realm, he thought I could handle it. After all, it was rare to find anyone who *had* had experience with this type of thing (especially in Arkansas). He said most psychiatrists and psychologists did not want to handle it, because it was outside their field of expertise. Merely knowing how to conduct hypnosis was not enough of a qualification. You had to feel comfortable working with the unusual, so you would not be disturbed by whatever came forth, and be able to conduct an objective investigation. I certainly fit that qualification, at least. I had worked for so long in the field of the bizarre and paranormal that I did not think I would find anything that would surprise me. If I could handle a man dying at the explosion of an atomic bomb (*A Soul Remembers Hiroshima*) or the actual observation of the crucifixion of Christ (*Jesus and the Essenes*), I should be more prepared that most investigators to handle the abduction of human beings by aliens from outer space.

At the meeting there were about thirty people present, and I worried about this being the proper atmosphere in which to conduct a regression of this type. It was certainly not the relaxed setting so conducive to successful hypnosis. In my work I usually go to the home of the subject, and the session is conducted in absolute privacy. At times there may be witnesses present, but this is always with the consent of the subject (often they are people the subject requests to be there), and these are normally few in number. The atmosphere is extremely important in order to put the person at ease. I told Lou this would be like putting the girl on exhibit in a gold fish bowl. I didn't know how she would react to so many people being present, and I thought the audience would surely affect any results.

I was also secretly worrying, because this type of case was outside my normal practice. I wasn't sure how to proceed. My methods automatically propel the subject backward into a past life. I would have to modify and change my working habits to keep her from going into the past, and concentrate on events in this lifetime. Since I have used many variations of my technique I knew I could find a method that would work. I would just have to change my procedure, and I didn't know the effects or the results it would have. My other methods are thoroughly predictable, although there will always be a rare individual who refuses to follow the pattern. In such cases the operator must learn to adapt their technique to fit. In this case there would be no time to practice or work out a new method. It would have to be done by trial and error, playing it by ear. With a roomful of people observing, the conditions were not really conducive to experimentation. Thus, when I conducted the session with the young woman it was done with apprehension, not because of the subject matter, but because of the changing of my faithful working pattern. I was again moving into an unknown area where the results were uncertain, for many reasons.

Amazingly, the diversion in my technique worked very effectively and we obtained a great deal of information. Those present did not know this was my first time to attempt this type of case, because the session proceeded so smoothly. For me it was a landmark case that opened the door to UFO investigation. It was my first introduction to little gray beings who removed people from their homes at night, tests performed onboard spacecraft, star maps, and encounters tracing back to childhood. It was also my first exposure to the fear and trauma felt by the subject. These feelings were so prevalent that the emotion blocked the obtaining of information. The young woman could only report what she saw and heard. She could not find answers to the many questions I asked. All of this only aroused my interest and curiosity. I knew I could develop a method to bypass the emotional state, and allow the subconscious to supply the answers. This method had worked in other cases, because the subconscious contains all the information. I saw no reason why it couldn't also work here, once I devised a method.

I was already working in the strange and the bizarre, because the contact with Nostradamus occurred during this same year (1986). This eventually resulted in the writing of the trilogy, *Conversations With Nostradamus*, over the next three years. Thus, strange and unusual events and uncharted territory did not frighten me. It only awakened my reporter's curiosity and desire to know more.

It was after midnight when I left the meeting to return home. I didn't relish the idea of driving home on my deserted country highway at that time of night after this type of experience. All the new and strange information came flooding back into my mind. I felt very leery, and cautiously looked at the sky repeatedly during the lonely drive. Did this regression mean there really were beings out there having contact with humans? What if they knew I had just done this session? Maybe they were watching me at that very moment. The thoughts created a very uneasy journey. It was about one o'clock in the morning when I pulled into my driveway with much relief. I knew I wanted to explore this field further, but I also knew I would have to come to terms with my own, very human feelings about beings from space dealing with humans. Naturally it aroused fear in me. We have been preconditioned through years of watching horror movies featuring strange and terrifying aliens' intent on taking over the world. These creatures had always been presented as a threat, not as helpers. How could I keep these feelings from being transferred to the person I was working with? I was well aware that when a subject is in hypnotic trance they are much more acutely aware of everything, including the mind-set of the hypnotist.

This case opened the door to work with other cases of similar types. It was the typical abduction scenario that has been repeated so often it has now become commonplace. As I worked I saw a pattern emerging, and when this pattern occurred repeatedly I soon knew whether I was working on a genuine case or a fantasy. The subject always saw the little gray beings with large eyes, and various types of medical tests were performed. Occasionally, another more human type was seen in the room during the testing. Often, strange insect type of beings were observed. There were always the curved room, the table, the bright light positioned over the table, and the use of unrecognizable instruments. Often there were computer type machines somewhere in the room. And many times the person was shown a star map or a book before they left the craft. They were always told they would understand and remember the book when the time was right. Many cases had their first contact in childhood; the age of ten seemed to be a crucial time period. I even found a few cases reaching back through three generations. The mother and grandmother of the subject reluctantly reported similar visitations and events. This gave me the impression of a laboratory experiment where several generations are studied and monitored over a long period of time.

During this time I was working with Phil and receiving the information that became my book, *Keepers of the Garden*. Some of the pieces were beginning to fit. That book discussed the Ancient Astronaut theory of the seeding of the planet Earth by aliens from outer space. I learned they had been watching us since the beginning of life on Earth. What could be more natural than that the aliens were still monitoring us and watching our development? To me, this was the reason for the tests and examinations. but it had to be done covertly so the person's life would not be affected. In *Keepers of the Garden*, I was told that the ideal situation would be that the person retain no memory whatsoever and continue their normal routine. But I was finding cases of people remembering traumatic and painful events, and often remembering them through dreams more than consciously. I was told that the chemicals and pollutants in our atmosphere, the drugs, medications, and alcohol in the person's body could affect the chemistry of their brain. This would cause them to remember bits, pieces and snatches of the experience, but they remembered in a distorted fashion colored by emotions. They were not remembering the actual event. Their conscious mind was changing the event into an emotionally charged memory. My job would be to get past the conscious emotions and talk directly to the subconscious, as I had in my other work, because I knew from experience the answers were concealed there. With the emotional conscious mind influence removed, the truth of the event could surface.

WHY?

Many investigators study only sightings and physical traces such as landings, and stop there. Other investigators study only abductions and stop there. I started with these and have moved beyond. I have discovered glimpses of a much bigger picture that is only now beginning to surface: a picture which our human minds can barely comprehend. It could be the biggest picture ever shown to humanity: the story of who we are, where we came from, and where we are going. Are we ready to learn the secrets of the story of ourselves?

It has been generally agreed upon by several writers and researchers into this UFO phenomenon that the aliens appear to be involved in some type of genetic manipulation, with or without our consent. It also appears they are not acting totally out of a selfish clinical motive, but are carrying out the orders of a higher authority. Much like the personnel of a hospital often appear impersonal as they perform their various tests and examinations. How many times have we met with the same indifference when we wanted to know the reason for hospital tests? When our children exhibited this same fear and curiosity, we hushed them by saying the doctor needs to know something, they wouldn't understand, just to be quiet and do as the doctor says, and it won't hurt at all. Even if we know the reason for the tests, we do not take the time to explain it to the child, because we think it would only create fear, and they wouldn't understand anyway. So we try to keep the child quiet until the necessary work is done. Then we often hear, "But, Mommy, you told me it wouldn't hurt, and it did." This creates the feeling of mistrust as though they have been lied to. In some cases this creates a fear of the doctor, nurse or hospital. Maybe we also misjudge the child, taking it for granted he will not have the mental capacity to understand, when actually this may not be so.

The aliens display the same attitude, as though they are dealing with a child or someone of substandard intelligence who wouldn't understand even if it were explained to them. The abductee reacts the same way as our children do; by saying the aliens have no right to treat them in this manner. They say the aliens do not respect them, and do not bother explaining what is truly going on.

If these examinations and tests are occurring at a large rate involving many, many people, I see it as being comparable to the coldness and aloofness associated with a crowded hospital that administers several hundred identical tests each day. After a while these tests become so routine and mundane they feel no need to explain. There is not enough time and not enough interest in trying to communicate with each individual. Then when an occasional worker does take the time to comfort and console, their kindness is remembered and stands out among the apparent disregard of the machinelike workers. I believe the attitude of the aliens therefore is not necessary disregard for us as a separate personality, but may be the same clinical attitude of overwork and being swamped by routine.

Many researchers have also struggled with the reasons behind the tests and examinations. Several different ideas and explanations have been brought forth, and several more will come forth in the future. Each person involved in this unusual field will formulate their own theories of what is occurring, based on their own research, and also based upon their life experiences, mindset, and expectations.

Many think gene manipulation or engineering is occurring, with various goals in mind. Some think ours is a superior race that has almost reached its perfection, and the aliens may be from an imperfect or dying race. Maybe they somehow have lost the ability to reproduce themselves and therefore need our species' sperm and ova to help perpetuate their own dying race. They hope to accomplish this by interbreeding, if not physically then clinically, and producing human alien hybrids. The idea is viewed with horror by human beings, and thus we consider anyone with this goal in mind to be also horrible.

My theories are different. I do not believe they are doing this for their purposes, but for ours. Of course, we have seen that there are several different types of entities involved, and there could be some negative types doing these things for their own gains. But I believe these are in the minority, the renegades or mavericks of the UFO groups. As I explained in my book, *Keepers of the Garden*, there is a higher power at work directing a plan that was fashioned for our world eons before the first human appeared upon our planet. This master plan was conceived and worked out by methods far beyond our comprehension. The beings were assigned the carrying out of various steps in this project. Each was responsible for its own small part, and really had nothing to say over the completion of the whole project. The entire scope was probably even beyond *their* comprehension. As they produced life on our planet, nurtured it and pruned it over eons of time, it was only a job, an assignment. They may have had similar assignments on various other planets at various stages of its growth. As individual beings died off their work was continued by others. This was a project of extremely long range, and one orchestrated in meticulous detail. Time did not matter, only the final goal: the creation of a species of superior physical and mental accomplishments. Such a project could not be accomplished overnight, and there was always the possibility of even such a carefully laid plan going wrong. It would have been impossible to anticipate every possible circumstance.

The fly in the ointment occurred when a meteor crashed into the Earth and introduced organisms that were foreign to our planet. In their own environment they had been harmless. But when introduced into the pristine atmosphere of Earth they multiplied and mutated into a volatile threat to the seedling human race. This created the introduction of disease into the human body. The ideal plan had been to create a perfect, disease-free functioning body with a long life span. There was much sorrow when this unforeseen development was discovered, and a meeting was held on the highest level of the counsel to decide what to do. There was much sadness and remorse because the grand experiment had gone awry. But it was decided that since so much work had already been done, it would be better not to throw out the entire experiment. It was decided to try to minimize the damage that had been done, and proceed by making concessions and moving forward with what they had left to work with.

In the early days as the human developed, there was constant care, pruning, and manipulating of the species. Gene manipulation and engineering have been a part of our species since the very beginning. It is not something new. That is why we are here at all, and not living in a cave and scratching out a living in the wilderness. The aliens have carefully bred and influenced the development of our brains, gradually introducing the amazing psychic powers and intuitive feelings that are common among them. As man developed away from the animalistic stage and became capable of handling his own life and affairs, the aliens were not allowed to have as much influence. It has been emphasized that this is the planet of free will, and it is a strict universal law that free will must be respected.

The task of gardener changed to custodian. Man was given many devices and knowledge to make his life easier, and then the new species had to go on their own. If they made mistakes and misused the knowledge, that was their right to do so, as long as they did not infringe upon the rights of others outside their own planet. The aliens were under strict laws not to interfere. Of course, the studying of the species continued. The experiment had to be checked from time to time to see how it was developing and adjusting to its environment. Corrections were made at the appropriate times through gene manipulation. If this has been occurring since the beginning of time, why can't it still be occurring? If they are acting under the authority of a higher power that we can't even begin to comprehend, who are we to say they have no right to do it? We do not tell a mother she has no right or authority to look after her child. I see it as the same logic.

As man progressed he influenced his environment to such an extent that it is greatly affecting his body. I think it is no coincidence that as man's environment undergoes these threatening changes, the tests and examinations by aliens have increased. Of course, they are interested in what man is doing to his body. They have always been interested. What could be more natural than to try to correct and adjust humans to cope with all the "stuff" we are pouring into our atmosphere? If this includes gene manipulation to produce a human better able to adapt, then so be it. I believe they are still trying to undo the damage done eons ago when the meteor introduced disease into their experiment. I believe they are still trying to return us to the original dream and design: a disease free human capable of fantastic feats and an incredible life span.

In *Keepers of the Garden*, I told about the other project of possibly creating a perfect human to live on a planet that is being prepared somewhere in the cosmos. A chance to begin again in a clean environment after this one has been contaminated beyond the point of no return, possibly by nuclear war or whatever. I believe this is one possibility, but it may not be the only one.

I had a strange occurrence in the autumn of 1988. During the night I had the distinct and unfamiliar feeling that an entire block of information had somehow been inserted into my head. The experience did not have any of the qualities of a dream. While it was occurring I woke up enough to comprehend the information. I knew it was a concept, not specific sentences or ideas, and it had been placed into my brain in a whole concise form. I have often heard my subjects talk of receiving concepts which they had to break down into language so it could be understood. I could now appreciate the difficulty they had. This was my first, and only (I think!), experience of this kind. I knew the concept dealt with the explanation for the UFO occupants' behavior, their reasoning, etc. I knew it was the explanation that should be included in my book on UFO cases, which had not yet even been started. I had not been aware of pondering this problem of why the aliens were using gene engineering, because I was involved at the time with the final editing of the first volume of the Nostradamus trilogy (*Conversations With Nostradamus*). I was just accumulating the information I expected would someday form a book on my cases with UFOs.

It was a concept, idea and explanation that was different from any I had heard expressed by the other writers on this subject at the time. It seemed very important that I remember the content, and the emphasis was that this was the information I had been seeking. I did not have time to analyze it, because it was too multifaceted. But I knew I would be able to retain it until the next day when I could put it into the computer. I fell back to sleep, and I awoke the next morning with a strange sensation in my head. Before I was fully awake the block of information came rushing back with the same intensity it had the night before. This was not normal, because usually upon awakening dream material fades quickly and is difficult to retrieve, even if only in images. This was not in images, but in philosophical thought. It was again stressed that it was important to remember and to write it down. I knew I had to get it into the computer before it evaporated. Of course, everyday life always gets in the way. The first order of business on that day was for my daughter and I to can peaches from our small orchard. Ripe peaches will not wait, even though I was distracted by information running round in circles in my brain. When the last jar was sealed and placed on the table to cool, I at last had time alone to work with the computer.

Of course, the next order of events is always to think of how to put it into words. This is often the most difficult part, because a concept can be whole and complete and resist the breaking down that is necessary to convert it into words. But I will make the attempt, being fully aware that I will miss some of it. It was an interesting idea, an explanation that I could construct the book around, and steer toward these preconceived conclusions. Even though at that time such a book was without form and substance, and only a faint shadow in the back of my mind. These beginning stages had to lie dormant in my files for ten years before becoming a reality. By 1998 I had accumulated a massive amount of information to form into a book, yet it definitely followed the concept given to me in 1988.

THE CONCEPT

It came to me that the manipulation of genes was for our protection, the preservation of our species, for the guarantee of our survival. Looking at it in this way it is an act of great kindness, and demonstrates an immense devotion to our care. In the Nostradamus books it is stressed that there is a very real possibility our way of life will be destroyed. It was foreseen that there is a possibility of the Earth tilting on its axis. During such a catastrophe there would be death resulting from many causes: flood, earthquake, volcanic eruption, massive tidal waves, every type of disaster known and unknown to man. Afterwards there would be death resulting from disease and starvation. Anyone who survived would have to be extremely hardy. I have complete faith in the human race. I believe we have the capability to survive. I believe, as Nostradamus does, that this would not be the end of *the* world, but the end of *our* world as we know it. It would be a complete changing of our way of life, but man has the wonderful perseverance to regain what he perceives to be important to that way of life.

This is something I do not like to think about and do not want to consider possible, but many experts have agreed that the possibility exists. Maybe the aliens are merely looking ahead and trying to anticipate every possibility. They do not want to be caught off guard again. By gene manipulation and engineering they may be, not only creating a human that can function in a contaminated environment with a body that can resist cancer and other diseases caused by these changes, but will also be able to adjust to a new life style filled with enormous stress. One of the subjects in this book saw herself amid a scene of sick and dying people trying to help in any small way. She herself was not sick, and was incapable of becoming ill. Her job was to help the others. Maybe she is one of the new breed that has been designed for this purpose, to withstand the ravages of the Earth shift and the major crises that could follow.

The theory I have developed from the information I have received is that they are extremely interested in our welfare as a species, because they have been our caretakers for eons. They are not about to give up on us now. Some humans are being prepared for survival on another planet that is being prepared for and to be populated by disease free individuals. It is designed to be familiar so there will be no shock as the people begin a new way of life, or continuation of the old ways, in a new and pristine environment. Others could also be being prepared for survival on *this* planet Earth after catastrophic changes render most humans incapable of functioning. I believe that in the future when we are able to see all the different facets of this phenomenon, we will realize the beings should not to be feared, but welcomed as our ancestors, our brothers, our custodians. Their purpose in the grand plan will at last be understood and become crystal clear to mankind.

OBSERVATIONS

Since I became exposed to this more radical way of thinking I have noticed I am observing things around me in a different way. It has affected the way I look at my fellow human beings, the way they live their lives, and how those lives relate to each other in a worldwide situation. As I note these things the logic behind the custodian theory becomes clearer and more plausible in my mind.

In some far off distant future time it is very possible we will assume the role of custodian for some other planet. The idea is not only possible; it is very likely to happen. Man is a very curious animal, as I am sure the aliens also were, who began their Earth caretaking project. It is inconceivable to me that once man has perfected space travel and conquered the distances between our world and silent dead worlds, that he would want to leave them the way he found them: dead and lifeless. In that far future time man would have the knowledge to introduce life as an experiment. He would introduce it in simple rudimentary stages at first; simple cells, to see what would grow in the conditions present, whatever the primeval "soup" would tolerate. After much experimentation this would lead to more complex life forms being introduced or genetically changed to fit the environment. I cannot believe that man, with his inherent curiosity, would do otherwise. He would reason that it could do no possible harm. The planet had no life to begin with or perhaps the most basic of cellular structure. Thus, man would have a barren planet ripe for experimentation, ready and waiting as a playground for future scientists to try the adaptation of life forms. Who could it possibly hurt? It would allow the application of methods forbidden on Earth, because there would be no such barriers on an alien world. Man, of course, would be under some governments or at least some superior's guidance and instruction. He would be following the orders of a master plan, because it would be far too complex for the average scientist working alone. Then there would be the caretaking, the pruning and the grafting, so to speak, to help the developing life forms adjust. These menial tasks would be carried out by the less educated (or even robots), because it would only entail the following of orders. This private project, known or unknown to the public of the home planet, could develop over countless years and be perpetuated by generations of scientists who considered the "new" world too valuable to cease experimentation. These scientists would be learning an incredible amount of new information that doubtless would be applied to help the welfare of the people of the Earth. The project could not be abandoned if it were also helping the lifestyle of home.

Over a countless period of time life would be established and start to develop its own characteristics. Perhaps life forms from Earth would be introduced and crossbred to genetically adapt. Eventually an animal with intelligence might arise. It would naturally be helped along with gene manipulation and the introduction of traits of our own race. Excitement would ripple through the halls of science as innovations were presented. The resulting creature might bear some of our characteristics, but probably would not be a carbon copy, because it had to adapt to its environment. Its eyes, breathing apparatus and circulatory system might be different, but it would still be considered a humanoid even though it probably could not survive on Earth. If the creature began to exhibit flaws that were inconsistent with the master plan, would the project be abandoned and the life form destroyed? I think not. I think man will still possess enough of the God spirit that he will consider all life to be sacred, even life he has created himself. I think he would try to help the species adapt to the flaws, or allow it to become an evolutionary dead end and expire on its own.

As the dominant species developed and began to show signs of civilization, supervision would then decrease. They would not need to be constantly watched. Besides, it might be an interesting experiment to see how the new creatures would develop on their own. What type of morals would they possess? Would they be inventive? Would they be warlike? In order to understand our own race we would feel obligated to allow these creatures to develop on their own and study which traits are naturally occurring and which are learned. But they would not be left totally alone. An advisor would come to live among them to teach them ways to make their lives better. This advisor would be treated and worshiped as a god even long after he had returned to his home planet. He had to have been a god because he possessed such wondrous powers and knowledge. Instructions would be given about the gathering of food, and ways to survive. Then in order to study the mental development the advisor could not interfere. Once the knowledge was given it had to be used in whatever way the new creature decided. If there was too much interference the experiment could be completely jeopardized. There obviously are too many different factors to list here, but this would be the general scenario.

It would be a continuing experiment and would never be abandoned by the home planet. Over succeeding generations it would continue to be listed in the annals of history. There would always be "Watchers" to observe and keep the records up to date. There would naturally be some of these new creatures who would be monitored more closely to see how the genetics were developing, and how they were being affected by their environment. If there appeared to be problems these could be helped by alterations. I don't believe we would consider this as interference, because under ideal conditions the creature would be unaware that anything was done, and could continue his life unaffected. It would be better at this advanced stage of the experiment for the scientist to remain behind the glass in the laboratory in order to remain undetected. Much in the same way rare birds are raised in captivity. After the egg hatches the handlers wear grotesque bird masks or hoods so the developing chick will not identify with humans. The scientists' theory is that if the bird identifies with humans it cannot exist on its own in the wild. It must identify with its own kind.

But what if the species took another turn and started to use his new found knowledge to invoke war? What if those war acts became so profound that the species created weapons of terrible power? What if they used their new inventions in reckless ways that threatened to destroy, not only themselves, but their entire world? Would they be allowed to do this? I think not. If the experiment had been protected and nurtured throughout countless centuries, would it be given up on, or would we take a chance on interference at that point? It would be a gigantic problem, and the decision would probably be the responsibility of the highest level of government on Earth. It might be decided to allow them to do what they wished as an ultimate climax to the experiment. But would we allow everything to be lost? Probably we could take cells and produce clones so we could have some examples of the species on Earth, or to start over on another barren planet. We would probably not allow all the work to be lost. But I do believe if the species threatened total destruction of their planet, we would have to do something to prevent it, because it could cause repercussions throughout the solar system and perhaps even neighboring stars and galaxies. This could not be allowed; it would cause too much disruption. At that time, I think we would finally have to break the golden code of noninterference and make ourselves known. We would finally tell the species we were their creators, their custodians and their protectors over eons of time. How would we be accepted? Would we be believed? Would it make any difference?

This entire scenario sounds like science fiction, but how do we know for certain it will not come to pass? How can we know for certain it has not already come to pass, not only here on our Earth, but on possible countless planets throughout the universe? As long as there is curiosity man will search. As long as he continues to search there are no barriers to what he will accomplish. The universe is and always has been his home. This is one important trait that has been inherited from our creators and our guardians. It is surely one important trait that we will pass on to generations yet unborn, whether on this planet or somewhere else.

*Knowledge is **not worth** anything if it can't be shared.*

CHAPTER 2
CONDENSED OR DISTORTED
TIME

Many investigators have explored cases of missing time, where several hours pass inexplicably without the person being aware of the lapse. I will discuss several later in this book. But I have discovered a concept which I find even stranger: cases of condensed time. This is where the events take place in far less time than it would normally take. Of course, both of these phenomena are examples of time being mysteriously distorted from the participant's point of view.

We are hampered by being trapped within our concept of linear time. It has been said we may be the only planet in the universe that has invented a way to measure something that does not exist. I have been told many times in my work that time is only an illusion, an invention of man. The aliens do not have this concept, and they have told me that man will never travel in space until he overcomes the erroneous idea of time. This is one of the main problems that keeps man trapped on the Earth. Even though we might understand this from a psychological point of view, it is difficult, if not impossible, for our human minds to accept. We are thoroughly entrenched in time with our life composed of and measured in minutes, hours, days, weeks, months and years. I do not see any way we can escape this concept and still function in our normal, workaday world. We believe that things must progress from point A to point B in an orderly fashion within a certain amount of time. There can be no deviation, no taking of side trips, because they do not fit in our belief system. Thus, our focus is very narrow. Anything that lies beyond that focus is said to be impossible and therefore it cannot happen, it cannot exist.

If we lived on a planet that revolved around its sun in a different manner, how would we measure time? Suppose there was always sunlight, or always darkness. Suppose the planet had two suns. Would they measure time in a different way, or would they decide there was no need for such an inconvenience? What about beings traveling on spaceships for long periods of time, hurdling through space with no reference points to distinguish day and night, and no reason to mark off the seasons and years? It is no wonder they do not understand our purpose for time, and often can make no sense of it. Under similar and even more radical circumstances we also might decide there was no purpose served by creating time and adhering so dogmatically to it.

Having no such restrictions they have been free to discover other dimensions and planes of existence that are hidden from us by our rigid time structure. Having made these discoveries they have found ways to dematerialize and rematerialize anything they wish to transport. They can slip and slide through cracks and crevices to other dimensions as easily as walking through a door. Of course, they may have been doing this long before our ancestors were living in caves, and we would have much catching up to do. But we will never find these cracks until we remove the blinders that tell us it is impossible. If another humanoid species has discovered the way, then it is possible for us. If they have been mentally feeding us information we have needed down through the eons of our existence, then they may be even now trying to relay the secrets of dissolving the barriers of time and show us where the golden doors lie.

There appear to be many metaphysical concepts that come easily to the alien mind, but are almost impossible for the human to grasp. The "nuts and bolts" investigator would like it to all remain simple: if they can't see it, measure it, touch it or dissect it, it doesn't exist. They are more comfortable with the concept of traveling so many miles an hour to reach the nearest star, and work at developing a fuel source that will do the task. It is much more difficult for them to grasp the concept of traveling by mind power, and moving in and out of dimensions. The solutions to the UFO riddle are no longer simple. The more we delve into the puzzle the more complicated and mind stretching the concepts become. Maybe this is why we were not given these alternatives until now. In the past our human mind had to get used to aliens traveling in UFOs in ways we could understand. For instance, using some type of conventional fuel source to go past the speed of light, in order to obey the laws of physics as our scientists understood them.

We have been spoon-fed over the years, and just given as much information as we could handle at the time. As we adjusted to each part of the concept and the idea no longer frightened us, we were then given a more complicated piece of the puzzle. I seriously doubt if we will ever understand the entire concept, just as we cannot expect a toddler to understand geometry or calculus. So we will probably never be given the chance. I have been told several times not to expect that all my questions would be answered. Some knowledge would be as medicine and some would be as poison. It would harm more than it would help. So I take what I am given, and I have found as I analyze and try to understand the concepts, I am then given more to digest. But it appears it is never more than I can handle. This is the way I have written my books, trying to present these ideas in a way that people can grasp them. Thus, there will be concepts in this book that I have not presented before. There is much uncharted territory that lies before the explorer, and I hope to journey there. We are taking our first baby steps into an unknown world.

We say these beings and crafts are not behaving according to the law of physics, as we know it. We say they are doing things that are "unnatural." This is the greatest skepticism about their existence. People say the feats reportedly performed by them are impossible. I think we shall find they are not an unnatural phenomenon, but a natural one. They could be obeying a new law of physics we have not yet discovered or even thought about. It is new only to us because it does not fit within our frame of reality, but to them it is quite natural.

According to the information I have received, the UFO craft are able to disappear from view or from radar screens etc., because they suddenly change their vibratory rate. If you observe how the blades of a spinning fan or propeller disappear as the speed of rotation increases, you will have a crude idea of how it works. We who are living in the physical on Earth are vibrating at a slower vibration. This will be explained further in my book, *Convoluted Universe*. Many of these beings are not living on other planets, but in other dimensions. In these other dimensions there are many other worlds (some physical and some not) that sometimes exist side by side with ours, but are vibrating at a faster rate. Oftentimes we are totally unaware of each other's world. The more advanced of the other worlds have become aware of us and often come here to observe. In order to do this they must slow their vibratory rate. It has been described as painful to do this, and to maintain this slower rate for any length of time. It could thus have the opposite effect on humans entering those dimensions.

Our vibratory rate would be speeded up, and have to be slowed down upon reentry.

Many of these beings have evolved to the point that they are pure energy and no longer require bodies. They can however manifest bodies when one is needed to interact with humans. I could not understand why beings who were pure energy would need spacecraft to travel in. Maybe they are not only carrying their environment with them, gravity, atmosphere, etc., to maintain life, but also carrying their vibratory rate.

There have been many cases of humans being taken onboard the smaller craft with no lasting effects on their body. Maybe this is why. The craft enter and function within our vibration rate and the humans can adjust to that. The little gray beings are usually reported on these smaller craft. They are a type of cloned or manufactured being that can obviously function easier at these frequencies than the other types of beings. They were created in the image of their creator, the tall gray beings, to be able to come to Earth and perform the menial tasks. The samples taken from humans, animals, plants etc. are then taken to the large craft for laboratory analysis. There have not been as many cases reported of people being taken onboard the larger craft or "mother" ships. These are usually located high in our atmosphere, because they are too large to land easily. But now, I think they are also vibrating at a different rate that renders them invisible. Maybe the beings onboard cannot adjust as easily to the slower vibrations, and prefer to remain in a comfortable environment. For the human to enter these craft their molecules have to be adjusted and their vibratory rate speeded up. They can function like this for a limited time, but it cannot be kept up indefinitely or the body would disintegrate. Upon reentry the complicated and difficult process occurs when the person's body is readjusted and the rate is slowed down. This can result in confusion, disorientation, temporary paralysis, and physical symptoms (such as bruising), as the body recovers from the trauma to its system. This could explain why there have not been as many cases of people being taken onboard the larger ships. The other experience with the smaller ships and the little grays is much more common. The average person may not be able to adjust to the physical changes necessary for the experience.

In 1998 the last American came back to Earth from the Joint Soviet mission onboard the orbiting space station MIR. He said the biggest adjustment was to get used to the oppressive weight of his physical body after being weightless for so long.

Missing time sequences are not always what they appear to be. It is assumed that the person has been directly involved with aliens or UFOs when there is a loss of time, especially if there was a light (or craft) sighted at the same time. I have found this is not always the case. In many instances the person merely blocked an unpleasant or traumatic experience from their mind, and it had nothing to do with aliens. This information can be accurately obtained when the trance is deep enough to contact the subconscious mind directly. It contains all the memories and will report what really occurred, without the emotional coloring of the conscious mind interfering. I always tell investigators to not jump to conclusions when subjects report missing time, or any of the other experiences that seem to fit the pattern. Always look for the simplest explanation first, before going into the more complex. In many cases the simple explanation is the answer. For some unknown reason some people prefer the more complex answer to explain events in their life. "I had missing time, so I must have been taken onboard a UFO." By some mysterious psychological process this abstract reasoning is easier to accept than a more mundane, but unpleasant one. In one of my cases the man had definite missing time, and it did involve contact with aliens, but it was a case of being in the wrong place at the wrong time.

Tom wanted to explore a period of missing time that occurred in 1972, in Massachusetts, which had always bothered him. He had been to a business meeting at a client's house. There were other people present and they had been served a very nice dinner. As the evening wore on it became quite late, and one of the women invited him to spend the night at her apartment, instead of returning to his home in the next city.

As the lady was driving that night, Tom remembered seeing a bright light in the sky over some trees. It seemed to make her nervous. He remembered nothing else until he awoke the next morning in her apartment. He had not consumed any drugs or alcohol, and he never could explain the missing time. Not long afterward the woman moved away and he never knew where she went. He remembered her as a rather strange woman; she was not friendly or very communicative.

The Custodians

Under hypnosis he returned to the scene, remembered the exact date of the occurrence, and described the delicious meal. He supplied many details that his conscious mind had forgotten. Many that were not relevant to what we were looking for, but it showed that all the information was there and readily available. The woman's name was Stella, and he said her car was a new 1972 Pontiac Firebird. It was almost midnight as they drove on a country road to her apartment, and he recounted their idle conversation. Then he saw what he thought was a fireball, or a "shooting star," out of the corner of his eye. They watched as the light in the sky became brighter and appeared to be approaching them.

The car's engine suddenly died, and the car stopped in the middle of the road. Stella was frightened, but curiously Tom reacted in a different way. He suddenly felt very tired, and was falling asleep. This was definitely not a normal reaction. I knew his subconscious had remained awake, and I would be able to ask it questions.

His subconscious told me that both he and Stella were asleep, and there was a brilliant light surrounding the car and coming in all the windows. The car doors then opened and their sleeping bodies were removed from the car. I asked who took them out.

"They *look* like people. One man has brown hair, and the other has blondish hair. They just take us out of the car, and they examine the inside of the car. Then they look at us. They have a *thing* they hold over us. And then they put us back in the car again."

He said they had held his unconscious body upright and moved an instrument up and down his body. It made a clicking sound as they maneuvered it. I assumed he would be heavy for them to lift in that way. He said he probably was, but they did it with little effort.

I asked for a description of the instrument. "It looks slender like a television antenna, about thirteen or fourteen inches long, with coils of wire around it. And it flashes color, almost a neon green to a rich purple blue. The colors surround the instrument when it passes over a person, and I can hear a clicking noise. I don't know what it's for though."

They were then put back into the car. The motor was now operating, and they were moving down the road. The men and the light were gone. Stella said, "Oh, I must have fallen asleep for a second. I must be *really* tired." Tom also felt as though he had dozed off. Stella then looked at her watch, and was startled when she saw

25

the time. "Oh, my goodness! It's two thirty! Didn't we leave there about twelve? Oh, I don't know. We better get going." They both dismissed it as they drove to her apartment. Tom felt very tired, as though drained of energy and exhausted. He dozed during the remainder of the ride. At the apartment she admonished him to be quiet so as to not awaken the neighbors. She showed him his room, and he collapsed totally on the bed. He didn't remember anything else until the telephone woke him the next morning.

I asked his subconscious if it knew the reason for the examination by the strange looking instrument. It replied, "Yes, I know why. It was because of Stella. She works for a company south of Boston that is preparing military secrets for the war in Viet Nam. And she has access to all different types of information. I think they really wanted the information from her, not so much from me. I just happened to be there at a time when they contacted her. They monitor her, and she has probably been contacted numerous times in her past. I knew something was wrong, because she always seemed on edge. She is suspicious and doesn't make friends easily. She also has moved a lot. Before she lived in Massachusetts she lived in California, before that she lived in Hawaii, and before that in Japan. She has traveled all over the world."

D: *Did they do the same thing to her with the instrument?*
T: I couldn't see what they were doing to her, because they were doing this with the thing to me. But I know they were doing something else. They have some type of contact with her.
D: *What was the purpose of that instrument?*
T: It was similar to a cat scan type instrument that we have now. It was examining my vital functions. It also measured my brain wave. They affect people by brain waves. But these people were not *bad*. They weren't cold or unemotional; they were just monitoring her because they were afraid she might be involved in something. It's kind of like espionage. That's one of the reasons they wanted to monitor her, because she knows a lot of information. Stella has a degree in radio-bacteriology, and a PHD in electrical engineering. She's a very intelligent woman.
D: *Were they trying to get information from her in this way?*

T: No. They already know all that she knows, because they can read her thoughts. But she's important to them for some reason or other. I don't know.

D: *Why would they be worried if she was involved in espionage? What difference would it make to them?*

T: She had that problem. She had been approached by people representing the Soviet bloc countries. They were going to give her a hundred thousand dollars, but she never took them up on the offer. She moved.

D: *Are these beings worried about her getting into some kind of espionage? Is that what you mean?*

T: No, they weren't worried about her getting involved in espionage or anything like that. She's one of the people they monitor, that's all. And she has access to all different types of scientific treatises and things of this nature. This is why she's monitored.

D: *This information you're telling me about her, is that something you knew, or is it something you're just now learning?*

T: Well, I knew she had a degree. And I knew she worked for a company outside Boston. And that it had something to do with electrical engineering. I didn't know she was involved in espionage.

D: *Then this is something you're just now finding out about her, that you didn't know at the time?*

T: Yes. She's really bothered by this monitoring, and this is why she travels all over the world. She's trying to get away from them. She left soon after that. I guess she moved from Massachusetts, because I couldn't get in touch with her.

D: *Then you didn't see her again?*

T: No, she had to go (pause, and then surprise) to Houston. Stella was transferred down to Houston. That's why she left.

D: *Okay. Did you ever have any experience like this again after that date, with the light or anything?*

T: No, never again. That was the only time.

I thought this was interesting, because it was a case of missing time where the subject was not the object of the beings' attention. There was ample room here for fantasy if the subject had been so inclined, but the incident did not even focus on him. Also it is interesting that he said he never had another similar incident. If he were imagining he could have expanded quite easily. As it was, there was no elaboration at all.

I came across three cases in 1988 and 1989 that suggested a distortion of time, and maybe even moving into another dimension.

In the summer of 1987 Lou Farish placed a small ad in a local free supermarket paper asking that anyone who had had unusual incidents relating to UFOs to call him. It was the first and only time he placed such an ad. A woman named Janet called him to relate a strange occurrence the night before in his area. The woman was very apprehensive and did not want to identify herself. She told him she had traveled from Little Rock to her home, which was past the Conway area, in only fifteen minutes time. As it is a distance of approximately 50 miles, the trip normally took 45 minutes. There was no traffic on the four lane interstate highway the entire way, which was very unusual. When she arrived home her dogs made a terrible racket, which was not normal for them. Lou said it seemed we had a case of condensed time rather than missing time. The only thing that might associate it with UFOs was that the woman had seen a huge bright light over some trees during the event. She was a businesswoman who did not want to be identified and seemed embarrassed talking about it.

Lou then went to her home to talk with her. He found Janet to be an extremely down-to-earth person who had never read or been interested in any way in UFOs. She was sure there must be a common sense, logical explanation for whatever happened, if anything. But she was having difficulty accounting for the speeding up of time, and the light in the sky. Lou asked if she would be willing to undergo hypnosis, but she was very much against it. I told him not to push it, to let her make up her own mind. But if possible, I would like to meet with her.

From time to time during the next year he occasionally had contact with her. She was grasping at all kinds of bizarre explanations to account for the light, even that someone may have been in the trees with mirrors directing lights upward. The explanations were more bizarre than the actual incident. But she was desperately trying to find an explanation she could accept. She also reported having strange dreams of a precognitive nature, and was exhibiting psychic tendencies for the first time in her life.

Lou kept trying to arrange a meeting between us, but it didn't work out. Each time she was doing something else that was more important to her, usually involved with her business. Obviously, the experience, although shaking, was not of predominant importance to her.

It was just as well that this time elapsed, because when I first heard of her case the idea of condensed time was a new oddity. But during the intervening period I came across two more cases which bore a distinct resemblance, and I thought there might be a similarity. Most notably Valerie's and Eddie's, reported in this chapter.

My meeting with Janet finally occurred during the Ozark UFO Conference in Eureka Springs in April 1989. She had reluctantly agreed to attend, and Lou introduced us. She said there were at least 30 other things she would rather have been doing that weekend, and attending this conference was not one of them. Her interest was simply not there. She had been listening intently to the speakers, and looking at the pictures and slides presented, but nothing seemed to be like her experience, so she just thought it was a waste of time. We sat in the lobby while the majority of the people were in the conference, so we could have a private conversation.

Janet was a very attractive blond, very much a lady, sophisticated but not overly so. Nicely dressed, and gave the impression she was used to mixing with a well to do, well educated crowd. Yet she seemed very friendly, and did not give the appearance of being snobbish. She relaxed noticeably with me, and immediately began pouring out her story. It seemed almost a relief to finally tell it. She seemed to sense that I would not ridicule her, but was there to try to help her. She decided to finally pursue it, because she had recently been having flashbacks that were adding extra details, and this bothered her. She was positive there was a logical explanation, and was convinced when she found it, it would stop bothering her. She carefully and exactly supplied the details.

I was certain she had checked the strange occurrence of condensed time, and she had. She seemed the type who wanted to verify every possible detail to satisfy her own curiosity. She had already double-checked with several people who verified the time she left a restaurant in Little Rock that evening. It was around midnight when she got on I 40, and drove down the freeway until she came to the road that turned off to her home. There is only one road in or out of that area, and there is always traffic no matter what time of the day or night. She is very familiar with every twist and turn, and knows every house along the way, since she drives this route almost every day. But that night everything seemed strange and different. There weren't any stars out, and she noticed it was extremely quiet. There was not even the sound of crickets. She distinctly noticed there were no lights in any of the houses, not even the outside mercury vapor lights which always burn. She knew this area very well, and there were always lights in the houses which could be seen for long distances. There was no sound and no sign of life. There was no traffic, which she considered to be very unusual.

Then she saw the object. It was huge, suspended just above the treetops ahead of her to her right. It was an enormous oblong shape, and glowing a very distinct bright orange color. The glow was contained within the shape and did not emanate outward. There were no markings, no windows, outlines or other lights, only the solid orange oblong shape. When she first saw it she thought it was the sun setting and the glow and color was coming from reflection off the clouds. Even though the sun had set several hours earlier, this was the first explanation that came to her mind. Then she thought of the possibility of a meteor flash or aurora borealis. She was trying to associate it with something logical, even though she had never seen anything like it in her life. She slowed the car to a crawl to watch it. Normally this would have been hazardous, because of the amount of traffic usually on that road.

As the car crawled along Janet was mesmerized by the huge light. She then saw an object in the road ahead that she thought was probably a dead animal. When she got even with it she stopped the car to look at it. She was amazed to see it was an ordinary house cat, frozen into an unusual position. It was sitting on its haunches, hair raised, paws in the air, and staring up at the same object that had caught her attention. The animal was not dead, but grotesquely frozen in this strange position staring at the object; almost in a state of suspended animation. This was the only sign of life that she came across, if you want to call it that.

She continued on still driving slowly and staring at the object. Then when she was alongside it went out, but in an unusual manner. The top and bottom edges slowly closed leaving a dark space once again above the trees. The two edges came together and blinked out. She demonstrated with her hands, and I got the impression of a giant eye just closing its lids. I questioned her to be sure it did not simply move lower behind the tree line and go out of sight. She said if that had happened she would have seen the light through the trees as it lowered. She was positive the lower and top edges simply came together and the light was out. There is the possibility that the object may have still been there, only now in a darkened state. Since there were no stars the object could have then blended in with the darkness. Whatever happened, she then speeded up and continued home more confused than ever. She said she never felt fright, only awe and amazement and wonder. Her calculating mind had been trying to figure out what it was.

When she drove into her driveway her pure bred dogs, which were enclosed in a strongly built pen, were having fits. They were barking and howling, clawing and biting at the fence trying to get out. She said they have never behaved that way before, since the breed was very mild mannered. They normally never even barked when she or anyone else came in the driveway. But that night when she arrived they went crazy. I asked if she noticed anything unusual on the car or on herself, and she said she had not.

When she entered the house she was surprised to see the time. She went through the house checking all the clocks against her watch, and they all said the same thing. She had arrived home much too quickly. She estimated fifteen minutes, which would have been impossible, especially at the slow rate of speed she was traveling. She woke her husband and asked him to tell her what time the clock said, and admonished him to remember the next day what time she had come home.

Janet said she was beginning to have flashbacks that related to the incident. She remembered that something streaked across the highway just in front of the car when she first sighted the object. Also, at the same time there was a sudden flash of light in the middle of the highway. She described it as similar to a mirror reflection that had flipped suddenly making a flash or glint of light. She had difficulty describing it, but it reminded her of the reflections in a hall of mirrors in the fun house at a carnival.

We never had a hypnosis session although I am convinced there was more to the story. She did not want to explore the incident further, because she had her life in order. She was very involved with her business, and didn't want anything to take her mind off that, or to create confusion in her life. She would consider the event a curiosity, even though she would probably never understand it, and continue on with her life. The most important thing about my work is that the person continues to live a normal life. I try to help them understand any experiences, and integrate them into their life. If the idea of uncovering more disturbs them, then it is best left alone. I have also told people who are looking for a hypnosis session out of curiosity, that sometimes they may discover things about themselves they wish they had left alone. And once the information is uncovered, it cannot simply be pushed back again. In this case Janet was probably very wise, because she did not want to cause disruption in her carefully organized life. This is as it should be. I respect the wishes of my clients.

In both of the following cases the subjects had vivid conscious memories of the event. These memories were enhanced and more details supplied under hypnosis.

Eddie was a manual laborer in his thirties, who was hesitant to even talk about his experience. He only did so at the urging of his girlfriend. Embarrassed and noticeably apprehensive, he felt uncomfortable with the tape recorder. I set it on the table, and told him in a few minutes he would forget it was even there. When interviewing people it is easy to forget details, and the recorder insures that the story will be accurate. It also validates conscious memories and keeps them separate from memories revealed through hypnosis. As we talked he relaxed and soon became oblivious of the machine.

He reported an event that occurred almost twenty years before when he was a seventeen-year-old high school senior living in a rural farm community in Missouri. After visiting with a friend in town, he was driving home in his old truck. It was late at night on a rural dirt road where houses are few and far between. When he first spotted the light he thought it was an outside mercury vapor lamp, which were new in the area. Some of the farmers were replacing the incandescent lamps with these, but it was in a place he wasn't accustomed to seeing a light. As he approached it he became increasingly aware that it was not an outdoor farm light, because it became brighter and was higher in the sky. It moved toward him until it stopped over him, and then followed the truck as he drove. He stuck his head out the window to watch it. About half a mile from home it suddenly moved ahead of him and hovered over a group of trees. At that time he could see it was a large lens-type shape. There were orange lights on the inside, and a rotating band revolved around the middle, causing the lights to blink. The bottom of it was a metallic silver color. His curiosity caused him to stop the truck at the bottom of the hill. He got out and sat on the hood of the truck to watch the strange object. It seemed odd to him that he wasn't frightened, but he presumed it was because he had been raised in the country and spent a lot of time outdoors. As he sat on the truck watching, a blue light came out of the bottom and lit up the tops of the trees beneath it. It hovered perfectly still, and although the band rotated, there was no noise. As an estimate of size he said it was about as wide as the room we were sitting in, which would make it about 25 feet.

He sat there for an estimated fifteen or twenty minutes watching it. During this time another strange thing occurred. A neighbor family came by in their beat-up pickup: two adults and a bunch of little kids who lived about three miles from his home. The kids were all sitting in the back of the truck. Eddie waved his arms and pointed upwards, frantically trying to get their attention. He knew they had to see him, because his truck was partly in the road. But they drove on without even slowing. He said it was almost as though he was invisible. Later he was tempted to ask them why they didn't stop, but he couldn't bring himself to talk to anyone about the incident.

When he arrived home, he ran up the stairs screaming. His parents were asleep, and he scared them by waking them so suddenly. He made them go to the window and look out, but the light had reduced to the size of a mercury vapor light. In an instant it blinked out and disappeared. Whatever his parents saw was a pale comparison to the large craft he had seen.

During that entire year there were many sightings in the area, some seen by police, but he never heard of one as close as he had experienced. He couldn't bring himself to talk about it, because he was afraid of ridicule. "I was the kind of kid that didn't need that kind of publicity." I could identify with that feeling, because I also live in an isolated rural community, and you are very conscious of what your neighbors think about you.

He said, "I've had to live with this for years, thinking I'm probably just nuts, or I had some psychological reason to fictitiously create this story. Although that's not true. I *saw* this thing. It's been a battle.

Not wanting to embrace the idea of what I saw, or admit what it was. That thing was so close I would say a good strong bee-bee gun could have hit it. Every time I tried to tell someone I felt that down deep the person probably would think I was crazy. I just didn't want to expose myself to that type of reaction."

This is the same feeling many people have about reporting what they have seen. Eddie had never read any books on UFOs prior to this event. As a farm boy he was more interested in hunting and trapping. It was years before he looked through books trying to find something that resembled what he saw. "I felt some kind of identity. I'd find pieces of it, but there was nothing particularly like what I experienced."

I got the impression Eddie seemed uncomfortable revealing as much as he did. I think he still felt he might be ridiculed, and he didn't want to be put in that position. I had the impression it took a lot for him to tell me, a stranger, about something he had kept hidden all those years.

He now felt relaxed enough with me to agree to hypnosis. I made an appointment for the next week, to see if we could get any further details.

Nothing much was added under hypnosis. He had remembered the event accurately. I decided to ask Eddie's subconscious for more details that his conscious mind would not have knowledge of. If the subject is in a deep enough level of trance this can be done, and often surprising answers will come forth. I wanted to know if anything had happened that Eddie was not consciously aware of. His answer was that there had been an infusion. He had been given fragments, pieces, bits of information. And he was given direction. He kept referring to infusion, and when I asked what he meant he used a word that is unknown to me. I can only spell it phonetically: contruvering. The word did not make any sense to me, and he also said he did not know what it meant. He said the bits and pieces of information were coming from the ship, and would help in his expansion and growth. It was a physical thing, and the information was being absorbed by the cells of the body, although he had no idea what the information was.

Many people have thought because they had a sighting, they might also have had an abduction experience that they did not remember. I have found that does not always occur. In some cases the sighting is simply enough, because subliminal information is passed without actual physical contact being made. It all occurs on a subconscious level. Thus, many people who think they have merely had a sighting, actually had much more, and have been influenced in ways they could not have conceived.

I asked why this had happened to Eddie, and the answer was that he was vulnerable. He was impressionable and naive, and this made the contact easier. It was more difficult to get through to people who are more material minded or worldly-oriented. I was told "vulnerable" or "innocent" were good descriptions of easy contacts. And surprisingly, it didn't matter if the person believed in these objects, because the goal was to get the individual's attention. The occupants were looking for an opening, a way to get into the being, the core of the person, so a seed could be planted.

I was curious about what type of seed he meant, and he gave a strange answer, "The seed of their being, of their oneness. I'm not separate. Oneness, not two, but one. The seed, or idea, is planted in the psyche by light infusion. It is in the cells, the memory of oneness. It can be planted anywhere there is an opening. We are all one with them. We are not created as two, but one. They want us to know this, and on this night he had an opportunity to see us. He was a good candidate to implant information in." There apparently were other times during Eddie's life when he was unsuspectingly taught. Since the lessons and concepts went directly to his subconscious, he had no conscious memory of them. He only remembered unusual experiences involving animals behaving in an abnormal manner. The contact usually occurred through the eyes of animals, because animals were willing subjects and could be used in this manner. Eddie saw, through the element of surprise, the spirit of oneness in the animal's eyes. In some cases it was not a real animal, but an illusion. This was done to find the vulnerable places in people. "The person must be quiet. The person must stop his world." They could make people see something that's not there, through the element of surprise. They take people off guard. But I thought people *aren't* on guard all the time.

The answer was, "You'd be surprised. People are always on guard. We have to find ways to take the person by surprise. When the person focuses on something, a craft or an animal, when we get their attention, we can stop their world. Then the infusion can take place. We use the element of surprise. If the person is going about their normal, everyday routine, we can't get their attention or focus, and it doesn't work. Their attention must be diverted in some way." I said that meant the beings had to be constantly monitoring, to find these little cracks. He said they are. This also could be an explanation of why they appear invisible to people who are not involved in the experience. *Their* world has not been stopped.

He said, "Not only could animals be used to accomplish this, but also dreams. In this case they would be controlled dreams and have unusual characteristics. Lucid dreams, the type that are more real than usual. Many times they are accompanied with physical sensations throughout the dream. These remain until the person is awakened. Many times they can be colorful dreams, or fearful dreams, but dreams of unusual character. It doesn't matter what the dream is about. It will be more vivid, and have the quality of vividness even after they awaken. The dream may have a fear emotion, because sometimes the dreaming person must be caught unaware, much the same way the awakened person must be caught unaware. Fear is the most powerful emotion, and can be used, at times, to generate the stopping of the world, both in the dreaming and the awakened. By creating a strong emotion it is easier for us to have contact. The element of surprise and the element of fear trigger the awakening. Fear is only used temporarily, and has to be used correctly. Fear is just an opening, but some people *cling* to it. For many people, it is easier to understand than the message. They really have no reason to fear, but they want to cling to that emotion. Many people require much fear to stop their world, but that is their own choice."

D: *It seems that the beings use emotions in ways that we wouldn't understand.*
E: We have used emotions to ways that we do not understand.
D: *Then there is really nothing to be afraid of?*
E: No. It is a gentle cracking of the shell. There is no harm intended.

The strange portion of this experience regarding the truck full of people has also been repeated in some of my other cases. The experience was apparently meant just for Eddie, because the other people were oblivious of the huge ship overhead, and also oblivious of Eddie. This was most unusual. I live in the country, and if you see someone parked at the side of the rural road, you always stop to see if they need help. This is only common courtesy, because houses are far between in the country, and help may be hard to find. You would never pass a stranded neighbor. It appeared he was invisible to them, caught up in his own little time warp where no one else was affected. A truly private experience.

After awakening Eddie remembered some strange incidents involving animals. Once while helping his father in the hayfield, he was driving the tractor when a dove flew down and landed on his right forearm. He felt that something happened at that time, because it was so startling. Another time he was sitting in a cornfield when a coyote came up and began walking around him in circles. This was highly unusual because coyotes will mostly avoid humans. In another incident while he was hunting in the woods a deer allowed him to walk up and touch it. It had no fear element whatsoever. At these times he felt as though something happened to slow him down. It made him look at things differently.

There are many stories in UFO cases where people report animals behaving in unusual ways. Whitley Streiber calls some of these cases "screen memories," when the person sees an illusion of an animal to cover what is really there. I think these display that the contact does not have to be physical or dramatic. It does not have to be actual contact with an alien creature. It appears that it can happen when you least expect it, in ways that are very subtle. It leaves a vivid impression on the conscious mind, but something more profound is occurring on the subconscious level while the mind is distracted and not monitoring the input.

I, myself, had an unusual incident with an owl that I have never forgotten, mostly because of the oddity of the event. I cannot remember the date, but I know it was winter, and I think it was before I became fully involved with UFO material, because I did not place any importance on it until the subject of screen memories came up later. This would place it about 1988 or so. I was driving home very late at night, well after midnight, from one of my metaphysical group meetings in another city. I live in a very isolated situation atop a forest-covered mountain in the Ozark Mountains. The isolation does not bother me; because of my constant traveling and lecturing I spend much time in the major busy cities of the world. After so much hectic activity I enjoy and appreciate my solitude when I return home. There are only about five houses in the four miles it takes me to climb my mountain. My house sits a mile from the nearest neighbor, so the road is very dark, and I am used to seeing wild animals in the area at night.

I had driven to the top of the mountain and just passed my last neighbor's gate. As I neared my place, at the boundary where my land begins, my headlights picked up a huge owl standing in the middle of the road. I drove right up to it and it wouldn't move. It just kept standing there, apparently mesmerized by my headlights. Its head was even with the top of the fender, so I could see it and its huge unblinking eyes quite clearly. I honked and came closer to it. I didn't want to hurt it, just to make it move out of the road. It then turned and flew very low to the ground with a large wingspan, and alighted just out of the range of my headlights. Once again I approached it and it wouldn't move until I got right up to it. Then it would fly a short distance again, alight and turn to face the car. This continued all the way to my gate. It would stop at various places in front of my car, and just stare unblinking at me. Each time it took several seconds to make it move. I laughed because it seemed very peculiar. I was not afraid of it. I kept talking to it, asking it to please move because I didn't want to run over it. I could have several times, because it would not budge until I came right up to it, and honked. This slowed me down considerably as it stopped and then flew low to the ground a short distance and landed again. Finally the last time it flew to the other side of the entrance to my driveway and just stood there while I turned in.

I told my son-in-law about its strange behavior, and he thought it was unusual because owls don't behave like that. He traps and hunts and is familiar with the behavior of the animals in our woods. He also said it sounded like a very large owl.

Later when the subject of screen memories, especially those dealing with owls, came up, I thought it was amusing. I didn't think it could have been one of these because I didn't feel any fear, only amusement. Also, I definitely knew there was no missing time, because I checked the clocks when I came in and stayed up for a while afterwards.

It was years later, in October 1996, when the event came rushing back to me with a tinge of apprehension. I had just completed a lecturing tour throughout Scotland and northern England. I had a few days in London with the luxury of not having any engagements, before continuing on to Dorset in the south of England to speak at a conference. My idea of relaxation is probably not what the average person wants to do. But I took advantage of the time off to go to the Natural History Museum in London. Museums and libraries are my favorite places. I wandered for hours from the main hall, where the giant reconstruction of a dinosaur stands, to the side rooms where every species of animal is preserved in cases. It was in the bird room where I was taken off guard. In one case all the species of owls were displayed. What shocked me and sent chills down my spine, was that *none* of them were as large as the one I saw on the deserted road years before. *None* of these could have been seen over the fender of my car. As I stared at them in wonder and perplexity questions flooded into my mind. What did I really see that night in the road? Did I have a similar experience to the ones I was investigating? Did something else happen that night? I never thought so at the time, and just considered it a curiosity. But now I know that if something else did occur it was a gentle and easy preparation for the work I was to do, and was definitely not to be feared. I am not saying this was an example of contact with alien beings. I am just saying that it bears an uncanny resemblance to the cases I have since investigated. If nothing else, it raises questions in my mind. Elsewhere in this book they say it can happen in the blink of an eye once they have your attention. It's strange how many things may be occurring to us without our conscious knowledge.

I investigated another case that occurred in the city of Little Rock, as a woman was going to work on a busy highway during rush hour traffic. She saw a huge capsule-shaped craft suddenly appear directly in front of her in the sky. She thought it would cause most of the traffic to come to a screeching halt. Instead everything was proceeding normally. There were joggers running by on the sidewalk, and she frantically waved and shouted at them from her car. She tried to get their attention, and kept pointing upward. They continued jogging as though she was invisible. She pulled her car over to the curb, and watched the craft do several drastic gyrations, and fly away. No one else paid any attention to it, although it was huge. She was not abducted, and nothing else happened during the event.

I investigated a case in 1997 half a world away in England that was identical in all respects. Do these aliens have the ability to create an individual experience that no one else is allowed to witness? A similar case will be explored in more detail later in this book.

Apparently there is a great deal happening to us on other levels. It only becomes uncomfortable to us when something happens to bring it to the attention of the conscious mind. I feel that since we are mostly unaware of it, and we couldn't do anything about it anyway, that we shouldn't worry about it. It would be too easy to become paranoid. Hopefully there is a plan to it all that we may discover someday; a method to the madness, so to speak.

These incidents, however, seem to be a different type of experience from Janet's. Eddie's world still had movement in it. Janet's did not. The world around her had stopped, while her private world continued. It was almost as though she was moving faster than the dimension she normally lived in. Everything in that world appeared to stop, because it was moving at a slower vibration. Almost as though she was slipping and sliding through dimensions. The following case is another example.

When Valerie first told me about her UFO experience I was not especially interested, because I was not working heavily in that area yet. It seemed like an ordinary sighting, until she started recounting some unusual circumstances. By the winter of 1988, when this session took place, I had become more involved in investigations. I decided to ask more about the case so I could have a record of it. I now can see that it relates to the two cases of distorted time I have already reported.

Thirty-something Val was a female barber in a small nearby town. I went to her house on her day off and asked her to repeat her experience for the tape recorder. It occurred around 1975 while she was living on the outskirts of Fort Smith, Arkansas, a moderate sized city on the central western side of the state. Some friends had been visiting her, and by two o'clock in the morning most of them had gone home. There was one girl left that Val had to drive back to her apartment in the city. She drove down some side streets and was heading for the highway when she first saw the strange object. It was a large luminous, white, glowing thing that was larger than the moon. Val pulled over to the side of the street so they could watch it. They weren't too far from an Army base, and thought it might have something to do with military night maneuvers. It had an umbrella type shape so she thought it might be a parachute, but it was soon evident it wasn't anything as normal as that. As they watched it suddenly shot right at them and hovered over the car. Frightened, Val put the car into reverse, turned around and headed toward the city. As she reached the highway the white glowing object moved and paced them on the passenger side of the car. It did not maintain any particular shape. It seemed to change, but remained a very white, luminous, glowing light. She drove faster, determined to reach the city as quickly as possible. Then she noticed a strange phenomenon. There was no traffic in either lane, and no lights. (This sounded surprisingly similar to Janet's experience.) The unusual situation continued when she turned off the highway and entered the city. She then saw that the street lights were going out one by one as she approached them, and yet she could see to drive. Nothing was moving, neither the grass nor the trees. There was only an eerie silence. They saw no dogs, no cats, no other cars, no people, no lights in any of the houses. It was as if they were the only people in the world, a weird "twilight zone" feeling. She described it as being in a vacuum: no sound, no movement, nothing. The street lights were off in the area they passed through, yet there was a soft radiating light coming from somewhere above them. They were determined to get someplace where there were other people. They went by a large shopping mall where there was an all-night restaurant. The object then hovered over the mall. As they drove by the restaurant they noticed there was no sign of life, although it was open 24 hours a day. There were no lights and no people anywhere. As they drove on they did not meet any cars or see any people. Even though it was late normally there was always someone on the streets in the city.

Out of desperation they decided to go to a friend's office downtown. He often worked late at night, and they knew he would be there. When they entered the office their world returned to normal. They didn't tell him the real reason they had stopped by, and they just visited for a while. Val then took her friend to her apartment.

As she headed toward the highway to return home the object appeared again, almost as though it had been waiting for her. Everything was normal during the time they were in the office, and when she drove to the apartment. But now the light was back again, pacing her on the driver's side of the car. When she hurriedly arrived home and drove into her driveway, the object swiftly sped away and disappeared in the night sky. Val said the way it moved in so fast in the beginning, and the way it sped away, it definitely appeared to be controlled.

After the discussion we decided to try a hypnosis session to find more details about the incident. She immediately began to recall minor things in detail: the girl's name (which she could not remember consciously), the exact time they left the house, the make and year of her car, and the fact that she was aggravated about having to drive the girl home so late at night. She noticeably breathed faster and was excited as she recounted the initial sighting of the object and the frantic drive toward the city. She said to her friend, "This is stupid, driving fast this way. If it wants us, it can have us." She was trying to get to town where there would be other people, so she could have witnesses. Her description of events was very close to her conscious memories.

V: We know if we can get into Fort Smith there'll be somebody. There's always a patrol car near the mall. There's always people eating at Sambo's. We've got to go by there anyway. It's real strange. Nothing is moving. There are no cars. There are no animals. There's nothing. It's eerie. It feels like we're in a time warp, like a twilight zone. But the streetlights; it seems like there's streetlights ahead of us, but there's no streetlights when we're there. It's like something is happening to the power. We get to the mall area, and it's right above the buildings. I want to think it's the moon, but a strange moon. It can't be, because it changes shapes.

D: *What shapes did it change to?*

V: I can't tell you exactly. It wasn't round to look at like a moon. It was more oblong, but it had no sharp lines. It was glowing and white. and in Sambo's, there's no one in there.

D: *Can you hear the motor on your car?*

V: No. We can't hear anything. I think our hearts are pounding so fast. (Laugh)

She said upon awakening that she could really feel her heart beating faster, as though she was experiencing it again, with all the physical symptoms.

V: Everything but us seems to be in a time warp. The car is working. We can hear each other. The car is being a car. But there's no other sound. It's very still. It's just very strange.

They did not see one car or one sign of life the entire way. When they decided to go to her friend's office, and turned into the street leading there, everything returned to normal. There were lights as there should have been. In the office they were tempted to tell her friend this crazy story, but it seemed too absurd, since everything was normal there.

After she dropped the girl off at her apartment and turned toward the highway going to her house, the object returned and the twilight zone atmosphere came back. Again, no noises, no cars, no lights and no people, although everything had been normal at the office.

V: I have to drive on home. So I do. And I still have this light traveling with me. It doesn't seem to be bad, but it's frightening. It's a strange thing that's happening. I made Glinda promise not to tell anybody. I didn't want them to think I was crazy. I didn't want to be locked away. I made *her promise* she wouldn't tell anybody. I went home, and when I turned into my driveway I was looking at the light. And it just went "whoosh" away from me, as fast as it had come the first time. And out of sight.

The majority of her memories under hypnosis were the same as her conscious ones. I knew the only way I would get further information was to ask to speak to her subconscious. I then asked it what occurred during the time she was driving and had the strange sensation of no lights or motion.

V: The examination. It was an observation of this entity. She was being observed through all of her journey. The trip indeed happened. But the ship was observing and picking up energy patterns and tests, while she was driving her car.
D: *How is that accomplished?*
V: Oh, it's not difficult.
D: *Was she taken physically?*

V: No. The equipment is technically very advanced, and far reaching. In fact, this happens often, that tests or an observation is made without the physical vehicle being removed.

D: *What is the purpose of such examinations?*

V: It's just informative. It's not bad.

D: *Why did she feel she was in a time warp?*

V: She was in a time warp.

D: *Can you be more specific?*

V: The energy and the power that were part of the transference of the pattern, was affecting her perception of the pattern. Affecting her perception of her surroundings, as if time had stopped.

D: *But yet she felt she was really driving.*

V: And she was.

D: *And she thought she was conscious of her surroundings.*

V: Yes. But you know now that more things happen on more than one level, Dolores. And that many things can happen simultaneously. You know that.

D: *I'm becoming more and more aware of that.*

V: And this is just another example of a simultaneous happening.

D: *I'm curious about the fact that there were no lights, and no cars or anything. Do you mean that time literally stopped outside of her immediate environment?*

V: Yes, but it did not hamper the rest of the world. The power that preceded these events simply stop gapped the happenings in the direct path. Do you understand?

D: *I'm trying to. As though everything was frozen?*

V: Yes. But it was so momentary that it affected nothing.

D: *Then other people's lives were not affected at all?*

V: Right.

D: *But were there really no lights?*

V: Yes, there were really no lights for an instant.

D: *And this was caused by the energy?*

V: Yes, that is correct.

D: *Would others have noticed that there weren't any lights?*

V: No. This pattern, this observation was happening with this one alone. And her friend.

D: *So if someone was outside looking at it, for them life would have gone on as normal?*

V: The time element was that there was no one on the outside looking in.

D: *You mean there wasn't anyone there?*

V: There was nothing. It was such an instant, such a flash, such a moment, that it was as if it wasn't.

D: *So in that moment there was no one else involved in this scenario.*

V: That is right.

D: *So time was condensed?* (Yes) *So actually less time passed than she thought.* (Yes) *So instead of a time lapse, it was a time condensation.*

V: Yes. For her it seemed as if it went on for a very long time, but however, it didn't.

D: *And in that instance what was transmitted?*

V: An observation of soul memory patterns. Light emitted. Conditions of concepts. Thought processes. Conditioning. What the human conditioning is, in terms of their ability to receive and to transmit. And the conflict of the patterns set in the conscious mind through conditioning and training. And the reality of who these beings are. Do you understand?

D: *Was there an exchange of information both ways?*

V: There was an exchange into the understanding that one of the things she has been clear on is that, even though it was very frightening, it was a tremendous blessing. It was a gift, so to say. It was an acknowledgment of more than the concepts of society had allowed. And an acknowledgment of a greater life. And more than is.

D: *Was there also an interplay between the friend? I mean, was it occurring to both people?*

V: It is difficult to say what the nudging did for this other one. I can speak more directly for this one. Obviously the observation had not only to do with the vehicle, but for the one with her too. It would seem only reasonable. Otherwise, she would have been alone. So it was an analogy, and a gathering of information.

D: *But was there also an interchange? In other words, were the beings also emitting information?*

V: Yes, on a deeper level. Not on a conscious level.

D: *But there was no harm.*

V: Oh, no. Oh, no. It is not harmful.

D: *This is what some people believe, that it is harmful.*

V: Yes, but those people are lost in a dream state. They are in the clutter, in the muddle, in many ways.

D: *Well, can you tell me about the ship, or the beings that were collecting this information?*

V: No. I could tell you that they were good. And that light that was glowing was representative of that light that was glowing.

D: *And information was transmitted to her for use in her life?*

V: Yes. There came an inner knowing about it, that actually embarrassed her because of her fear.

D: *But it is only human to be afraid of what we don't understand.*

V: Yes, but she likes to be brave.

D: *Was there any particular reason she was singled out, or did she just happen to be in the right place?*

V: Many light ones, as that light is transmitted, are being picked up, so to say, beamed up. These souls are connecting to their brothers, to their sisters, to other beings of God, even before their consciousness is awakened.

D: *So it was not because she was just there. There was more of a plan to it than that?*

V: There always is a plan.

D: *I have been working with some people who have had experiences since childhood.*

V: And was it because they were just there?

D: *No, not in their case.*

V: No. Do you think that with anybody?

D: *I don't know. I am trying to learn. But apparently it was good. It was for her benefit.*

V: It was for her benefit. Everything has to do with how we use it and what we do with it.

D: *And it was good that she also transmitted information they could probably use in their understanding.*

V: Oh, yes. Their understanding is beyond. There has been much information come into this one. But information is usually nudged from another knowing.

D: *Something has been bothering me. I seem to have only had contact or experience with positive experiences. But I have heard of others who have had negative experiences. Is that because there are also negative beings?*

V: I am not of that opinion. I am of the opinion that the reason they are clouded with negative ideas and stories, is that it comes from that consciousness that is giving those stories. That it is so colored in all of their own creation.

D: *Then do you think fear and similar emotions have colored their perception?*

V: Of course. Fear is the only thing - and the list that comes below fear - that creates that which is dark, which is negative, which is less than love and life and God.

D: *Do you think they actually had experiences, but their conscious mind perceived them as negative?*

V: I think that it is possible, but then I am not all knowing.

D: *Then there will also be asked the question, if the conscious mind can be fooled into thinking it's a negative experience, can it also be fooled into thinking it's a positive experience?*

V: No. It cannot be fooled into thinking it's a positive experience. You see, here is the difference. That which we perceive as positive, we perceive as good, we perceive as God. That which we perceive as negative is the illusion. The dream state. So, if we perceive it as positive, as good, as God, then our perceptions are correct. If we perceive it as negative, then it may have been negative, but only in the way it has been turned. The way it has been perceived and used. The lack of understanding. Do you understand?

D: *Yes. This is the way I believe. Except that some people think they have been harmed by these beings.*

V: There are some people that believe they have been harmed by these other beings, and by their neighbor, by their friend, and yet it is their perception. We have to understand and come to a place of knowing that all is good. And that if we perceive it out of fear, it can be nothing but negative. Fear colors and discolors. I can only tell you what my deepest soul says. And that deepest soul says, if we respond from fear, it will be negative.

D: *Maybe that is why I've only been involved with positive experiences.*

V: I think you have been well chosen.

D: *I have also been told of genetic experiments and genetic engineering. And that some of the results do not appear to be human.*

V: I believe the genetic experiments are happening on this planet, but it is happening with mankind. Man is stepping beyond his spirituality.

D: *That's an interesting concept. You mean there are people on Earth who are experimenting along these lines?*

V: Yes, but it will not be allowed to go on. The information I have is that, there are indeed beings from other planets on this Earth plane, to serve humanity. They are advanced in many ways to humankind. Man is a co-creator with God, the creator. And in his creation he can create all that his mind will allow him to. And that is created out of love or out of fear. That one that comes from another place, another planet, our brothers and sisters, comes out of love. Out of love for mankind, for this planet Earth, and for the universe itself. They come at a time of our need. They come at a time of our awakening.

Val's subconscious said she never had an actual physical encounter with the craft or the beings. The only contact was this interchange of information.

When Val was awakened she remembered the first part because it was a very real reliving of the incident. But she had no memory of the last part, the conversation with her subconscious. She listened to that part of the tape, and was surprised by what she had said. This is very typical. When the subconscious gives information the subject will not remember it. It always sounds as though another entity is speaking, and it always refers to the body it occupies in the third person (he or she), instead of I. It is always very detached, and can thus be analytical and objective.

CHAPTER 3
THINGS ARE NOT ALWAYS
WHAT THEY APPEAR TO BE

Whitley Streiber was the first author to use the term "screen memories" in connection with UFOs and aliens. This is a memory of an event or a thing that is not accurate. Something has been superimposed over what is actually occurring, and the mind interprets it differently. Often it is interpreted in a safer and gentler way, so the person will not be frightened or traumatized. When I heard of this, I suspected it was part of the subconscious mind's defense system, its method of protecting the psyche from anything it considers harmful to remember, or to see in its actuality. Often these screen memories involve animals. I have had several cases where this appears to have occurred, where an "overlay," as I call it, has been placed over the actual scene. For some reason owls feature prominently in this phenomenon. In *Keepers of the Garden* Phil was startled on a road late at night when an owl swooped over the highway and then over his car. Under hypnosis we discovered it was not an owl at all, but an alien craft and small beings on the highway that forced him to stop. His subconscious had disguised the scene in a softer way so he would not remember what had actually occurred.

In the case I am about to relate "overlay" memories seem to be involved with missing time. I had known Brenda for several years, and she was the main connection in my work with Nostradamus. We were very involved in that work when I also began to work as a UFO investigator by using hypnosis in suspected abduction cases. One day in January 1989 when I went to her house for our regular session she wanted to tell me about an unusual incident that had occurred in March 1988. She considered it odd, but for some reason had not mentioned it to me before. She thought I would be interested now because I was becoming more involved in the UFO phenomenon. She did not know if it was connected with UFOs or aliens, but it definitely involved missing time, and an owl.

She was driving home from work in Fayetteville, a drive that normally took about a half hour, and was within sight of her house in the country when the incident occurred. The sun had set but it was not yet dark. She came around a curve and there was an owl sitting right in the middle of her lane. It was not the normal type of brown owl that is usually seen in our area. It was brilliant white with silver highlights on its chest, and its eyes were very black. It was absolutely beautiful, and she slowed down so she wouldn't hit it. She assumed this was the type called a "snow owl," which is normally seen in colder climates such as Canada or the northern states. A zoologist friend told me later that it is possible for a snow owl to be seen in Arkansas in the depth of winter, but there shouldn't be any as late as spring. This would have been a rare occurrence, *if* it were a real owl.

When she first spotted it, it was sitting facing away from her, but it turned its head to look at her. Then it flapped its wings and flew up straight toward the truck. Its wingspan was as wide as the windshield. It startled her, and as it skimmed over the roof of the truck Brenda twisted around to look out the back window. But there was nothing, no sign of the owl, no sign of any type of bird. When Brenda turned and looked out the front window again she was shocked to see it was dark outside. It crossed her mind that it had certainly gotten dark fast. Totally confused, she had to turn on her headlights to drive the last quarter mile to her house. When she entered the house she looked at the clock out of habit. Instead of being around 5:30, as it should have been, it was almost 7 o'clock. What had happened to an hour and a half? She was positive of the time she left work, because she did not work overtime until summer.

She thought it was a peculiar incident, and she had heard that sometimes when something odd like that happens, something has been blocked from your conscious memory.

I asked if she had noticed anything else that was different. The main thing she remembered was having a strange effect on electrical appliances for a few days afterwards. This had occasionally happened to her in the past. She can't wear a watch because of her electrical field, or whatever it is. But the sensations had never been so profound or lasted for so long. This time everything electrical was malfunctioning. For several days her TV would go in or out of focus whenever she moved. At work the computer kept flipping, and the clocks and calculator were doing weird things they weren't supposed to do. She thought her electrical field was interacting more strongly than usual with appliances, and she was more sensitive to sound. Her natural hearing extends into the upper ranges beyond normal hearing. She can hear higher frequencies, and for several days she was particularly sensitive to these higher frequencies that most people can't hear. The telephone was one of the peculiarities. She said it makes a high-pitched beep just before it starts to ring, and most people don't hear that. So she was answering the phone before it started ringing. This was confusing her boss, who said, "Please, Brenda, settle down. Let the phone ring before you answer it."

She could also hear a high-pitched screech that certain security systems make in stores. It sounded so loud to her that it hurt her eardrums, although no one else could hear it. She tried to stay out of the shopping mall until things returned to normal.

At home if she picked up a clock to wind it, that was enough to destroy the clock. At work the clocks were electrical, and she did not have to touch them. Just being in the same room with them was enough to cause them to do strange things. Those clocks never totally recovered. The clock on the microwave at work also created a problem. It emitted loud beeps when she started to punch in the numbers on the timer. She did not have to touch it, she just had to reach towards it. These strange effects on electrical appliances continued for four days afterwards and then settled down again.

We decided to devote this session to discovering what, if anything happened during that missing time, instead of doing our regular experiments with Nostradamus. She didn't think it would bother her if she found out something unorthodox had occurred.

When we started the session I took her back to the latter part of March 1988, and she immediately entered the scene where she was driving her truck home. Along the way she discussed her day's work, and that she was worried about her mother, who had recently been in a car accident. These were her thoughts as she drove. She was also tired, and anxious to get home, take a hot bath and relax.

She was almost home when she came around a curve and saw something standing in the middle of her lane. She stopped the truck so she wouldn't run over it. In her conscious memory of the event she thought she only slowed down, but she now said she came to a complete halt. Another surprise was that what she saw in the road was *not an* owl.

D: What is in the road?

B: It's hard to say. I suppose if we lived in olden times I would call it an angel.

D: (Surprised) An angel?

B: A being from a higher plane perhaps? I see a man standing in the middle of my lane. He glows white ... all over. And his clothes appear to be white as well.

D: Do you mean the glow is like an aura around him?

B: Sort of. (She had difficulty explaining.) It's kind of like a black and white picture that's been a bit overexposed. You know, very light colored all over and white radiating out from it.

D: It's not like a glow from a light?

B: Well, it's hard to describe, because it's sort of like that and it's sort of like an aura. And sort of like an overexposed picture, or all of them rolled into one.

D: And his clothes are white too?

B: At least that's the way they look to me. It could be that I'm not able to perceive the colors correctly, since he has so much light around him. Even his hair glows white.

D: Can you see what his features look like?

B: That's hard to do because there's so much light. From the best I can tell they resemble classical Greek features like you see on classical Greek sculpture. Very even, with level forehead and a nice straight nose, and very balanced features.

D: About how tall is he?

B: Six feet, six foot two.

D: He's large then.

B: He's a good sized fellow, yes. He's standing there looking around. And I can see rays coming out from his eyes. When he's looking towards me I can't see them. But when he looks off to the side I see these rays coming out from his eyes. I do not know the purpose of these rays. And he sees me. I've stopped so I wouldn't hit him. I didn't want to do him harm. And he came over to the truck. As he walked around toward the driver's side, he did a gesture over the truck. He waved his hand just once. (A motion with her left hand, a slow wave.) He did it parallel to the hood of the truck, and then swooped it up parallel to the windshield. His hand was about six to eight inches above the truck when he did this.

Apparently this was what her conscious mind recorded as the owl flying low over the truck. It was obvious that the false overlay of the white owl came from her conscious mind, because in trance she had no hesitation in identifying it as a person. She never once mentioned an owl.

B: And I rolled down the window to see if he needed a ride or anything.

That seemed to be a strange reaction upon seeing such an unusual person. It would have been normal if it appeared as a physical human, but this did not. The expected reaction would have been to gun the motor and get out of there. It certainly seemed unusual to roll down the window to speak to the glowing being. Obviously it did not inspire fear in her, and she felt no danger. I asked her if it bothered her.

B: It was strange, but I was curious about who he was and what he was doing. And I figured if he meant me harm, he would have zapped me already. I figured with him glowing so much and with light coming out of his eyes, if he wanted to zap me from where he was standing, he probably could.

D: *So you're not afraid of him.*

B: Well, I was apprehensive, maybe a little nervous. But I wasn't panicked or anything like that. And I asked him if he needed some help, or if he needed a ride somewhere. And he said, "Oh, bless you, child. I appreciate your offering. My transportation's right over there." He gestured toward a hill that was beside the road.

D: *Could you see anything?*

B: No. I just saw the hill. It has quite a few cedar trees on it. From the way he gestured I got the feeling that if there was anything there, it was on the far side of the hill, maybe just over the crest. Where it would be out of eyesight anyway.

I have driven that road many times going to Brenda's house. And after this experience I took particular note of that hill. It is not far from the road in the middle of a farmer's field. There are a few trees on top, and no houses near it. But it is not very high, so a craft could not be very big if it hid behind it out of sight from the road. *Unless* he had also rendered it invisible to humans.

B: I asked him, "Who are you? I can't help but notice that your appearance is different from mine. Are you an extraterrestrial visitor or are you from a higher plane?" And he said he was from the council of elders. I asked him, "What is this council? Councils are usually to advise or to run a group or something." And he said that various visitors had been to various parts of the Earth and were bringing back conflicting reports about how far Earth had developed. There is a group that is in favor of open contact with humankind, and there's another group that is in favor of leaving humankind in ignorance, as it is now. And since he is part of the council of elders, they decided he would come on his own to see how things were on the Earth. It is rather a covert type mission, a fact-finding mission, you could call it. So they would have more information to base their decision on, whether to leave Earth in ignorance, or to contact humankind and bring them into light and health and knowledge.

D: *Is that what you meant by "ignorance"?*

B: Well, even though humankind suspects, and some wish and dream that there is extraterrestrial life, for the most part, so far as the officials in the governments are concerned, there is no such thing. That's what they mean by ignorance, by not accepting that fact. They have been thinking of contacting humankind in a way they could handle, that also would prove beyond a doubt that there is extraterrestrial intelligence. And they're living their own lives until such time as humankind catches up enough to be able to join them.

D: *Is he having this communication with you by speaking words?*

B: Not really. I guess you could call it "vocalized telepathy." I could hear him very clearly, as if he were speaking, but his mouth wasn't moving. I am assuming he was projecting his thoughts toward my mind, but I could perceive it as a very pleasant-sounding voice.

D: *Then what happened?*

B: He said he had to continue with what he was doing, and that I needed to go home. There was nothing I could do to help him. Then he waved his hand once in front of my eyes. And when he did that - I suppose with the mental powers he had - I could no longer see him. And I no longer remembered the experience as it had happened.

D: *I wonder why he was out there in the middle of the road?*

B: I never did find out for sure. I got the impression he'd been going to different places and observing humankind and everything that was going on. And I had the feeling he was curious about what would happen if he were to have a chance meeting with an average human on the road. Whether I would panic and try to run away, or be scared and try to harm him or anything like that.

D: *Well, there probably are people who would have done that.*

B: That is true. But I guess you would say he was taking an average sampling. He was appearing to various humans here and there, and then making them forget the experience. But he was taking note of their reactions to his appearance. To get an idea of how humankind in general would react to definite knowledge of extraterrestrial life.

D: *When he was by the side of the truck, could you see any more details about him?*

B: Well, everything was very white and glowing. His style of clothing was basically loose and comfortable. Rather like a caftan with a poncho over it or something like that. And he had a sash tied around his waist. His clothing seemed to have several pouches and pockets, so he could carry things with him. And it looked like he had cloth boots on his feet, and although the cloth was about an inch thick it appeared flexible and soft. He had flowing robes on, but two or three layers, so it looked like he'd be warm, for the time of the year. It looked like they were made out of finely spun wool or something similar.

D: *Did he have hair?*

B: Oh, yes. It looked like straight white hair, trimmed on the front, and maybe shoulder length in the back. He was glowing so much that I couldn't really tell if he had any particular colors around him. His skin and hair looked white, and his eyes looked silvery. And he was clean shaven.

D: *Did he still have the rays coming out of his eyes?*

B: No, not when he was talking to me. But when he was looking around the landscape, he had the rays coming out of his eyes.

D: *But nothing about it was frightening. It was just strange.*

B: Really strange, but I really enjoyed it, because he didn't seem to mind my asking questions.

D: *What other questions did you ask him?*

B: I asked him if there really was life out there, or if that was just wishful thinking on my part. And he said, "Yes, there really is life out there, and it is very varied." There are many different kinds of life with all types of appearances and abilities. And several different races of beings are looking forward to humans finally developing reliable spacecraft, so we can join them and be part of the galactic community. And he said that different races have particular characteristics. Some are more belligerent than the others, and some races tend to be lighthearted and humorous. And then he said something I thought was strange, yet promising, too. He said, "But you'll learn all about that in a while." So I took that to mean perhaps within my lifetime humankind would reach out to the stars.

D: *I wonder where this council is located? Did you ask him that?*

B: He said it didn't have a particular location. They simply met wherever all the members decided. I got the impression there was one particular ship that was theirs. It's a very large ship, and they tended to meet on this ship most often to conduct their business. But the council members are from all different planets, to represent several different races.

D: *But you said he had human features.*

B: Yes, he appeared human. I asked him, "Life out there in the stars, does it come in all different unimaginable forms and features, or are they basically humanoid?" He said we would find life both ways: similar to us but a little different, and so totally different that it would be hard to believe they really are intelligent life.

D: *You said you saw his hands. Did they seem like human hands?*

B: They were very large, with long fingers. On the piano keyboard he could *easily* span a twelfth or a thirteenth without even straining, the way I can span a ninth or a tenth. (She was using her pianist's background to make a comparison.) And his fingers were long in proportion to the size of his hands. But the best I can remember, he had the same number of fingers as we have. And since he wore flowing clothing, I could not tell if there were any particular physical features that were different from us. The main thing I noticed was that he was larger than average. But then I figured that where he came from they probably have a higher standard of health. And so people would probably reach a larger average size.

D: *Do you mean he was taller or just bigger?*

B: Just bigger. Taller, broader shouldered, large hands. He had beautiful teeth. I don't think he ever went to a dentist in his life. He seemed to be very wise and gentle. And he said one of the things that frightened some of the other races is our tendency to be somewhat aggressive, and maybe a little belligerent sometimes. He said if we can learn to control this, our future will be very bright.

This seemed to be the only information she could supply about the strange encounter. I knew that I could always get more by speaking directly to her subconscious mind. So I asked to speak to her subconscious. I have never been denied access.

D: *I am curious about this being that she saw. In actuality, did he really look the way she described him?*

B: In actuality, he *did* glow the way she described. But there were some visible physical differences that he caused her to forget, or not to see to start with. I suppose you could say he had a charm cast upon himself so he would appear fully human.

D: *Can you tell me what he really looked like?*

B: His hair was white and flowing, and longer than she remembered, and the hairline was more receding. He had a very sharp widow's peak, where she perceived him as having a straight hairline like that of a young man. And he did have large hands, but they were bony, and his fingers had an extra joint in them. Instead of the fingers ending where ours do, it was as if the middle joint had been repeated. To where they bent differently than our fingers do.

D: *How many fingers did he have?*

B: He had four fingers, but he also had a double thumb.

D: (This was a surprise.) *A double thumb? What do you mean?*

B: Two thumbs. His hand was longer than ours, because it had more bones in it. He had one thumb in the normal position and another above it. There was plenty of room for two thumbs before the fingers started. (All of this was accompanied by hand motions.)

D: So he had two thumbs and four fingers, making six fingers altogether.

B: Yes, on each hand. With long, narrower fingernails than ours. At the base where the cuticle is, it was a very sharp U shape instead of squared like ours are.

D: Was his face different?

B: It looked harsher than she remembered. He realized she might find his appearance frightening. His eyes were very large and glaring, because of the power emanating from them, with very bushy eyebrows above them. And actually, his eyes were totally white. There was no iris or pupil to be seen.

D: I have seen blind people like that. Is that what you mean?

B: Yes. Except that this white glowed with light, because of the power emanating from him.

D: What about his other features?

B: His other features appeared quite normal. His cheeks were rather craggy, sunken in. And he had a very strong jaw line. It was hard to tell about his ears because his hair covered them.

D: And his skin was actually white?

B: I don't think it was really. There was so much light glowing, it was hard to tell what color it actually was. But because of the contrast between his hair and his skin, and between his eyes and his skin, it appears that his skin was darker. But it glowed with light, so it looked lighter than it really was.

D: Did he have a nose and a mouth like ours?

B: Yes. He had a nose and a mouth, but it's hard to say whether the teeth were the same, because he did not open his mouth when he was speaking. He was speaking by projecting his thoughts.

D: But she saw teeth.

B: Because the image she saw would occasionally smile. And the real image was very solemn.

D: So his face didn't have expression.

B: Oh, it had expression, but it never involved showing the teeth. He would quirk his eyebrows and tilt his head and such as that, but it never did involve smiling. His face did seem more narrow in front. The way his face slanted into his mouth was sharper and narrower than our faces. Ours are kind of flat by comparison.

D: Was he wearing the type of clothes she described?

B: He wore clothes, but they were much more complex than she described. He had a lot of metalwork and such worked into his clothing.

D: *What was that for?*

B: Various instruments and such. Some of it was just adornment. Some of it represented his rank. And some of it was remote controls for a ship and such. This was in his clothes, in his belt. He had something like a bandoleer crossing his chest, (her hand motions indicated there were two straps) that was loaded with metal things.

D: *Instruments and stuff like that, you said?*

B: More like buttons and switches and things. And it looked like small bottles, but they all had purposes. It wasn't just ornamental. If it were instruments, they were very miniaturized.

D: *So even the clothes were different than she thought they were.*

B: They were similar, with flowing sleeves and hemline. She just didn't see the instruments and what she would call the "gizmos." He did not allow her to see the gizmos.

D: *Was there a reason for that?*

B: Yes, because humankind is technologically immature. And if they are exposed to too much foreign advanced technology too quickly, it could be disastrous.

D: *Man is always trying to learn new things. Do you mean we couldn't understand it or handle it or what?*

B: Couldn't handle it. The equivalent from Earth history would be whenever sailors discovered a new island in the South Pacific, and gave the chief a gun as a gift. The chief was proud of his gift, and waved it around, saying, "Hey, look what I have." And it accidentally went off and hurt somebody, because he didn't have the knowledge of how to take care of it and use it.

D: *I'm thinking of the word "discipline."*

B: No, that's not the right sense. He didn't have the understanding of how something should be applied. Because once you understand how something should be applied, the discipline comes naturally.

D: *So they figure it's better not to show us too much at once.*

B: Exactly. We are considered to be an intelligent species and very highly curious. And they know if we see something and remember it, we'll try to figure out what we saw and then try to reconstruct it.

D: *Did he really have rays coming out of his eyes?*

B: Yes. The way their machinery is constructed, it can work *through* the body, not just through the machines. It can also use the body. And the rays coming out of his eyes could have been from either a machine that was scanning the landscape to analyze what things were made of, or it could have been rays from a machine that was tuned to find a particular element of something. There are many different things it could have been.

This sounded similar to the cases in my book, *Legacy From the Stars*, where machinery and the body were combined. In some cases the body was wired so that it could operate the spacecraft by moving muscles. Many of the aliens in that book literally became part of their ship. I thought it might be an eerie extension of the new Virtual Reality games where machine and body are working together.

This now appeared to be a case of not *one* but *two* "overlays." The simple version of the owl that her conscious mind remembered was totally different from the two supplied under hypnosis. Apparently these alien beings have the ability to make us perceive things in many ways. Only hypnosis can reveal what truly lies beneath the surface. Can we ever know what is real and what is an illusion?

D: *It seems strange that he didn't know she was coming along in her truck.*

B: But he did know.

D: *Oh? I thought he was surprised.*

B: No. She was the one who was surprised. He knew that she'd be along. And she was one he wanted to have contact with.

D: *Was there a reason he wanted to have contact with her?*

B: Yes. The council of elders keeps track of certain ones on the Earth, so that when the time is right to contact humankind, these will be the ones contacted first, if it occurs within their lifetimes. For several centuries they have done this. One of the humans they felt was the most promising was Leonardo da Vinci. And so as each generation comes and goes, there are particular ones they watch. In case it happens during their generation they have already decided who they want to contact first.

D: *Was there anything particularly different about her that they were watching her?*

B: They look for a combination of features in the people they would like to contact first. The people must be highly intelligent. (This would fit Brenda, because she has the I.Q. quotient of a genius.) And open minded and willing to learn new things. (She certainly is open-minded or she would never have agreed to our strange experiments.) As well as being spiritually advanced and in contact with the higher planes. Someone who is trying to improve themselves and who is open to new things. Someone who, even though they have obstacles in their life, overcome these in a positive way without negatively affecting others around them. Some people overcome their obstacles by tearing those around them down. But that's not the type of person they want. They want people who overcome their obstacles through positive means.

D: *Do they keep in touch with these people or watch over them all their life?*

B: Yes. They keep an eye on them all their life. And from time to time they contact them. Sometimes they allow them to remember, but most of the times they cloud their memory, so as to not complicate their day-to-day life.

D: *Has Brenda been contacted before?*

B: Yes, she has. Particularly when she was a young child, but she doesn't remember. They contacted her to help her start preparing, in case the time comes during her lifetime.

D: *This same type of being?*

B: Sometimes a being like this, and sometimes a being of a different appearance, because it would be someone from a different race of beings. But it would usually be someone that was in close contact with the council of elders. They work together.

D: *How do they keep track of someone? People move around so much. How can they locate them?*

B: They are able to perceive your mental emanations. And your aura is very visible to them. Plus some of these individuals are highly developed enough to perceive on higher planes than humankind can. So once they know what your aura and your higher self and your mental emanations look like, it's very easy to track you down, because everybody is unique, and no two people are alike. They have machines that help with this. They put the information into the machine, and tell it to scan this planet. Where is this person with thus and such type of aura, thus and such type mental emanations? And the machine zeros in on the location.

D: *Then they didn't have to do anything to her physical body in order to find her.*

B: They don't have to do anything physical to her body every time. Now the first time they contacted her when she was a child of nine, they did inoculate her. Rather like a vaccination, you could say. It's hard to explain.

D: *I'm thinking of a shot or something like that.*

B: Yes, it's very similar to that. And sometimes this inoculation will leave a scar or some sort of marking on the skin. They inoculate a substance into the body that helps heighten the perceptions. It helps make the person more sensitive to asper abilities, because those abilities are very important in the galactic community.

D: *That's a strange word to me. "Asper" abilities?*

B: That's a very common word. It's just another way of referring to all the extrasensory abilities.

D: *I was thinking of aspirations.*

B: You're thinking of the wrong word. (She spelled it.) "Esper," esper abilities.

D: *It's a word I'm not familiar with.*

B: She's familiar with it. That's where I got it.

D: *Oh, you got it from her vocabulary. - Well, in what part of the body would they give this inoculation?*

B: In her case it was here where this bump is on her left forearm.

Brenda held up her arm, and I could see a very small bump.

D: *How was that given?*

B: It was given at night while she was asleep. And if you ask her when she's awake, she'll tell you when it happened, because it seemed very odd at the time it appeared.

D: *Was an instrument used?*

B: Yes. It appears to be something like a silver tube. And the end they press against the arm appears flat or maybe slightly curved inward. But when you press it against the arm, something in the tube pierces the skin and inoculates into the blood stream. But it doesn't hurt.

D: *But it leaves a little bump?*

B: When it heals there is a bump left where they give the inoculation. When she's awake she can describe how it first appeared and how it healed. And in addition to the substance they inoculate, it appears there is also a small silver ball. But it's actually a very small instrument that will help their machines keep track of the person, because it tunes in on their mental emanations. And if contact is made during that person's lifetime, they can activate this "thing" they left in the body. Then it will also act rather like a translator. So she can project her thoughts and communicate, and hear their thoughts. And if vocal communication is used she'll be able to understand them even if they're speaking an unfamiliar language. When the sound hits the brain, it will be transferred into comprehensive symbols that she can understand. This thing in her body will be able to do this. I call it silver type because that's the way it appears. It's not really made out of silver. It's maybe an eighth of an inch in diameter, and it's located in the flesh of her forearm, beneath the bump where they inoculated her. It's in between the two bones, the radius and ulna, down there in the muscle. It was injected with the inoculation. They do it in one trip, so they don't have to physically enter her dwelling again. They can then keep track of her through their instruments.

D: *Are there any other foreign objects in her body?*

B: Not at this time.

D: *Was there at one time?*

B: Not that I know of, but there is the possibility there might be some put in her body in the future for various reasons.

D: *Is this one in her arm causing any physical problems?*

B: No, and it shouldn't.

D: *What about x ray? Could that pick this up?*

B: It might, although it's unlikely. The way it's positioned between the two bones, one of the bones would probably block the view of it in the x ray. They try to position these so they would be difficult to find, because they don't want them taken out. The way they are installed, I guess you could say, they can transmit to a nearby nerve, in order to have contact with the brain.

D: *I have heard of other people having things in their head.*

B: Something might be put in her head in the future if the occasion warrants it. But for the time being the council of elders prefer to have the ones they are watching be totally free agents.

D: *What is the purpose of putting one in the head?*

B: I'm not sure. Of the various races and groups of humanity that are out in the galactic community, different ones have different aims and different goals. And they use different instruments. So they might go about contacting humankind in different ways. Although the contacts are supposed to be coordinated through the council of elders, some of these groups use their own instruments rather than the ones the council of elders approve.

D: *Doesn't the council mind if they do these things? Isn't it against their regulations or something?*

B: Some of them are against the regulations and some of them are not. It depends on how it's done, and if any harm is done to the subject. Also what kind of effect it has on the subject.

D: *Can you see what the beings look like that put that in her arm when she was nine years old?*

B: They were a very gentle type of people. It's hard to see what they look like because it was nighttime when they did it. They are different from the person she saw on the highway. For one thing they had no hair on their heads. Their heads were very smooth. And they seem to be kind of silvery colored. Their hands were different, because they have three fingers and a thumb. They are not as large as the person she saw on the highway. These people tend to be long boned and slender, very delicately built. They have dark eyes, but that's all I can tell because their faces are in shadow. But they tend to be long limbed and skinny, and they look emaciated by human standards, because they're so thin.

D: *You said these are a gentle people?*

B: Yes. They have great intellectual curiosity. And they're doing this on the instruction from the council of elders. And the council of elders, as you will remember, includes many beings of many different races. There are an infinite number of types of beings, because there's such a variety of life when you take the universe as a whole. Just in this galaxy there are many different types of living beings that have different appearances, different cultures, different abilities, different ways of looking at things, different ways of building things. When you see how some of the races appear, you can understand how the different legends about gnomes and elves and such got started. Because in ancient times sometimes the visitors were not as careful, and someone would see them without having their memory clouded, and it would start this rumor about people of a particular appearance. And so when you hear these legends of people who are either extremely tall and grotesque looking or very small and delicate looking, they are most likely from some of these different races that have visited in the past.

D: *The council is the one that tells these other beings to go and do these things?*

B: That's the way it should happen.

D: *It doesn't always happen that way?*

B: Not always, no. But they try to keep it coordinated through the council of elders, so as to do the least harm.

D: *I'm finding a larger majority of people have had contact with these different beings, than we thought at first.*

B: Yes, because the time for making open contact with the Earth is closer than ever before. And it is quite possible that it might happen during the lifetime of the present generation of the ones they've been watching. They're really hoping so anyway, because many are anxious for humankind to join the galactic community.

D: *We have been hearing about people who say they were abducted. Do you know anything about that?*

B: Now it is true that occasionally they will make a closer physical-type examination of a human being, to keep track of how the science of medicine has progressed and how human beings are still evolving. They want to be prepared for the type of human beings there will be when humankind joins the galactic community. Because when this occurs they want to offer eradication of disease. In order to do that they have to examine humans first, so they can develop the cures to these different diseases. Then they can offer the cures to us when they contact us openly.

D: *That makes sense. How are these physical examinations carried out?*

B: Usually with light and certain kinds of energies. Similar to the way we use x-rays to examine bones. They have various frequencies of energies that can examine particular things in the body, and tell them what kind of shape it's in, or what stage of development.

D: *Is this done in the person's home in their bed?*

B: No, they have to take them into one of their ships where they have their instruments set up. These instruments emit specific energies to examine specific things in the body. And since there are so many of them, they are not easily transportable. They could probably do a partial examination in your home, but it would not be as thorough as they could do aboard their craft.

D: *This is what I think people are calling abductions.*

B: It's not meant as an abduction. If they were going to abduct them they would take them to the ship, fly off, and never bring them back to Earth again. This is just an examination, so they can continue to collect the information they need. And in return mankind will offer the galactic community our individual accomplishments: our curiosity, our intellect, our love of arts and music. And the way we like to build things and figure things out. That's what we can contribute to the galactic community.

D: *I've also heard that some of these different beings seem cold, as though they don't have any emotions.*

B: Some of them do appear that way, simply because they're concentrating on an intellectual type pursuit, so they'd have no reason to show any emotion. And some of the beings are just naturally reserved, and rely more on telepathy to express their emotions, rather than physical gestures.

D: *I have talked to people who have a great deal of fear after seeing these beings.*

B: Yes. And that is unfortunate, because they really don't mean us any harm. The ones that feel such fear are usually people who are not as open-minded as they could be, or not prepared for the experience. And so instead of thinking of it as something wonderful and a new experience to cherish, they think instead of late night monster movies and bug eyed creatures coming after them. (*I laughed.*) And so they get scared.

D: *This is a perfectly normal human reaction though.*

B: That depends. If the human has been trained from childhood to react that way, then, yes, that's a normal reaction. But if they have been trained from childhood to react with wonder and curiosity instead. It depends on the exposure they get to such things when they are children. And what kind of attitudes their family have.

D: *There has been talk of people seeing beautiful blond beings. Do you think they are real, or are they just a type of illusion?*

B: There is a race of beings that have white hair and some are very beautiful. This being that she saw was a member of that race. And so it could be that they have seen these people. But at the same time there was probably an element of illusion to make them appear more beautiful, so people would not be afraid. They are made to see it as beautiful, according to human terms, so they will react more positively.

D: *That makes sense. Humans are basically fear oriented animals.*

B: It doesn't have to be that way.

D: *I have a few more questions. When her truck was stopped on the road and the being was talking to her, what if someone else had come by? Would they have seen this being?*

B: They would not have seen the being or her truck either one. They would have passed her, for the road was straight there, but they would not have been aware of passing her. They would have thought they were just driving straight, because they would not have seen her or the being either one.

D: *I wondered if they could hit the car, because she was stopped in the road.*

B: No, they would have just gone around her and kept going, but they never would have known it happened.

D: *How was that accomplished?*

B: The same way it was accomplished when she saw a different appearance for that being. He altered her perception of what she was seeing. They can do this to any human. So they just alter their perception of what they see. If someone came along, instead of seeing a truck stopped in the road with someone speaking to the driver, they would see just the open empty road. And they would just keep driving.

D: *I see. And they arrange this so no one will be hurt in the process.*

B: Right. Because they do not want to harm anybody.

D: *But anyway, during this experience she had in March, there was an actual physical being there, but he not only made her perceive him differently, he also blocked the memory and put in the image of the owl. Is that correct?*

B: Yes, as a matter of protection, both for her and for him. He wanted to be in contact with her, but he did not want to complicate her life. So he had her perceive that she had seen a very beautiful owl in the road. That way it doesn't really affect her life. But at the same time, he altered her perception of how she saw him, so it would be a gentler experience for her. So she would be more open minded toward the experience. Because had she seen him in his true form, she might have had a stronger element of fear. He was trying to keep it as pleasant for her as possible.

D: *That makes sense. But it won't bother her to remember it this way, will it?*

B: No, not at all. She has such a great desire to remember it. And I think that is good. I permit it myself. She should remember all this when she wakes up, because it will help her to continue to prepare for when the time comes. She is ready for this information. That is the reason she remembered about the owl, so she could use the techniques that are available to draw forth this information. And so she will remember everything.

D: *Brenda said that for days afterward she experienced problems with her hearing, and something was affecting electrical appliances and such things. What was causing these things?*

B: Due to her interaction with this being her aura had absorbed some extra energy. Much of this energy was used within her body, but there was still some excess. And her aura was throwing off this excess energy rather like invisible bolts of lightning, so to speak. As a result, her ears were ringing and doing strange things. And she was hearing very high-pitched sounds. And with having this extra energy about her body, it was interfering with the functioning of electrical things.

D: *Was this just because of being in the proximity of this being?*

B: It was due to the fact that she is receptive to higher things. Therefore, she and her aura are open to higher energies. And so when she was in the proximity of this being, in addition to absorbing spiritual and mental knowledge from him, she also absorbed some auric energy. There was excess energy that could not be utilized right away, and so there were these side effects. It's like when you send too much electricity through a wire, you get a spark.

D: *Was this affecting her own health in any way?*

B: Not negatively, no. The extra energy within her body did help with some healing processes going on, because there's always some healing being done within the body. And so it didn't interfere with anything that needed to be done. It was just a matter of affecting the hearing some and affecting electrical things around her. She was not too astonished, because for most of her life she has affected clocks around her. And for a while when she was in high school she affected vending machines also. And she has always had sensitive hearing. So these effects did not alarm her, because they were similar to things that happened to her before. But they were still a little different and slightly more intense. The effect with her hearing comes and goes, sometimes for just a few minutes, for part of a day, or like that time, it lasted for several days. That's what annoyed her so, because she was used to the effect on her hearing fading away quickly. Now in her case, the effect she has on clocks and time pieces is a permanent effect peculiar to her.

D: *Because of her energy field?*

B: Partially because of her energy field, and her psychic abilities, and partially because of the way she perceives time.

D: *What do you mean?*

B: Most people in her culture, because of the way they have been raised, are very conscious of time. Of minutes, and hours and of, "Gee, I have to be at thus and such a place in five minutes." Due to her interests and the way she was raised, she developed a more holistic view of time: thinking in terms of seasons and years and centuries, rather than in minutes and hours. So since she takes a different view of time, it has an effect on timepieces around her. She lives time in a different speed, so to speak.

After the session I recorded her conscious memories.

D: *Your subconscious said when you woke up you would tell me about your forearm.*

B: About the bump on my arm? (She unbuttoned and pulled up her shirt sleeve.) It's been there since I was nine years old, so that would be almost twenty years.

The bump was located about an inch and a half below her elbow joint on the inside of her left forearm. It was about the size and appearance of a wart, but it was smooth and had a pink color. Warts are usually rough. I touched it and it didn't feel solid underneath, like a growth or cyst would be.

B: I think there might be a tendril connected to a nerve, because sometimes if I rub it a certain way I feel tingling down in my wrist.

D: *Do you remember when it appeared?*

B: Exactly. Thanksgiving weekend 1969. We had gone to my grandma's house for Thanksgiving. At that time we lived in Houston, and my grandmother lived in Louisiana. We were leaving on Sunday to go back to Houston, and that morning when I woke up I noticed a puffy place had risen on my arm during the night.

D: *Was it like an insect bite?*

B: No, not at all. It was white, like an air bubble under the skin, raised like a dome, but very puffy.

D: *I'm thinking of a blood blister, but that is usually blood colored.*

B: It was more like a water blister, except this didn't have fluid inside. It was not clear, but very white and rough-textured. When I woke up and discovered it, it was only about a quarter of an inch across. But during the day it kept spreading and growing. It was the size of a dime by midday. It was higher than a blister, about three times higher than it is now. I showed it to my mother and grandmother, and they couldn't figure out what it was. It didn't hurt, but it tingled a little. I knew it wasn't a spider bite. There was no redness and no pain. They decided not to mess with it, and it would probably go away. As we drove home that day, I noticed it kept getting bigger. By the next morning when I woke up to go to school, it was the size of a quarter. Finally, when I woke up on the third day the puffy part was gone. I had an open running sore on my arm the size of a fifty-cent piece. The center of it was where this bump is now. It looked the same as when you skin your knee, and you accidentally rub the scab off, and you have blood and goo and liquid. And it kept crusting over and cracking and running. And around the edges of the sore it was raised like a ridge. It stayed that way for about three weeks. It was an open running sore, and very sore and tender inside the perimeter of this circle. Finally it started shrinking very gradually. Meanwhile, the inside dried out to where it was like a crusty sore. It took about six or eight weeks to shrink. It started going in, but the ridge stayed for a while. I kept a Band Aid on it to keep from bumping it.

D: *If it was as big as a fifty-cent piece, it seems it would have left a scar.*

B: Yeah, you would think so. But it shrank in until it was very small. And then one morning I woke up and saw that a layer of skin had grown over it. And when it healed it was basically the way it is today, just this little bump. There used to be a little branch off to one side that shed off a couple of years later, but that little bump basically stays the same. Occasionally it itches, and sometimes the top layer of skin will peel off, especially if I've been out in the sun.

D: *Did you ever go to the doctor about it?*

B: Yes, I did, and the doctor couldn't figure out what it was. The only thing he could think of was some kind of fungus infection from a cat scratch, but I had not been around any cats. It has been the same for nineteen years, and has caused no problems except occasionally it itches or tingles.

So the small bump on Brenda's arm seemed to be a mystery. There is probably no way we could ever find out if there really was a device implanted in her nineteen years ago, or whether it was still there. As long as it is not causing any physical problems it is probably best left alone, and will continue to remain a mystery. Some people want to have implants removed once they discover them. But I am of the opinion that if the extraterrestrials want them there they will simply replace them.

These strange cases did not only occur during my early investigative days in the 1980s. I will include a recent case that shows the ability of extraterrestrials to create an illusion on a much larger scale than individual animals.

During 1997 Clara had written and called several times asking for a session. There are so many people now wanting sessions that I have stopped doing them at my home. I don't take new subjects unless I am going to be giving a lecture in the city where they live, and then only provided I have the time. I have stopped doing them on the day I am going to give a lecture. I find the energy is divided if I do too many different things on the lecture tours. I only do sessions on days when little else is planned. Clara said she had first met me at the Shanti

Cristo conference in Santa Fe, New Mexico, in December 1996. At that conference I only had sessions with people who had set up appointments beforehand, so there was no time to schedule any others. I usually tell people they will be put on my list, and the next time I am going to be in that city we can schedule an appointment. Thus I did not remember Clara, or our conversation. She found out I was going to be in Hollywood in May 1997 for a conference, so she called and asked for an appointment. She lives near San Francisco, but she was willing to drive down to Hollywood. Under those circumstances I felt I could not refuse her.

The conference turned out to be a disaster. Lack of publicity and planning were the main reasons. Although the speakers were all there, there were no participants. Several talks were canceled because there was no audience. It was the worst one I have ever attended, but as a result I had more time on my hands than I had anticipated. My friend, Phil, turned the trip into a sightseeing trip, and showed me the Hollywood I had wanted to see ever since I was a teenager dreaming dreams in a darkened movie theater. I never had the time to really see it before, as I was always confined to the hotel or convention center. When my lectures were finished I always went directly to the airport. We decided to make the best of a bad situation, and I really enjoyed seeing the glamorous side of the town. Thus, when Clara arrived at my hotel room for the session I was relaxed and had plenty of time to spend with her.

Clara is an attractive blond in her forties, seemingly active, intelligent and in good health. During the talk beforehand, when I try to determine the problem or the reason for the session, she said the main thing troubling her was an episode of missing time that had occurred a few years before. She occasionally goes to Hawaii for conferences relating to her work. On this occasion she was driving on the island of Maui. It was almost dusk, but still light, and she was looking for a hotel she had seen on earlier trips. It was located on the beach, and she wanted to eat supper there and enjoy the ocean view. As she drove along looking for it, she discovered she had gone past the entrance. She decided to drive a little further to find a place to turn around and go back. This part of the island had lush tropical growth and palm trees shading the two lane road. A few houses sat back from the road and were hidden from view. She finally found a driveway to turn around in, although she mentally noted that she had never noticed it before when she drove the same route. When she pulled in she found herself in a small housing development composed of modular homes. They were sitting among palm trees in very pleasant surroundings. She pulled her car in and was turning it around. And that was the last thing she remembered.

The next instant she found herself on the other side of the island driving down a busy four lane highway. It was now pitch dark, and she had no idea how she got there.

A year later when she returned to the same island for another conference she drove down the same road looking for the group of houses, out of curiosity, because the strange incident never left her memory. She drove all over the area, and although she found the hotel again, she never found the housing development of modular homes. This had confused her ever since, and was what prompted her to have a session. She wanted to discover what happened that night, and how she so mysteriously got to the other side of the island with no memory of driving there.

She proved to be an excellent subject. I had no trouble getting her immediately into a deep trance, and she was quite talkative after she entered the scene. It was made easier because she remembered the date of the event. I counted her back to March 1994 when she was on the island of Maui in Hawaii. She found herself standing in front of her hotel, the Maui Sun, about to walk through the glass doors. She had just arrived for an annual workshop where she liked to combine relaxation with work. She admired the outstanding color of the flowers surrounding the hotel.

D: *Well, you have checked in now at the hotel. And I want you to move ahead to the night you were going to the restaurant you wanted to eat at. Is that in the same hotel or a different hotel?*

C: A different hotel.

D: *Is it very far away?*

C: Hmmm, maybe a couple of miles. Two or three miles. I've never been there to eat before. I've just passed by it. It's right on the water, where my hotel is up the hill a little. And I really wanted to experience sitting in the hotel with the windows all open, and hearing the water crashing on the beach. I've wanted to go there for a long time, but it just never happened.

D: *Well, are you driving there now?* (Yes) *What time of the day is it?*

C: It's just about dusk. I don't know what time it is by the clock, but it's kind of like twilight.

D: *And you think it'll be dark pretty soon?*

C: Hmmm, probably. I don't think much about it.

D: *Well, you're approaching where the hotel is. Tell me what you're doing.*

C: I'm driving on South Keyhey (phonetic) Road. And it's getting darker. It's hard to see because there are no streetlights. And I'm going past the Astland. That's a really big place, and I miss that driveway. It's a circle. There are a lot of trees. And the driveway seems like ... well, not camouflaged, but I miss it. (Aggravated) I just can't see it. So I go on down further, to find a place to turn around and go back, because I really want to eat dinner at that hotel. (During this part she seemed at times to be talking to herself as she drove, and then also answering my questions.) I'm driving. And I find this place ... Okay. So I see this place. It's a cul-de-sac. Yeah, this looks like a good place to turn around. Hmmm. I've never seen this place before. (Confused) Hmmm. It has beautiful palm trees and flowers. And it has a fence, but it's one that I can see through. And there are all kinds of ... (had difficulty describing) modular homes, or homes like ... very fancy mobile homes. Yeah, okay, this is ... a beautiful place.

D: *And do you find a place to turn around there?*

C: Yeah. It's like a cul-de-sac, and I'm turning my car. (Softly) And I see these bright lights. (Pause, then confusion.) It's like ... blinding lights.

D: *Where are they?*

C: (Her breathing became faster.) They're coming down from the sky. And it's ... it's ... kind of like a funnel of light. A funnel, with the wide end down toward me. It's like a ... (Confused)

D: *With the point pointing upward?*

C: Yes. It's almost like ... from the sun, how you see through the trees this bright, bright light. And I feel a lot of very powerful energy from this light. (Deep breaths)

D: *Is it a solid light?*

C: It's like beaming light. Streams of light.

D: *Out of the bottom?*

C: (It was evident from her voice and her breathing that she was experiencing something unusual and mildly disturbing.) By the bottom, yeah.

D: *Are you still driving your car?*

C: No! I just am. I just am.

D: *What do you mean?*

C: (With disbelief) It feels like I'm part of this light.

D: *Are you still in your car?*

C: No. I feel like I'm floating. And like I'm part of the light. (Deep breaths.) I'm just light. It seems like a transcendence of time and light. Like I'm moving. I'm going somewhere, but I don't know where I'm going. And it's okay.

D: *It's a feeling of movement?*

C: Yeah. Of floating. Of moving. (She was definitely caught up in the experience.) Through colors, through time, through space, through .... (Deep breaths.) It's very pleasant. As through time and space.

D: *But colors are all you can see?*

C: (Sluggishly) Colors, and golden light. And it's very peaceful. (She let her breath out in a very relaxed manner. She continued to breathe deeply and comfortably.) The feeling is that I'm everything, and everything is me. All that is, is there. All that is, is here. All that is, is.

I am going to stop the transcription of this session at this point, because it soon began to involve complicated concepts. The entire session will be reported in my book *Convoluted Universe*, in which I will expand into theories and concepts this book will only touch on. It will be the sequel that will broaden into mind boggling ideas. It is sufficient to say that Clara was not transported to a craft, but to a planet in another dimension. I only include this case here to show how even surroundings can appear as an illusion.

At the end of the session I was communicating with her subconscious.

D: *Are you in a position to explain what happened when she was driving down the road in Hawaii, and came upon that housing park?*

C: She was sent there at that time and that place, because that was the place that materialized for her benefit. Afterwards it was not appropriate at the time that she return to that particular place. So she was taken to a place she knew on that highway. So that the car would be there, and she would know how to get to where she was going.

D: *Then the return had to occur at a certain place in Hawaii at that time?*

C: Not necessarily. That was just a place that she felt comfortable with in the physical body. And the place (the housing development) that was created for her to be, was a place of great beauty for her. And so it was a place where she could be totally and completely relaxed, so the transference could be accomplished.

D: *Then her physical body was returned to the car, and the car was physically taken to the other highway?*

C: That is correct. It was just simply dematerialized and then materialized back at another place.

D: *Is this common to move cars and people from one place to another?*

C: Oh, yes. Oh, yes.

D: *It happens often then?*

C: Very often, very often.

D: *When it happens, is the physical body dematerialized and rematerialized also?* (Yes*) And no harm occurs to the body?*

C: No harm. It becomes pure energy.

D: *And she and the vehicle were just moved from one place to another.*

C: That is correct.

D: *So when she came to, I guess I should say, when she was once again conscious, she was in a different place on the island.*

C: Right.

D: *And was driving at that time.* (Yes) *And she had no memory until now of what happened.*

C: That's right.

D: *Is this the only time this has occurred in her life as Clara?*

C: It has occurred many times. But this time she was at a place and time in her life when she was open to investigate, to see what occurred, and how it may have occurred. The other times were not a time when she was ready to have an understanding. Or she was not at a growth time in her Earthly physical life, that she could have an understanding of what was happening.

D: *So this was a time when something unusual occurred, and made her remember it.*

C: That is correct.

D: *Is it all right for her to know the information now?*

C: Yes. She should know the information. She has been longing to know the information. She will understand it now.

D: *And it can be a benefit, because we want no harm at all.*

C: Yes. It is to be a joyous benefit for her.

I then asked the subconscious to recede, and I had Clara's personality incorporate fully back into her body. The release or change is always noticeable, because the subject breathes deeply at this point. I oriented her to the present time, and brought her back to full consciousness.

So things are not always what they appear to be. Can we ever be sure that what we see and experience is real? At least it appears to be done in a subtle and gentle manner so the only effect will be curiosity, and then (usually) dismissal of the incident as an oddity. It would do no good to fear something so benign, especially if there is no way of anticipating such an event, and certainly no way of controlling it.

THE MYSTERY CONTINUES, AND CONTINUES TO DEEPEN.

CHAPTER 4
HIDDEN INFORMATION IN DREAMS

When is a dream not a dream? When is it an actual memory clouded over by the subconscious so it will appear as a dream? What is a dream anyway? How can we ever know the difference? And finally, is it important to our well-being to know the difference anyway? Maybe such things are better left alone.

In my work many people do not report any actual physical contacts with aliens or sightings of craft. Instead they are often bothered by strange and unusually vivid dreams. These are usually dreams that had a different quality about them, and dreams they cannot forget. We all, from time to time, have remarkably sharp and clear dreams that seem very real. And we are usually glad they are not real. We also have dreams that we remember long after they have occurred. This is a normal part of our shadow world we call "sleep," and it is often our subconscious' method of interpreting events in our waking life. It is also a way that the subconscious is attempting to deliver information to us via symbols. What makes dreams about UFOs, aliens or space flights different? And why should we even pay any attention to them? I have always said, "If it's not broke, don't fix it!" If the person is functioning normally, and not having any memories that are creating problems, it is better to leave it alone and treat it as merely an interesting curiosity. There is no need to make life more complicated merely for the sake of curiosity. Remember, once you open that box you cannot close it again. You cannot forget what you bring forth as a memory. And it may affect your life forever after. I always wish for my subjects to be affected in a positive way by any information uncovered through hypnotic therapy. Thus if any information is uncovered through exploring the subject's dreams it must be incorporated into their life in a positive manner, so they can deal with it and return to living a normal life. This same rule applies to people who have conscious memories of interaction with aliens.

This life is the most important of all, and they must continue to live it as normally as possible. So it is the therapist's responsibility to help them deal with anything that is uncovered, and put it into perspective.

In my book *Between Death and Life* we found that the soul (or spirit) actually never sleeps. Only the body gets tired, and the soul would get very bored waiting around for the body to awaken. So while the body sleeps, our soul or spirit, the *real part* of us, is having many adventures. It may travel to the spirit realm to meet with the master teachers and guides, to obtain advice or to learn more lessons. It also may travel to other parts of our world, or even venture outward to other worlds and dimensions. These travels are sometimes remembered in snatches, especially in the common dream of flying. That essential part of us always returns to the body when it is time to wake up, because it is connected by the "silver cord." This umbilical is not severed until the physical death of the body frees the spirit.

Before I began UFO investigation I never thought of the *physical* body actually going somewhere during the sleep state. After all, the body would awaken if it were moved, wouldn't it? This has been part of my education to investigate these other strange possibilities. In these cases I have tried to carefully question to be sure the experience was an actual physical experience, and not an out of the body spiritual experience. They can be similar, but the description is different. In an OBE the person may remember the sensation of leaving their body. Often they can look down and see their sleeping body lying on the bed. They describe their reentry into the empty shell after their journey. They often describe seeing the "silver cord," the umbilical that connects the spirit to the body. Sometimes they describe a tugging sensation of the cord pulling them back if they have been away too long. In my work I discovered it is possible for the body to exist without the spirit residing constantly within it. It is maintained by a life force present in the physical, but it cannot continue to exist indefinitely without the presence of the soul.

The other experience, of the actual physical body traveling, is described differently. My first case of this type was a wonderful black man, John Johnson, a psychologist who often traveled with me to interview suspected abduction cases. In those early days of my investigation everything was new. I felt we were plowing new ground. I had not yet discovered the patterns that I now observe. This only comes from investigating many cases. Since I am not a psychologist I relied on John's expertise when we conducted a first time interview with people who thought they were having alien-type experiences. He asked questions I would have never thought of, questions that told him about the mental health of the subject and their family. Sometimes when we got in the car to go home, he told me the subject was disturbed and he suspected child abuse in their past. In other cases he suspected the person was fantasizing or looking for attention. I gained invaluable lessons as I learned from him some of the signs to look for. Mostly he would say the family was normal and appeared to definitely have had an experience they believed was real. If he thought it was worth following up, we arranged to return, and either he or I performed the hypnosis. I greatly valued John's help and advice during the three years we worked on these cases. He traveled many miles with me to investigate these unusual topics, in spite of his weak heart that caused him much pain. It often seemed as though he was taking heart medication like candy, but he said working with me was what kept him going. Our working relationship only ceased when John died of heart failure in 1990 at the age of 53.

Shortly after I met John in 1987 he told me about his own strange experience, which he wanted to explore under hypnosis. It had occurred in 1981 while he was traveling on a tour in Egypt. He was rooming with a stranger (arranged by the tour) in a hotel in Cairo. He could remember nothing about the night except that he awoke standing over the other man's bed, which naturally startled the man awake. He could not remember getting up or how he got there. All he remembered was something about a blue light. I suggested that he may have been sleep walking. It is very common to do that if you are trying to sleep in a strange place, especially if you are tired from a journey. He had thought about that explanation, but discarded it, because he had no history of sleep walking. He was positive he had gone somewhere, and he wanted me to help him uncover where.

Before we began the session he confided that he was worried that his heart might give him problems while he was in trance. He listed symptoms to watch for, and to bring him out if they occurred. I told him I was convinced that nothing of that nature would occur, and I was correct. He went through the session beautifully. Since I knew he was a hypnotist I was positive it would not be difficult to put him under. Because he knew the procedures he gave me his full cooperation.

Once he was in trance I took him back to the day he arrived in Egypt. He had just deplaned and was preparing to go through Customs. When working with cases that involve the present life there can be apprehension involved in remembering the event. Many hypnotists say the subject will experience anxiety about returning to the time of the event. I have found no resistance when I take the subject, not to the exact time of the event, but to *before* the event occurred. This way you can sneak in the back door, and lead up to it from behind. After he relived being in the airport and going through Customs with the tour group, I moved him ahead to his hotel. He gave exacting descriptions of the hotel and the meal he ate before retiring to his room. He was so tired from the long trip that he had no trouble falling asleep.

As I have said before, the subconscious never sleeps. It is always aware of what is happening. I knew if anything had occurred during the night the subconscious would tell me about it. If it was only a dream or sleep-walking, the subconscious would also tell me that.

D: *Did anything unusual happen during the night?*

John's answer was a surprise to me. "I was called out."

D: *Can you explain what you mean?*
J: I was called out, and I exited through the roof, through the ceiling of the room.

At the time, I assumed he was describing an OBE. "Do you often do that?"

J: I have on occasion done that.
D: *You said someone called you. Do you know who it was?*
J: No. I don't recognize that voice. I've never heard that voice.

I asked him to describe what was happening.

J: I just float up. And I float *through* objects, through solids. I've done it before.

John then found himself in a dimly lit circular room. He was standing before a huge glowing white tablet. The estimated size was fifteen feet tall by eight feet wide. He sensed he was not alone in the room, but his attention was focused on the large stone. "I'm studying the block. There are lessons incorporated in the block."

D: Have you seen that block before?
J: That particular block, no. But I have seen other objects. Not crystal in form, but I have seen other objects with writing on them.
D: As you study it, can you share with me what it says?
J: No. I have no recall of what it is. As soon as I read it, I forget it.
D: But it's important that you read it, and then another part of you remembers? (Yes) Is that why you were called there, to read this?
J: I assume that was a part of my reason for being here. Another reason is to learn.

I kept trying to get him to share some of the writing with me, but to no avail.

J: I do not recall. I learn it, and in a millisecond I have forgotten it. It becomes a part of me.

In one instance he was standing before the stone studying it, and the next instance he was back in his room at the hotel. "I'm back in my room. I'm not in my bed. My bed is over there. I'm over another bed."

I was still assuming he had an OBE experience. "Then did you just stand up whenever you came back into the body, or what?"

J: I did not come back into the body. The body was with me.

This surprised me, and took me off guard, since it was the first time I had heard of this. "You mean your *physical body* went through the ceiling? Isn't that a little unusual?"

J: (Matter of fact) No. I go through the walls sometimes.
D: I mean, if someone were to look at the bed that night, would your physical body have been lying there? (No) Do you know how that was possible to do that?

J: Teleportation.

D: Did you do it on your own?

J: No, I cannot do it with my own will. When I was called out it was made possible.

This rather shook me up. I was having difficulty thinking of sensible questions.

D: This round circular room that you found yourself in, was that a physical solid room?

I was thinking it may have been on the spiritual plane, perhaps at the schools or the Hall of Learning, described in *Between Death and Life*.

J: Yes, it is solid.

D: Your body was solid? And the floors, the walls and everything in that room were solid?

J: Yes, they are all solid.

D: Do you know where that room was located?

J: No. But I can tell you what I see in the room. (He was again visualizing it.) As I face the tablet there are panels to the right, and a railing. The panels are elevated maybe twenty-four inches from the main surface of the floor, and there is a walkway there. There are panels and gauges. I don't understand any of them. I'm not shown them. I just see that as I scan the room.

D: Is there anything you can compare them to?

J: I can't tell. I am seeing the dials and gauges from a distance.

D: Is the railing around the side of the room?

J: Yes, it surrounds the room. This part I am in is like a sunken room. It is lower than the rest of the room. I feel a presence, but I am unable to look in that direction. There is little illumination in the room. The major source of illumination seems to be this crystal tablet. I see some purple (pointing) right over there, but I don't know what it is.

D: Have you been to this place before?

J: I have been many places. I don't know that I have been to this particular room before. It is new to me. I don't know my way around. I am not familiar with this room. I have been to many rooms. Maybe just one time in that room was enough. I have been in many chambers only one time.

D: *What about the place where the room is located, have you been there before?*

J: I don't know. I only see the room. I'm not anywhere else. When I came here, I came *to* the room. When I leave, I leave from the room. I don't go anywhere else.

D: *How long have you been going to these different places?*

J: All of my life.

D: *But you said they were not the same. How were they different?*

J: Sometimes I'm in an auditorium. Sometimes I'm in a smaller room. Sometimes I'm in a library. Sometimes I just have a sense of motion. It can be a floating sensation or an accelerating velocity as I soar. In the past when I did that, it would be because I had nothing else to do during that particular period. I had nothing to learn. I had no work to do, so I was on my own. The feeling of freedom can be exhilarating. Sometimes on these little journeys I see beings. They look like human beings. They are *dead* though, but they *were* human beings. They are dead only in the sense that they are not of this world any longer.

These places sounded more like the spiritual realm where the soul journeys at night (and in between lives) to study and learn.

D: *During all of those times, was it your physical body that experienced this?*

J: Sometimes it was my physical body. Sometimes it was my astral body. It is difficult to say when these experiences were physical, because there is no way to validate that information. This experience in Egypt definitely involved my physical body.

D: *I suppose it's very similar, because in both cases the main part of your intelligence is present.* (Yes) *When you had this experience of going through the walls and the ceiling in your physical body, what did that feel like?*

J: A sensation only of motion, just motion. I don't recall it. I'm just there. I don't know what I did.

D: *But when you came back and you found yourself by the roommate's bed, did you see anything unusual in the room?*

J: I saw a blue beam coming from the ceiling.

The Custodians

D: Bright blue?
J: No, no. Pale blue. It's a little darker than a robin's egg.
D: What do you think the light was?
J: What do I think it was? It was a slide. It wasn't really a slide. But I see a slide as though it was made available for me to come back into the room. I can see it now. It comes from the ceiling to the floor, and is about three feet in width. It brought me back into the room. It has something to do with the breaking down of molecules of the body. I can think of no other way to accomplish that feat.
D: Where do you think the light came from?
J: I have no idea. But I was in it when I went out, and when I came back. It gives one a sense of *nurturing*. It's a good light.
D: How long did it last in the room?
J: Just long enough for me to see it, and then it was gone. And I found myself back in the room standing by the other bed, as though I had been *deposited* there. It startled my roommate awake, but I had no memory of how I got there.

Since it seemed we could obtain no further information about the experience I instructed him to leave the scene he was watching. I brought him up to the present time (1988). Before the session John had asked me to find out about his health problems. In other sessions I have asked the subconscious to tell me what was wrong with the body, and prescribe remedies. It has always done so in an unemotional and detached manner, as though speaking about a third person. This brief portion shows how truly objective the subconscious can be.

D: (I was speaking to John's subconscious.) He is concerned about problems he is having with his physical body. Would you be able to scan his body and tell us about some of these problems?
J: I am not deep enough to conduct that scan. That scan requires a depth that will enable one to circulate throughout all of the organs in the body. I have not achieved that depth. I have incomplete conditioning for me to achieve that depth.
D: Would the subconscious be able to look at the body objectively and give us some information anyway? It doesn't have to be thorough. We would appreciate anything you can tell us.
J: Yes. (Pause) Presently. that heart is dying. It shall stop one day ... soon.

His total unemotional objectivity surprised me. "Is that the most important problem of the body?"

J: Yes. It keeps the body functioning.
D: *Is there anything that John can do to help the condition? Do you have any suggestions?*
J: (Emphatic) No. When his time comes, he goes.
D: *There's nothing he can do to help it?*
J: No, no. There is nothing he wants to do. He is satisfied. He has come to terms with it.

I gave suggestions for well-being and health, but I knew these would be futile. If the subconscious was positive there was no hope of recovery, then there would be nothing to be done by mortals. When John awakened he remembered nothing of what his subconscious had said. This is often the case. The subject may remember some of the session, but the part when I converse with their subconscious is blank. I thought it best to let John hear it from himself when he played the tape recording.

Instead he wanted to describe what he remembered about the room. Most of it was the same as the session. "I couldn't see the dials and gauges and stuff clearly, because I was maybe twenty feet away. It was a *large* room, and it was *tall.* You know, this sounds crazy, but at one point I wondered if I was inside the Earth. Seriously. One thing that made me think that was because the walls were craggy, like rock. As a matter of fact, it was more like a cave. The floor even seemed to be rock."

A week later John called to discuss the session after he had a chance to listen to the tape. The first thing he did was announce that there was no way he could believe his physical body was taken from that room. He could not believe it happened with the breaking down of the molecules or any other way. He was laughing when he said that, and I laughed along with him, saying, "Hey, you're the one who said it, not me." He said he could believe it if he heard someone else say it, but not himself. He really made a joke of it, but I suspected he knew enough about hypnosis to realize it had to be true, or he would not have said it. He was just trying to justify it to himself, the same as all the others who have these experiences. They will try to find alternate explanations for their conscious mind to accept. So it apparently doesn't matter even if you are an investigator and are familiar with the techniques and hypnosis itself, the reaction is the same.

John worked with dying hospital patients and tried to prepare them for the world they were about to enter. He did much good before it came time for him to make that journey himself. And then, as his subconscious said it would, his heart simply stopped. I learned much from John about investigative procedures. I will always miss his advice, but I am grateful I was honored to know him for that brief time.

John's experience showed the difficulty of differentiating between encounters with aliens and astral traveling. I began to pay attention to my subject's unusual dreams while working with Phil on my book *Keepers of the Garden*. He had no conscious memories of alien encounters, only traumatic dreams. When we explored these we found actual encounter experiences going back to his childhood. Some of the details uncovered established a pattern I would see repeated over and over again.

The fact that I got together with Carrie at all is too farfetched to ever be considered coincidence. My friend, Connie, had mentioned her longtime artist friend who lived in Houston. Carrie had had strange dreams and (supposedly) visions that suggested contact with aliens. Connie thought I might like to work with her, but it seemed highly unlikely as Carrie lived so far away. She was kept on a short leash, as her husband did not allow her to travel away from home. She had not visited Connie since she moved to Arkansas, even though Connie was an old and dear friend. Then the strange coincidence stepped in to bring us together. Connie went to Houston to visit Carrie, and became deathly ill. The only way she could return home to Arkansas was for Carrie to drive her. Under the circumstances her husband gave his permission, and she made the journey.

Connie called me on a Tuesday night after arriving back home. She wanted me to come to her house to meet Carrie so she could discuss her experiences, and perhaps have a regression. She knew she would never be in our area again, so this would be her only chance to meet with me. I was due to leave Thursday morning for a convention in Little Rock, so Wednesday was the only available day. We met on that day for supper, and then I asked her to tell me about her experiences for the tape recorder. She had memories of dreams associated with aliens, but she mostly wanted to find out about an out-of-the-body experience and a vision she was shown. It had made a great impact upon her life, although other people made light of it. I told her I would work on anything *she* wanted to. I believed it was more important to help her than to find another interesting piece of information dealing with UFOs.

The out of body experience occurred in 1978 as she was preparing to go to bed. She knew she was not asleep yet. She had put on her nightgown, and was sitting on the side of the bed, when she heard a deep voice from up in the corner of the room, saying, "Carrie, come with me!"

"And he didn't say it out loud. It hit right here," she pointed to her forehead. "And I felt myself like a wet towel. You know how when you put a towel in water and lift it up it all sticks together and it's heavy? Then I felt myself just float up and out of my body. And all of a sudden I was floating with this grayish, misty, no form, nothingness sort of thing. When I came out of myself, I saw that. It was this misty thing with no form, and it had black eyes. Deep, loving eyes. And all of a sudden we weren't in the room anymore. We were floating up above everything."

From this perspective Carrie was shown five scenes in succession. They seemed to apply to future events in her life, and she was shown them in time sequence. To me they seemed full of symbolism, similar to the type our subconscious uses in dreams. Over the years since this experience some of the events had already come to pass in Carrie's life, except the one that had left the greatest impression, and had caused the greatest fear and confusion. She had never been able to forget it.

She saw a body of water. She couldn't determine whether it was a lake or an ocean, but there were hills and trees that came down to the water's edge. She was floating above it looking down on it. The water had a greenish color, and was in tremendous turmoil, as though from a storm. All the sky was greenish, and there were huge waves. Then she saw thousands of dead fish floating belly up in the water. Two white birds were flying over the water when they suddenly fell from the sky.

She was then shown a partially demolished city. There were hundreds and hundreds of people in different stages of illness. And she saw herself among them feeding them and trying to care for them. The words came into her head, "And some can eat, and to some it will turn to vinegar in their mouth." To me, this sounded Biblical. During this sequence she knew she wasn't sick, and she knew she couldn't get sick.

As she protested, "Why *me*?" the answer came. "This was not shown to you for you to fear. Do not be afraid. This was why you were sent to Earth. You must be prepared for these coming times." It then repeated, "Do not be afraid," three or four times.

Carrie continued, "Then all of a sudden I found myself back in my room sitting on the bed. I looked to see if my husband was awake, and he was lying there snoring. And I was shaking as I looked around the room. Nothing had changed. I got up and walked out to the den, smoked part of a cigarette, and put it out. I was sweating. I was scared to death. I was not scared of what I saw; I was scared because I knew I wasn't asleep. I didn't know what had happened, but I finally crawled into bed and went to sleep."

"The next morning I called four or five ministers. I started out with that, thinking something had come to me to tell me about the future. Well, I found out very quickly they were *not* whom I should have called. Their first suggestion was that something was mentally wrong with me. So I learned there are some things you cannot discuss with others. I knew it was *not* a dream. I stayed frightened for two or three years, because I knew these things were going to happen. It was not something I believed would happen, but I *knew* was going to happen. It didn't help when some of the first events began to occur."

She indicated this experience was the main one she wanted to explore under hypnosis. She was positive the other (alien suggestive) experiences were "just dreams," although they were disturbingly vivid. I encouraged her to tell me about them anyway, just for the record.

She described a dream, or "nightmare," that was so vivid she had never forgotten it. It occurred in early September 1963 when she was a nineteen-year-old student at a university in Texas. In the "dream" she found herself in a curved room between rows of incubators. She called them incubators because they had babies in them, but they were not like any babies she had ever seen before. She had drawn pictures of them and said she would send these to me. The babies had huge heads, and huge eyes, which was in sharp contrast to their tiny, shriveled bodies. They were completely submersed in fluid, and she knew they were growing in it. The babies were communicating with one another through their minds, and they had a huge vocabulary of sophisticated words. The babies in the different incubators seemed to be at the same stage of development. Their skin was luminescent, pearlized, whitish, and appeared almost transparent.

A woman then came into the room, and dropped a capsule on the floor. It resembled a time-release capsule, except that it was clear. This was put into the fluid to grow the babies. I thought she meant that the capsule contained something that was added to the fluid to help the baby develop, but she emphasized that the capsule *was* the baby.

"That was like the seed that grew the baby. They put the capsule in the fluid, and then the baby grew out of that capsule and continued to grow. But she dropped this one on the floor. So I leaned over and picked up the capsule and put it in my pocket. I wanted to tell someone about it, and show it to them, because I knew that was how they did it. Then there were other people in the room saying I shouldn't have the capsule. I was scared, because they were mad at me. At that point I woke up."

Carrie continued, "Anyway, that was my dream, and I've never forgotten it. I had snatches of the same dream the entire time I was attending college. I had the feeling I was working in this nursery at night, instead of sleeping. No wonder I was tired when I woke up. I don't know whether this is UFO related. I'm an artist. I'm a creative person. It could be that, or it could simply be dreams. If we have the session I may not remember anything more than I've told you about any of this."

Connie sat in on the session with her friend. Carrie gave me the approximate dates she wanted to zero in on, and we agreed to try to cover all the incidents, if possible. I knew from past experiences that if the incidents had merely been dreams, the subconscious would tell us so. We would not know until she was regressed to the dates. Carrie proved to be an excellent subject, going quickly into a deep trance state. I took her to the evening of the out-of-body visions, sometime during the last week of July 1978. Although she had not consciously remembered the date, under hypnosis she immediately supplied the exact date: July 26.

She was describing getting ready for bed that night, when she became upset. She cried out as though frightened, and then began to sob openly. I gave calming suggestions so she could tell me what was occurring. The sobbing stopped, and between sniffles she explained that she suddenly felt very heavy and the sensation was frightening. Everything was very dark and she couldn't see anything. Then something was telling her not to be afraid, and she was encompassed by a great feeling of love. Then the darkness changed to gray, and gradually scenes began to come into view. She appeared to be floating above the scenes, and it was an unusual feeling. She was aware that an entity was with her, but it appeared as just a gray, misty thing without form and substance. The only thing that was recognizable was large eyes, and even they seemed to float in and out of focus. The scenes that were shown of her future were identical to her memories of them. There were no new details added.

The scene that disturbed her the most was the last one of the people dying in the large city. She cried and her voice quivered as she described the scene. "It's sad. There are so many people dying. Some of them won't get well, no matter what I do. I'm giving them something. And I'm holding them in my arms, and I'm touching them. And some of them die anyway. It *hurts* me to see this. I can't help them *all*. I'm giving them something that this misty thing said to. It's some kind of food. I don't know how they got sick. But they're hanging off balconies. And their skin is a funny color. They're kind of grayish, yellow or blue. They're just sick looking. It's ugly, and all are bald, and skinny." She was crying, "I'm not skinny. I *can't* get sick. He told me I couldn't get sick. I have to take care of these other people. Some of them are helped, and some are not. There are just so many of them. I don't think it was a war that made them sick. It was some kind of nuclear stuff. I don't know whether it was water, or what happened to them. It was like a cloud, but there was no war. It was like a storm. That's probably what killed the fish I saw, too. It had something to do with water, like rain."

She was becoming so emotional that I thought it best to remove her from the scene of hopeless despair that she could do nothing about. "I can't help them all," she insisted, "but they *cry*, they *cry*. There are so many that are sick. I don't know who they are. I don't recognize anybody. But I feel so sorry for them, and I love them." She protested, "I don't know why it's me. Why do I do that? The misty thing is telling me I'm not supposed to be afraid of it. I was sent to Earth for this. I don't know why *me*. - Oh, he has pretty eyes. I feel such love from him. Then it's like he touched me on my forehead, yet he didn't have any fingers. And all of a sudden I was back in my body. I got up and went out of that room."

She stared out of the window at the dark night sky and nervously smoked a cigarette, trying to make some sense out of the experience. "I know I wasn't dreaming. I've never dreamed sitting up before. I remember *everything*. He said I *had* to remember it. It's supposed to really happen, but I don't know where."

Since she was so upset I thought it best that we leave that scene and move on to the next experience. Obviously we couldn't get any more information about it anyway. After calming her and giving relaxing suggestions I moved her backward to September 1963 when she was a college student. She immediately returned to that time and described her dormitory room in detail and discussed her roommate, who was also her best friend. I then directed her to go to the night she had the strange dream about babies. She immediately began describing what she was seeing.

C: I'm in a room. And I'm like a . candy striper.
D: *A candy striper?*
C: Yeah. You know, those girls that work in hospitals.
D: *What makes you think you're like one of them?*
C: Because I'm in a nursery. It has babies. I'm wearing an apron with pockets. That's why I look like a candy striper. - But I'm scared of the babies.
D: *Why would you be afraid of a baby?*
C: Because they're funny looking. They've got big eyes. And they're really smart.
D: *How do you know they're smart?*
C: Because they talk to one another.
D: *With their mouths?*
C: No. They're in water. All up above their head. They're submersed in the water. It's like they're thinking at one another, but I can

know what they're thinking. One of them knows I have the capsule. And it's gonna tell.

D: *What capsule are you talking about?*

C: The one that fell on the floor. It's just a plain old capsule. It's like a pill. And you can see through it.

D: *There's nothing inside it?*

C: Well, there's something inside, but you can see through that too. I can't see what it is.

D: *You said one of them says they're going to tell?*

C: (Childish) Uh huh. He's going to tell on me. And he's mad at me. I can hear it in my head.

Carrie described the containers that held the babies as something like vats with rounded edges. They were constructed of a material that resembled clear plastic. She knew it was different from plastic, but not hard like glass. There were many of them in the room. She tried to count them, and thought there were at least fifteen, maybe as many as seventeen, of these containers. They were sitting on something because she could look into them without bending over. "And they're all hooked together with a clear tube. That's what keeps the water filled. The tube goes to *all* of them: between each one and into one and then the other, like a hose. It comes out of the side of the wall, where there are knobs you turn and buttons you push. I don't know what they mean. I don't have anything to do with that part. This lady comes in and turns knobs and makes *sure* that the babies are okay. She likes the babies, and talks to them. My job is to watch the babies, take care of them. I have to check the water. There's a temperature or something on the side, which I have to check. The babies have big heads, and a little body. I don't like them. They're ugly."

D: *Are they always in the water?*

C: Uh huh. I've never seen them out of the water.

D: *Have you seen this before?*

C: Sure. Lots of times. That's why I can work there.

She described the lady as a normal looking human, although stern and strict-looking. "She's my boss, but I don't like her. She's mean. Except she's not the big boss."

The Custodians

D: Who is the big boss?

C: The man in the other room.

D: Do you know what he looks like?

C: I'm not sure. I don't go in there.

D: Is there any other furniture or anything in the room?

C: I don't see any furniture. It's just the babies in these containers. I have to walk up and down between the babies. I have to check the temperature and the water, and make sure it's high enough. Some of the babies have their eyes closed, and some have them open. They all look alike. Ugly. Some of the containers are empty. That's where you put the pill.

D: Can you tell how that's done?

C: She puts the pill in about an inch of water. Puts some water under it, through the pipe. And then she puts some other stuff in the water, but I don't know what it is. She brings that with her. It's in a *little* bottle. And she puts in a pinch of stuff, like when you cook you put a pinch of this and a pinch of that in it. And then she lays the capsule in it. Then it dissolves, and starts growing this baby.

D: Does it take a long time?

C: No. I'm not sure how long, because I'm not there all the time. But I know it doesn't take very long.

D: Do you think these are human babies?

C: No, because they're ugly. They would be *sick* if they were human.

D: What do you think they are?

C: I don't know.

D: Well, have you ever been outside this room?

C: Yes. I don't know where we are, but it's big.

D: Would it be like a hospital?

C: (Pause, then carefully.) I don't know. Sort of, I guess. It's like a military thing.

D: Why do you feel it's military?

C: You have to take orders. You just don't go anywhere you want to.

D: How do you get there?

C: You just wake up, and there you are.

D: How long do you stay?

C: Oh, overnight at least.

D: Then what do you do when you leave there?

C: You go to sleep. You wake up. And it's a dream.

D: You said you've been doing this a lot?

C: Oh, yeah! I think since I was fourteen or fifteen. They don't let everybody take care of the babies. I don't know how I get here. But I have to work with the babies.

D: *You don't have any choice?*

C: No. You can't leave that room.

D: *Do you know what they do with the babies?*

C: They grow up to be people. And they're funny looking.

D: *Have you seen what the adults look like?*

C: They're tall, and really thin. They have long arms. I haven't seen them up close.

D: *What do their faces look like when they're grown up?*

C: Just like they did when they were babies. Ugly. They have big eyes. And a skinny jaw, hardly any. And their eyes .. their eyes are like oil. They change color. They're black and they're wet.

D: *What colors do they change to?*

C: Purple, blue, like oil.

Apparently resembling an oil slick which has variations of color in it.

D: *What color is their skin when they're grown up?*

C: I think the grown up babies are funny looking, purpley, grayish, sick-looking. The babies are almost like you can see through their skin. So transparent you can see their veins. And kind of like that for a big person too.

D: *Do they wear any clothes when they're grown up?*

C: I can't tell. He's skinny though. His arms are long. They come down long on his legs. When I saw him he was far away. He was standing at the top of the stairs looking down.

D: *Does this room have stairs?*

C: No. That was outside the room. You can't go outside the room. It was out the door where you're not supposed to go. I looked when the lady went out the door.

D: *It sounds like that part must be larger.*

C: It is. It's big.

D: *Then he was too far away to see his hands. Can you tell how many fingers they have by looking at the babies?*

C: The babies' fingers are really long. And they have a thumb, but it's up funny on their hand. It's up further by their wrist.

D: *How many fingers do they have?*

C: I don't ... I hate to touch one.

D: *Have you had to touch them?*

C: Yeah. You have to straighten them out in the water. If they get turned bad, you just reach in and turn them over, so their heads lie back. So they don't turn over and get tangled. They lie on their arm or something the wrong way, because their bodies won't work. I have to put my hands in the water to turn them. And the water feels funny, almost like there's a lubricant in it. That's my job, but they don't like me much. They just stare at you sometimes.

D: *Where did these babies come from? Do they have mothers and fathers? (This was a question Carrie had written down before we began the session.)*

C: They come from a capsule.

D: *Where does the capsule come from?*

C: Somebody makes it.

D: *In another room or what?*

C: Must be. It's not in there.

D: *How do you know they're in that capsule?*

C: Because they start to grow out of the capsule, with a little head and a little body.

D: *Well, do you know why they're growing these babies?*

C: I don't know. I just take care of the babies. They don't hurt anything. They just grow up to be people. Big, funny looking people.

D: *Have you seen them when they are taken out of the water?*

C: No. I don't get to hold them then.

D: *So you don't know how you get to this place? You just wake up there? And then you go to sleep, and wake up in your own bed in the morning? (Yes) And you never know when you're going to go again?*

C: No, you don't.

It was increasingly apparent that I could not get any more information about this, because she did not leave that room. I ended the session and brought her to full consciousness. It had been obvious from her body and facial signs that she was in a very deep state. She did not move at all. Only her face showed expression. Even when she was crying she made no other movements. When I began to count her out of trance she became aware of her physical body again, and jerked and jumped noticeably. After awakening she had no memory of the session at all.

After she was fully awake I had her obey a suggestion I had given her to draw a picture of the babies. Carrie was an accomplished professional artist, and had drawn pictures of them after the original dreams. She now made a rough sketch which I later compared to the copies she sent me. There were a few differences that she explained as she drew the sketch. When she drew the hand of the adult being she drew three fingers, and said the hand was almost as long as the forearm. In her original drawing she had four fingers. This time she said the three fingers felt right, and she was going to leave it like that. When she drew the picture of the incubators, she said, "This time I have the urge to add something here on the sides. It's as though something was connecting them. I didn't put that in the original drawing." While she was drawing the vats and the connecting hoses, she suddenly cringed and exclaimed, "Oooo! I just remembered. I put my hands in that water."

We laughed. This was obviously a detail she did not remember from the original "dream," and it revolted her. The last picture she drew was the being she had caught a glimpse of when the other woman opened the door. It was standing at the top of some stairs and had a light behind it, so she couldn't make out the features. But she knew this was one of the babies in adult form. When she was in college she had painted a picture of this adult standing at the top of a spiral staircase looking down on a group of people. She didn't know where the idea came from. She called it "Dante's Inferno," and she won an award for it. Although she had the painting for several years she can't find it now. As she now sketched the drawing for me she had the impression that it was not a staircase but some kind of light beam (maybe spiraling as in the picture she drew of the interior of the craft). She promised to send copies of the other drawings she had made from memory, although it now appeared we had more details than were in the originals.

I left Connie's house at midnight with Carrie still asking questions about the session. I told her Connie would have to tell her about it. I had to get home since I had to drive to Little Rock the next morning for a convention. I knew I would not arrive home until one o'clock in the morning, but it was worth it to speak to this woman.

In the years since this incident I have found that some other investigators have obtained copies of the baby picture. Some of them are saying it is an example of human alien hybrid experimentation, but that theory goes totally against what Carrie said under hypnosis. She insisted the babies were not human, but alien. The drawing she sent me of the interior of the craft indicates that she must have been outside the room at some time during this ongoing experience.

I have been showing these pictures at my lectures for the past several years. I always described that drawing as the interior of a huge mother ship with many levels. Now as I write this I wonder if there could be another explanation. Could she have been in an underground experimental facility? The thought came to mind because of her mention of a military type environment, and the fact that there was another seemingly human worker there. She never said where it was; only that she woke up there. She never could say how she was transported there. I have assumed it was a mother ship because, in my experience, that was the only thing conceivably large enough to house such a facility. Now I wonder.

The vision Carrie reported of the disaster scene has been repeated through other subjects, not in exact detail, but describing similar scenarios that something drastic had happened to the Earth. I have even had similar cases in foreign countries while doing UFO regressions, from people who have no knowledge of American "trends" in this field. My mail also attests to the fact that many people have had similar visions, through strikingly vivid dreams, out-of-the-body experiences, and simply flashes of insight. Where are these scenes and visions coming from? Are they real glimpses of the future? Or are they probabilities and possibilities on the time lines, as described by Nostradamus in my trilogy *Conversations With Nostradamus*? If they are possible futures, then they can be influenced and changed by the mind of man. Is this the reason for revealing them to us?

When I called Carrie to ask permission to use her story in this book, she told me she had gone to a psychologist about five years ago for an unrelated personal problem. During their sessions she told about the strange dream. The psychologist's explanation was that Carrie must have been sexually abused as a child. It didn't matter that

Carrie had no memory of any abuse, that *had* to be the answer. Carrie didn't see the connection and neither did I, since there was no sexual connotations in the "dream" or the visions. Some psychologists and psychiatrists, when confronted by something unusual, instead of exploring a different explanation, will not deviate from the "book." In their training there can be no other explanation.

Drawing by Carrie of the inside of the ship.

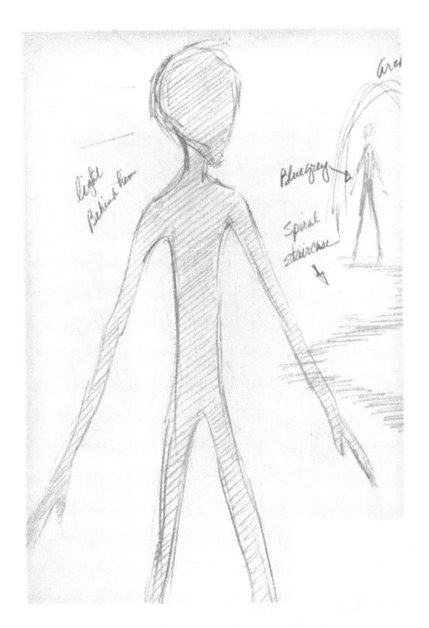

Carrie's drawing of the silhouette of the alien.

Carrie's drawing of the nursery inside the alien ship.

Carrie's drawing of one of the Aliens.

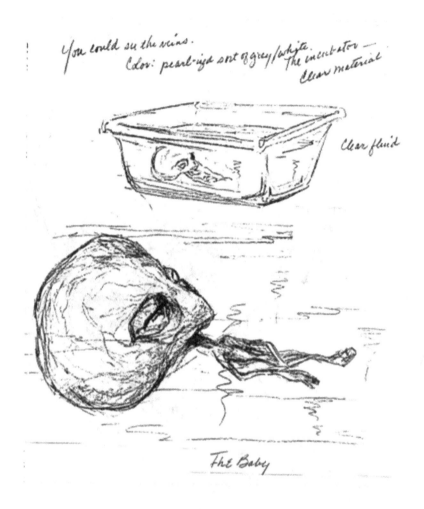

You could see the veins.
Color: pearl-ized sort of grey/white. The incubator —
clear material

Clear fluid

The Baby

Carrie's drawing of the Alien baby.

My friend, LeeAnn, was another case of information being hidden in a dreamlike state. She was a woman in her early forties, who taught learning disabled children in Florida. Her mother and father were old friends of mine, and she came to Arkansas every year to visit them. She had been interested in psychic phenomenon, and more recently in metaphysics. Her parents did not understand any of this, so when she came for a visit we spent much time together discussing these things. At this time in the summer of 1988 we followed our normal routine.

We would go to the local restaurant, find a table in a corner, and talk for several hours, often until they closed. Her parents could never understand what we could find to talk about for so long.

During the discussion she described some strange experiences that had occurred about six months before. She thought they might be out-of-the-body experiences, but the more she talked I recognized symptoms of a classical UFO abduction. She had not read any UFO books before the incident. Afterwards she read an Ashtar Command book, and thought if her experiences had something to do with space people, this was surely the type it had to be: the beautiful blond, blue-eyed benevolent beings. I wanted to be sure she really wanted to explore it, because I had the feeling if it really was the classic type case she might discover something that would disillusion her. She was excited about trying it, apparently convinced it would be a wonderful experience. So we scheduled the time for the session, allowing for the whole afternoon.

LeeAnn's aunt and uncle were also friends of mine, who definitely would not understand any of these weird things their niece was interested in. Since they were out of town we knew we could have their house to ourselves with no interruptions. We settled down into chairs in the living room, and I had her tell me her memories of the experience for the benefit of the tape recorder. I always like to record the interview first so we can know the conscious memories. Otherwise, the subject might say later that nothing new was revealed, that they remembered everything. Hypnosis always adds details that are not known at the time of the experience.

She called it a dream, because she didn't know what else to call it, but it had qualities that did not suggest a dream.

She remembered the exact night, and the circumstances leading up to the occurrence. LeeAnn, her husband Mike, and their son, Adam, were planning to visit their in-laws, so she was doing the laundry late at night. Mike and Adam were asleep, and she was folding the clothes in the guest room. The first thing she noticed was little shadows out of the corner of her eye. She had seen these on several occasions, and they never seemed to be associated with normal things in the room that would cast shadows. They would be on the floor or along the wall, always at a low level. When she tried to fixate on them they wouldn't be there. They were only visible out of the side of her eye. These shadows have been reported by other people, usually at the beginning of an alien encounter. Of course, they could be associated with ghosts or spirits, but they seem to have an increasing association with aliens.

I have a theory about this, but it cannot be proven at the present time. There is increasingly more speculation that aliens and their craft are coming from another dimension. If this is true, maybe the shadows are the beginning stage when they are just starting to enter our dimension, and have not quite materialized yet. My assumption was backed up by her remark, "I was seeing these little shadows again, and I thought, Just leave me alone tonight. I don't want to be bothered." That seemed an unusual thing to say without thinking, unless her mind associated the shadows with some type of entities.

After folding the clothes, she took a shower and decided to read for a while. It was around one o'clock in the morning when she laid down to read, but instead fell immediately asleep. She thought she was dreaming, but it seemed to be an OBE, because she was suddenly above her body looking down on it.

"The most fascinating and most exciting thing was that as I looked at my body, I was viewing it as an empty shell. And actually *knowing* what it felt like to have a body without a soul. To see a total nothingness, a total void, an emptiness, and knowing exactly what that felt like, for the first time. I was really excited about that. I was not in two places at once. I could see my body on the bed, but I'm sure I wasn't in it."

Then the situation changed. She felt a sense of urgency, and had to return to her body because she felt she had to get up and go to the bathroom. She was back in her body, but before she could get up she heard a loud, high-pitched sound directly in her ears. She described it as the sound a Skil-Saw would make, high pitched and shrill. The part of her mind that was still semiconscious was trying to reason, "It's nighttime. What goofy neighbor is running a Skil-Saw at this time of night?" She said you have to define things in terms that you know. Yet she knew it was not the first time she had heard the sound. There was the feeling of familiarity, as though this had happened before.

During the following years I was to discover other cases where the person heard a motor sound (often high pitched) at the beginning of an experience. This is another aspect that was to fall within a predictable pattern. But her next remarks were unusual and unpleasant for her to remember.

She had the sensation that she was no longer lying in her bed, but was hanging upside down by her feet. Then she had the feeling of her private parts being poked and prodded. It didn't seem to be a sexual feeling, more like it was being done by some sort of instrument. Then the urge to urinate again. Another part of her mind was saying, "I'm going to wet this bed. I felt like I was hanging upside down, but relating it to sleeping and being in bed. I thought, this is weird. I wanted to get back, because I knew if I didn't I was going to wet the bed, and the bed would be a mess."

Then she had the feeling of something (an instrument) being put down her throat, and she started gagging. And she thought, "They're going to kill me. I'm going to gag to death." Next the awful feeling of her dinner coming up in one round *blob*. She could actually smell the sickening odor of bile. Then the thought, "Now I know the bed is going to be a mess. Not only am I going to wet the bed, but now I'm throwing up. This can't be a dream. It's too real!" Her sense of smell was so acute that it had to be actually occurring.

Yet the sensation passed as soon as it began, and she found herself lying down again. She wanted to wake up, and she looked to where the sliding glass doors would have been in her bedroom. "The room was bright, and my conscious mind thought, 'Gee, why is the room so light, when I know it's dark out. Why is that light coming in through the sliding door when I know I didn't leave that door open?' So I looked outside, or I went outside. I don't remember. There should have been a patio and a screened-in pool out there, but there wasn't. Where my swimming pool should have been, there was a table. And it was a white, very bright light. This was surprising, because I really thought I was in bed in my room. Instead of a patio and swimming pool there was this bright room. And I remember seeing people. They were brown-skinned and not wearing any shirts. And I thought, 'What happened to my patio? And if that's my patio, why are these people around that table without shirts on?' It was as if I was observing things from two parts of my mind, and none of it made any sense."

Those were the last things she remembered. "I felt calmer. I felt back together again. I knew I was awake, but I didn't open my eyes right away, because I didn't want to *see* anything. I don't know how long I laid there, but when I opened my eyes I saw the room was dark like it should have been at nighttime. And I thought, 'God, I'm back in my room!' And I was lying on my stomach, and I never sleep in that position. But my body was so relaxed. I can't recall ever waking up in such a relaxed position. And the bed was not a mess. There was no throw up, no urine, the covers were neat as though I had hardly moved. And the clock read 3:00, so two hours had passed. I did not feel the urge to go to the bathroom. The first thing I did was check the sliding door, and it was just as I had left it. I checked on my son, and my husband, who was snoring away on the couch. Everything was as it should be. I then turned on all the lights, and went into the kitchen and had a cigarette. As I sat there in my kitchen smoking I looked at the ceiling, and thought, 'Doesn't that look nice? That physical reality.' And I felt the table, 'Oh! Doesn't this feel nice? It's physical and solid. Isn't it good to be here?' I guess I thought it was a strange out-of-the-body experience. I had learned that it's nice to get back in, and it's nice to be part of this world. And it's nice having a physical body, and to appreciate the physical body I have now. That was what I was feeling when Mike got up, and wanted to know what I was doing awake. And I said, 'Aw, honey, I just had a weird dream.'"

If this had been a nightmare induced by digestive or gastric distress, why did she feel normal upon awakening. There was no sickness or vomiting.

To add to the confusion of the strange night, if she had really been physically poked and prodded, she should have felt some irritation in those parts of her body the next day. Instead she felt fine, although confused. So she concluded it had to have been a dream.

After the discussion we went into her aunt's bedroom to have the session. When she had entered a good state of trance I instructed her to go to her home on the night of the event in January 1988. She was reliving folding the clothes. She thought it was interesting that she was actually seeing the scene.

L: I can see the bedroom. I can see what I have on. I can really even see the pictures on the wall, rather than remember them. This is like a remembrance, but can you visualize the remembrance? Is that how it's supposed to be? There's a difference between seeing and remembering.

I had to get her mind away from trying to analyze the situation, and back on just reporting what she was seeing. If the subject continues to analyze they can switch into the judgmental side of their brain, and alter the hypnosis process. I explained that it was easier to remember this way.

L: But there's no involvement.
D: *If you don't want to be involved, you don't have to be. You have that choice. You can watch as an observer if you wish. It's all up to you. You're in control.*

She returned to describing the room. And then noticed the shadows.

L: They always are just low to the ground. I can never really tune in on them. They are not like shadows on the wall. Those are fixated from objects. These just seem to be there, and then they fade away quickly.

After she finished folding the clothes she wanted to go to bed because she was tired. She went to sleep immediately, and when I asked if she slept all night long, she whispered, "No." But instead of telling me why, she began to display distress. Her facial and body movements indicated something was going on, but she wouldn't speak. Finally she sighed deeply and said, "I don't want to recall it." I gave comforting suggestions and insisted that she was perfectly safe, and it would be all right to look at it as an objective reporter. This took several minutes of talking in order to gain her confidence. Her breathing was deep and irregular, and I knew something was occurring. All during this time when she wouldn't talk she kept reaching out with her hand and touching my arm gently. It was as though she wanted to make sure I was there, and she was not alone. She continued to do this at regular intervals. It seemed to help for her to know that I really was there and had not left her. She seemed to be so caught up in what was happening it was distracting for me to ask questions. That seemed to bring her focus back to me though. She was definitely watching and experiencing something, and didn't have the impulse to talk. Finally she burst out, "This is nuts!" I assured her that I had heard many strange things, and anything she said would not surprise me. I tried to convince her that if she would begin telling me about it, it would become easier.

L: You're there? Okay?

D: *I'm right here. And I'll be with you through the whole thing. You won't be alone. It doesn't matter how strange it sounds. What are you seeing?*

L: (She finally began to report.) I'm inside. I'm not at home. And they're talking, but I don't know what they're saying now. I don't like it there.

D: *What does it look like?*

L: We're enclosed. It's a room. I don't like how it smells either.

She was making definite facial expressions as though she was smelling something unpleasant and offensive. A wrinkling of her nose, etc. When I asked her to describe the smell, she had great difficulty, but was also determined to get it correct. This was made more difficult because she could not accurately associate the odor with anything familiar. "Not clean. Rotten. Not like dead stuff. It doesn't smell like compost. Not like fish rotten. It's just pungent, if that's the word. A higher frequency of rot, although that makes no sense. Like slimy rotten. It's not like anything I have ever smelled before. Not like bile either. Worse than bile." She made a disgusted face, and seemed uncomfortable with it. So I gave suggestions that she would not be disturbed by the odor as she described the events. In this way we could block it out so it wouldn't physically bother her.

L: It's a room, but it's not like I thought it would be. There are people here. Ummph! (Smiling) It's not Ashtar.

I wanted her to describe what she was seeing, but she fell silent and became an observer. She was in obvious distress from something she was witnessing. I could discern this more from her facial and eye movements than her body movements. Her breathing was loud and uncomfortable. The main body movement was when she reached out to touch my arm; to be sure I was still there. She was absorbed in experiencing whatever was going on.

Suddenly she blurted out, "Why don't they stop it? Their poking. It's like I feel it more than I see it." I patiently tried to persuade her to tell me what was happening, and it was as if my questioning pulled her attention back to me. "Their eyes are very big," she said with a deep sigh. "It's not like I hoped it would be. I hoped it would be a much more spiritual encounter. An intellectual encounter." After a pause she continued, "It's not happening anymore. I think I'm on a table now." She then began to describe the occupants of the room. "Their heads are a light brown, but not beige. Tan is a good color. I guess they have on suits, but their head is always uncovered. Their arms are longer than ours. They're not tall. They're not hairy. They look similar to the "Communion" kind of people, except they are more wrinkled. Their eyes are almond shaped, and in proportion to the rest of their face, their eyes are big. Larger than our eyes, and there is no white. Their pupil is very large, and the iris is real dark, almost blacky brown. They really don't have a nose, just holes, with no extension or whatever it would be called. They also don't have ears, just holes. Their mouths are not like ours, no lips or teeth."

D: Where are they more wrinkled?
L: Their arms are more wrinkled. And their necks are wrinkled, like leather. You know, like those dogs that have the wrinkles?
D: Rolls?
L: Rolls is a good word. There aren't any in the shoulder area, but wherever there is a joint for movement there are wrinkles. By the elbow, and on the inside of the forearms.
D: Are their faces wrinkled?
L: No, their face is smoother and tight, like a nice leather handbag kind of smooth. Not soft like skin is soft, more of a leathery appearance, but their neck is more wrinkled, and skinny.

She described their hands as having three fingers: an opposing thumb and two fingers. She tried to see their feet. "They have joints like we have joints. They have shoulders, elbows and knees. But their feet are not like our feet. They're flatter. They're not as high as our foot would be, and the heel is wider. And I don't see toes."

There have been similar descriptions of the aliens' feet, most notable the one in *Legacy From the Stars*. In that book the description was of something like duck feet or mittens: a flat structure, but without webbing.

D: Did they have any nails on their fingers?
L: I don't remember. But if I had to guess, I would say no.

This goes along with all reports. The being usually has no hair, so it would also have no nails. Nails are composed of the same cellular structure as hair, so it appears that this type of being does not have the gene to produce hair.

L: They were poking. I didn't like that at all. Not at all. Now it's okay. It was disgusting in terms of just being prodded at and poked, and being stuck with. It's worse than when you're having a child and they're poking and prodding.

I tried to get her to tell me where they were poking and prodding, but she was uncomfortable discussing it. So I asked if they had used anything, and she tried to describe instruments she had seen. "They're cold, and smooth. I guess metal like. Not stainless steel. You know how when you go to the gynecologist, sometimes the instruments are cold? But it wasn't gynecologists' instruments. One was long like a straw tube, with some kind of structure on the end, like for scraping or something. That was for their examination in the lower part."

LeeAnn then described where the instruments were kept, "There's a counter area that's made out of some white material. Everything in the room is very *built-in*. The counter part, the drawers, everything, slide in and out of this wall surface. If you needed to place something upon something, you would pull it out from the wall. I guess they have it that way so whenever they're traveling or whatever, they don't have *objects* within the room, necessarily. Everything is pushed *in*."

I asked for description of other instruments, but she switched her focus to the surroundings. "I don't like it here. The room is round. It's light in the room. Did I say that? I'm not lying down anymore, but when you're on the table there's a light above. But then they *hang* you upside down." This was apparently the part that disturbed her, and she couldn't describe it while it was occurring. Now she was able to tell me about it because that part was over. "You feel like you're in stirrups. And you feel like you're a hunk of cattle there. Hanging from your feet, and your head is down."

D: *Not a very comfortable position.*
L: No. (Pause) I don't have any clothes on right now. I didn't have any on when they were doing that. But it's okay now. That smell's

gone too. That was bad, that was different. That was somewhere else, a different room. This room is clean.

D: The smell came from somewhere else?

L: That room wasn't clean, wherever that was. This room is clean clean. It doesn't smell any more. Except ... you shouldn't do that to people. You shouldn't probe. I mean, it's like there is no respect for your body. Ha! What a big shock, LeeAnn! This isn't how it was supposed to be.

D: How many people are in there?

L: There's one person that did the probing. And then there are two other people - people? Ha! - just standing and watching and talking. But I don't know what they're saying.

D: Are they making sounds?

L: Yeah, they're making sounds, but I can't even describe the sound. There is a tonal structure to their language, versus words. Similar to musical tones, but their speech pattern's more hollow sounding. Like if you were talking through ... (had difficulty describing) ... a machine that would replace your vocal cords. But it's a hollow sound. Like you were piping your voice through an organ, but not an organ. An empty kind of sounding. Not a computer. Kind of a mechanical sound. Hollow.

I could understand this definition, because I knew a man that used a machine to replace his vocal cords that had been removed because of cancer. His words could be understood once I became familiar with the sound. But it had a monotone, vibrating effect.

This description was similar to Penny's in *Legacy From the Stars*. She also said she heard the beings making strange musical tones instead of words.

D: Do all these people look alike?

L: They look basically the same, but their eyes are different.

D: In what way?

L: Their eyes are different or their face is different, in terms of the sensitivity. Like all Caucasians look the same, they're Caucasians. All blacks look black. There are similarities, right? But you tell people by their eyes or whatever. And there are very soft eyes right now. You see, now I feel okay. I'm not up there anymore. And the one I'm looking at now has very soft eyes. The same shape, but they're more ... *caring*. He was there before, but watching. He wasn't the one doing the probing.

D: *Could you see anything else that they did?*

L: Yeah, I guess I did. I don't like talking about it.

D: *All right. I just wanted to get all of it out now, and then you wouldn't have to do it again.*

L: We won't do it again, okay?

D: *That's true.*

L: No, we won't do it. I'll talk about it instead of doing it again. Okay?

D: *You can do that. Just talk about what happened.*

L: Okay, I get the feeling - no, I don't get the feeling - I see. They took fecal material. And it looks like they're shooting some kind of laser beam or something into it. They're over there in the corner. It's not really a corner, because the room is round. There's a sound coming from the machine. It's kind of like that sound I heard, but not quite like I remember. It's a high frequency that I guess you would get from a light beam. (This may have been the Skil-Saw noise she heard when she thought she was in her bed.) They took samples of waste material. I can't see what they are doing with it. I don't choose to see. But I think ... *something* thinks, "Why even bother with what they're doing? What's the purpose of it?" The one was *nice*, the man ... the *being* with the nice sensitive eyes. At least they have that much respect. After I was down from hanging like that. Hanging, I didn't like that. He was there to at least calm me down, not that I felt anxious. I just felt like, "Why are they doing this sick stuff?" And it wasn't like *perverted* sick. It was like investigating, I guess, in terms of science, versus being ... (She had difficulty explaining) violated. But at least it's good they have the sensitivity to calm you down after the examination.

A similar caring individual has been seen by other subjects and is reported in my other books. They often describe it as a "nurse" type that calms them down, sometimes just with the expression in its eyes. Some say that, even though they could not distinguish a sex, the being had a feminine feel to it.

D: *You said they had suits on?*

L: Yeah, the ones that stunk did. They had the blue suits on. These other people in the experimental room had on the same type of white jumpsuits. It's a more sterile environment. They had a high neck on the suit too, because they had long necks. Part of the neck was covered. The rolls were above the neck of the suit. (I was picturing a mandarin-type collar.)

D: *Did you see any type of insignia or anything like that on their suits?*

L: Let me see. (Pause) Take this with a grain of salt. This is what popped in, okay? It's a circle. And above the center point are three wavy lines. It's a calming symbol, I guess.

D: *Where was this symbol?*

L: Oh, you'd wear it on your chest. (Her hand motions indicated it was on the left shoulder.) I think it was on the white uniforms.

I gave her instructions that she would remember the symbol and be able to draw it for me upon awakening. I then wanted to know if there was anything else in the room that she remembered.

L: The lights in there. I don't know where the light was coming from, except for that main light over the table. It was big and round, but it wasn't a fluorescent light. It didn't have the heat of the light like when you are at the dentist. You know how that light gets hot? It didn't have that kind of heat, or like I would imagine a light in a doctor's operating room has heat coming off it. This light was right like that, but you couldn't feel any heat being given off. The room was light, but I don't know the source. It seemed to be coming out of the walls, but I couldn't see any light fixtures that I could recognize, so I don't know the central point or source it was coming from.

This description has been repeated in other UFO cases, that the source of light seems to be coming from the ceiling and walls, as though the entire surface is illuminated.

L: This room has a bar bolted into the wall, that is similar to the stainless steel type for the handicapped to hold on. Not a bar, but a pole that runs circular around the wall. It's fine textured as stainless steel is, but it's not cold. The walls are curved, like in a big circular room. I say "big," but it's not really big. It's not massive. If you're lying down and you look up, there is something like an observation room where people or beings could look down, and observe what was going on within the confines of this examining room. I want to say it's glass. It's clear, but probably not glass. But something that would probably prevent germs from spreading, or extra things being exposed to whatever was happening. Almost like an observation deck you would see in a hospital. But in hospitals I think observation decks are set farther back. This is not like that. It's like glass windows, and behind it you can see people standing and observing. But not like in a hospital that you would see on TV with the students standing around and observing. It's different from that.

D: *Are the beings behind the glass the same type as the ones in the room?* (Yes) *Are there any other objects in the room that you can see?*

L: I want to say ... it's not a computer like we think of, with a typewriter and screen. It's not like that at all. There are monitors, I guess, but not like our monitors. These are more or less built-into the wall to do whatever they do. They appear to be made of that same metal, like stainless steel, and have panels and buttons beside them. There are different work stations around the walls of the room. One work station has a very complex-looking microscope, and whatever they are working on is shown on the screen above it. And another work station has a pair of very delicately balanced calipers and cantilevers for handling and dealing with extremely small objects that are too small to use your fingers. A miniaturized tools-type of thing. There are colored lights on the panels. And there are sounds that come from them.

D: *Like machine sounds?*

L: No, not like our machines. The frequency of the sound is higher. There must be some correlation between the sounds you hear and the different light patterns that appear, but I don't know what.

D: *Are there any other sounds?*

L: Sounds? Yeah. You know what that is? That must be the sound. I said the sounds in this examination room were higher frequency sounds, like a dentist's drill. That other sound - although this wouldn't make sense, but I'm going to say it anyway. That buzzing, Skil-Saw sound - this is real. That must have something to do with the engines or something. That's putting this whole thing in Earth terms.

D: *But the other computer type machines are making a different kind of sound?*

L: Oh, yeah! That sound is much more melodic. It's not changing, but it *is* more melodic. It's not like a Skil-Saw sound.

D: *All right. I'm going to ask you now, how did you get there? You can just watch. You don't have to experience it again. How did you come to be in that room?*

L: I'll tell you what I want to say. Take it with a grain of salt. This is the only thing that seems to make sense. What came to mind was that I had to be teleported or lifted up through some method. Not by a space craft coming into my bedroom and doing whatever. No, again I'm going back to a light beam effect. But I don't even know about that, because it's as if I have two minds working here right now.

D: *Just say whatever comes to mind. Don't worry about analyzing it.*

L: (Big sigh) It was like I was beamed on board through whatever means. But the physical body didn't break down like in Star Trek. It must have been some kind of light beam effect, I guess, because I'm thinking about physical realities, like the structures of your house, and thinking about returning. It must be that they encompass your body with this physical light beam. And maybe break apart its molecular structure, so it could be encompassed. So it wasn't a solidness. And then the light beam doing whatever it does to the solidness of the body, and taking the whole molecular structure via the light beam.

D: *Don't worry about it making sense. This is what comes to mind, and that is what we're working with.*

L: This is what comes to mind, yes.

D: *And the whole time you were there you only saw these beings that looked alike?*

L: I want to say there were two groups of people or beings. The second group were the experimenters. The first group were the ones with the blue uniforms. They were more bug-like. They weren't the same body size as the others. They didn't have chests. They were more long and thin, and more flattened. And their appendages were longer.

D: *What do you mean, bug-like?*

L: They weren't the same. Their eyes were bulging, and located on the sides of their head. The head was predominately eyes, bug-like. I don't remember seeing a nose or a mouth, but I assume they had to have a mouth. And they didn't have a chest. You know, these other guys have chests, like we have a chest, with a bone structure. They were more like a big kind of ... I want to say "praying mantis" or "walking-stick" in terms of structure. But large like a person of our size. And frail - but I was thinking they couldn't be as frail as a praying mantis kind of frail. It was a drab looking, insect-looking, type of being, with really long gangly-like arms. Not human like in any way, shape or form.

D: (I was trying to get more description.) *Were their heads also bald?*

L: No, they were different. They were more like a fly. Blacky, browny, straight and brittle hairs, but not a lot of hair. Like a fly has hair on its legs. Brittle hair that stands up stiff, not soft hair. You know, with those weird eyes that are baldy like you'd see in the movies, and appendages that hang.

This description fit the being that Phil saw on a spaceship in my book *Keepers of the Garden*. This type has also been seen by other abductees. A similar type is reported by Beverly in Chapter 5.

L: These people - they're not people - don't even seem to be ... evolved. I can't say what I mean. They don't seem to be intelligent. They seem to be more bug like. Drones, that's a good word. A drone.

D: *When did you see them?*

L: They were involved in the beginning, I guess. I think they're the ones that had that smell. They must be. They must be some lower life form or something that's used for a certain purpose. These creatures were in the beginning of the experience, that I didn't recall before. Like you'll be telling someone a story, and then something that happened in the beginning pops in. Well, they were in the beginning. I want to say they were like recruiters. (Chuckle)

D: *Ah, that's an interesting word.*

L: And they took me through a hall and into the room with the smell. (She wrinkled her nose again.) Right now I get a flash of their quarters, I guess. I don't know why I was there.

D: What did it look like?

L: I can tell you ... if the smell would just .... (It was bothering her again.)

I gave instructions that the smell would not physically bother her while she talked about the creatures.

L: It just focuses your attention. Not that I can even smell it now. It's *dark* there. It's not like the other room. This one is dark and ... damp. But how can it be damp? I don't understand it, but that's the feeling I get. I see ... I guess it's clothing. Suits of some sort. They're on the floor, just like firemen's suits. You know, when we used to go to the firehouse as a kid, and the guys would have their boots and everything all in a pile. All *these* clothes are piled, but there are no *real* boots. The clothes are some kind of cloth, but more like a petroleum made product material.

D: Is that the only thing you can see in that room?

L: Yeah. I'm sitting in there for a while.

D: Did you have your clothes on while you were in there?

L: Yeah, I did. I have my nightclothes on. Ha! I had on my nightshirt to sleep, and it says on it, "You can't sink a rainbow." That's funny. (Chuckle)

D: Then it's the same one you had on when you went to bed. All right. Let's go back to the other experience. At least that one being was nice afterwards. Did he do or communicate anything to you?

L: Yeah, there was a stroking of the arm, a touching of the face, and eye contact. I guess for a calming effect. I hear ... I *could feel* the sounds. No, he's not talking. When he's calming me he wasn't even transmitting the kind of weird verbalization that was going on before.

D: Was that all that happened there? (She sighed deeply.) *I think it was enough though.* (Chuckle)

L: Yes, I think. I don't want to remember any more.

D: That's perfectly all right. But then you were brought back?

L: Yeah. How was I brought back? (Pause) Now there's communication between us, as I'm standing there in their white room, and I have my nightshirt on again.

D: What is the communication?

L: I don't know. I can see myself, and I'm pleased. And I feel all right now. I can't remember.

D: *Was it important?*

L: I don't know. I hope it wasn't.

D: *If it was important your subconscious will remember it anyway.*

L: It was more or less ... I'm going to say it. I don't know if it's true or accurate. A farewell greeting and, yes, "We'll see each other again." That kind of a deal.

D: *All right. But then how were you brought back to your room?*

L: I'm walking with the *nice* man through a hall. And through the stench. And now we're outside the stench room. (Pause) I can't remember. I can't even see it. But it has to be that same kind of beam source, whatever it is.

D: *Do you think that's how you got back to your room?*

L: I don't know how else. (Chuckle) I'm sure the vehicle didn't land on my house.

D: *(Laugh) Do you remember seeing the outside of the craft?*

L: I could see it now. It was - not round - it was more elliptical shaped. (Hand motions) This way would be elliptical, the underneath would be more rounded.

D: *But then you ended up back in your room, and everything was fine, wasn't it?* (She gave a positive exclamation.) *It wasn't so bad then. It was all over with. How do you feel about it?*

L: Now? I didn't like that experience when I was viewing it. And I don't like thinking about it. But right now I sound angry, don't I?

D: *A little bit.*

L: But as I pull myself back and look, I wasn't after it was over with. How do I feel about it? Do you really want to know? I think I made it all up.

D: (Laugh) *But does it bother you that it might have happened?*

L: Does it bother me? (Thoughtfully.) No.

D: *I was thinking that might be the reason they didn't let you remember, because they didn't want it to bother you at the time and afterwards.*

L: That's true.

I then brought LeeAnn forward and oriented her. Before waking her up I gave many suggestions for well-being so this experience wouldn't bother her.

After the session we got a drink and relaxed for a bit before I gave her a tablet and marker and asked her to draw what she remembered. She apologized that she was no artist.

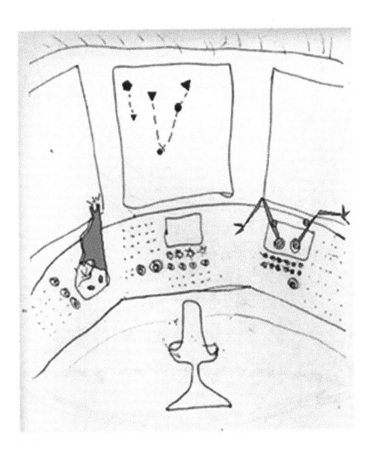

Drawing of the instrument panel, microscope and calipers, by LeeAnn. Many other subjects saw similar scenes: control panels and screens mounted on curved walls, instruments with handles to manipulate small objects, microscopes that projected cells, etc. onto the larger screens. Often star maps were seen on the screens.

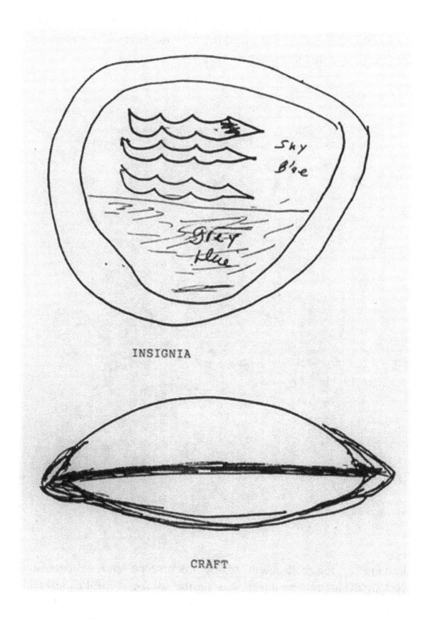

INSIGNIA

CRAFT

Drawing by LeeAnn of the insignia and craft.

LeeAnn remarked sarcastically, "What happened to Ashtar? I would rather be traveling with Ashtar."

We laughed, and I knew she would be all right, even though the experience was not what she had expected. She then spent quite a bit of time trying to define the awful smell that still lingered in her memory. That seemed to bother her, and she was determined to find some kind of comparison.

"That smell ... not like anything I ever smelled. You know how rotten eggs smell. It wasn't like that, because that is like a sulfur smell. It wasn't organic. You know how things that are organic may smell really terrible when they rot. It was a different smell. This smell is like ... a burning ... like a metal. We used to live in Chicago right by the steel mills. And it reminds me of the smell when they burned metal. It was like the smell of zinc. How does zinc smell when it burns?"

I had no idea. "I don't know. But it was like a burnt smell?"

"Not *burnt*! It was like a rotten, sour smell, but like it has to do with a metal. I want to say zinc. That keeps popping in. Yet I don't know how zinc would smell if you burned it. Or like slate. How would slate smell if you burned it? But it wasn't like a body decomposing. It wasn't like garbage or anything organic. It wasn't sulfur. I keep wanting to say it was more metallic instead of organic."

"If it's any consolation, other people have smelled strange things, and they also have difficulty describing it."

An offensive smell was reported by the first case I ever investigated. The woman, Christine, became almost physically ill when she first entered a craft. She was overwhelmed by a smell that she found difficult to describe. The closest she could come was that it reminded her of something electrical burning, like a burnt-out engine. She did not think it was coming from the beings themselves, but instead from a room where the power supply was located. When she asked about the power source, they told her she would not understand unless she had a knowledge of electro magnetics and crystallized structures. There was no visible way to open the door that led to that room. But she saw the beings pass their hands over certain controls, and doors would open and things would move. There, of course, is no way of knowing if the craft these two women saw were the same type, but it is an oddity that they both described a disturbing smell.

LeeAnn explained her difficulty and reluctance to describe events to me in the beginning of the session, when she was experiencing the physical examination. "It was like I didn't want to get involved. I'd see a glimpse of it or know what was happening. It's like this other side of me was saying, 'You don't want to do that. You're not going to recall any more.' At one point it was like, 'Oh, take me out of here.'" She chuckled.

I explained, "Your subconscious safety factor will do that if it thinks you're not ready to look at it."

It was important to note that LeeAnn went into the session expecting a totally different experience, and that gave it more validity. If she was going to fantasize, she would have been on the ship with the blond, blue-eyed Ashtar. She would not have fantasized something so unpleasant.

I saw LeeAnn again a few days later before she returned home to Florida. I wrote down most of our conversation later while it was still fresh in my mind.

She said she had spent the time puzzling over the session. It was as though two parts of her brain were battling each other. The first thing she said was that she wanted to apologize to me. I was surprised, what could she possibly have to apologize for? She said she was apologizing for telling me all those lies and making up that weird story. (I knew better but I let her talk.) Then she said the other part of herself wanted to know why she made up such a perverse story. She was expecting a beautiful experience. If not a religious one, at least an intellectual one. She was reasoning that this meant she was a perverse and sick person, in order for her to lie like that and make up such disgusting things. This battling between herself went on for two days. But she now felt better. She had come to the conclusion that no, she was not perverse and no, she was not sick. She knew she was normal. But the question still prevailed, "Where did it come from? What did it mean? Was it real?"

I told her she had been expecting to fantasize, and have an enjoyable experience. The real story had been a shock to her. In order for her to fantasize a story that was admittedly perverse and sick, she should have gotten some enjoyment or excitement from the perversion, instead she felt only disgust and repulsion. To me this added validity and dispelled the fantasy theory. The idea did occur to her later about the possibility that something may have been done to her son also. This thought made her feel physically ill in the pit of her stomach. As though, "What kind of a mother am I if I couldn't protect my son." And, "What kind of creatures would want to hurt a child." She also wondered about his psyche and any trauma that may have been done to his subconscious. We discussed this at length. I had suspected her son may have been involved because of the other cases I had investigated. I did not mention the possibility to her because I didn't want to trouble her. She came to the conclusion by herself. The important thing was that her son did not seem to have any conscious memories of this sort of thing, and it was better left that way.

About a month later she called me from Florida and spent almost an hour discussing all of this. She was still having trouble dealing with it and putting it in its place. The only person she told about the experience was a psychologist friend, who reassured her she was normal, and this was merely a fantasy. When LeeAnn asked why it was so unpleasant, the woman explained it was because of her strict Catholic upbringing, and the idea had undoubtedly been embedded in her that sex was dirty. I thought that was an interesting explanation, because the incident did not necessarily focus on her sexual parts. Of course, LeeAnn did not accept the explanation.

LeeAnn mentioned another unusual aftereffect. One day when she was downtown she was looking at a large white building with smoked windows, common to that area of Florida, because of the heat. As she looked up at it the image of the white room with the observation window came into her mind. And she once again thought about the beings up there watching her. Then she told herself that was crazy. When she looked at the building again, she saw there were only people on the other side of the window doing exercises.

I thought she would begin to put the experience into place and deal with it. It was just such a strange and new idea. She is an intelligent and very stable person, and should be able to handle this with no problems. But she could not yet bring herself to listen to the tape (Similar to other people I have worked with). I told her this was common and it too would pass.

LeeAnn called again about a week later, late at night. The first thing she said was, "Tell me the truth. Did that really happen to me?" This was a difficult question. It would have to be answered carefully so as to not have any effect on her everyday life. I told her that reality was hard to describe. I spent a long time discussing this with her and telling her it didn't really matter one way or the other if it were real. The important thing was how the memory was affecting her. She finally decided she was not going to read any more about UFOs. She was just going to stick to metaphysical books for a while, because maybe she was thinking about it too much and dwelling on it. I agreed it would be best to get her mind off it. She was leaving for a vacation in Canada, and I thought this would be perfect. She said she had a nightmare the other night and it had also seemed very real. So she convinced herself that if that nightmare (which she was positive was only a dream) seemed so real, then the session was also relating to a dream. Nothing more, nothing less. I told her if this made her feel better, then that was the right way to look at it. This is also the way Phil chose to handle it, just to believe that he had a wild imagination.

Her description of the examination showed that the experience is not always related to sexual parts, as in cases involving the removal of sperm and ova. The beings also study waste products (feces and urine) and food before it is fully digested.

Maybe this was the reason for hanging upside down, to more easily remove the food from the stomach area. Although it is distasteful to us, it may have genuine scientific value to them to study these things. We cannot judge what we do not fully understand.

These unusual cases have continued through the years. By the end of the 1990s I was traveling to several foreign countries, and investigating cases that had been screened by other investigators and psychologists. I never knew what the case would entail, and by 1997 I had become adept at detecting fantasy cases and those individuals wanting attention. Edith was one of several I worked with in November 1997 in the south of England. During the initial interview it was established that she had recently suffered from bulimia. Even though she insisted it was no longer a problem her doctor was alarmed that her blood count was far from normal. I suspected that Edith had psychological problems, and this was further reinforced when she explained the reason for the self-induced bulimia. She was a forty-year-old woman (although she didn't appear that old) with grown children, who had recently married a young man in his twenties. Her relatives seemed to be the basis for many of her problems, including this one. They berated and criticized her by saying, "What can he see in an old woman like you?" She already had a problem with self-esteem that had reflected in her inability to hold a job. These remarks did not help the situation, so she became bulimic in the hope of making herself more attractive. I personally couldn't see the purpose for doing it, because the young man had fallen in love with her the way she was. Why did she feel the need to change? I suspected she needed more psychological counseling than I could give her, especially in the limited time that I would be with her. My main concern was her belief that she had had UFO and alien experiences. Of course, with any work of this type you must take the whole personality into consideration.

She explained that she had been having strange dreams that she thought might be related to either aliens or spirit manifestation. Her family was of no help whatsoever, because they did not have any understanding of the paranormal, and constantly criticized Edith because of her interests.

The main experience that she reported occurred during the past year (1997). She had awakened to see a figure in her room that approached her bed. Then she remembered nothing except the dream that followed. She was lying on a table with figures surrounding her. In a dreamlike stupor she heard them discussing her. They said something about a mistake, and that there was too much blood lost. She determined from this that they had done something to her, that they had taken blood from her, and this was causing her present physical problems. She wanted me to find out during the session: Why did they take her blood, and what were they going to do with it? She was convinced that if the experience was real, it was a negative one.

When I began the session I didn't know if anything would come out, because I really believed the woman's problems were caused by deeper psychological causes, and the alien connection was merely an excuse to blame them on something outside herself. If this were the case then her subconscious would tell me.

When she was in a deep state of trance I directed her to return to her apartment on the night of the event. (She was positive of the date because she kept a diary, and the events were recorded in it.) She had awakened from sleep because the room was cold. Then she announced apprehensively, "There's something there. It's looking at me. It's watching me. It's by my bed."

She described an object about nine inches across resembling a glowing orange and yellow light, with a large crystal or diamond in its center. Frightened, she was peeking out of the covers at it when she noticed others had entered the room. One was tall and resembled a human with pale skin. He was accompanied by three small creatures that resembled white glowing globs. She was not frightened by them, only amused. She thought they were very cute as they touched her arm and face with ice cold fingers. The tall one was now holding the strange glowing device. A shaft of cold light came from it and was aimed at the center of her forehead. He explained to her that it would not hurt her; it would only make it easier to transport her out of the house. She was told to lie very still as she was encased in a beam of light coming from above, and then began to float off the bed. Somehow they were then outside and floating upward. At this point Edith expressed difficulty breathing, and I had to remove the physical sensations. The next instant she was inside a huge ship, although she did not remember entering it. She was taken to a bright room where the light seemed to emanate from the walls and ceiling. Inside the room were many more creatures which she described as different from the little white soft ones that had accompanied her. "They're uglier. But they're not really ugly, just different. They're chunkier, a purpley-brown color with bigger fat heads. The little light ones look softer. These have skin that looks rough." She couldn't touch one to find out, because now she was lying on a table and unable to move.

They then brought a machine over to the side of the table. She was apprehensive as she saw a light come from the machine and enter her body between the ribs on her left side. She exclaimed, "It hurts, but it doesn't hurt!"

The tall being mentally communicated with her that it would not hurt her. They were going to repair damage that she had caused to her stomach. She wondered why they were going in between her ribs, instead of through her mouth. He explained that it was easier going through the side. The mood then suddenly changed to one of anxiety when she mentally heard the beings say there was a mistake. There was more damage than anticipated. They were worried, because there was much more bleeding in the stomach. There was more to fix than first thought. She had already lost a great deal of blood, and was getting weak. She heard the words, "You must not damage your body. It is special." They then used the light to seal off the bleeding.

I was curious about why she had not noticed the effects of internal bleeding. They said she would have eventually, and it might have been more difficult to repair by that time. They then inserted a white liquid into her arm through something "like a needle, but it's not a needle." They explained that "they were putting in better blood cells to counteract the damage. Something to make the blood cells work better. To make the blood have more oxygen."

When they were preparing to leave the craft the tall one communicated to her that he would come again and check on her. She felt comfortable with him and thought she knew him. He said they had been together before she came into this life. And he was really very old.

The next instance she found herself back in bed in her home. Her mind was filled with questions that quickly dissipated as she drifted asleep. In the morning there was no memory of the event except the dream that suggested they had harmed her by removing her blood. It was now obvious that they tried to help her, and she had caused the damage to her body herself through the constant vomiting created by bulimia.

Her doctors were concerned, because her blood count was so low they couldn't understand how she was functioning at all, and said she should have been unconscious. Her subconscious communicated to me that there should be no worry about the abnormally low blood count. That was now normal for her, and she was able to function quite well with it. "The blood count means nothing. It's just a low count. A low count is normally an indication of oxygen. Her oxygen supply is greater even though it is smaller." The damage to the stomach area had been repaired, and the doctors would find nothing with their tests. It would probably just be recorded as a mystery, and as long as Edith was having no physical problems it was best left alone.

This case shows the problem between the conscious mind interpreting a disturbing dream and arriving at the wrong conclusion, and the correct understanding of the situation coming from deep trance hypnosis. When we discussed this after she was awake she could understand that her perception of the memory of the dream was false. The beings on the craft had not harmed her, but actually had repaired the damage she herself had caused through her vanity and self-doubt.

CHAPTER 5
BURIED MEMORIES

Just as dreams can sometimes hide real experiences that are deep in the subconscious, so can memories be distorted through time. As children we perceive things in a simpler, more naive way. What is often traumatic to a child is viewed differently by the adult that child has become. Often the memory of an event is buried because it was traumatic or painful to remember. Under hypnosis when the memory is found and relived, it is often seen to not be so threatening after all. It can be looked at and understood by the adult. I have had clients who wanted to remember a forgotten incident. They thought because they had forgotten it or suppressed it that it must have been something very terrible. Under hypnosis it is often found to be an event that could easily be explained. For instance, a misdeed or an act of mischief that caused the parents to be angry. It does not have to involve physical punishment to cause the event to be suppressed. Often it is the mere fact that the parents were angry. Add to this, the now popular explanation that somehow UFOs and aliens were involved if something has been suppressed. In nine cases out of ten I have found no alien involvement at all. This is why I tell investigators to always start with the simple rather than the complex. In other words, look for the simplest logical explanation, before bringing in the bizarre. When using the deepest levels of hypnosis the real truth will always surface. It cannot be hidden, unless telling lies or fabricating is a normal part of the subject's life. In which case they could lie or fantasize, because it is part of their nature. But such cases are rare, and their story does not hold up. If they are fantasizing the story will not remain constant, but will change with the retelling. It will be embroidered as new details are added. Also the story will not fit the pattern I have discovered. There is always the possibility that I do not have all the pieces that make up a pattern. Someone could come up with a story that presents a totally different side that I have not explored. Thus I must be open to that possibility, and not close all the doors automatically. But even if a new way of thinking is introduced, there will still be elements that fit the pattern. It is obvious that the job of an investigator is not easy, especially if it is combined with therapy. It is only because I am open to all possibilities that the following cases emerged.

Fran was a divorced woman is her forties whose most distinguishing feature was her bright red hair. She was very content with her executive position with a prestigious firm. She came to me in 1988 because she had some unusual vivid memories that she wanted to explore under hypnosis. She was raised on a farm in Mississippi, and had not been exposed to stories of UFOs in that type of rural area. She did not have access to any type of occult or supernatural book or topic. Yet it was in this environment that the events occurred, and the memories were obscured and clouded.

Fran remembered several sightings of strange lights over her house when she was growing up, and her car being followed by lights when she was older. Since there was no logical explanation for them, she assumed they might have been UFOs. Strangely, she experienced no fear when these events occurred, yet the people with her were terrified. She had no other conscious memories of anything of this nature, so we decided to explore these sightings. I have conducted many of these types of sessions where the subject just added more details about the sighting. We were not expecting anything unusual to come forth.

She had one personal problem she thought we might look for if the session went in that direction. It was what I call "a karmic relationship" problem. She seemed to have had friction with her grandmother since she was very young. She couldn't understand what caused it because she loved her grandmother, but she had the feeling she had done something to offend her. This type of situation is best handled during past-life regression to previous lifetimes, if the cause of the friction cannot be located in the present lifetime. So I was not really concentrating on it. I merely made a note of it, and thought we would pursue it if we had time.

Fran proved to be an excellent subject, and surprisingly spontaneously regressed to an unusual event in her childhood. I decided to stay with it and ask questions, because normally the subconscious does not bring up an incident without a reason. She was once again a child of seven years old. Her mannerisms and facial expressions were amazingly correct for the age she was reliving. At that young age she was sitting cross-legged in the middle of her bed playing with a set of little china dishes. It was a special event because she was not allowed to play with them, since they belonged to her grandmother. But she thought it would be difficult to break anything if she played with them in the middle of a big bed. She giggled gleefully as she handled the little pitcher and cups and saucers. She remarked, "They don't belong to me. I play with them. Father is here, and he is showing me how to have fun with them."

It turned out that the person she was talking about was not her biological father, but he had asked Fran to call him "Father." Apparently he was not a stranger, but someone who came to see her regularly. I asked for a description. She described a very tall and thin being standing at one side of the bed. "He has on a cloth that just hangs over his body. It doesn't look like clothes like I wear at all." She hesitated about describing his physical features. "It's hard to look at him. His face looks like when you mold clay, and you mix it real slick. He doesn't have any hair or any eyebrows. His eyes are big and dark ... but it really doesn't matter."

He was teaching her how to levitate. He placed his hand over the top of her head, and she felt a tingling as her body and the little dishes rose into the air. She thought it was great fun, and was laughing and talking to him. At that moment her grandmother burst through the door very suddenly. She had heard the talking, and wanted to find out what was going on in the room, thinking that her granddaughter was into some kind of mischief. When she came through the door so suddenly, it broke Fran's concentration. The little dishes fell together and broke. The grandmother couldn't understand how she had broken them, but she was very angry with her, although Fran insisted that she hadn't done anything. Strangely, the grandmother didn't seem to see the being. Did he disappear at the moment she came through the door, or what?

Fran had spontaneously regressed to the incident that had caused the anger between her grandmother and herself. The little girl felt angry at being unjustly accused of something she had not purposely done. Of course, even if she had explained about "Father" the grandmother would not have understood. Fran would have been accused of fantasizing or lying. As an adult she consciously knew something had happened in her childhood, but she could not remember the incident before hypnosis.

I wanted to know more about this being. The child Fran replied that he had been with her as long as she could remember. He would often meet her in the woods, and walk and talk with her. "He shows me how to listen, and hear. Things big people don't hear. He shows me how to see, colors and things that the big people can't see. It's beautiful."

D: *When he comes to see you, how does he come?*
F: (Confused) I don't know. He's just standing there. And sometimes I discover he's there, and I walk up to him. Sometimes I know he's going to be there. I don't know how I know. I know in my mind that he's going to be there.
D: *Do you ever meet him anywhere besides the house and the woods?* (She hesitated to answer. She had probably never talked about this to anyone else.) *I'm just curious. You can tell me things that the big people don't believe. It's good to have someone believe you, isn't it?*
F: Yeah. He believes me.
D: *I bet he does. But have you ever been anywhere else besides the house and the woods with him?*
F: I think so. There's this light in the woods. It's a big light. There are stairs that go into this light. He's with me, and we went up the stairs.
D: *Where did the stairs go?*
F: Into the bottom of this big light.

She described walking up steps made of light. At the top of the stairs was a metal doorway. It looked gray like metal, although it felt soft when she touched it. He wanted to show this place to her, but explained that she couldn't stay very long. There was a hallway, and doorways going into rooms. But the doorways looked strange to her, composed of different layers. "There's an area where I'm not supposed to go, into the big room. This one is okay."

In the room she was allowed into, there sat a metal looking cylinder supported on a form fitting platform. "It's real shiny. And that other metal on the doors was not shiny." I was trying to get an idea of the size of the cylinder. "It's not quite big enough for me to get into. If I laid down, it would probably come up to about here on me. (Her nose.) But I couldn't get into it, because it's not big enough around. There's supposed to be some kind of animal in there."

The being was carrying some eggs he had taken from a bird's nest in the woods. He told her he had to put them in the room. "That's how I got to go."

D: *What did he do with the eggs?*

F: (Her voice was childish.) Oh, he put them away, in a ... in that thing. (pointing to the left side.) I don't know exactly what that is over there. It's strange looking. It's got some light to it, but it looks like cloth of some sort. But ... it's not like normal cloth. And he puts the eggs over there. I wonder why he did that?

D: *You mean like a curtain?*

F: Yeah, kind of. But this is different. It's got light in it. He says it's to help them hatch. Oh! It keeps it warm. I like to see things like that.

D: *Then he brought the eggs in to watch them hatch, and that's why you got to see that room.*

She tried to explain in her childish way that there were more of those tanks in other rooms, and the baby birds would be put into one of them to keep them safe.

F: They have different things, different animals in the tanks. I don't think they come from here. That animal. He didn't come from here.

D: *Where do you think it came from?*

F: The stars. That's where father comes from.

D: *That would be a long way, wouldn't it? Did he say where?*

F: He said I wouldn't understand. He just said the stars.

D: *Well, that would explain why the animal would be safer inside the tank.*

F: I suppose so.

D: *Did he show you anything else?*

F: No. We have to leave. We have to go back out. It's just time to go.

D: *That was fun, wasn't it?*

F: It sure was. I want to go again. (Giggle) He likes my red hair.

D: He does? Maybe he likes it because he doesn't have any.

(She laughed.)

D: Do you go back outside?
F: Yes. The stairs are like white light. It's different, but you can step on it. When I was back in the woods, Father tapped the center of my forehead with his finger, and I keep hearing the word "Forget."

I tried to find out if she ever saw him again, or had any more adventures with him. But sadly, he told her he couldn't come any more after the incident with the dishes, because he had gotten her into trouble with her grandmother. He said she would have to forget all about him. I sensed that he had a genuine affection for the child, and really didn't want to leave, but felt compelled to. He seemed to be enjoying the interaction with her, and the teaching he was exposing her to. If she had any other involvement with him I was unable to find it in her memory banks. Either the suggestion to forget about him worked, or he didn't return.

The remainder of the session concerned the sightings she had, and only mundane information came forth.

Beverly was an artist in her forties. She officially called herself an artist, but that type of occupation doesn't always pay the bills. So she had turned to sign painting in order to make a living, and to her surprise she was successful at it. However, she still pursued her painting in her spare time. She lived in an unusual house that was built totally into the side of a hill in our Ozark Mountains. It was like living in a cave. The only hint of the outside came from light shining through the door and windows on the front wall. This was where our sessions took place in 1988. Beverly wanted to explore her past lives in hope of finding explanations for problems with her health and money (the lack of it). This was what we intended to do, but often the subconscious has other ideas. In which case I always go with it, because there has to be a reason for the subconscious bringing something up. Usually it is something the subject needs to know about, rather than the intended purpose of the session.

During our discussion before the session Beverly told me about some strange experiences in her childhood that she had never forgotten. They did not worry her. She mainly considered them a curiosity. "When I was in first grade there was an incident when a girl friend of mine, Patricia, and I supposedly ran away from home after school. There was a huge wooded field across the street from the school, and that's where we went. I have no memory of what took place in there, how long we stayed or anything. But our parents were looking for us. I didn't know how much time had passed, because I didn't have a concept of time back then. I lived six blocks from the school, and we were half way home when my mother found us. I have no memory of what took place during that time at all, except that we really got fussed at for being gone so long. They said school was out at three o'clock, and it was almost dark when we got home. They were ready to call the police. The thing that strikes me about it is, if that was my first episode of running away, I should have remembered what I did. At least parts of it, but I don't. All I remember is us going across the street and into the woods. And I don't remember anything else, except being found later and getting into trouble about it. I don't remember having a good time or not."

While she was reminiscing about her childhood, she brought up other strange memories. "My room was at the back of the house. I liked to be by myself. And I would often go there, shut the door to get away from my parents, sit on my bed and daydream. At least I thought I was daydreaming. I would be sitting on my bed and the next thing I would kind of jolt and I would come back to awareness and be on the floor. My mother said I had probably fallen asleep and fell off the bed. But I knew I wasn't asleep. This went on all through grade school."

We spoke about many events in her life during the preliminary discussion. This is when I get to know the person, and try to find out what they want to explore during hypnosis. Sometimes their remarks are relevant, and sometimes not. In this case there were several unusual memories that I made special note of. Beverly's discussion about her childhood triggered another memory: a negative one dealing with nightmares.

"When I was as young as I can go back to remembering, and this has to be three years of age, I had nightmares of giant insects. I know the age because I remember a dog I had then. These giant bugs would get on my bed with me. They didn't hurt me, but they reminded me of walking sticks. They had long bodies and little thin frail feeler type things like insects, and great big eyes."

The term "walking stick" caused me to take notice, because of the other cases involving this type of extraterrestrial. Was she describing alien beings, or just remembering a child's vivid imagination? I didn't want to give any clues of insect type alien beings I had already heard about. I wanted her to give her own descriptions.

"They weren't round insects like spiders, they were elongated. There are some bugs that are made that way. One of them is the walking stick, and the other one is the praying mantis. They had appendages up on the front of their body, and on the back of their body. And they were as big as I was. Of course, I was a little girl. They didn't hurt me, but they really scared me when they would get on top of me. I had a twin bed, and with me lying on it and them on top looking at me, they were bigger than me. Their body didn't touch my body. Their feeler legs or whatever lifted them up above me, so there was a space between their body and my body. There would usually be two or three in the room, but at least one, and they were just looking at me. I had those nightmares from as young as I can remember, all through my early childhood. At that time I had never even seen a movie, much less a scary show." They were a dark color, and had big eyes similar to an ant's, but she knew they were definitely not that type of insect.

"I would wake up screaming many times. Sometimes I would get up and go out in the backyard to get my dog and bring her back to bed with me. Mother wouldn't let the dog in the house. I was scared of the dark, but I would go out in the dark night and bring my dog back and put her under the covers with me. Then I'd sleep okay. Where I lived houses most of the time had roaches, because it was a hot, humid climate. But I didn't dream about roaches. I spent my summers with my grandmother in the country, but I never had the nightmares there."

As Beverly kept associating through memories she brought up another strange experience that had left such an impression she had never forgotten it. It occurred when she was an adult, married with a son and living in a suburb of Houston in the early 1970s. Their house was the only one on the street that didn't have any trees in the backyard. That was not important because they intended to put a pool in the backyard anyway. Beverly's bedroom was in the back of the house, and she and her husband were asleep when she was awakened by an unusual sound.

She laughed as she said, "I just knew in my mind it was a flying saucer. And I thought, 'Oh, it's just them again.' Don't ask me where that thought came from, because I have no idea what a flying saucer would sound like. When I woke up and heard that noise, I just knew that's what it was. Robert was still asleep, and he never did wake up. I thought it very strange that he didn't wake up and hear it, but I wouldn't disturb him. And I did not get out of bed, to my knowledge. I don't know how long I was awake, but I went back to sleep without ever getting up. Now, normally, I should have gotten up. Most people, if they heard something in the backyard, would get up and go see about it. But I didn't, to my knowledge."

I asked her what it sounded like, and her answer was very familiar. "It was like a whirring noise, like a high-speed plane." We tried several associations of sounds before she found one that was nearly correct. "It didn't sound like an airplane propeller. You know how a children's top sounds when you spin it on a table? A singing or whooshing. A high-pitched spinning sound, like wind swirling real fast, then magnify that sound a little. It wasn't very loud. I mean, it wasn't as if the whole neighborhood would have been awakened by it."

I suggested the sound of a helicopter, but that would have been louder and a different pitch. Another association, "Or like a washing machine when it's on spin cycle, except that I knew it was faster. And I'm sure I was not asleep. I laid there and listened to it, and I thought, 'Well, it's just a spaceship in the backyard.' I wasn't scared. I just went back to sleep, as far as I know."

This did seem like a strange reaction. Normally the first thought upon hearing an unusual sound at night would be that someone was in the backyard and they might break into the house. Your first reaction would be fear, and then you would probably get up and look out the window. I agreed that all of these memories were indeed strange incidents. I made notes of them, but our first concern was finding answers for her current problems, not the exploration of UFOs, which she said she was not interested in anyway.

Beverly then changed the subject and went on to discuss her many physical problems. All her life she had strange and unusual symptoms that were difficult for the doctors to diagnose. "This got to the point where it had become a joke. They never knew what was wrong with me. Even when they ran many tests they couldn't agree on what it was. They were never sure about anything. It was the same thing when I went to large hospitals for diagnosis. They assured me they would find out, but then backed down when they couldn't pinpoint it. That was frustrating, to drive thirteen hours and be charged two thousand dollars for medical tests, and they still can't tell me what's wrong with me." Some of these problems existed at the present time, so this was one of the areas she wanted to explore. She wanted to find out why she had so many physical problems, and where they came from, presuming that the cause of this type of karma could lie in another lifetime. Her continuing money problems were also a concern to her. So when we started the session health and money were to be our main focus. The childhood memories were only interesting sidelines.

After Beverly was in deep trance I used my technique that should have put her automatically into another lifetime. Instead she saw only various whirling colors. This often happens and can be moved beyond. After giving her deepening suggestions, Beverly began describing a scene from her present lifetime. She was once again a child of six reliving her first day at school. With high pitched giggles she talked about being left behind in the bathroom, and becoming lost in the corridors of the big school. It wasn't frightening, it was an adventure. With childish mannerisms and speech patterns she went into much detail about her teacher and her friends in the first grade. There was also much description about the physical layout of the school. The subconscious never brings up an incident without a reason. So it occurred to me that this might be a perfect opportunity to explore the memory of running away into the woods across from the school.

D: *Well, are there woods around the school?*
B: Uh huh. They're over across the street, not the busy one but the side street. It's kind of spooky in there. I don't go in the woods. But I could!
D: *What's spooky about it?*
B: It's dark where all those trees are. But there's not anything in there, just a lot of trees. It gets dark early, too.

D: All right, Beverly, I want you to move forward in time to when you went into those woods with your girl friend one night after school. What was her name?

B: Patricia.

D: All right. It's that evening, and school is out. Have all the kids gone home?

B: No. They're out on the playground. We're just wandering around.

D: Had you ever been in those woods before? (No) *Why did you decide to go in them on this evening?*

B: (Soberly) We're running away from home.

D: You are? Why are you doing that?

B: Because we don't like it there.

D: That's a rather drastic thing to do.

B: Well, it'll serve 'em right.

D: Why did you want to run away? Did something happen?

B: No. Nothing. We just decided that we would because we didn't like it at home. Besides, we should be able to go places sometimes, now.

D: Why now?

B: Because we're big, and we're in school.

D: Aren't you afraid you'll get lost?

B: Well, we'd probably go back home. I don't know if we would stay away forever. I think some of the kids have crossed the blacktop road before. It's not a real street. You know, it's just that road. But I think other kids have done it.

D: Well, tell me what's happening.

B: We just wandered inside. The trees are really big. There's no grass. I mean, you can walk between the trees. It's got pine needles and stuff like that on the ground. It's not grass like in your yard.

D: What did you do in the woods? (Pause) (Her facial expression and eye movements indicated something was happening.) *What is it?*

B: (Confused) I don't know. (A long pause.) I don't think I'm supposed to talk. I don't think I'm supposed to do anything. I don't know where she is, but I don't think we're supposed to do anything.

D: Where who is?

B: Pat.

D: Isn't she with you?

B: (Pause) I can't see her. I think I'm frozen.

D: *Your mind isn't, and your mind can speak to me. And it won't bother you at all. It knows things and it can talk to me.*

B: It's like ... it's wiped clean. Like windshield wipers do.

D: *What do you mean?*

B: I don't know. (Hand motions) It's curved. (Hand motions) It's just out in front of me. And I'm not supposed to do anything.

D: *Can you see through it?*

B: I don't think I'm supposed to look.

D: *I don't want you to do anything that will get you in trouble. I'm just curious. Where did it come from?*

B: (Pause) I don't know. I was just walking in the woods, and I think it's pinkish. (She was becoming frightened.) It's like a shield. (Her voice quivered and tears came from her eyes.) In front of me. (She was now openly crying and sobbing as a child would.) It makes me feel like I can't move. (Obviously upset.)

I talked to her soothingly so she would relax and stop being emotional. After a few minutes the loud sobbing stopped. I tried to reassure her that she could talk to me and tell me what was happening. She began to calm down.

D: *You said it is a pinkish color?*

B: Yeah, it's something pinkish. And it's like it numbs everything. And my mind. It goes from one side of me across the front to the other side.

D: *Just over your face or what?*

B: I don't know. It's all of what I know.

D: *In other words, that's all you can see right now.* (Yeah) *And what happened as you were walking through the woods?*

B: I think we could see some sunlight in there somewhere. I thought it was bright. And it was pretty, I thought. The sunlight was coming down through the trees. I don't think it was all over, I think it was over to the right.

D: *But you know, sunlight does that sometimes. Then what did you do?*

B: I think we just looked at it.

D: *Was it sunlight?*

B: (Puzzled) I don't know. I couldn't ... this pink thing ... just couldn't do anything anymore. It's like it stopped everything. (Hand motions) Except it came from here across here (Across her field of vision). It didn't touch me. And it's slick, but I can't see through it. It just made everything stop. It made my head stop. It doesn't hurt. I can't feel anything. I can't see anything, except this pinkish thing. It's all in front of me, like a shield.

D: *Can you feel anything under your feet?*

B: I'm not aware of my feet. I just feel numb.

D: *Can you hear anything?*

B: No. Everything just stopped. Like a still shot. I can't see anything beyond this ... (Sigh) pale yellow, pinkish ... it seems to just freeze everything.

D: *All right. But remember, it's only temporary, and it won't bother you at all.*

Beverly was unable to report any sensations at all, as though all of her physical senses had been literally frozen. I soon realized the futility of pursuing this. Her subconscious was not ready to release information yet. I moved her ahead to her next sensation, whether hearing, smelling or feeling. Surprisingly she suddenly began to giggle.

B: We're running out of the woods. Giggling. We got out. (Laugh)

D: *What do you mean?*

B: Well, we just got out of there. (Big sigh and a laugh.) We got out! (Pause) My hair was curly.

D: *What do you mean?*

B: Well, we had curly hair. We were giggling and running out of the woods, and our hair was bouncing. (Big sigh) And we did it. We went into the woods, and we came out.

D: *Did anything happen while you were in the woods?*

B: I don't know. (Puzzled) Probably something.

D: *What do you mean?*

B: Well, you know how when you go into where you haven't been before; you wonder if you can get back out. And we did.

D: *What did you do in the woods?*

B: Just played, I guess. I don't remember. We just, I guess, went in and wandered around. (Sigh) I have to go back across the street.

It was dark in the woods, but it was light on the school ground when we went in. But now it's getting really dark, so we better go home.

D: *I guess you better go before you get in trouble.*

B: I think we're already in trouble.

D: *Did you decide not to run away?*

B: Yeah, I guess so. I think we have to go home. I don't know if we're ... oh! I think they came after us. Our mothers. They're coming after us. Almost up to the school ground.

D: *Well, you weren't gone that long, were you?*

B: I don't know. It's probably ... maybe six o'clock. Supper time or something. It's getting dark.

D: *Was it worth it?*

B: I guess so. They really didn't fuss that much. Maybe because Pat's mother was there, too. My mother would have if she'd been by herself. Probably. And Pat lives on the right hand side of the street when we're going home. And I live on the left.

D: *Well, did your mother say anything?*

B: Yes. (A whiny, scolding, childish tone of voice, with appropriate gestures.) "Where have you been? I've been lookin' all over for you." She didn't give me a spanking. (Giggle)

D: *You had a little adventure, didn't you?* (Uh huh) *All right, Beverly, I want you to leave that scene, and drift away from there. Had you ever seen that pink shield at another time in your life or was that the only time?*

B: I don't think I saw the pink shield. I don't remember a shield. Sometimes I just went off, and I didn't know anything, like everything just stopped.

D: *I'm going to count to three, and I want you to go to one of those times that you had that feeling, even if you didn't see the pink shield. And you will be able to explain how it happened, and where it happened. I will count to three, and we will go to another time, if one exists, when you had that experience. 1, 2, 3. What are you doing? What do you see?*

B: I think I went out the window of my bedroom. (Puzzled) Just went out the window in the air.

D: *Climbed out the window?*

B: No. Just ... just sucked out.

D: *How old are you?*

B: Eight or nine. Ten, maybe.

D: *Was the window open?*

B: Yeah. It was open. It's in the summer time. And I was sitting on the bed, and I just got sucked out the window.

D: *Is that unusual?*

B: (Laugh) It sounds a little unusual to me. (Sigh) I think it has happened more than once. It was evening. There's a vacant lot next to my house. And sometimes I sit in the floor, and lean on the window sill, and look at the people and the cars going by at night.

D: *And then what happened?*

B: I don't know. I just went out the window and then I came back in.

D: *How did it feel when you went out?*

B: It felt like ... a whooshing ... just whooshed out the window. (Puzzled) I don't know how I do that. Right through the screen.

D: *Through the screen? What would that feel like?*

B: (Puzzled) I don't think I felt it.

D: *All right, I want you to go with that feeling, and you are going through the screen. Let's follow you as you go out the window like that. And tell me what's happening.*

B: I think I'm talking to somebody. It's somebody about my size. But I don't really see them.

D: *How do you know they're there?*

B: I don't ... really. I think there's just one, right here on my right, talking to me as we're walking through the air. I can't see it. I just get an impression, a feeling. Just kind of a rounded head. Everything's fine and we're just talking. I don't remember looking and seeing particularly.

D: *You said you feel like you're walking in the air?*

B: Yeah. Right across that lot next door. I think it's floating. I'm not really aware of much below the middle of my body.

D: *What are you talking about?*

B: I think just greeting each other. It's friendly. It's like we're doing this again. It's like somebody I know.

D: *It's familiar to you?*

B: Yeah. It's like it's the same person, because it's not new.

D: *Where are you floating to?*

B: (Sigh) I don't know. That's as much as I see. It's like I know we're going somewhere, but I don't know what else.

D: Can you see buildings?
B: There aren't any buildings. It's a vacant lot. There are two or three houses a block or so down the street. I can see lights in the distance. But it's mostly just ... space.
D: Do you feel like you're very far off the ground?
B: Yeah, it seems like I came out the window, and went up just a little higher. Probably four or five feet. Up above window level.
D: And you're floating with this other person.
B: Yeah. I mean, it's not a real person. It's not a person. It's roundish. It's like a person, but it's not colored like a person. It is gray brown; its skin is wrinkled and tough like elephant skin. In fact, it reminds me of the ridges on an elephant's trunk. He looks strange, but I feel great love. He's familiar to me. He's not a stranger.

This description was similar to the "nurse" creature Phil saw on a craft in *Keepers of the Garden*. It was also wrinkled, and gave the feeling of caring.

I gave instructions that she could remember what occurred during this strange event. That the memories were there and it was probably time for them to come forward. Then she suddenly announced that her head was hurting, and she pointed to the right temple area. "Like a headache. Like it's been squeezed or something." I gave suggestions to take away any discomfort. Then I told her that the memories could come forth, and we could look at them and examine them as a curiosity, and as an observer, if necessary.

B: I think there's probably something there, but I don't believe there really is. You can make up stuff like that.
D: What do you see that you think you're making up?
B: Well, it's probably like a game that you make up. That you go through the air with this little creature thing, and then you go in this space craft.
D: Well, tell me what you're seeing. We won't worry about whether it's a game or not. If it's a game, we'll play the game. We can have fun playing the game. What do you see?
B: Well, we know that's where we're going. He was sent to get me.
D: Did he tell you this?

B: Well, I just knew that. I don't know how I knew it. I just know I went through the window and he was there. Then we were going back for some kind of visit again. There is something like a space craft over on the right. And it's lit up against the back part of that lot. It's a big lot. But that's all I see.

D: *What does it look like?*

B: It's round and flat and shiny.

D: *Round like a ball?*

B: No. It's like a disk. It's thin. And it's rounded on the top. Kind of flat looking on the bottom, but it's not very thick. And it's shiny. Kind of glowing. Fluorescent looking, almost. Silvery white, all over.

D: *I wonder if anybody else could see it if they looked.*

B: I don't know. There's nobody else around.

D: *What if your mother came in the room while you're gone. Would she see you in there?*

I was trying to determine if it was Beverly's physical body that went through the window, or her spirit form.

B: No. I'm not in there. But I don't think she ever does that. Or if she did, she just thought I was in some other part of the house. She wasn't really looking for me or anything. I know I always shut my bedroom door. And I don't think I stay gone very long.

Apparently she perceived it was her physical body having the experience.

D: *How big do you think that disk is?*

B: As big as a house. Well, maybe it's not quite as big as a house. It's a lot bigger than cars. Maybe if you put three cars in a circle, it would be about that big.

D: *Tell me what is happening.*

B: I think it's just stopped. I don't see ... continuing this. I don't see a continuance. I saw just what I saw. Like half way across the lot, and I saw the craft on the other side, and that's where everything stopped. I don't see anything else.

D: *You don't know if you went any closer to it or not?*

B: I don't know. I think I probably did. That's where we were going.

The Custodians

D: What is the next thing you remember?

B: I always fall off the bed on the floor. I always do that when I come back. I'm on the bed and I fall off on the floor. Every time.

D: How do you get back to the bed?

B: I think they just dump me there. And then I fall off on the floor. It wakes me up then.

D: How long have you been having these experiences?

B: At least a year or two, I know. It's been going on a long time. Ever since I got my own room, I know. I don't remember it happening before I got my own room. But now I don't remember where I slept before I had my own room. I think probably one summer it happened more often.

D: And it's always the same, floating out the window, going out so far, and coming back?

B: Uh huh. But I didn't get back the same way I went out. It seemed like I just *dropped* into my bed. And then fell in the floor, because I'd always think, "What am I doing in the floor?"

D: Did your mother ever hear you hit the floor?

B: Yes, she did! She heard this thump. She came in and asked me what I was doing. And I told her I just fell off the bed. I guess she saw I was okay. But I know she heard it in the other room.

I then had her leave the scene she was watching, and I asked her to drift back in time.

D: I want you to drift back to the time when you were little, and you used to have some very strange dreams. Do you want to talk about them?

B: Well, they were real scary, because these things came into my room at night. I was in a twin bed against the inside wall. And it was dark in my room. They came in after everyone went to sleep. And they crawled around and looked at me. They had great big eyes, and they were like giant insects. That's what I thought they were. There was a window on the other side of the room. Sometimes light came through it, and I could see some of them on the floor. And I could see them at the foot of my bed. They would get over my face and my chest. And I'd open my mouth to scream, but nothing would happen. But when I'd start to really wake up, then I could scream.

D: *How big were these?*

B: They were bigger than I am. They were big enough to almost fill up my bed. Their heads were even with my head, on top of my body.

I gave her instructions that she could see the scene again very clearly, but it would not bother her. She could watch it as an observer if she wanted to.

D: *Where are they, as you're looking at them now?*

B: Okay, there's one that's light colored or either the light's hitting it. And two of them, on the floor. (Hand motions.)

D: *On your right?*

B: My bed was against the wall, it wasn't in the middle of the room. And so the rest of the room was to my right. And there were one or two of them in the floor, with this moonlight or something coming in. We had Venetian blinds, and they didn't close real tight. And then there were one or two at the foot of my bed. They would either crawl up to me, or their bodies were long enough that their faces were right above my face, looking at my eyes and my nose and my ears and stuff. And they could spread their legs or whatever and hold their bodies up above me without touching me. So their legs were long enough to hold them up off me. But they touched my face sometimes.

D: *Tell me what they look like.*

B: They had a great big head, and great big dark eyes. And their bodies were spindly. And it seems like their arm things were the same length as their leg things. They were like insects. Like grasshoppers or something that have legs on the front and legs on the back. They were sleek, streamlined slick. Almost like a tube of long body, with these legs or arms or whatever coming out of it, like insect legs. I think the ones on the floor were a little different. They were lighter in color. And I think they were shorter, and had fatter bodies.

D: *Did their face look insect like?*

B: All I remember is the eyes. And this great big round head like an ant's head. It was round and came to a point, and had great big eyes. The ones in the bed were dark, the ones in the floor were light. I know they were different colors.

D: Can you see any hands?

B: No, because if they have hands, they're down on the bed and I can't see down there because I'm looking up in their faces.

D: Because you said they touched your face sometimes.

B: They did! They had fingers. They pulled my eyes open. They poked around on my face. All I can see is fingers, skinny, skinny fingers. Doing like that, on my face. (Hand motions, like a touching or stroking of her cheeks. The memory made her upset and she started to cry.)

D: I wouldn't like that either. Was that all they did?

B: (Crying) That's all I remember. (Crying, emotional.) And then I'd scream and scream and scream.

I calmed her down by speaking to her like you would to a frightened child.

D: Did you ever notice how they got into the room?

B: (Surprised) They must have come in through the window. It seems like my door was always shut, because when my mother ran in there when I was screaming, she'd always have to open the door. I don't think they went out the door.

D: What happened when you started to scream?

B: I think they left. I don't know that I was trying to scare them away. I was just scared, so I was screaming. And I think I would have been screaming before if I could have, but I don't think I could. Then I'd get to where I could scream, and then they'd be leaving. And I guess it woke my mother up, and she'd come in there. But she never saw them.

D: Did you ever tell her about them?

B: I think I told her giant bugs were getting me. She just told me I was having nightmares, and to go back to sleep.

D: Yeah, it sounded like nightmares really.

B: Sometimes I knew they were coming, and I'd go get my dog. They wouldn't come when I did that.

D: How would you know they were coming?

B: I just knew when I went to bed they were going to show up. I just knew it.

D: Maybe the dog kept them away?

B: Either that, or I never did wake up when I'd cuddle my dog. Or I didn't wake up like I was having a nightmare.

D: *When that light shone through the window, was it a bright light or what?*

B: It seems like it was pretty bright. I thought it was moonlight, but you know it could have been that thing up in the sky shining that light in through the blinds.

I thought we had explored enough for this session.

It was strange that this same type of blockage occurred while working with another UFO subject on the next day. She experienced a dark vortex of energy that seemed to freeze or stop things. She also could not remember past a certain point. It is interesting that this same type of blocking should occur in two separate people within such a close proximity of time.

In later years (1990s) of my investigations this occurred from time to time. Sometimes I could recognize it as an attempt by the subconscious to block the information if the subject was not ready to investigate something like this. Other times I wondered if it was caused by post hypnotic suggestion from the aliens themselves to keep the subject from remembering past a certain point.

In the sessions that followed with Beverly we were able to erase the block and discover what lay beyond that barrier.

A few weeks later we met again, and had another session. We were still trying to find something that would explain her health and money problems in this life. This time the block that had been present the last time was gone. At the beginning of the session her subconscious offered her two separate past lives to look at. One was in a desert land. The other one appeared to be dated around the Civil War. I let her make the choice, and she went easily into a lifetime that apparently ended around the turn of the century. It was not very interesting to me, it was rather mundane, which is normal, but it did have some information that was important for Beverly.

She next went into the other life she had glimpsed, the life in the desert. She was a middle-aged man, a member of a group of nomadic desert dwellers. They traveled taking a herd of goats with them. The goats were important for their survival because, besides providing food, they were sold in the towns or traded for necessities. I took her through important events, and she was in a marketplace selling and trading for goods to carry with them. She liked the freedom of being able to wander, and being free from laws and restrictions imposed by city life. When asked for a name of the tribe, she came up with the name "Teleg," but she wasn't sure if it was the name of the tribe or the town or her own. She thought they were located in Egypt. Much information came forth, but it was a dull existence.

The surprise came when I moved her to another important day in that life. I normally take the subject through an entire lifetime, touching on important days and then ending with their death. Occasionally they will leapfrog into another unrelated life. This is common and shows the instability of the subconscious to hold on to one lifetime when this experiment is first tried. When the subject exhibits this, I usually go with it because the subconscious may have something more important it wants to bring forth. Normally after a few sessions the subject can hold to one lifetime and explore it in detail. Apparently Beverly's subconscious thought there was no reason to continue to explore the desert life. It decided to jump forward into something it considered more meaningful. I could have returned her to the desert life for more information, but I decided to go with the subconscious this time. Since it had presented a block in the prior session, I thought it might be getting ready to open the door.

I asked her to leave the marketplace scene, and to move forward to another important day in her life. *"What are you doing now? What do you see?"*

B: I'm out on the driveway at my daddy's service station.
D: (She obviously was no longer in the desert life.) *Oh? Where is that?*
B: Just down the street from my house.
D: *In what town is that?*
B: In Shreveport.
D: *What are you doing out there?*
B: Playing with the guys that work there. They're teaching me about Harry Truman and the ABCs. And to count.
D: *Oh. How old are you?*
B: Five or six.
D: *Is your name Beverly?*
B: Uh huh. They're teaching me how to spell that too.

D: Do you go to school yet?

B: No. But I'll know more than the other kids when I go to school, cause Eddie teaches me. Eddie's a black man. I don't know why they call them black, cause they're brown.

D: Yeah, they are. Well, you're lucky if someone's teaching you. You will know more than the other kids, won't you?

B: Uh huh. And I'm happy. I like Eddie. He only has one hand though.

D: He does? What happened?

B: (Matter of fact) The other one got chopped off.

This typical childish honesty can sometimes be surprising.

D: Oh? And you said your daddy has a gas station?

B: Uh huh. And Eddie works for him. Eddie's about as smart as my daddy.

D: Well, I think that's nice that he's teaching you.

I decided to try for the scene in the woods again, now that the barriers apparently were down. She was obviously in a much deeper state. She was exhibiting the personality of the little girl, even down to her facial expressions, hand gestures and body mannerisms. I structured my speech and questions as though speaking to a child.

D: Let's move ahead to when you're in the first grade, and you're going to school and you're learning things. Move ahead to the day that you went with your friend into the woods next to the school. Why did you do that? Didn't you want to go home?

B: No! We wanted to stay out and play some more.

D: Do you like school?

B: It's okay. I met a lot of new people. And it's easy. All we do is color in books all the time.

D: Aren't you learning your letters and things?

B: Yeah. But I already know 'em. I'm the littlest one in school, but so far I know as much as they do.

D: Well, who's with you?

B: This one teacher that's getting married, and I can't think of her name. But I can see her face. She's got brown hair and she's going to get married and her name will change. And there's Clinton.

There's another teacher. And my friend, Patricia. And some boy named Bobby.

D: *These are in your class?*

B: Out on the school ground.

D: *Well, then did you go over into the woods?*

B: Yeah, when school was out and everybody left, Patricia and I did.

D: *Tell me about it. What were the woods like?*

B: (Softly and childishly pretentious.) They were scary.

D: (Chuckle) *But was it a good scary?*

B: Yeah. And the trees are real tall. And we are just giggling, because we're doing something we're not supposed to do.

D: *Have you ever been in the woods before?*

B: Not over there in those woods. I've been in some little, little woods. But this is woods for a long, long ways.

D: *Aren't you worried you might get lost?*

B: I'd come back out the same way we came in.

D: *What do you see as you walk?*

B: Well, we see a lot of trees.

There was a long pause. Her eye movements indicated she was experiencing something.

D: *Is Patricia about your age?*

Her voice was quieter as she answered, "Yeah." I knew something was happening, but I had to be very careful not to lead or suggest.

B: (Cautiously) I think there's something in there in the woods. It might be mice. Might not be. Might be big insects.

D: *What do you see?*

B: I don't see anything, but I just know there's something in there. I can hear it.

D: *What does it sound like?*

B: (Pause) It's just movement. There's something moving around in there.

D: *Are you going to find out what it is?*

B: I don't know. I don't think we better go any further. I think we better stay right here. I see a light.

D: *Where is it coming from?*

B: It's coming from in the woods, coming out toward me.

D: *How big is the light?*

B: It's not real big. But it's blue, blue white. It's coming forward.

D: *About as big as a flashlight?*

B: No, it's bigger than a flashlight.

D: *Like the headlight of a car?*

B: Kind of. It would be that big, yeah.

D: *But headlights aren't that color, are they?* (No) *Is it coming fast or slow?*

B: Slow. But I don't know what to do. (Sigh) I have to be brave.

D: *What do you want to do?*

B: Well, I don't think I can do anything. I don't think I can run. I think I'm already caught.

D: *Why don't you think you can run?*

B: I just don't think I can. I think it's too late. It's like I'm in a snare trap or something. I don't think I can back out now. It doesn't feel like I can turn around or anything.

D: *Is the light still there?*

B: Uh huh. I think we're going with it. Yep, it's pulling us to it.

D: *How big is it now?*

B: It's as big as I am.

D: *At first you said it was about as big as a headlight?*

B: That's where it was coming out of, but it shows out a big light. When it gets to where it's as big as I am, I can't go anywhere. It's all around me.

D: *What about Patricia?*

B: I don't know. I guess it's around her, too.

D: *You said you feel like you want to go with it?*

B: I think I have to. I don't think I can get away now and run. Besides, it would just catch me if I did. I'm walking forward on the leaves, but it's like the light is making me do it. It's bright, and it makes me not able to see stuff. But it's okay. It's not hurting me.

D: *Tell me what happens.*

B: Well, we get up there and we go inside this little building. It's filled with light. I couldn't see it too well. It's about like a car. Bigger than a car, I guess.

D: *What kind of a shape?*

B: It's round, like half of a ball.

The Custodians

D: How do you go in?

B: Through one of the window things. They have a whole bunch of slots or window things that you can go in.

D: Is it on the ground?

B: No, it's not on the ground. It's above the ground. Sort of. It's low, but it's above the ground. You just sort of float up to the window like thing and go in there. And then they put me to sleep.

D: What did you see before they put you to sleep?

B: Little people. They don't look very much like people. They look like little creatures. They're not much bigger than me. But they're nice. Might be make believe friends.

D: Could be. Can you see their faces?

B: Little bug faces, except they're light. I mean, they're not dark like bugs. Kind of pinkish grayish color skin, like little kids' skin, but buggish lookin' faces. You know how bugs look ugly in the face?

D: Do they have any hair?

B: No. None of them have any hair. And they just make me go to sleep.

D: Could you see what their eyes look like?

B: They're great big round eyes, like black buttons or something. Great big ones.

D: What about their nose and mouth?

B: They don't have noses and mouths, much. Maybe. They're just kind of ... buggy faced. You know, they don't have features like we do.

D: Did you notice anything about their bodies?

B: Kind of ghosty-like bodies. You know, I don't think they have legs. I think they just kind of float around. Maybe they have legs, but they're not legs like my legs. Their bodies and their arms and legs, too, are real skinny. I don't know how they can hold them up. That's why I said they kind of float. And it's all pinkish in here. The color, the light, is all pink. I guess it's pink for little girls. I don't know.

D: That would make sense, wouldn't it? Could you see how many fingers they have?

B: Oh, they have ... either three or four fingers.

She held up her fingers, folded the little finger down and held it down with her other hand. Very childish gestures.

B: They don't have a little finger. They have a thumb and ... two, no, there must be three up here. There's a boy in my school that's got six fingers. And these people just have four. Lester is his name. He's got six toes and six fingers.

D: *And these people just have three fingers and a thumb. So it can happen.* (Uh huh) *Are these little people wearing any clothes?*

B: Nope. They don't wear clothes like animals don't wear clothes. Don't see anything, you know.

She said this kind of secretively. Was she referring to genitals?

D: *Do you see anything else in the room? You said there's pink light?*

B: Yeah. Lots of lights everywhere. And lots of tables. Not a lot of tables. Some tables. Like the doctor's table. Like examining tables. And then there's another room. It's a little room. And it has these magnifying glass things on the other table in that other room.

D: *What do you mean, a magnifying glass?*

B: They look like those things that stick up in the air and then come back down. (She was making hand motions.) Like the light bends. Not bends, it's got a crook in it. It goes up and then it comes back down. And they can shine it wherever they want to.

D: *Oh, yeah, you mean they can move it around. A big light like doctors have?* (Yeah) *And it magnifies?*

B: I think it does. It's in that other room. Over there. (She swung her hand and arm out in one swift motion, to point to her left.) Where that other little table is. And the light is on that long stick thing that comes out of the wall.

D: *You said there are a lot of lights? Where are they?*

B: They're in the walls. It's real shiny. It's like, you know where lights are hidden in a room, but it's still all lit up? Well, it's real shiny and lit up, but I don't see where the lights are.

D: *Like they're behind something, you mean?*

B: Yeah, or they're just coming out of the walls, except in that other little room where that big crooked light is. It's where they examine you. There are tables in there, too. I don't know what they use those tables for, because they didn't ever put me on that table. Maybe they use that for grown up people.

D: Does it look bigger?
B: Yeah. The tables are in a circle in the middle of the room.

I asked her to explain.

B: Well, they're long tables. And then there's another one, and another one, and another one. Maybe they're not tables to examine on. Maybe it's some kind of boxes for something. They go all the way down to the floor. It's like solid, where you could put stuff in it. Like with drawers and stuff.
D: What do those tables look like they're made out of?
B: Stainless steel. Real shiny.
D: If they're in a circle, is there anything in the middle of the circle?
B: No, there's not anything in the middle. But you can walk in, and be in the middle of them, like between the tables.
D: Well, do you see anything else besides the tables?
B: I see the drawbridge.
D: What's that?
B: It's the thing out front that closes the door.
D: Is that what you came in on?
B: I guess so. It was already open when I came in. But I know it's out there, and they close it up.
D: Do you see anything else in that room?
B: Around the wall there's all these dials and knobs and stuff to turn and run the ship. They go all the way around in a circle. All of it looks ... like an airplane. It's too complicated for me. There's some stuff that looks ... I mean, it doesn't look like a real TV set. It's not a box. It's like a panel, or screen that you can see stuff on. They don't have them on. I imagine they do turn them on when they're flying around though. - You know what I bet those things are in the middle? I bet they're beds for those little guys. I bet that's what that is. They probably sleep on the top, and keep all their stuff in the bottom of it.
D: That makes sense, doesn't it? Well, is there anything else in there that you can see?
B: Nope. I'm ready to go, really.
D: What do you mean?
B: I'm ready to leave. Ready to get out and go home.
D: Did you say they made you go to sleep?

B: They take me in that room. And I'm so sleepy I can't keep my eyes awake. And then by the time I get in there I'm ... I don't remember. I'm just asleep.

D: *What did they do to make you sleepy?*

B: I think they shine those lights on me. It just makes me go to sleep.

D: *Well, did you get up on the table by yourself?*

B: No, they must have put me up there, because I was too asleep. I was like just ... floating up there. But they were sort of lifting me. And then I was just zonked out. I think the lights do it. The lights are real strange. They do all kinds of things. When you get in the light you can't go anywhere else. And then when it pulls you in, you have to go with it, 'cause you can't do anything else. And then inside, I know it was all pinkish, but still whitish, with kind of yellow pinkish in it. That's because it's so bright. It's like sunlight that's yellow pinkish. You know not painted yellow pink. But it can make you go to sleep, or wake you up. It must be able to do all kinds of stuff.

D: *But even if you went to sleep, you still remember, and you can tell me what happened when you were on the table.*

B: (Softly) They leaned over me. And they pulled that light down. And they showed it all over my body.

D: *What were they looking at?*

B: (Childish) Just to see what I was made out of. Then it was like it was in the bedroom when they crawl all over my bed.

D: *Are these the same ones?*

B: I don't think it's the same ones. They're lighter. (Emotional) I think they're just looking, but I can't move. I can't talk.

D: *That's all right. You can talk to me.*

B: It's not like it's really hurting, but you can't move. It's sure scary. (She was ready to cry.) And they touch me, but that's not why I can't move. I can't move anyhow. It's like I'm frozen.

D: *Do you think it has something to do with that light?*

B: That light or that table.

D: *What does that table feel like?*

B: I don't feel it, cause I'm not really lying on it. I'm above it. It looks to me like it would be cold. But it's like I'm just lying there in the air.

D: *What are they doing as they look at you?*

B: They're making little noises. (She made little chirping or high-pitched chattering noises.) Like they're just talking up a storm.

The majority of cases report that the creatures communicate mentally or telepathically, and do not make any sounds. But a few, in this book and my book *Legacy From the Stars*, report a high pitched, sometimes melodic, oral communication.

D: Can you understand them?
B: No. (She made some more of the chirping sounds.) Just like little ants. Little busy ants.
D: That's a funny way to talk, isn't it? What else do they do?
B: Nothing. They got through, and they put that light back up in the wall. It fits up in the wall somehow.

Her voice was not as upset now. As though as soon as they finished she calmed down.

B: It was like they were all around me. You know, it's like being suffocated.
D: Why are they that close?
B: They're looking. I think they're looking all the way through me.
D: All the way through you? Do you think they can do that?
B: With those lights they can. Yeah. All the way through. That's why I'm not on the table, so they can do it underneath, too. They can do that with the light. Then they were starting to back away. And it was like I was in this pink sleep. And I was coming off the table area and back down. (Hand motions)
D: Floaty like that?
B: Yeah. But then upright. Then kind of carried in this light back into the other room. And then I left.
D: Did you just walk out the door?
B: Yeah. Walked down the ramp. And I was back down in the woods.
D: I wonder why they were doing all that?
B: I don't think I can wonder too much. They do all this little gibberish. The only time they talked was when they were examining my body, so I think it had something to do with that. But it's like they make you numb, and you can't think too much, or wonder too much. Especially when you're little, because

they're bigger than I am. But if that was a grown person, they wouldn't be bigger.

D: *They didn't look very strong, but yet you think they picked you up.*

B: The lights did it.

D: *Well, is this the first time you've been to that place?*

B: No. But that's the first time I've gone there from the woods. The other times they just came and got me out of my bed.

D: *Then this place is familiar to you? (Yeah) Well, do you know if Patricia was still with you?*

B: I don't remember Patricia till we were running out of the woods. But that room was not very big. I don't know where she could have been. I didn't see her. But those lights do all kinds of stuff. So it ... (puzzled) she could have been there and I didn't see her.

D: *But did you wake up when you went outside?*

B: I remember walking down the ramp, and being in the woods. And then I don't remember anything for a few minutes. And then Patricia and I were running out of the woods giggling.

D: *What happened to that big light that looked like half a circle?*

B: I don't know. We left it back in the woods.

D: *But you said they'd come in your room and get you?*

B: Uh huh. That was scary. I didn't like that at all. Sometimes they do it in my room, and just scare me to death. Other times they take me out of my room.

D: *How do they do that?*

B: Out through the window.

D: *Carry you out through the window?*

B: (Aggravated) They don't have to carry me. That light just takes you. It's like being on an escalator, except it's all light.

D: *Is the window open when they do this?*

B: It doesn't matter whether it's open or not. If it's not open, we just go through it.

D: *That's like magic, isn't it?*

B: Uh huh. They're magic.

D: *Well, do you think if somebody were to come in the room when you were gone, would they see you in the bed?*

B: They wouldn't let anybody come in. They don't ever get caught. I think they make time stand still. I think that's what they do.

D: *Did they always look alike?*

B: No. There are some others that look a little different. They look like caterpillar bodies with arms and legs.

D: *Do you mean long and thin?*

B: Bumpy bodies. You know how caterpillars have bumps on their backs?

D: *Yeah, like ridges?*

B: Yeah. Those guys are just messengers. I know they are.

D: *The bumpy people? What makes you think they're messengers?*

B: The only time I see them is when they're taking me from my bed on this light to this room, and then they're gone. That's the only time I ever see them. And *they* talk to me. They don't talk with their mouths. It's like they're nurses. You know how a nurse takes care of you when you're walking down the hall? That's how they do. And I think that's all they do.

D: *What do they say to you?*

B: "How are you today?" They don't say it. They just think it, and you know they're thinking it. And it's like they're being nice, 'cause they know they have to take you there.

This type has also been reported in other cases, for instance, in my book *Keepers of the Garden*. It is interesting that they call it a nurse because of the caring feeling about them while the others are cold, distracted and often disinterested. The subjects say this nurse type has a feminine feeling about it although there is nothing to indicate sex.

D: *What kind of faces do those people have?*

B: They're like the other people, but they're darker, and coarser. They're not as smooth. They're not as refined.

D: *Are their faces bumpy, too?* (No) *What kind of eyes do they have?*

B: They have great big black eyes, too.

D: *It is just their skin that is different?*

B: Well, I think they're fatter, too.

D: *Do they have any hair?*

B: No, not any hair, but kind of like when you're just getting a beard. It's all over their bodies, just little short stiff hairs. Not very close together, just here and there on their little brownish colored bodies.

D: *Rough, bumpy bodies.*

B: Real rough skin. Not like cow skin either. Maybe more like pigskin. I think they're some kind of workers.

D: *None of these people wear clothes, do they?*

B: No, no. They don't have to.

D: *Well, how do they bring you back to your room?*

B: I don't know. I always just wake up and I'm there. I guess they bring me back the same way, but see, by then I'm asleep.

D: *Well, do these people do the same thing with that light on that table every time you go there?*

B: I don't guess it's always the same thing. Sometimes they mess with my hair. They take pieces of it, and they take some of my blood.

D: *How do they do that?*

B: They just zap it out. You know how you suck through a straw? Well, this was a little tinier. They wouldn't suck it or use a needle or anything, they just made the blood come up in a little stream for them to get it. Right through your skin. I couldn't see an instrument. I didn't think they had one.

D: If the blood came out through your skin, where would it go?

B: Into some little ... thing. A little jar. (Hand motions) And they took some of my pee pee. They just got down there with a jar, and just did it.

D: *They know how to do all kinds of things, don't they? (Yeah) I wonder why they keep doing that?*

B: I guess they're trying to find out more stuff. They don't keep me very long. I guess they don't want my parents to know, or anybody else either, because nobody seems to know about them. You don't talk about them. I don't talk about them. It's like that's just ... over there somewhere.

D: *It's separate from you, you mean?*

B: Yes. And so they don't keep me very long, because if they did they'd probably get found out. Maybe they're not getting it all done at one time, is what I'm thinking. Since they don't keep me very long, maybe they keep bringing me back to do something else.

D: *That makes sense. But the main thing, they're not hurting you, are they?*

B: They're not hurting me, but I don't like it when they get me on that table like thing and then they're all over me.

D: Yeah, and you can't move. That would be a little scary. I guess they've got reasons for what they're doing.

B: It's not any of my business. I think it's pretty tacky though, because they're sneaky about it. But it's like it's a whole other world. And they don't talk about that with this world. I don't know why, but that's just the way it is.

D: Well, if I come to see you again, will you tell me some more things?

B: I guess so.

D: Because I'm interested and I like to talk to you. And I don't tell anybody else. There's no way I'd get you in trouble.

B: You know, I don't much think you'd get me in trouble any more. I don't think they're even coming around anymore.

Her voice was now more mature. She had apparently left that child behind.

When Beverly awakened the only thing she remembered about this session was something about the desert and a pinkish light. That was all.

Because a terrible storm broke out before I could leave her house, I stayed and ate supper with Beverly. She wanted to hear part of the tape. As she listened it was as though she was hearing it for the first time. She was dumbfounded. She had absolutely no memory of any of it, and kept saying she had to be making it up.

We met again a few days later for another session. Because of the breakthrough in the last session I wanted to concentrate on her UFO experiences. I wanted to find out about the time in Houston when she claimed she heard a spacecraft in her backyard, but instead of getting up to investigate, she went back to sleep. She was also aggravated because her husband did not wake up.

When she was in trance I told her to go back to sometime in the years 1973 to 1975 when she was living in Houston, Texas. I asked her to return to the night when she had the unusual experience of hearing a noise in her backyard. When I counted her she returned automatically to that night. The year was 1974, and she was getting ready for bed.

B: We have a really big bathroom that opens into the bedroom. An archway.

D: And now you've gone to bed. Did you go to sleep right away?
(Yeah) Did you sleep all night long?
B: No. Somebody came into my bedroom.
D: Someone you knew?
B: No. It was a figure. It was almost ghost-like. It was big, tall. I think it was a male figure. And it was willowy.
D: What do you mean by willowy?
B: Like it could wave in the wind. It was almost like see through.
D: Like it didn't have much substance to it?
B: Yeah. Tall. Whitish looking. Almost like a ghost, but it wasn't a ghost. Grayish-white. And it seemed to just hover in the doorway inside the room.
D: Then what happened?
B: I just laid there and looked at it. It came into the room, between that doorway and the closet door. I know it was closer to the bed. (Pause) And I was scared.
D: Yes, I think you would be. You weren't expecting that. Then what happened?
B: I don't know. Just ... (Sigh) I know there's something in the yard.
D: How do you know that?
B: It has a light. It's like a glow. Something landed in the yard. (With resignation) And I guess it's a spaceship, and it's glowing.
D: What makes you think it's a spaceship?
B: I just know it is.
D: Couldn't it be a car or something?
B: Not in the backyard. There's no way to get to it with a car. It's all fenced in with a high wooden privacy fence.
D: Couldn't it be someone out there with a light or something?
B: I don't think so. It's sitting low on the ground. I just see the glow through the ... there are bamboo type shades on the big triple window.
D: Does the light look very large?
B: No. It's really very small. My backyard doesn't have any trees in it. We probably have the only backyard out here with no trees in it. We're thinking about putting a swimming pool in.
D: Did you hear anything?
B: I don't know if I heard anything outside. It's like when you know there's some sound, but you don't hear it with your ears. It probably was what roused me awake. And then I felt this thing in

the room. It was on the opposite side of the bed from where I was sleeping.

D: *On your husband's side?*

B: Uh huh. But he wasn't awake.

D: *What kind of a noise woke you up?*

B: It's like a high-powered drill, or a high-powered saw, or something like that, but not as heavy. It's a lighter sound than that, but it was the sound of spinning fast.

This certainly sounded familiar.

D: *And you think that was what woke you up?*

B: I think so. I mean, it wasn't loud. It was like when you feel a presence and you know there's someone there. And it kind of startles you.

D: *So it wasn't the sound by itself. It was the sound and the feeling of a presence.*

B: Yeah. If that sound had been something else, that degree of loudness would not have normally woke me up. But there was a feeling that went with it.

D: *Do you think this was why your husband didn't hear it?*

B: Probably. He says he sleeps lighter than I do, but apparently he doesn't.

D: *But whenever you saw this figure, you also saw the light in the backyard about the same time?*

B: I think I was facing the doorway, so I saw the figure first. But I could tell behind me, where the window was, that there was a glow coming through the bamboo rollups.

D: *It couldn't have been the moon?*

B: It kind of showed through like a moon would, except it wasn't from way up high. It was like a concentrated light. You know, how the moon gives light all over?

D: *Yeah. But I think it is interesting that you thought it was a spaceship.*

B: It was a spaceship.

D: *Well, what happened then?*

B: The figure was close to my husband's side, but it didn't bother him. It was there for me. I know that, because this has been going on a long time.

D: It's not something new. Then what happened?

B: I don't know. It just stops right there. I'm lying in the bed on my left side, and I'm facing the doorway looking at this figure, and knowing that this glow is out there in the backyard. It's just frozen right there. And it scares me. You know, (Sigh) there's a feeling of fear inside me.

D: That's why I think it's important that you look at it and find out what happened. Then you won't have to be afraid of it anymore. Once we find out what happened we can move past it and put it to rest. You're able to see it because your subconscious records everything, even though the body consciously doesn't remember. So something happened to block out the conscious mind right at that point. What happened? What did the figure do?

B: The figure went around the foot of the bed and out the window. And I followed it. (Nonchalantly) I walked right through the window.

D: This is similar to what you used to do as a child, isn't it?

B: Uh huh. I think that's why I feel scared about it.

D: Why did it make you scared this time?

B: I think it always makes me scared. The whole thing. You're not supposed to be able to go through windows.

D: That's true. Well, do you think it's like a dream where you can do things like that?

B: Maybe. Maybe my spirit's going out, and my physical body isn't. I don't know. (Sigh) Maybe they make me de-materialize? (She was unsure of that word.) And re-materialize. Maybe my body does go.

D: Do you think if your husband woke up that he wouldn't see you in bed?

B: He won't wake up. (Contemplating) My body must go. If it didn't go, why would they care if nobody else woke up or came in there? They did it when I was a kid, you know, in my bedroom. And they do it in my bedroom here. My bedroom's way at the back end of the house. It's a beautiful bedroom, but I've always been scared in it. It's so far away from the rest of the house.

D: Where did you go when you went out the window?

B: Out in the yard. To a spaceship. It's a little bitty round ... well, not real *little*, it's big enough to get into. It must be something they send out. You know, there are bigger ones, this is a little one.

And it's silver, and dome shaped on the top, and it has this rim around the middle of the - not the middle - about three quarters of the way down the dome shape. And then it has a little belly underneath it. Not a fat belly, but a little shallow belly, on the bottom. The bottom isn't as much of a dome as the top is. The whole thing is only three or four feet tall.

D: *Where's the glow coming from?*

B: From that rim that sticks out. It's as if it's lined with something and it puts out a glow.

D: *Then what happens?*

B: We went up in the air and left.

D: *What was it like on the inside?*

B: It was little, and kind of cramped. I'm just supposed to go in and sit down, and they fly off. It's almost like a lounge chair. I don't mean a yard chair, I mean like a dentist's chair or something that you lie back in.

D: *Well, did the being come in with you?*

B: (Surprised) I think he's too tall to be in here, unless he .... I think what was in the room was the *essence* of the being.

D: *Do you think that's why he was wispy?*

B: Uh huh. I think it's like he *projected* part of himself into the room. But his heavier body was out in a spaceship. There's either two or three others in here with me. They're small.

D: *Are they also sitting down?*

B: No, they're walking around. There's not much room. It's shorter than the fence, and the fence is a six-foot fence. I guess there's room for them to walk around. They're not tall like that projection was. They're shorter. I have to sit down. Well, I guess I could stand up, but only in the middle. (Beverly is a short woman, only a little over five feet tall.) They don't seem to have to sit anywhere. They're doing things. You know, walking around and punching buttons and looking at screens.

D: *Where is all that?*

B: It's in the inside walls. It's like a little cockpit.

D: *Is there anything on the screens?*

B: Maps and graphs. I don't really see them, but I know that's what's on there. I mean, I've glanced at them.

D: *You mean like a map of land ....*

B: Of the sky. I guess it's like an airplane map would be, you know, to fly. There's bound to be pathways that are used over and over, in an airplane. And so what's on the screen is some sort of pathway to get somewhere. It's almost like a graph. Maybe it's some kind of radar. It has vertical lines and horizontal ones, like graph paper. There are some screens that don't have that. They just have lines, intersecting and going off in different directions. And I don't know what they mean. The screen's white. The lines are all the same dark color. Maybe it's a computer system. That's what the screens look like, kind of like a computer screen. Everything's built into the wall. The wall is rounded.

D: *All right. What do these little beings look like?*

B: They're gray. They're short, three or four feet tall, and kind of nubby skinned.

D: *Nubby? What do you mean?*

B: They're bumpy. They're not smooth or soft looking. Well, they may be soft, but they're nubby. Like ET in the movie, but not that extreme. It *looks* rough, it may not be. In fact, I think that it probably *isn't*, when you really touch it, but it has the effect of looking thick and rough.

D: *Can you see their faces?*

B: Uh huh. They have little faces. No hair. I don't think they have any ears, or if they do, they're sort of recessed in. They don't stick out like our ears. They have eyes that are similar to my eyes. They're not big black eyes. They have the white of the eye. They have a nose and a mouth.

D: *Like yours?*

B: No, their faces are nubby, like being an old, old person with a really wrinkled face, millions of wrinkles all over their face. Except their heads are really little, bigger at the top than the bottom, almost coming to a point at the chin. And their faces look sort of squashed in. Like a Pekingese dog has kind of a squashed in face.

D: *I understand what you mean. Can you see their hands as they work the buttons? (Uh huh.) How many fingers do they have?*

B: They have five fingers.

D: *Five fingers? Four fingers and a thumb?*

B: Uh huh, but they're longer than mine.

The Custodians

D: Can you see their feet from where you are? (Uh huh) *What do they look like?*

B: They're almost webbed like. They have five toes. And their feet are big compared with their bodies. They're wide in the toe area, and there's webbing between them. But not like a duck. That's too much webbing. This is just a cross between our foot and, say, the webbing on a duck foot.

This type of foot was also reported in *Legacy From the Stars*. A similar type shaped like a mitten with the bones of the foot appearing as ridges beneath the skin.

D: Can you see any way of distinguishing sexes?

B: No. I think they're messengers or workers. I don't think they're robots. If they were they'd have to be an awfully sophisticated one. I think these are alive.

D: Are they communicating with you in any way? (No) *But you sit down in that chair. Then what happens after that?*

B: Well, it takes off. Up out of the yard, off to the left.

D: Can you feel the motion?

B: Very little. I feel a lift up off the ground. But after that there's very little .... You don't feel any kind of motion. You may feel a turn. But as long as you're going up or in one direction, straight ahead or back or whatever, you don't feel any motion.

D: Can you hear anything?

B: No. It doesn't take very long. It goes to another ship up in the sky.

D: Are there any windows that you can see through?

B: Yes, I didn't know it until we got inside. There are some windows that are like little portholes. And they're all around the part of the dome where the ridge comes out from it. And I guess lights were coming out from that. Above that little platform like thing, and I think probably below it, too.

D: But you couldn't see anything out the windows when you were flying?

B: I was facing the middle of the room. And, no, I couldn't see anything. It's like being half asleep.

D: Then they go to a larger ship, you said?

B: It goes *into* the larger ship, from the side. Like there's an opening. And it goes *into* it. And then the dome lifts off. (Trying to be correct.) The top lifts off. Or part of it. Maybe all of it. I'm not sure. Either all of the dome part or half of it lifted back, that exposed it to where it was open. And then you just get out and walk down a hallway.

D: *Are they walking with you?*

B: Uh huh. The hallway is very sleek. Very streamlined. Light colored walls. I don't think they're white, but maybe an off white. They're a light shade of metal or fabric or whatever it's made of. I don't know about the floor. And it is like a runway in an airport, sort of. A tunnel like, but big. They put me in a room. It's just a small room, and they put me in there. There's no table. But it's so they can come in and look at me.

D: *Who can? These little people?*

B: No, it's not the same people. They go to their ... bosses, I guess. And they come in. I think this is like a psychological examination. There's no exchange of words. They just surround me, and examine my brain. They're insect like. I guess it's the same thing I used to see when I was a kid, but they're not really insects. Their limbs are very flexible, very bendable, and very angular. They're maybe a foot or so taller than the little nubby people. Maybe my size, my height. They're whitish gray, so they're lighter in color than the little nubby things. They're... what was it you called it a while ago? They're not as substantial. Wispy. The little nubby people are not wispy. They are nubby.

D: *You said the one in your bedroom was wispy.*

B: Yes, it's like these. Maybe they project themselves through these little nubby people.

D: *You said they had angular like appendages. Do they have fingers or hands?*

B: Yeah. There's a thumb, and three fingers.

D: *Are they wearing anything?*

B: No. Clothes would be heavier than they are, it seems to me. Clothes would have more weight and substance than their bodies. Or if they do have a covering, it's like part of their body.

D: *It's not anything they can take off, you mean?*

B: Well, maybe they could take it off, but when it's put on it becomes a part of what looks like their body. I don't know if they're made that way, and they don't wear any clothes. Or if the outer thing that I see is part of the clothing, and would actually be removable.

But it doesn't look different from what they look like. There's not a break where clothing starts and skin or flesh or whatever begins.

This has also been reported in other cases. Some of the alien creatures have delicate skin that is easily damaged. From the instant they are born they are encased in a membrane type substance that remains around their body their entire life to protect the skin.

D: *You said you were never sure how many appendages they had because the bedroom was dark. Can you see now?*
B: There's just the two arm like ones and the two leg like ones. (Motions) The legs bend upward at such a sharp angle, and then the bottom part of the leg goes down, but it almost looks like there are other legs underneath. And the arms do the same way. They're thin and very angular. They can almost bend flat. (Motions)

She seemed frustrated because she was having difficulty making it clear what she was seeing.

D: *All right. Is there anything else in the room?*
B: There is nothing. The room is just a cubicle, a box type room.
D: *Is it light in there?*
B: Yeah. The light seems to emanate from the walls. There's no light fixture. Here they would either turn the walls on or turn them down, like you would turn the lights on or dim them. I don't see a knob anywhere, but I think that's the way the walls function.
D: *It's as though the whole wall is a light?*
B: Right.
D: *And you said they were surrounding you, as though it was some kind of a psychological examination? How do you know that?*
B: (Sigh) Well, I don't know it. But for one thing, they were just looking at my head. They weren't touching me. I know they project somehow. And I don't know if they were projecting themselves into my head, or if they were pulling stuff out of my head into theirs, or both.
D: *Could you see pictures in your head while this was going on?*
B: No. I just knew. It was like a pull between my head and this other being. And then I'd feel a pull between my head and another being. And it was like that was going back and forth all the time.

The Custodians

D: *How many are in there?*

B: Must be about five. (Pause) Four.

D: *Four? And you're feeling like a pull between all four of these.*

B: Uh huh. I don't feel it all at the same time. I feel it more from one side and then from another. I think it's because I'm turning and being aware in that direction. I think it's going on all the time. We're all standing up. And it's like they're wandering through my head.

D: *But it's not bothering you, is it?*

B: No, the whole thing's just uncomfortable. It's not painful, but they're doing things that don't normally get done. And so it bothers me. I don't like it.

D: *Kind of like a nuisance?*

B: More than that. It's like a dread. It's like I'm at their mercy. It's like when you're in a hospital having a baby and they're going to tell you everything to do. And you're in the act of having it, and you can't do anything *but.* My mother always told me, when you're having a baby, you're at the mercy of the world.

D: *Uh huh. There's nothing you can do about it.*

B: Nothing you can do. And this is that kind of feeling. I don't know what they want. I don't know why they keep doing this. And I don't even know what they get from it. I'm not getting anything in my head.

D: *So you think this has happened before?*

B: Oh, yeah. It happened when I was a kid. But it seems like most of the time they were examining my body, the physical stuff. Maybe they've learned all they can learn about that, or maybe this is just a different time. Who knows? But it's like they can go inside my head, and pull out information, or look around and see what's in there. And I can't do anything about it.

D: *But it's not physically bothering you, or mentally, really?*

B: Physically, it's not bothering me. Mentally, well, it's like you have no privacy. It's like being stripped naked physically, except that it's worse mentally. You're totally exposed. And it's not just the present they're looking at. When they get into your brain, they look at everything. The past is all there. There are no secrets at all.

D: *You mean all your memories?*

B: Uh huh. And your knowledge.

D: I wonder why they would be interested in your memories?

B: I don't know, except it's like the whole story of your life is in your head. You're the one that knows it. It's not the gray matter that they're looking at. It's the essence of your beingness that they're examining. And so it's not just for today. When they get the mind, they examine it for ten years ago, for fifteen years ago, or the week before last. They pick it. They find what they want to look at, or they wander through and see something else. And information, your knowledge, which is stored in your mind. And your feelings.

D: Your emotions?

B: Your emotions, yeah, probably more than anything else. Why do they care what I did on my tenth birthday? And physically they've looked at all of that. Probably, it's mostly how the brain works, how the mind works, and how your feelings function.

D: What are they doing with the information?

B: Putting it in their own mind, I guess. I don't know.

D: There's no machinery or instruments or anything?

B: No. It's all through mental telepathy. But it's almost as though I can see light waves go back and forth, between my head and their heads.

D: Kind of like electric currents? (Yes) Have you ever tried to communicate with them, and ask them why they're doing this?

B: Not this time. I can't remember right now if I ... it would be pretty stupid if I never had. But if I did I don't think I ever got anywhere, so I just quit.

D: I'd think you would be curious.

B: Well, I was curious. There's no reason to communicate, because they already know.

D: But you don't know.

B: They know I'm curious. They know questions are there. They know that I don't want them to do this, but they do it anyhow. There's no point in asking. They'd let me know if they want me to know. It's like there's no point in making any kind of wording whatsoever about it. It's all in your head. And they know what's in your head. And what they want me to know, they would let me know or they wouldn't. My asking would not be effective. So there's no point in doing it.

D: Except to satisfy your own curiosity.

B: But it wouldn't satisfy it, because they wouldn't answer it. They want to find out what's going on inside our heads. Why, I don't know ... I guess because we're a different species. If we were on some other planet, we might be doing the same thing to whatever was there.

D: *That's possible.*

B: We do it here. We experiment with animals.

D: *Well, does this go on for very long?*

B: Twenty minutes maybe.

D: *Is that the only thing that they do? Just this interchange ... not really an interchange, just a one way type of communication.* (Yeah) *Then what happens?*

B: They leave the room. And then the three guys that brought me down from the ship come and get me, and we get back in the small ship. And we fly back.

D: *You didn't see any other part of this larger ship?*

B: No. I just know it must have been much bigger than the one I came in, because the whole small ship went inside, and that appeared to be a small portion. You know, how we talk about having a base out in space that a whole colony of people could live on? I feel it was something that was, if not that large, pretty close to it. And I don't know why I think that, because I didn't see the rest of it. It's just an impression.

D: *Then what happened when they brought you back?*

B: I got in the small ship. It's like a shuttle, or like a helicopter would be to us. And we left in it. I don't remember getting back to the ground or getting back in my bed.

D: *You don't know if it landed in the backyard again?*

B: Probably it did, but I don't see it. I don't remember it. In fact, I don't guess I remember anything. The next thing it's morning. I think they have the ability to shut down the function of your brain. Or to open it up and expose it, like cutting open your stomach, but it's not done physically.

D: *But it didn't hurt anything.*

B: No. Not physically. Nothing was painful. I mean, it's not like your skull got ripped open.

D: *Did you have any aftereffects the next day?*

B: The next day I remembered this figure in my room. I remembered thinking it was a flying saucer out there waiting for me, but that's all I remembered about it. And I wondered if I dreamed it. I don't remember having any physical side effects, but I think I have headaches while they're doing this.

D: But it's all right to look at the experience, and talk about it. Then we can put it all in the past.

B: Maybe. But it's in the past already. So there's not a whole lot to be done about it.

D: That's true. But the main thing is, that it didn't bother you. Isn't that true?

B: I think it bothered me. I think it still bothers me. And what it does to your head. It's like you have to live a lie. I mean, you can't go around lying twenty-four hours a day about stuff. So I think what happens is, you just forget it. You block it. And then that does, I think, psychological damage to your head.

D: What do you mean, living a lie?

B: Well, you have to go around acting twenty-four hours a day like this didn't exist. I mean, nobody else thinks it exists. Nobody else talks about it. And if you know that it does, then you have to live a lie to fit in with the rest of the world.

D: Because they wouldn't believe you?

B: Of course they wouldn't believe me.

D: But a lot of it you didn't remember yourself, did you?

B: Right. But that's what I'm saying, it is too difficult to live a lie twenty-four hours a day, especially when you're young. So I think the mind just obliterates it. Either they do it, or your own mind does it. I don't know. I think they do a lot. But I think psychologically, too, that our own minds cover it up in order to live with it. It's like mass ignoring. I want to say "mass ignorance," but it's not ignorance like we think of the common use of the word "ignorance." It's mass "ignoring of."

D: I wonder how they know where to find you?

B: They always know. I don't know if it's something they do to you, or if it's with their minds. If with their mind they scan where you are, and it just pops up. I mean, that could be. I don't really know how they know. Except they seem to know everything. Well, I say that, but obviously they don't know everything. They wouldn't be investigating if they knew everything. But they know so much more than I do, that it seems like they know everything.

I was getting ready to move her to another scene when she abruptly interrupted. "Maybe there's something about me, and anybody else they do this with. And there are other people they do it with."

D: You think so?

B: Oh, yeah. I've seen them with other people on a spacecraft just like they had me. I don't know what all was going on, but I know there were other human beings on there.

D: When did this happen?

B: It's happened more than once. I just know there are other people they do this to. I was talking about how they find you. You've seen these great big world maps that they put up on the wall? And they put all these red dots in certain places, or purple dots or whatever? I think there's something about us that either beeps or flashes or lets them know what people they've been examining. Now I don't know if it's some *thing*, or whether it's because once they've examined you, you become like that. To where you send out some sort of light signal or auditory signal. To where, like a computer scanning, it would just find you, like a warfare missile would find a target. I mean, there's some sort of radar. Some sort of thing where you can find things. Even we can do that. And so there's something that enables them to keep tabs on anybody they deal with. You're probably tagged in some way, like we tag pigeons, I guess.

D: All right. We can find out. I want to talk to your subconscious. Is Beverly tagged in any way, physically? Was anything physically done so they could locate her again?

B: Yes. I think it's in her nose. I think it's in the center here. (She pointed to the bridge area of her nose.) Of the face and the nose.

D: The bridge area? (Yes.) *What is there?*

B: I don't know whether it's a round thing like a bee-bee, or whether it's a little square, almost like a piece of paper. But it's not paper. It would have to have more substance than that. It's just laid inside there somehow.

D: What purpose does it serve?

B: It sends out some sort of signal.

D: Does it bother her in any way?

B: Yes, it gives some sort of head problems, headaches, sinus. I think any time there's anything foreign in the head, or anywhere in the body, there's going to be a slight problem. And this is foreign to us, to have *anything* there. It's not meant to do anything like that, but I think that it does. Just like if you were wearing contacts or something foreign in your eye.

D: *You mean it would not be intended to cause any problems. But just because it doesn't belong there, it could cause slight problems as a side effect.*

B: Yes. And then it would depend on the rest of your health how much that bothered you.

D: *When was that put there?*

B: I think many, many years ago at a very young age. Very young, maybe not even out of the crib.

D: *So it's been there all that time. But the subconscious can help alleviate any problems that would be caused by a foreign object?* (Yes) *Because there's nothing we can do about it. If it's in there it has to stay.*

B: I think there are accommodations that can be made that help counteract the results produced by that.

D: *Is this the only foreign object she has in her body?*

B: I'm not sure. There may be something in the brain. And it's a monitoring device. I think it's in the right side. (She put her hand on the right crown area.) Maybe toward the back.

D: *What type of device is that?*

B: I think it monitors the brain wave activity.

D: *What does it look like?*

B: I don't know what a microchip looks like, but I get the feeling that it must be like a microchip that is used in computers. Something tiny. Maybe not quite thin like a piece of paper, maybe it has a little bit more thickness to it, but very tiny.

D: *Is that one creating any problems?*

B: Not noticeably so. I think the awareness that all of this exists creates more problems than the objects themselves.

D: *Then do you think it's better if she doesn't know about it?*

B: No, when I say "awareness," I don't necessarily mean *conscious* awareness. There's an awareness where she knows about it, *period*, and always has. And that has promoted enough emotional anxiety to be a problem to her.

D: I see. We don't want to cause her any discomfort at all. The main thing is for her to be healthy and happy.

B: Well, I don't think you can ignore it.

D: That's true. But maybe we can help to alleviate any problems or side effects caused by it. So I would appreciate it if you can help her in any way.

B: I think probably acceptance is the only answer. I don't know what else to suggest ... even though maybe I do know more than I think I know. But it's so much less than they know, that I'm dealing with something that's beyond my ball game.

D: That's true. In those cases it's better to ignore it. But physically we want to try to alleviate any problems that these objects might cause.

I then brought Beverly back to full consciousness and oriented her back to the present day. I gave her suggestions to help her stop smoking, as she had requested before we started the session. The only memory she had upon awakening dealt with some of these suggestions, and remarks her subconscious made about her difficulty in stopping the habit. She did not remember anything that had been said about the objects in her head. I thought it best not to tell her about them at the present time. I knew when she listened to the tape recording she would find out about them. Maybe she would be able to accept it at that time. I didn't want to discourage or frighten her.

I never had another session with Beverly. She decided she did not want to explore the subject of UFOs again. Apparently her subconscious thought she had discovered enough, and did not want to complicate her life. Probably for the same reason she put the tape recordings away and never listened to them. Amazingly, many of my subjects never can bring themselves to listen to the session. When it is over they put it behind them. Maybe it is just as well.

We never did find the causes for her strange ill health. Maybe this was one of the reasons for the alien monitoring. They may have been trying to understand it also. She went on with her life as sign painter and part time artist, so these strange sessions apparently had no ill effects.

For years, especially after I became involved in UFO research, I have kept notes about unusual incidents that have occurred in my own life. I never know if they are paranormal or not, but if they are unusual enough to get my attention I write about them. I never know whether they will have future use or not. I do the same thing when I am working on a case. I keep copious notes so that the event comes alive again when I want to include it in a book. That is where the details in this book have come from.

While compiling the cases to be focused on in this book I went over my notes, and discovered something that happened to me that reminded me of Beverly awakening and seeing the strange light in her backyard. I had thought Beverly's reactions were strange because she did not get up and investigate. In my incident I displayed the same nonchalance, and accepted the unusual as normal while it was occurring.

The majority of these cases occurred during the late 1980s, especially the one involving Beverly. My notes say that my incident occurred in December 1988 during the height of these investigations. At the time I did not make any connection.

My notes:

December 18, 1988. About 3 o'clock at night I got up to go to the bathroom. As I walked from my bedroom down the short hall to the bathroom, I noticed that a bright light was shining through the large picture window in the front room. It illuminated most of the objects in the room and shone on the wall of the hallway. I said to myself that there must be a full moon, because it can shine in with that type of brightness. I hadn't noticed it in my room though, but the drapes are drawn in there to shut out any light. While I was in the bathroom, I was facing the wall of the hallway, which I could see through the bathroom doorway. The light from the front room was shining on part of the wall. I wasn't even thinking about anything, when all of a sudden the light went away, and everything was plunged into deep darkness. It was not like it had been flicked off. It was more gradual than that, although rapid. It appeared that the darkness moved from the right to the left quickly obliterating the light. There was only one more brief flash, and the entire house was very dark. I immediately thought that clouds must have drifted across the moon and obscured it, although they would have been fast moving clouds. That could have happened if there was a strong wind. When I left the bathroom and went back to my bedroom, I pulled the drapes aside and looked out.

There was no moon, no clouds, and no wind. It was a calm, clear starlit night. I wondered if I had gone first into the front room instead of the bathroom whether I would have seen anything outside the big picture window. I often do that, go to the window and look at the moon or stars. But the urge to go to the bathroom prevented me doing anything else. The way the light disappeared suggested movement, as though it had moved from left to right across the window. This would explain the movement in the hallway of the darkness coming from the other direction.

My house is built in an unusual way. It is two story and the living room, bedroom and kitchen are upstairs. The living room has a large picture window that faces the sparsely populated rolling hills. I have considered the possibility of cars passing on the road in front of my house, but I discarded this theory. The road is several hundred feet away and the house is shielded by a thick line of trees. I have watched cars go up and down that road many times, and the reflection of their lights on the wall is always sporadic and blinking, caused by shining through the trees. The outline of the trees is always visible on the wall when they go by. Even when a car comes up the driveway and parks in front of my house the lights are different. I have observed this many times. This was not a car, either on the road or the driveway. It had to be a very bright light shining in from a higher angle in order to illuminate the entire room and hallway.

Almost a week later when the moon was really full, I watched to see if it would create the same effect at night. I found that at this time of the year (winter) the moon travels directly over the top of the house, rather than in front of the window as it does in summer. Thus, the moonlight shines in the window at a different angle. It did not create the effect I saw. I still wonder if I would have seen anything if I had been able to go to the window sooner.

I am not saying the light I saw was a UFO, but it shows that we do not always behave rationally when awakened in the night by strange lights or sounds.

CHAPTER 6
THE LIBRARY

Information can be gained in many different ways when the subject is put into the somnambulist state of trance. Often it comes from reliving their own experiences in past lives, but this is hampered by the restrictions of being confined to a body in a particular life. They can only recount what they personally know and have been exposed to in the lifetime. I have found the best information comes when the subject is taken to the in between lives state, the so called "dead" state. Then the restrictions of the physical body are removed, the blinders are taken off, and they have access to any information they may wish to explore. I discovered a wonderful place on the other side in the spirit realm where there are no limitations to knowledge. This is my favorite place to do research: the library. This has been described in many different ways by my subjects, but I believe they are talking about the same place. They are only placing it within their perceptions. Many have described it as an actual building where information is available in many different forms, according to the advancement of the seeker. There are books on shelves that can be read, or the person may enter rooms where the information is displayed on the walls around them in holographic 3 D images. In many cases there is a guardian or caretaker of the library who greets us when we enter, and theoretically checks to see if we have permission to use the facilities. He will then lead us to the proper section of the library where the information we are seeking can be found. In a few cases my subjects described the library differently, but I believe it is still the same place on the spirit side.

One subject's description: That library is my favorite library of all the worlds.

D: I have been to the library. Can you tell me what your library is like, and I will know if it is the same one?

The Custodians

S: It is white. It has no ceiling. It has no roof. It has columns. The books are on shelves, and enclosed in glass cases. There are books on every subject known to man in all his forms. There are books that record histories of *all* worlds that have ever been in existence. There are books that point to the worlds that will be *coming* into existence. It houses the past. It houses the future. And it houses the present, because they are all one.

D: *Is there someone that is in charge?*

S: (Enthusiastic) Yes!

D: *I call him the "guardian." Is he the same one?*

S: Yes. I call him the "caretaker" of the books, but his purpose is the same as the guardians. But there are a number of different libraries. Each has its own caretaker. Each has its own information. Just as there are groups in this world, there are groups in that world. Each group in that world has its own system. Just as ethnic groups have their own customs, groups there have corresponding systems. For instance, there is a medical library, only for persons who are interested in learning medicine. There are libraries concerning the stars, for people who want to learn astronomy or astrology. There are whole libraries, entire libraries, covering just one topic. In these places we can indeed learn many things. Or we can learn what is meant for us to know, because we can only know so much. There is much material that is not meant for us.

D: *Yes, I have heard that before. That some knowledge is as poison instead of medicine. That we wouldn't understand it, it would hamper us.*

More information came through in 1987 when the subject went to the library to seek information. His answers were extensive, and have been incorporated with other subjects who have accessed the same records. Since the material is so similar I have compiled it to read as though one person is speaking, but it actually came from several people. All of this information came through before I started active investigation.

S: I'm just coming into the rotunda of the library.

D: *Is the guardian of the library there?*

S: He's coming toward me now. He's a light being, arrayed in a white robe. He has a hood, and his face is almost beatific. It's beautiful. He just shines with all this light, and it's pulsating with colors around him.

D: *We would appreciate it if he could find us some information on the phenomenon known in our time as UFOs or Flying Saucers, Exterrestrial craft. Can we have access to that information?*

S: He's taking me into the viewing room. You're in the center of the room, and everything is happening around you. It's like a holograph. You see the scenes from all sides, and you view it like that. And he points to different things on the screen. He says there are many interesting things about these craft, as you would call them, but they're all part of the plan. He says there are many, many, many more planets in the universe that have evolved higher forms of life, than you people in the testing school of Earth understand. He's showing me ... (In awe.) I'm seeing ... oh, just countless and countless stars. It's very serene and beautiful. He's showing me Earth, and he's pointing at different stars. And he says, "Higher forms of life live in this area ... over in this area, and in this area." He's showing me *beautiful* pictures of other worlds. There's a gorgeous purple colored planet, and he says this is where many UFOs have come from. And he says these beings have to reproduce a vehicle. They can travel from their planet in *spirit* form, but when they come toward the Earth atmosphere, they have to incarnate in a vehicle. Mainly like we call a "spaceship."

D: *You mean they create this after they enter our atmosphere?*

S: Right, because the Earth is such a different density and vibratory nature from their own planet.

D: *Do you have any idea where this planet is, or how far?*

S: He's saying something about Betelgeuse. I think it's a constellation or a star.

D: *Why are they coming here?*

S: The librarian is discussing all this with me right now. He's saying, they're coming because the Earth is going to become part of the spiritual universe. And many beings have gathered from all over the universe to see this momentous event.

D: *You mean they're just here to watch?*

S: To analyze and watch.

D: *Well, if they journeyed here in spirit form, and formed this ship, did they then become physical themselves?*

S: They had to form the ship to enter the Earth's atmosphere, because Earth is a different vibration from theirs. So this was a way they could land and see what the Earth is like. It would be similar to when we go to the moon, we have to bring oxygen and things of this type.

D: *This is confusing because I thought if they were in spirit form ... but you mean, more or less, they are transporting their bodies. And then they create this?*

S: Yes, because it's very hard for them. The vibratory nature of the planet is changing, and they are going to be on hand to watch this. But they could not function in the vibration, so they have to protect themselves, and they use vehicles like ships.

D: *Do they have physical, solid bodies?*

S: Not on their home planet, no.

D: *What about on this planet?*

S: On this planet they cover themselves in something like a body casing, so they can function in this vibratory nature.

D: *What does this body casing look like?*

S: They try to appear as humans. And I am seeing that they have beautiful faces and eyes and blond hair, but their skin is almost a gold color.

D: *Then what are they on their home planet?*

S: They have more of an energy body that can take any shape it wishes.

D: *And these beings are just watching?*

S: Observing is the better word. They do try to contact other people at different times.

D: *What would be the purpose of that?*

S: To let them know they are being observed. They're here for the momentous occasion when the Earth becomes more enlightened, then becomes part of the spiritual universe.

D: *And they want certain people on Earth to know they are observing?*

S: I really can't answer that question.

D: *You don't know, or you're not allowed?*

S: The librarian says, "Everything has a purpose. Do not question." He says everything will be revealed eventually. There are other beings too. In time their appearances will have a purpose, but right now that information can't be clarified. But there is a definite purpose behind why they are here. It can't be revealed right now.

D: *Well, can we ask him specific questions? Will he show you the answers?*

S: It depends on the question. He says it's very important to understand that at the rate of your mental abilities, you might not understand everything that this channel is using. He says some questions cannot be answered at this present rate of your evolvement.

D: *Then he will tell us if there's something that can't be answered. All right then. Can we examine this solar system?*

S: He's pointing out the different planets aligned around our sun now.

D: *How many are there?*

S: He says in time before the Earth ends there will be sixteen planets that will be discovered as part of this solar system. He says there will be one huge planet discovered about 2040. Then there'll be another planet found about the year 3000. And then there'll be another planet discovered, and this will be the final planet. This will be taking place about 6000 years from the time of Christ.

D: *Do these planets have any life on them now?*

S: He says all planets have life, but it might not be life forms you are familiar with in the terrestrial world.

D: *Are there any that have human or humanoid inhabitants?*

S: Not in this part of the solar system. Earth is the only one.

D: *Have there ever been in the past?*

S: Yes. He says at one time there was humanoid like life on the planet Mars. He's pointing to that right now, because it is a red planet. And he says there was a human spirit like on the planet Venus. He says all planets, though, have spirit entities on them, which are like the guardians and watchers.

D: *Do these spirit forms ever take on a fleshly body on that planet or elsewhere?*

S: Most of the spirits on these other planets are of a higher vibrational rate than you of the Earth. It's painful for them to come to the Earth, because they have to lower their vibration, so they do not incarnate much on the Earth plane. But *have*, both in the present and in the past, as well as the future. But it's very hard for them, because this can be very painful to lower their vibrational rate. It's like trying to condense a tornado into a glass.

D: *Good analogy. You said there was a human form on Mars at one time?*

S: Yes, but this was a long time in the past: almost seventy-five thousand years ago, in our Earth reckoning. Life forms existed on the planet Mars, very similar to terrestrials, but due to their misuse of energy ... they were not in tune with the spiritual progress that is taking place in this part of the solar system. And as a result they were banished to another part of the universe.

D: *Are there any remnants of their civilization?*

S: Man will discover evidence of their civilization when he explores that area. But this information will not be allowed to the general public.

D: *Why will it not be allowed?*

S: He's saying, man is still functioning through his sense of greed, and his sense of power and dominion. And as a result, information of this sort is only for the few for power and dominion.

D: *What is the nearest star system to ours that has intelligent life capable of space travel?*

S: Aldebaran.

D: *What about the craft and the beings that seem to be visiting us now?*

S: There are extraterrestrials that are watching the planet, but they do not try to interfere that much. They do come with a sense of peace and good will for man, because they're trying to help the evolution evolvement rate of their terrestrial brothers. Many of them come from Aldebaran, Betelgeuse, and Sirius, the dog star. These entities from that area are part of the same galaxy that Earth people are from. At the present time they are watching the evolutionary rate of the planet Earth grow to a high degree, to take its place within the galactic federation. This is a spiritual confederation of advanced beings centered in light and love, and we are part of that plan. He says that not all beings who come to the Earth are positive. There is one group that you would consider negative, but they are in the minority. They belong to another federation.

D: *Can you tell us what these beings look like?*

S: One common characteristic is that they have reptilian type features. Their eyes are more reptilian-like. He's showing me a picture of one right now. He says their original evolution was through the reptilian family. What Earth people would call "reptilian like." Their skin is not smooth like our skin is. It has a rougher texture, but not exactly scales. They have large eyes, with a slit type pupil. And they don't really have a nose or a snout, but they have nostrils. And their mouth is very small actually. They don't eat like we do here on the Earth. It looks like they inhale essences that help them survive. He's showing me different sizes of different members of this whole race, and their bodies range in size from about four feet all the way to eight feet.

D: *Do they have limbs like we do?*

S: Yes, they have limbs. And they have lizard like finger type things, almost like a bird's talons, but they're not talons. They taper.

D: *How many fingers do they have?*

S: It depends on the species, from which system. Some have four, others have three, and then others have six.

D: *Do they have opposable thumbs as we do?*

S: The ones that have four digits do. The others don't.

D: *What about hair on the body?*

S: They really don't have hair like we have hair. They don't have fur either. They have protective coatings in different areas of their body that are more hardened skin than hair. For example, the skin around the reproductive system area is very hardened, because when they do engage in reproduction, this brings out their hardened senses, and they can be rough with each other. This is why that area has evolved to be tougher.

D: *Do they have separate sexes?*

S: Yes, they have separate sexes, but there's some hermaphrodite in the three-digit ones. Both male and female of the ones with three digits can incubate young. They appear reptilian like, so in their reproductive system they bear eggs. He's showing me an image of that now. He says this is how they give birth. They bear eggs and these are placed in special chambers they have in their bodies.

D: *Do they have ears?*

S: He says their sense of hearing is very acutely attuned. They have shell like things in their skulls. They're not like ears, but they can hear a wider range of pitch than we can.

D: *What about their ships? What type of craft are these mostly seen in?*

S: Their craft has more of a cylinder shape. Some are cigar shaped. Other ones appear as an egg or globe shape. They use an organic material from their world to build their crafts. It's a combination like rubber, plastic, fiberglass and metal mixed together. It's a very hard type of substance, yet it is organic, and it can go through many different heat exchanges to cold extremes. And it goes through a great distance of time, because their home planet is on the other side of the universe. It's a very resilient material. It goes through a lot, so it can expand and contract. The craft are powered by a solar collector, since they've learned about solar energies. We would call it solar energy, but to them it's star energy. They focus beams of light from different stars to make their craft travel. They call it a star collector, because in their travels they use different stars as a guidance system, to get where they want to go. They come from quite a distance from this planet, and they're just roaming in this part of our galaxy now.

D: *How long have they been here?*

S: They have only roamed this area for the last thousand years.

D: *How can we tell the difference between the positively oriented and the negatively oriented extraterrestrials?*

S: That's a very interesting question. You'll feel in tune with the higher beings that have a sense of kinship with the Earth people. There will be a sense of love that you will feel a sense of happiness, and a sense of camaraderie. The beings from this other federation are basically very cold, clinical, and you will feel fear. Fear will be very predominant.

D: *There are reports of tall blond aliens. Do you know anything about them?*

S: The ones that are more humanoid-like are part of this galaxy system.

D: *Do they have any bases here?*

S: They have used two of the moons of Uranus. He's showing me Uranus, as a base station for their explorations in this part of the galaxy.

D: *Do any have bases on Earth?*

S: The humanoid like have bases. He's showing me there's one located in the ocean. He's saying their craft can go into the water. This is located near the Caribbean Ocean. And there's another place that is high up in the mountains somewhere. Yes, it looks like South America that he's showing me, near the Amazon River. And then there's another place that he shows me in Australia or New Guinea, somewhere in that area near the ocean. These people, he's saying, are very much full of love and light, and are trying to help mankind. They've been coming to this planet for thousands and thousands and thousands of years. We would call them "The Watchers."

D: *Do these people ever have contact with humans?*

S: Yes, for specific reasons. Either to be instrumental in helping their spiritual growth, or to relay information about new inventions and things of this type. They will be of service as the Earth shifts.

D: *The ones that are more humanoid, what about their craft?*

S: They are normally the traditional saucer shape, basically made from some type of metal. It's a very shiny, shiny type metal. I don't know what kind of metal it is. He's saying, in the future you'll know about these craft and this metal, but it's not mined on this Earth. There's no metal comparable. And they power it by thought energy. That's the phrase he's giving me, "thought energy." It gives a rapid sense of propulsion by group thought energy. It's collected and stored as energy into batteries, and this motivates these ships.

D: *What material or type of substance are these batteries composed of, or how do they operate?*

S: (Smiling) He's just put a big, huge blueprint before me. I can't understand it. Thought is energy, he is saying, and people of the terrestrial form do not realize how powerful it is. It's hard for you to understand, he says. It's not collected in batteries, per se. I don't understand what he's trying to say. He says it's hard for your mind to grasp what it means. In time people of the Earth, humans, will expand their consciousness so they will understand this phenomenon. But at this present rate of evolution, you're not ready for this information.

D: *Do the Watchers travel through time as well as space?*

S: As advanced beings, they are capable of traveling through all sense of space. And time is space.

D: *Have any ships ever been captured, or crashed on Earth?*

S: Two of the reptilian-like ships have crashed on Earth. One near the Arizona desert, and the other one in the Indian Ocean.

D: *Were they retrieved?*

The Custodians

S: The one that crashed in Arizona was retrieved.

D: *Any occupants aboard?*

S: Two burnt bodies were onboard.

D: *What happened to them?*

S: He is saying they have now been cremated, but they were observed by scientists. He says the American government and the Soviet government have had many contacts with extraterrestrials, both of the reptilian-like as well as of the ones from this part of the galaxy. They do not release information to the masses for fear of panicking the people. In the Soviet Union, at one point, a radio telescope operator was communicating with an extraterrestrial source, but his superiors stripped him of his rank, and reassigned him. They reassigned him to a mental institution where he went through shock treatments, which now have ... (as a question) have collapsed his mind? Hmmm. This was done because he was releasing information to the Soviet underground about this, and they felt this would panic the nation and they would not have control and power any more.

D: *What type of communication did he receive?*

S: He established a type of code with them, through electronic pulses.

D: *Similar to our Morse code?*

S: No, it wasn't like Morse code. He's showing me something like light energy translated into pulses on a radar like screen type thing.

D: *The Watchers you spoke of, do any of them live within the Earth?*

S: No, they don't live within the Earth. They live within their ships.

D: *I meant, are there people living inside the Earth? Going along with the theory of having a hollow Earth.*

S: No. He's showing me a picture of the Earth. And he says, there were bases carved out at one time, which were used eons ago. They were rediscovered by these Watchers. It's like explorers in their pursuit of mountain climbing, going back to a cave occasionally, but they don't really live in them. They really don't want to live on Earth. It's not very important to them. They do explorations here, but mostly there's a communication line between these other star systems.

D: *What about the cases we've heard of ships that appear to be collecting energy or water at different places on the Earth?*

S: They're not collecting water, they're not collecting energy. They're actually charging the electrical field, and picking up communications, energy. They're monitoring different forms of life that exist in the ocean: whales, dolphins, sharks. They're taking experiments, that's what he's showing me. They also monitor our communications, our electronic capacity and our nuclear power, when they appear over different installations that deal with communications and power.

D: *They give the impression they are somehow dependent. People think they are taking on power from the electric stations and things like that.*

S: (Smiling) He says, no, that's not true. These beings are so evolved, you people are back in kindergarten while they're high school level.

D: *What is the mode of their interplanetary or galactic communications, considering that they must travel such enormous distances?*

S: Again, thought power is used.

D: *Relating to that same question. Why don't they respond to our interrogations via radio frequencies?*

S: He says they have in the past. We just talked about this phenomenon that took place in the Soviet Union. But, again, man is not ready. That's what he says, "Man is not ready," or he's afraid of having higher advanced beings dominating him.

D: *Well, the picture we get, basically, is that there are two major types, the reptilian and the Watchers. How many others are visiting Earth?*

S: These are the two major groups that are manifesting in this part of the galaxy at the present time. There are even more advanced beings than the Watchers, that occasionally travel to this planet. But they only come, oh, once every ten thousand years.

D: *Did any of these people have anything to do with the creation of human life on our planet?*

S: Yes, the Watchers have helped form man. He says you would consider these as angelic beings. And they have appeared as angels to people in the past. And, yes, they have helped form life on this planet, and evolve it to a higher degree. They are still helping at this present time, to help man's evolutionary rate. They are attempting at this time to create a more perfect human body, in terms of immunological response to disease and initial resistance to disease. So there will eventually be those or that stock perhaps, of human bodies that would be most resistance to most form of disease on your planet now. The intent of this genetic engineering is to, in essence, create a more perfect physical body, such that the spirit, once raised in awareness, can more perfectly translate into these more perfect bodies. A more perfect spirit requires a more perfect body.

D: *Then they are actually helping more than they are harming, aren't they?*

S: Indeed. There is no intent of harm in any of this.

D: *Some aliens seem able to enter houses where they don't even trip burglar alarms. They just appear there. How are they able to do this?*

S: They have an anti-matter energy that they use to do this. Where they seem to disseminate and break down, and then reappear. And this is how they can also transport.

D: *You mean they break down the physical body?*

S: Yes, break down the physical molecules, and then reassemble them.

D: *It would seem this would cause trauma.*

S: Oh, yes, it does. This is one reason why most of the time the people don't remember afterwards. The aliens have taken their memory away, because usually it will be very traumatic and painful for people to remember these type of experiences.

D: *Well, in that way it would be a kindness.*

S: The Watchers have come to help in the evolution of man from his primitive beginnings to his spiritual glory, so he can take part in what they call the "federation," this galactic federation of advanced beings. Some of the other beings have their own purposes. They're networking throughout the universe, to explore, to see what is out there, to see what they can use for their own life systems on their home planets. So they've been *allowed* to come here in the last thousand years to see what is on the Earth that could be of valuable use to them. These have taken things from the Earth: crystals, different types of stones, especially magnesium. This is why they appear over areas of Africa and Asia, especially around India. They've taken certain minerals from the Earth that are very valuable for their own life forms, that are not found on their planet. Also they have taken plant life, and genetically engineered it, so it would fit their home environment, which is very different. It has a different atmosphere, gravity and density, but they do need plant life on their different worlds.

D: *Why can't the Watchers keep the negative aliens from coming?*

S: Because they are still exploring, they haven't conquered worlds yet. There are other worlds besides ours, that are at similar evolutionary points, throughout the universe. He's showing me another planet that looks similar to Earth, but it lies near a star that is very distant and isn't even named. It is very similar to Earth, and they've been watching that planet as well. These aliens will have to become more warlike, and more obsessive to expand their territory within the universe, before the Watchers can really do anything.

D: *Did ancient civilizations on the Earth have contact with these beings?*

S: Oh, in the times of Atlantis much of the information about crystals and energy and light and sunlight, solar energy and things like this, was freely traded with extraterrestrials. The Watchers took an active part in the development of that civilization, as well as the civilization of the Lemurians. They also interacted with the civilizations of the Egyptians and the Babylonians, and the people of the Indus River Valley. They were all connected with the Watchers at one point or another.

D: *Were the Watchers the only ones visiting Earth then?*

S: Yes, they were the only beings allowed to come on this planet.

D: *Are the Watchers all of one type, one race?*

S: "Terrians," as he calls us, are of the same genetic makeup. They're humanoid-like. They might have a few differences, like different types of eye color, and different types of bone structure. And two or three organ systems that are very different from humans of the Earth, but on the whole, genetically, they're very much in tune to the people of Earth, because we're all part of one galaxy. And they are watching as the Earth moves from our barbaric level into a high vibratory level, to take its place within the galactic federation. There are about thirty-six planets in this federation at this time. Earth will be the thirty-seventh, and there will be two more.

D: *Do the Watchers know what is going on in the rest of the universe?*

S: The guardian says they have perfect knowledge. And they're in constant communication with their home bases and with all other bases. They have ... the best word I can come up with is "osmosis." They have perfect knowledge of time and space, and what is going on at all times. They use telepathy rather than speaking, to interact with each other and other beings. They are very advanced in this regard. They can send energies over great distances, or periods of time and space. If we were in this level we wouldn't have any wars or any conflicts, because we'd all be in tune. They are all attuned. That is the word that he uses: attuned.

D: *Are the Reptilians different in that respect? In that they do not have this same type of communication skills and knowledge?*

S: He says they have developed clicking signals that they use. They sound like clicks, which can travel and be amplified by instruments within their bodies as well as within their space craft. This transmits over great arcs of time. They use star power that they bounce off these different click signals. And this is how they can transmit information from one end of their galaxy to the other.

D: *Are there any humanoid aliens living among our human population on Earth?*

S: Yes. He says some of them have incarnated to be of service as Earth goes through her change in her rapid deployment to the higher vibratory form.

D: *I mean, are any of them living among us in their own form, and not as an incarnation?*

S: Many souls have come from these areas and have incarnated on Earth. Yes, but there are also humanoids from the Watchers that have lived in their form on Earth. There are only though, about thirty-six, scattered throughout the world. And they are monitoring, especially, our growth and capabilities in nuclear as well as in laser and destructive technology.

D: *Then there aren't so many that we would find any of them.*

S: Six are gathered in our southwest, three are gathered in our northeast, one is in the northwest, two are gathered in the central portions of our country, and another one is in what would be Florida. Two are gathered around the radio telescope that is in Puerto Rico. And the rest are scattered throughout the world.

D: *Are they in communication with each other?*

S: Yes, they keep a monitor on what is taking place with all types of energy developments.

D: *Have these humanoids interbred, or had offspring with the human life forms on Earth?*

S: They were forbidden to do that. They did that in the past. This is how man grew. They mated early with animal like forms and helped human like forms to evolve. But they didn't mate, per se, they used what we would call genetic engineering. He's showing me laboratory type conditions. And this is where man came from. He's showing me the Biblical quotation, "The sons of God took up with the daughters of men."

He was referring to: Gen. 6:2. *"The sons of God saw the daughters of men that they were fair, and they took them wives of all which they chose." Also Gen. 6:4. "There were giants in the earth in those days; and also after that, when the sons of God came in unto the daughters of men, and they bare children to them."*

S: This is where this passage came from, describing what took place. And now they can't do that anymore, because that is against free will. You see, the Watchers respect our free will. However, the Reptilian beings look at us as a lower life form. They evolved out of a reptilian like mode, and, as a result, they're not very highly evolved on what we call the "spiritual evolution" scale. The guardian says the Watchers are of a higher spiritual energy, so we can repulse the negative beings by allowing ourselves to function in a higher spiritual mode. The Reptilians are definitely repelled by a higher spiritual force, and they will be unattracted to this type of energy.

It's an interesting observation that the negative element of these extraterrestrials is reptilian. The Bible is replete with symbols of serpents, asps, dragons etc. that are always representative of the negative influence.

In this portion the guardian of the library spoke directly to us.

S: It is important for you to know that after the coming period of turmoil and the Earth changes there will be much smooth sailing.

There will be much learning. There will be assistance involving interplanetary travel. You will begin to know more about your universe, and all of the many others. There will be assistance from those in other space realms, and you will join in with that. There will be a communion, a *knowledgeable*, on both sides, working together. You have not had that before. Other entities in space have known about you, but you have not known about them. And that will happen. There will be smooth sailing. Quite a relief after the turmoil that has been taking place.

D: *Why are they giving us this assistance?*

S: They would give anyone this assistance. You will do the same when you are in a position to do so, because we were all part of the *one*, and we are all related. You have been unaware of that, because you have been in such an infant stage. You will be growing out of that and into an awareness that we are all one. Something like when the Age of Reason came about with humans.

D: *You said we are all related. Do you mean physically too?*

S: Are you talking about the physical look?

D: *The genes or whatever.*

S: Yes. They all had to come from somewhere, and we are physically related. And even more importantly *metaphysically* related. You all started, and from your history all you know about is here. But there was a beginning before that, or there was *existence* before you were ever here. And that's what your history books don't know about.

D: *One line of thinking is that we all evolved and started here on this planet. We were created through the evolution of the species.*

S: Yes, through some mishmash of gases and mists and solids bouncing around together, and accidentally popping up with something they considered had life. That is not true. There are many, many, many planets - if we shall call them that - out there that are not experiencing any lifeform whatsoever at this time. If and when they do, it will not be because it just happened. It will be because it was done in some way. Either the planet will undergo a change to where it can support life, or if it already can, seeding, so to speak, will be put there so life can then evolve.

D: *Do you mean there is never life that is just indigenous, that just begins by accident on any planet?*

S: *Correct. Life does not begin by accident.* And indigenous depends on how far back you want to go. You see, if something has been around since before your history of it, you consider it indigenous. But that's simply because your history is limited, not because it was necessarily indigenous. It depends on how far back you want to go.

D: *Then it would be safe to say that all life, plants, minerals or whatever, have to begin by being brought in? (Yes) It never just evolves by itself?*

S: No. Nor will it ever. That would be quite erratic. Quite - I don't know what the word is - very disorganized, very uncontrolled, without union. It would be a very big mess.

D: *I was thinking that in the natural cooling of a planet, with the mixture of gases and everything, that life could evolve spontaneously.*

S: No. It does not happen that way. In the cooling of the gases and/or whatever that you are referring to, the habitat might become *supporting* of a lifeform, but it wouldn't just develop by itself. Life is so precious and important. You do not realize how carefully it is actually handled. It would not be a system set up to just spring about all of its own accord, with no one else knowing about it or having anything to do with it. That would just not be the way it was done. There is much caring about lifeforms on any planet. And they are carefully planned. The setting is organized, and the setup handled well before it ever happens. So much importance is placed on *life.*

D: *I was thinking of the enormity of a project like that; of all the people that would be involved.*

S: Those are things I do not know all the answers to. I know that it is of far greater magnitude than you can even imagine.

D: *I'm thinking of all the uncountable worlds there could possibly be, and then the amount of individuals that would have to carry out such a program.*

S: That's true, but they're not exactly individuals. There are great powers. Greater than I know of. So I cannot speak of that.

D: *I'm thinking of the individuals that would be sent out to do these different jobs. But you mean it's something besides that.*

S: There is something above and beyond that, yes. I did not know you were referring to the *physical* counterparts of this. Is that what you mean?

D: *I guess. The ones who would be responsible for doing it. It seems like such a large program.*

S: It is a matter of consciousness, not so much of people sent out to do it. It is true there are those sent out to do things of this nature. There is also a consciousness implanted, so to speak, that could be done in mass, rather than individually sent out. Both could take place.

D: *I'm thinking of individuals having to go and do different things. I know they would have to have orders from someone else, or someone who knew the grander plan.*

S: That's what I thought you were talking about initially, of which I have referred to. That is so far beyond me that I know of no way to even give insight on an answer.

D: *Then the mass consciousness would be more like a spirit.* (Yes) *It couldn't physically manifest something.*

S: Yes, consciousness can physically manifest something.

D: *It could manifest life?* (Yes) *In what, beginning stages?*

S: Actually it could in any stage, but it wouldn't normally be done that way, so *randomly.* I speak of it as an "it," and it is not an "it." Consciousness could manifest itself as anything at any time instantaneously, and with no effort. You're not aware that the levels of consciousness you operate under is the power of consciousness, but it is so. And you are like babies just creeping into that realm of awareness of your consciousness, and what it amounts to. But if consciousness wanted to manifest itself as an entire planet, peopled with many, it could do it. It just *wouldn't* do it that way.

D: *I think you are referring to what we think of as God in our belief system.*

S: That may be true, but it's more than just a belief. It is a manifestation. Believing does make it so, to an extent. But consciousness is there whether you believe it or not. It's just that your ability to know it is diminished, if you can't believe it.

D: *So life can occur through this consciousness and also through the manipulation of other individuals?*

S: Yes. And that would be the more appropriate manner. You see, consciousness isn't out there to just manifest. It *never* stops. Consciousness doesn't take back. When it manifests outwardly, that continues *forever*. So consciousness would be somewhat cautious about randomly making another planet and throwing a lot of people on it, because it couldn't "disappear" it. It could withdraw itself, its focus, *from* it. But what it had manifested would then have consciousness of its own, and would continue on and on. So a higher level of consciousness would not be so thoughtless and erratic or irresponsible as to do things like that. It would create joy, comfort, love, and all of the things that we think of as positive. It would not do something that would leave some entire planet not knowing what to do next.

Another subject described the library in a different way.

S: I am in a place that is similar to ... the closest concept I can find is a library. It's located on a different spiritual plane than the one I just left. If you wish, I will describe this library to you. Nothing can improve upon the card catalog in this library over here. This library does not have books in it, per se, but it has kernels of knowledge. That knowledge floats in its own space, shining brightly like a spark of light. They are all around you and you are surrounded by these bits of knowledge. And when you decide you want to learn about a certain type of knowledge, the energy of these bits of knowledge is drawn toward you. You see these lights moving toward you, and they rest upon your head, so to speak, because we're not physical here. And you can absorb the knowledge from it.

D: *That would be much faster than reading from a book. It's not really like a library that I would picture with books on shelves.*

S: No, but it's the closest concept I can find. It has all knowledge. It's just a matter of my ability to be able to link up with it. So you're not limited by the place, you'll be limited by me if there are any limitations. I can find what we're looking for, but will I be able to observe it in a way to help you understand? That is the limitation. The knowledge is all here, sparkling and shiny and ready to be learned. If the answer happens to be located somewhere else, I will project myself there instead. It is no problem.

After she awakened she retained a vivid impression of this library and wanted to add more information about its appearance.

S: The plane of that library is like an energy field shaped in the form of a huge sphere. And inside the sphere is the plane of the library. The sphere isn't to keep anybody out. It's just a matter of keeping the information organized and contained in this area. I guess you would call it a magnetic indexing system that attracts information to it, then zaps it and it falls in the right place. And when you make use of the library, your consciousness or whatever is floating in the exact center, and every bit of information is floating around in these different shapes of light. Sometimes they're tear dropped shaped or round or almost like Christmas tree ornaments. And they're all sparkling with light of different colors. And somehow the shape of the light, the color of it, and how it sparkles, tells your consciousness what kind of information it is.

D: *I wonder what the difference is?*

S: I guess it's like the difference between books on animals and books on governmental procedures or what have you. Just different subject matter. And I got this feeling that if you didn't really have anything particularly in mind you wanted to learn about, that one of these shapes would spark something. But if you were wanting to find a particular piece of information, then whatever light that is concerned with that information comes over and kind of merges with you. And when it separates, you've learned the information from it. I had this feeling that I had a new parcel of knowledge gained thereby.

D: *I guess your subconscious just draws whichever piece of information it desires.*

S: I guess. And the background is a dark midnight blue, so the light really shows and glows.

D: *How do you go into that sphere?*

S: You think yourself into it.

D: *Just go right through the wall of it or whatever.*

S: Yeah. I have this feeling that you think, "Now I want to be in the library," and when you open your eyes, you're there. It was very beautiful. The library is there to be used by all. And those on the physical plane that manage to contact this library are welcome to its knowledge.

So this was my favorite place to search for knowledge, just as I enjoy going to the University of Arkansas Library to research my books. I am definitely in my element when I can spend an entire day within the halls of knowledge. When I could take a subject to the spirit realm I always had many questions to ask about many topics. After I began doing UFO investigation I took advantage of the opportunity to find knowledge in the library about UFOs and abductions. When I later combined this with the actual hypnosis sessions it was not contradictory, but similar, and added an extra dimension to trying to understand the phenomenon. Some of the information came through in 1985, 86 and 87, before I began my actual investigations, when I was still in the curiosity stage.

A female subject was in the library observing outer space. It seemed to be a perfect time to ask questions about aliens and UFOs.

S: I am looking at this galaxy. This part of the library has a holographic effect, so I feel as though I am actually in among the stars. I have been meditating, and gazing at these stars as I meditate. And I've been looking at the various planets and the life on these various planets.

D: *Can you tell me some of the things you see as you look at the galaxy?*

S: Well, I see Earth. Earth is like a green jewel. And there are other stars with planets like this star. Some of them have life and some of them do not. And the life is at various levels of development.

D: *Can you see the other planets in our solar system?*

S: Yes. There are ten of them. There are the nine that you know of: Mercury, Venus, Earth, Mars, Jupiter, Saturn, Uranus, Neptune, Pluto. The planet the scientists have hypothesized that is beyond Pluto. It is there. The scientists have attached a name to it, but this instrument finds it difficult to pronounce. I'm not sure I can get the tongue around the name. This other planet is very far out, yet the sun is the center of its orbit. The sun just looks like a bright star to it, because it's so far out. It really receives no heat from the sun to speak of. But it does orbit about the sun, so it would be considered a planet of this solar system.

D: *I would like to ask questions about what we call UFOs, and Flying Saucers.*

S: Extraterrestrial Traveling Vehicles, yes.

D: *That's a more accurate term.*

S: I am aware of the concept of the phenomena that you are speaking about. There are various types of UFOs. They have the same basic shape, because there is an intergalactic civilization that travels faster than light through warps of time. And the vehicles need to be the same basic shape in order to survive the journey. But there are details that are different, because they come from the different nations that make up this civilization. The various UFOs come to Earth for different reasons. One set, the very oldest set that comes, keeps an eye on the development of the Earth. Earth has been their pet project, you might say. And this particular nation I'm going to call them is a nation of thinkers and experimenters. They wanted to see if the predicted results would happen if they did a certain action at a very malleable time of the planet's history.

D: *What action was that?*

S: It's been a steady pattern of mild interference since before there was life as such on Earth. And the Earth was like a fertile womb. Life was developing here, but they speeded up the process by seeding the Earth with proto life. So they could control the development and see what direction it would take, rather than letting the Earth develop its own natural life by itself. You could call these people the archaic ones. They have kept an eye on the Earth the whole time to keep track of the development of things. And to occasionally give things a little nudge here and there to keep them developing in the direction they want to develop. Other vehicles that come here are from other nations of this civilization, and they come here for various reasons. One nation sends five vehicles on a regular basis to see if comparable technology has been developed here, so we would be ready to join the civilization, or at least open trade with some of the member nations of this great civilization. One nation apparently has a more paranoid mind set, and it sends vehicles just to explore the military installations to make sure we're not going to do any damage to the rest of the universe through our weapons development, and through our military, scientific exploration. There's another type of ship that comes, and I say "type." They're all basically alike, but I'm talking about the different ones that come predominantly from the different nations. There's another type of ship that comes just out of curiosity. They're always trying to find out everything that's going on with everybody. They knew from the distance Earth was from the sun that it could support life. And as they observed the planet they discovered there was indeed life here. But they saw what had happened regarding the political and religious structure, and they knew it would not be a good idea to come into direct contact with the life on this planet yet. Mostly because of the delicateness of the situation and the explosive violence always so close to the surface. And they've been keeping watch because they want to be in contact. They feel that the two civilizations together could build something really great, and develop into a galactic power. They see that we are trying very hard to develop, but we're not quite ready. It has to wait till the right time, and so they are waiting. They will make a test contact to see how well humans have developed. They come at different times, and disguise themselves so they can mix with the people. With their psychic abilities they can get a feeling for the general currents in social and mental developments. Occasionally they take a human and give them a physical examination, so they can keep track of how our life sciences are developing, since they've put great emphasis on that on their planet. They have a theory that, according to how advanced the life sciences are and how they take care of the race in general, regarding feeding, medical care, general health and nutrition, that this is paralleled by technological developments.

D: *These aren't the only ones coming to Earth, are they?*

S: No, no. There are many others that have been observing Earth, but they are the closest ones. They're the ones that would be most apt to make successful contact with us first. They mostly do passive observing. They really don't directly interfere with any humans very often. It used to be once a century, but lately since the life sciences have been developing at an astronomical rate, it's been more often. They feel that the time is very close when they can successfully contact humans, and start sharing their technology. These are the groups of UFOs that do travel to your planet. The physical types, because I feel you're asking for information on vehicles whose dimensions closely overlap your dimensions. Their dimensions are close enough to your own so you're able to perceive them without difficulty. There are several, several, several UFOs that you never perceive, simply because their dimensions do not overlap enough with your own. These UFOs' dimensions of length, height and width correspond very closely to your perceptions, but their dimension of time is different from yours. Consequently, time seems to be, from your point of view, distorted about them. They appear to travel very fast and very swiftly, because of this distortion of time. At the same time, when any humans have close encounters with these, time feels like it stretches out indefinitely, because once again time is being distorted.

D: *What area does this type of vehicle come from?*

S: It's hard to say, because there's quite a striving interstellar community in the galaxy. And they can come from several different areas, depending upon why they want to come to your planet. They all know of each other's existence. And many times they'll have very close contact with each other, depending on which group it is. There is one group from a different arm of the galaxy, that has quite a distance to travel to get to Earth. They have a great deal of interest in Earth, because they put some early colonists on the Earth millennia ago. And so, in a sense, human beings are their descendants. There are several different groups interested in the Earth. Earth is not the only planet they're interested in, mind you. Several different groups are interested in the development of various planets, for various reasons, depending on what stage of development the planets are going through. And so naturally the groups interested in the development of Earth are the ones you would have the most contact with. And some of these groups have gotten together and put a temporary quarantine on this area of space, to give Earth time to do her own development, because right now mankind is at a crucial stage. Just an eyeblink ago, regarding universal time, mankind entered the nuclear age, and that is always a crucial time for any culture. At this point they know they dare not interfere or everything could fall apart into ruin. And they have to sit back and wait, to see how a race newly introduced to nuclear power is going to handle and deal with it. If they deal with it successfully, then the quarantine is lifted, and they start sending technical advisors to coach the planet and the race, to get them ready to join the galaxy community. Advisors will be sent to spark new ideas, to answer questions, and to show the scientists some of the areas they thought were impossible to research, because of the currently formulated scientific laws that are actually not impossible at all. The main way mankind will fit into the plan of the galactic community is: they will be the major ones to approach and encounter new universes, and the galactic communities in these new universes. For mankind will have the questioning mind necessary to learn and understand these new universes, but will have the strength of not being unduly influenced by them.

D: *So there is a higher power, so to speak, that watches over all of this.*

S: The older powers. The older a power is, the higher they are in the hierarchy of the galactic races.

D: *We're interested in reports of aliens abducting people and taking them onboard their ships. Do you have anything in the library about those type of beings?*

S: Yes. Centuries upon centuries upon centuries upon centuries ago these beings came to Earth in their ships. I call these the Archaic ones, or the Old Ones. They "seeded" the planet so intelligent life would develop here. And so they come back to take crop samples, so to speak, to see how it is turning out for their "project." They are watching what's going on and how things are developing, because they want to create more intelligent life in the universe by "helping it along sometimes." The best way they can do that, they feel, is by getting the information from one of the more intelligent species on the planet: human beings.

D: *Could you tell me something about the archaic race? You said they were around before there was life on Earth?*

S: Yes. Their technology developed to a galactic level when life on Earth was at its very beginnings. They had to work with the Earth itself, because the planet was having problems with extremes of climate. And they worked with the Earth to help balance the climate so that life could develop. Occasionally the Earth gets out of balance again, and they have to put it back into balance. That's what caused ice ages in the past.

D: *You mean they were actively involved in the climate?* (Yes) *What about being actively involved with the species?*
S: Yes, they have done genetic manipulation. When the species is developing, you have to try to speed up the process of their development.

I had already discovered this in my book *Keepers of the Garden,* but I always like to verify these theories through other subjects when the opportunity arises.

S: That's one reason modern man developed so quickly. They discovered this anthropoid animal (the ape), and they saw the potential in the genes and the greater brain capacity. They saw the dexterous digits of the hands, and they knew it would be very easy to develop tools and hence technology. This type of digits is important for the beginning development of technology. They started manipulating, and the first thing they did was to change the skeletal structure to free the hands for making tools. Then after the hands were free and used to make tools, they started working on increasing the brain capacity, so they could develop the technology they were now physically able to handle. They then started intensive genetic manipulation to speed up the process as much as possible without endangering the race. They had a laboratory type location to do this, but they left the humans involved in their natural setting. They took the sperm and the ovum, genetically manipulated it in the laboratory, and then came back and artificially inseminated the females. They were continuing to do this until modern times, which was recorded in ancient histories as visits of angels and such.
D: *What about before life reached that stage? When it was in the very beginning cellular stages? Did they have anything to do with things at that time?*
S: Oh, yes, the whole time, at all stages, to help life develop in viable directions.

I was again checking information I had already received, but I was trying to ask questions as though I knew nothing about it. If several subjects supply the same type of information, and there are no contradictions, it gives it more validity.

D: Can you tell me something about when they first began?

S: When it started as single celled animals, they encouraged them to proliferate into several different types to make it a balanced ecology. And whenever any of the particular types of single-celled animals showed a tendency to try to clump together into multi celled organizations, they would encourage this. And that gradually developed into multi celled creatures, et cetera. And so they'd been encouraging it all along, not radically, but gently to make sure it continued to develop in a positive direction. Because they had observed many instances where a planet would develop life at the single-celled stage. The single cells would start to clump together, and somehow they would not be successful, and would fall back apart into just single-celled animals. And then after a while, the single celled animals would start to die off and the planet would be lifeless again.

D: Then they were doing genetic manipulation at that time also?

S: More like selective breeding at that time. Encouraging the best cells, the ones with the most potential, to breed. Much like you take the best animals, say, horses, and breed them to develop a particular trait.

D: Then they would allow the other ones that were not developing correctly to die out.

S: Yes. They did not do anything with the ones that were evolutionary dead ends. They ran their natural course to the dead end, and died. One of the things that excited them about this planet, it was so rich in the variety of molecules and chemicals that could combine in infinite variations. When they started working on the climate, they made it favorable so these different compounds could combine into complex forms. At this point they started actively - interfering is not the right word - actively participating. And they helped these complex forms to combine into more complex forms. They had to do much delicate chemical engineering at this point. And they gradually developed into ... first into viruses, that type of creature. And from there they developed into one-celled animals.

D: Do you mean like the amoeba and that type?

S: First they developed into viruses. As you know, the virus, when it's in a liquid medium, in water, it conducts itself like a living creature. When you take it out of water and it dries into a crystal, it just sits there. This was kind of an intermediate form. And from there it developed into larger one celled animals.

D: *And then through a natural evolutionary process they began to change?*

S: Yes, they were using the natural evolutionary process, but they kept urging it into positive channels so it could continue to develop into more complex organisms without falling apart. And so it's like tending a hydroponic garden.

D: *Did they stay here the entire time they were doing that?*

S: This was when they were set up on the moon, so in effect they were here. Since they were still dealing with the planet's climate, it was safer for them to stay off the planet as much as possible. But they had to take samples of the lifeforms, see how they were developing, and balance the chemicals accordingly, when the lifeforms were in the seas. And so they were nearby observing everything very closely while they were doing all this.

D: *That must have taken a great deal of time.*

S: Yes, it was a long range project.

D: *So they were more or less based there, and they kept going back and forth. Is this what this archaic race normally did, travel to planets looking for suitable life?*

S: No, it's just one of the things they did. They had several major projects, but that was the one that most immediately affects us. They did this, because when they were first starting out, there was a race that helped them along. But by the time they came to galactic power, that race had died out. This archaic race is very advanced and very old, as far as civilization is concerned. One reason they have been trying to develop these other races, and helping other ones to continue to evolve on their own, is to help make this galaxy into a balanced community, capable of interacting with other galaxies and eventually with other universes.

D: *When they were doing these manipulations, and developing the species, did they ever have any mistakes, any problems?*

S: Yes. From time to time they would see that one particular branch would be developing in a way that had not been anticipated, and it would cause a problem. Or it would not develop the way it should have. At which point they would either try genetic manipulation or, if the mistake was too bad, they would leave that particular species alone, and let it live out its normal evolutionary span. They would not interfere with it, but they would not actively kill it off either.

D: *Is the archaic race still actively dealing with humans and changing us by manipulation?*

S: Yes. The main thing they're doing now is trying to expand our life span, and trying to help make human bodies in general healthier and stronger. They're also helping the medical profession by making discoveries easier to find. They do this psychically by giving them the ideas.

D: *I have been told it is time that the people knew how the human race began, and how things started.*

S: Yes. Your scientists theorized the theory of evolution. They're on the right track. They just don't know all the facts, and they don't know all the forces involved.

D: *Wouldn't life have evolved by itself without the interference of the space people?*

S: That's a very iffy proposition. It might have evolved spontaneously, but it would have taken much longer, and there would have been many false starts. Some life would have evolved, and then it would have died out. And it would have had to start from scratch again, until finally the right combination started developing.

D: *Do you think we would have ever developed to the human stage if it had been left alone?*

S: Maybe eventually, but it would have taken hundreds of thousands of times longer than it did.

D: *Then there are some life forms on other planets that are indigenous, and have not been interfered with?*

S: Certainly. All the life on a planet is indigenous to the planet. It was just treated as though it was in a greenhouse. When you plant a plant, say, a tomato plant outside, it develops and grows and produces tomatoes. You put it in the greenhouse, it grows and develops and produces tomatoes. It just does it faster.

D: *Do you think we ever would have developed the intellect that we have now without the direct manipulation of the genes?*

S: That's very questionable. The potential was there, but whether or not it would have been triggered spontaneously, is a whole different matter. But they thought the potential was there, so they made sure it was triggered right away.

D: *Do you think this gene manipulation happens a lot throughout the universe?*

S: I'm sure it does. Of course, if there is life here, this proves that life developed spontaneously at one point in time, and developed to an advanced stage where they could start manipulating other life developments. So it does happen spontaneously. There are many places where they'll see that life is developing quite well, and they really don't need to interfere with it. Either because they have a more pressing project to work on, such as Earth, or what have-you. And they just keep an eye on it to make sure nothing happens to actively destroy it.

D: *Then it must have happened spontaneously at some time in the past.*

S: Oh, yes, it has happened several times. Otherwise where did life begin originally? It had to start somewhere.

D: *Do any of these that are watching us come from our own solar systems?*

S: Not directly from the solar system. Now some of the watchers have bases in the solar system and they travel from these bases. They have rotating personnel at these bases, but you cannot say they are from this solar system. They're just working here, and they're from another part of the galaxy. Some of their favorite places to establish these bases are on the larger moons of the larger planets, particularly the moons around Jupiter and Saturn, because they are close enough to the sun to have enough solar energy to run their technology and machines. And they're within easy observing distance of Earth, but still far enough away to not be discovered by, what they call our "budding technology."

A thought here about another short session in the early 1980s where a man saw himself on what appeared to be an alien barren planet. He and others were in a cave with some machines and talking about us, the people of Earth, saying that they were observing us. At the time it sounded strange, but now I wonder if maybe he was seeing one of these bases.

D: *What about our moon?*

S: They used to be based on our moon until the twentieth century. That was the ideal place. They were right there on top of us and they could, figuratively, not have to get out of bed to observe us. And they left automatic machinery there. They set up automatic beacons and automatic observing equipment there, which they can tune into with their equipment when they want a closer view. They visit it occasionally for upkeep and maintenance. But they don't keep any personnel there, because with humans actively exploring the moon they don't want direct contact with humans yet.

D: *Is there any chance of our people finding this equipment?*

S: Not really. The moon is quite large and it's been very sparsely explored. They have protective energy shields to deflect the energy of human's instruments, so they're not aware they're observing them when they do observe them.

D: *Then there is nothing they could see through a telescope?*

S: Ordinarily, no. One of the probes almost discovered the equipment, but the people who owned it saw it in time. And did something to the probe so the scientists just interpreted it as a momentary blip.

D: *A momentary malfunction or something. But mostly their bases are on other planets.*

S: Correct. On the moons of other planets. Sometimes people have seen through their telescopes what appears to be ruins and such on planets in this solar system. These can be truthfully attributed to past observers, and their old abandoned observation stations.

D: *Are there any bases on Earth?*

S: Not large establishments. There are, halfway houses, you would call them, that are established on the planet in remote areas to use whenever they're sending an observer into the population. Not to contact the humans, but just to observe the humans and pick up psychic feelings from them. They come to this halfway house first, and live there for a little while to get adjusted to the climate, the gravity and the air and such. So they can act more human when they're among the humans. If they want someone to stay for long term observation they will disguise them as a doctor, or someone in a capacity that would actively help humans during the process of observing them.

D: *But these bases would be in isolated places?*

S: Ordinarily, yes. They are usually in mountainous areas where the isolation is greater, without the climate being too harsh. It would defeat the purpose to have the halfway houses in harsh climates, because they would be adjusting to an abnormal climate. They want the halfway houses to be in areas where the climate is moderate or even close to normal. So this would be the mountainous areas, in the valleys between the mountains, where there is a lot of greenery and temperate climate.

D: *Do these beings and craft ever come from anywhere else besides planets?*

S: What do you mean? Planets are the only place they come from. They all live on planets.

D: *They all live on physical, three-dimensional planets?*

S: Yes. They may not necessarily be in the same three dimensions we're in, but they're all three-dimensional planets. They all appear physical to the people who live on them, because they are used to that particular set of three dimensions.

D: *I was really thinking of the fourth dimension, I guess.*

S: Some of the planets involve the fourth, fifth and sixth dimension, or the twelfth, thirteenth and fourteenth dimension. But it's different sets of the various dimensions because there are an infinite number of dimensions. And these planets, in addition to being scattered all amongst the different galaxies, are also scattered all amongst the different dimensions, to keep everything balanced so things won't get too crowded.

D: *I've also heard that they come from different planes of existence. Would this refer to the same thing?* (Yes) *We're thinking that these ships and the people on them are just coming from nearby galaxies and planets like ours.*

S: No. That's one of the reasons those distances in space seem to be so vast. Because there's nothing there in this set of dimensions, but there are things in other sets of the other dimensions.

D: *Then it's not just empty space.*

S: Correct. It simply is incapable of being perceived from these dimensions.

D: *But if someone was to go through them, would they realize them as physical, even though they can't see them from Earth?*

S: There's no way they can be perceived, because they're not in these dimensions.

D: *All I can do is write this down and let those who understand it understand it, if I can't grasp it all.*

S: Those who are better educated may have a more difficult time understanding because they are more fixed in their ideas.

I wanted to get the conversation focused back on something that would be easier for me to understand, rather than these complicated concepts that just gave me headaches, and left me feeling like my poor brain had been bent like a pretzel.

These type of concepts and theories will be continued and explored further in *Convoluted Universe*. Suffice it to say that there are countless worlds around us that are invisible to us because they are vibrating at a different frequency. The inhabitants of those worlds perceive their surroundings as physical, and are as oblivious of us as we are of them. Yet some of the aliens that have mastered space travel have learned to go back and forth through these different dimensions simply by speeding up or slowing down their vibrations.

D: *In relation to our solar system, can you tell me anything about the asteroid belt?*

S: Yes. There was a planet there when the planets were developing. It was at the time when Jupiter almost developed into a sun, into a twin star to orbit around the sun. It would have been a smaller sun. There was powerful stress from Jupiter and with another large planet, Saturn, being nearby, the planet between Jupiter and Mars could not handle the stress. On the one hand, it was being pulled to revolve around the sun, yet at the same time Jupiter was tugging at it to cause it to revolve around Jupiter. And so the stress ripped it apart into shreds.

D: *Jupiter is a giant planet, and it had too much gravity. Why didn't Jupiter go on to develop into a twin star?*

S: It was not quite large enough to initiate the necessary nuclear reaction. If the nuclear reaction was initiated it would probably sustain itself, but it did not quite have enough mass to initiate the nuclear reaction to cause it to become a star. The archaic race could have initiated nuclear reaction, but they felt it was not necessary to have two suns in this system. They felt it would adversely affect the new life developing on Earth.

D: *Yes, we would have had a sun on both sides of us. I wonder what effect it would have had? It would have made us hotter, wouldn't it?*

S: No, but more radiation.

D: *Jupiter has accumulated moons, so it does have the gravity to pull things in.*

S: Yes, it's almost like a miniature solar system in itself with the number of moons it has. The archaic race decided they would leave the decision to humankind, because they knew when humankind developed to galactic level they could trigger Jupiter into another small sun. It's still at the stage where you could trigger it, even though it has been considered a planet. But they thought they would leave that to the discretion of the dominant lifeform that developed.

D: *What would be the reason for wanting to do that?*

S: For extra living space. We could develop space colonies on the moons about Jupiter.

THESE EXCERPTS ARE BUT A SMALL SAMPLE OF THE KNOWLEDGE THAT CAN BE OBTAINED WHEN ACCESS TO THE LIBRARY IS OBTAINED.

CHAPTER 7
THE ALIENS SPEAK

When I first began to work with Suzanne in October 1986 she was bothered by several allergies, and we were looking for the source of her problem in past lives. She went into deep trance immediately and was an excellent subject. The sessions were highly successful. We had explored several lives and the information proved helpful. Her problem with asthma was traced to another lifetime when she died as a child from pneumonia. In the present lifetime anything that interfered with her breathing brought on the subconscious fear of death, and triggered an asthma attack.

When our next session brought forth space aliens, it was a surprise because we were definitely not looking for it. Suzanne had never experienced any sightings, dreams or any interest in UFOs, so this was the last thing she expected to find in a session. It was the beginning of my having direct contact with aliens, and having them speak directly to me. It was a spontaneous occurrence that was to establish a continuing pattern that would produce startling results.

We had almost finished a hypnotic session that brought forth a life in England in the 1930s. After her death in that life I took her to the world beyond to get information about the afterlife. This is my pattern when I have a good subject capable of deep trance. I try to gather information about different topics and then later combine and compare them for validity. Thus when I asked her to describe what she was seeing after her death, I already had an idea of what I expected her to say. In the beginning her voice was sluggish and she spoke slowly.

D: *Can you see anything there, or is there anything to see?*
S: (Pause) Well, I see ... a computer board.

That was a surprise. It was not at all what I was expecting based on what my other subjects had seen. These many other reports were combined and explained in my book *Between Death and Life*.

D: A computer board?

S: There are some beings. It is like they're monitoring something. They have controls and switches, and they're sitting in chairs and looking at something. I can't see exactly what they are monitoring. There are many things, maps and .... Now I'm above it all. Earth. I see the continents. And they're monitoring what's going on down there in the ocean, on the continents. They are observing it. They know more. I'm learning. And they're letting me watch. They do this because there's another force that guides them, and they are messengers for this force. They do it to help mankind.

I thought she was probably seeing the computer room on the spirit plane. The room I was not allowed to enter before. It was restricted because all the elements of a person's life are accumulated there, and the specifics relating to their next reincarnation are studied. Since I had directed her to go to the spirit (or so called "dead") plane, I was trying to compare her answers to what I already knew.

S: They understand more easily. Knowledge and technology are more advanced on these levels. A much higher level of understanding is taking place.

D: Can you see what these beings look like?

S: They're dressed in white. They look white all over. And they have a round head and look shorter, like a space body. And they have bigger eyes. They're sitting in chairs and moving things: dials and the switches. They have a big window to look out. It's in a round circle. There's a structure in the middle that is an orb object.

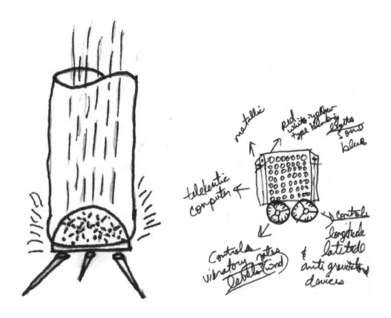

Drawing of orb object and control panels.

Half sphere flat edge on bottom. Seemed to be supported off floor by legs. Transparent inside a sparkling crystal seemed to be moving. Sparkling tiny pieces constantly in motion. Long tube coming from ceiling to enclose top part of sphere. Tube solid but transparent. Light (?) coming down through this. It had something to do with propulsion of the ship, and it also directed cloaking device. She was surprised when she said that. She didn't know where that remark came from. This device was located in the center of the ship.

D: *Then this is a physical craft?*
S: It can be seen or it can be camouflaged. It depends on what their primary mission is, what is to be monitored. The crystallized orb gives this craft energy to propel itself. And it also controls the anti-gravitational devices for this craft.
D: *You said they were allowing you to see this? Is that unusual to allow you to see what they're doing?*
S: (Mechanically) We have contacted before. They have monitored me before. They have probed me. And they do not mind because

I am a brother, and I come in peace. They want assistance from beings like myself.

D: *Do they care if I know these things?*

S: No. Not now. They want information translated.

D: *Would they be willing to share information with me?*

S: Yes. It has begun. They will use me to communicate.

D: *I would like to have information, and I want them to understand I would only use it for good. Do they know that?*

S: Yes. It is only for individuals that can do something with it. Who can apply it in a productive way. If not, it would be useless information.

D: *Do they understand how I want to use it?*

S: They're very telepathic. (Softly) They're making contact. (Then the voice changed and sounded mechanical, robotic once again.) We are scanning.

After a pause I felt as though I was being scanned. It was a tingly feeling throughout my body, especially in the head area. I do not believe it was mental suggestion on my part, because I didn't know what to expect. The feeling was definitely physical, and unexpected. I tried to remain calm, although this was very disquieting, so I could give them a clear impression of myself. But I had the feeling that it wouldn't make any difference. I felt they could see to the core of my being, and nothing could be hidden or falsified anyway. They could probably see me and my motives clearer than I could myself.

S: Certain phenomenon must be explained more clearly. And you are a bridge for information. You have the ability to write. This is necessary.

D: *This way it can be communicated to other people.*

S: I see a being. All white body. Short. Long, thin arms. Big head. Big dark eyes. I see his full body now. His legs. I don't see any clothes on him though. And he's kind of looking at me. He is looking at me.

The side of the ship she could see had a curved wall. Beings sitting at seats in front of screens and knobs and controls were oblivious of her. Only the one being was aware of her. She was unaware of his status on the ship. He communicated telepathically with her. She later explained that the beings had bald heads but appeared different from the cover of *Communion* because their eyes were not as slanted. Their bodies were similar to *Close Encounters* except not as childlike. Their limbs were stockier, thicker, more clumsy.

D: *Would he be willing to share some information with us?*
S: He wants to channel through me.
D: *How do you feel about that?*
S: I'm happy. (Laugh)

Ordinarily a statement like this would have unnerved a hypnotist, and they might be uncertain how to proceed. But I was working on the Nostradamus material at the time, so I had become accustomed to speaking with disembodied entities. My main concern was always the welfare of the subject. Once this was established, my curiosity took over, and I was filled with questions. I have found this is the easiest way to secure the connection, just start asking for information.

D: *I'm curious about him. What is this place?*
S: It's a craft.
D: *What is this room we are in?*
S: There's only one room. - He's trying to blend with my energy right now. He's trying to integrate. (A series of big deep breaths. Then a deeper voice.) One moment please.
D: *What? (I was startled. The voice was not Suzanne's.)*
S: One moment please.
D: *All right. But remember we are protecting her.*
S: Yes. No harm. No harm. (More deep drawn out breaths, then a mechanical sounding voice.) She must remove herself temporarily for this transmission to be more complete. She's blocking. I'm trying to remove blocks in her consciousness. She is not used to this type of experience. That's part of the block. She's not used to removing herself consciously from this vehicle.
D: *But this is natural. This is why we have to take it easy at first.*
S: I'm helping her. It will take some time, but it's a start. I can partially integrate through her. But it must be more complete to get the most accurate information, without her thoughts combining and altering this information. Do you understand?

D: Yes. That's why we want to be careful and do it slowly, so it will be more effective that way.

I was being the Mother Hen. I wanted to protect her as she went through this strange experience.

S: She must get used to integrating a higher type of vibration. Her will is open to this type of suggestion and communication. She's not blocking that way, but it's more of a physical block. Energies just used to being there. It needs to get used to being in an alternate state of consciousness. To wait there while communication takes place. Do you understand?

D: Yes, I do.

S: So I can give you partial information at this time, but I'm still working on her vocal communication. And the mental images ... she needs to get used to that type of transmission. I'm still more combined with her consciousness now, but in time she'll be able to remove herself more fully for temporary communication.

D: Okay. We're patient. Can you show me some of the things in that room and tell what they are used for?

S: The words are difficult at this time to convey exactly. Some of these questions you may want to repeat later, to get the correct wording. But I will try to come close to it in words she can describe. They may be similar but not exact.

D: The language and the words are always difficult.

S: We have a computer I'm showing her that has many lights on it. Like a square board, with little round lights completely covering it. Like a game board, or she's thinking in lines, in rows. Up and down, vertical, horizontally, completely covering a square type of silver board. These lights are all lighting. Red lights ... blue ... the colors mean different things when they're lit. And they are controlled by circular dials that have markings on them when turned to different positions. This is a main type of computer for our ship. It has a name, but I'm having a problem getting the name through. Something she says sounds like "Telekinetic board." It sounds similar, but it's not quite the right word. We're trying to convey to her something that sounds like "telekinetic." And there are what you describe as lines. Some are long lines, some are very short lines. These spaces between the lines going around the outer edge of the dial mark certain latitudes, longitudes, altitudes. They control these elements for maneuvering this vehicle. She just sees the surface of it. I'm trying to give her as much visualization as I can. There is a silver outer part to the computer. It's not really square. It's built *into* the craft. So she isn't able to see ... although she's now visualizing, behind all the little lights are many wires, or what you would see in a microcomputer if you opened it up. You would see many electrical type of connections, many wires, but made out of different materials than you find on your planet. It's a very complex system. You do not have a computer of this type, to our knowledge.

D: *What is different about it?*

S: The material it's made out of, what it's capable of doing. It controls antigravitational - she can't get the right word - maneuvers of the craft. There are people on your planet who are experimenting with antigravitational craft, but not at the level we have already developed it. They got some ideas from finding pieces of crafts that have crash landed on this planet. It's been kept secretive, I believe, by your Air Force. Not many people know, but they have copied the pieces as much as they can without the proper materials. They could only go so far with it, but they don't have the speed. There are so many things that will take evolvement for these things to be accurate. And certain materials will have to be used to produce these certain effects. That is one of the reasons we have chosen to communicate at this time to help man *to* evolve and advance at a more rapid pace. To help him explore other dimensions, to be able to travel to other dimensions and planets with more ease. I will go into more detail later about the intricacies ... Words ... that word. Again, it's not exactly what I'm trying to say here. But we'll go into more detail about the technical aspect of it. Her vocabulary for electrical types of things is not very expanded. That's why I must integrate energy more fully in her, because then I could convey it in more detail. Her consciousness is not very mechanically minded in this particular lifetime. I know that women of your species don't have a tendency to be that way. It is more what the men or male part of the species does. The ability is there, but the training has not been there. So if I communicate more fully through her, then I can get details to you more clearly. Which I think you would prefer.

D: Apparently the materials are very important.

S: Yes. Just as certain metals are used in your society for electrical purposes, for making computers. If it was made out of wood, as an example, it wouldn't work as well as made out of a metal type substance. So the material does play a significant part in the makeup of how these computers and generators, as you would call them, work. Some of these items can be gathered at other planets when you're able to transport there, whether in space shuttle or I see that as the first step for advanced transportation on a large scale. When these substances can be gathered from other planets, I think you will find many uses for them that will advance this society technologically and scientifically.

D: Do you think we could find substitutes on our planet that might duplicate some of these processes?

S: There are ways of alchemy. A mixing of certain metals, mixed differently than you might have thought. Yes, there are more possibilities than have been discovered thus far.

D: It would be developing a totally new metal then?

S: Yes. And it must be done a certain way, a certain temperature, a certain mixture. Substances can be created that are similar, not identical. You must use the resources that you have here.

D: Maybe we can come close anyway.

S: Yes, that's another reason this communication is taking place, to help man with some of these discoveries.

D: How large is this craft, if it only has one room?

S: (Pause, hesitating as though unsure.) Again, her estimate of size is limited. (Laugh) I want to say ... 3000 of your yards, what you call "yards," in diameter. Something in that range. Um, 300, 3000, um, ask again later on this. (Laugh) I think if she is shown a scale of what 300 yards would be, she would know whether it is 300 or 3000 of your yards.

D: Well, can you tell her what the outer shape of this craft looks like?

S: It's round in shape, with an oval top. A little flatter on the bottom than it is on the top, but like a bowl turned upside down. Silver, metallic. Windows on the side rim, around the edge. There are lights on this craft that are used at certain times.

D: I think you already told me something about the power source. It is located in the middle of the room? Is that correct?

S: Yes. The cylinder. Like a crystal orb. It generates the power for the craft. It's in a circular, clear kind of shaft. The top part of the orb is a half-cut circle, like a half cut ball.

D: *I'm familiar with some of the workings of crystals. I know there are many ways they can be used. Is it one large crystal?*

S: It is taken from crystallized substances from a different planet. And it is sculpted into an orb, like you might sculpt a crystal ball out of quartz. It is not see-through, yet there are things inside it, even in the orb shape. It is a transmuter for energy.

At first when I transcribed this tape I thought she intended to say "transmitter," but when I looked up the definitions I saw the difference between the words. A transmitter sends out something, where a transmuter *changes* or transforms something from one form to another.

S: It looks as if there are different colored lights flashing inside the crystal. It is not completely clear. In other words, there are shapes and forms inside it. Lights.

D: *And this is the main power source that operates everything on this craft?*

S: It is a major power source.

D: *It's not the only one?*

S: No, the computer controls other power sources. In case any power is damaged in any way there is another backup. A source that can replace that same amount of energy. So we are usually able to return to where we came from. It is a very rare thing that a craft crashes. And usually in that situation there are atmospheric conditions that played a part. The problem is not in the craft itself so much as atmospheric conditions combined with a mistake. One of the beings on the craft programmed something wrong. So the combination can exist in them.

D: *Then it is possible for your people to make mistakes?*

S: That too is very rare. We don't see it as what you call a "mistake," but there is always room to learn more. Things happen, but we adjust to the situation at that time.

D: *So you're not infallible, in other words.*

S: No. And it's just a normal process of being a living being, but we don't view it as a mistake that requires punishment. You beings seem to feel that when a mistake is made the feeling of guilt must be experienced. And then sometimes a punishment added to reinforce the guilt, so the mistake won't be made again. But we don't feel this is necessary. Whenever what you would call a "mistake" happens, we automatically compensate for it. The person is aware it has happened. That's all that's required, is that they are aware of it and best they will learn from it. These feelings of guilt, the punishments, are one of the major things that keep Earth beings - I will call them - from progressing at a more rapid rate. They're "hung up" on these type of phenomenon, and they keep themselves from progressing. It's an obstacle. And when these obstacles can be removed, a person or an Earth being can pursue more of his dreams. He can actualize things, make them happen more easily, because he's not holding himself back. Most of the illness stems from this. This planet is wrapped up with that same type of reinforcement. A real conditioning that is taught at a young age. It has to do with limitations. People have to learn how to overcome their limitations if they want to progress more rapidly. It helps if this conditioning is begun at a younger age, because once these behavior patterns have set in, it is not easy to dismiss them.

D: *This craft that you are on, can it travel by itself through space?*

S: What do you mean, by itself?

D: *Well, I keep thinking it's not that large. Does it come from another craft, or can it go back and forth to your home planet by itself?*

S: I'm being very basic with her at this time. I'm integrating this energy. I'd like to express things more ... flamboyantly, as you might call it, more boldly. But, to get back to your question: We must be able to return in case anything happened to the craft we were going to. If we couldn't return, we would be stuck in this atmosphere. And our bodies are not made of cells conditioned to this planet, to the atmosphere. We can come out of our craft for short periods of time. But even then we have to use a type of protection, because of the bacteria here. It is alien to us. And so in our craft, we set our dials to a vibration of a location, and we just transport there. It's like one big jump and then some short jumps, past the speed of light. There are other type beings that may do this differently, but as far as beings of our type, we can always go back to our home planet, if the planet has not been destroyed because of any atmospheric conditions or whatever. We thought this was wise in our thinking.

D: *Yes. But I'm getting the impression that you don't always do this. You said something about going to another craft?*

S: There are other crafts, which you would think of maybe in those words, a "mother craft." We have bigger craft. Different craft are used for different purposes. Smaller craft are used for monitoring things usually. Bigger craft are more for observations or telepathic communications. So it depends on the purpose of what size craft is used.

D: *Can you give me an idea where your home planet is? It may be difficult.*

S: Beyond what you call the North Star. Headed in that direction. Five stars past it, in a line. (Pause) I want to say "Centra." The planet sounds like it. She's not getting the word exactly right. Centeria? Something that sounds like it. Oh, I think it will come out more exactly later.

D: *Is that within our galaxy?*

S: No. Umm, it's light years beyond it. There are systems of an alien nature to you that are in closer range.

D: *Then you're from another galaxy, would that be right?*

S: I seem to get no and yes. It's a no and yes answer, because we travel to many galaxies. There is a home planet, but we aren't there very often. We're always traveling, exploring, and spend most of our time in crafts. We send information from our explorations back to the home planet, but we don't always go right back to the planet. We can send information without having to be there.

D: *Is this done telepathically or ....?*

S: Partially. But there are transmissions set up on our craft. And there is a transmission receiving type of instrument. It's like a thin metal pole set up on the home base, like you would think of as an antenna. And that's just set for our craft, and the information hits this thing, this pole. And is sent down and is decoded from beings there and recorded in our, what you would call, history books. And our scientific data on different lifeforms in the universe.

D: *And that pole antenna type thing is on the home planet? (Yes) Are you able to transport physical objects as well as messages over that long of a distance?*

S: No. Certain things we'll analyze on our craft. Then the information is sent. What we discover from our research on the craft, that information is sent in more of a word form or a communication type of form.

D: *Then you don't actually have to transport physical objects.*

S: No, that is usually never done. We would transport ourselves and the craft, but even that is a rare thing. We're able to maintain our craft in what you call "Earth space" for long periods of time. Time is not as you know it, to us. And we can travel many light years very easily. We've found enough resources in the galaxy to maintain our craft, and keep energy going through it. So it does not get worn out, as many things on this planet seem to wear out. The materials used in our craft last much longer. More durable, as you might phrase it.

D: *I have so many, many questions. I would like to ask about your body. Do you need any kind of sustenance, food, as we would call it?*

S: Fluids. There is a fluid we intake. The environment gives us things that sustain us. The atmosphere in our craft is kept at a certain temperature, consistency, so it maintains our physical vehicles so they do not deteriorate. We don't grow old as you know it. We stay in one form. When a being is "born," as you call it, it does start as a smaller form. When it reaches maturity, it stays in that form. There is not old age duration. We can maintain ourselves through our mental abilities, like using a visualization to keep oneself young. It is similar. It is almost programmed in us to be this way. If one of us is injured in any way, or has come into an atmospheric condition that starts to cause any type of deterioration, then we have a special fluid from our planet that is taken into our systems to help repair this. But it is only used for emergencies of this type.

D: *Then you don't need it all the time to survive?*

S: No. The atmospheric conditions inside the craft are set at certain temperatures and velocities that - I can't think of the right word. A certain atmosphere is created, and it will maintain our physical form. That is one reason we can't stay out of the craft for long periods of time, because it has a deteriorating effect on our forms.

D: The air, the atmosphere on Earth, you mean? (Yes) *Then you don't need food or anything like that, except this fluid. Do you drink that fluid?*

S: It's rather like drinking it, I guess, but it could be injected into us. It doesn't have to be drank, as you call it. There really isn't a need for food, as you know it.

D: Then the fluid is not taken through your mouth?

S: It can be put in that way, but more injected into the mouth instead of drank. It's as if you were giving somebody - what she is thinking - like an IV or something. A tube put in and something put through it. You see, that's why it's for emergencies. There is some plant life on our planet that can be taken into the system, but it's not necessary. Our systems, or our "bodies" as you call it, have everything we need to sustain it if the atmosphere is right. You see, when one intakes food it produces a growing effect which produces an aging effect later in the human form. That's one of the reasons we can maintain ourselves at one size, because of not having this intake of food that changes sizes in our bodies. It would produce an aging effect later.

D: That's an interesting idea. But what is that fluid composed of, roughly?

S: Nothing found here on this planet, but perhaps there could be something I could compare it to. She's getting a picture of a red type fluid, but it's not blood. More of a vitamin type substance. Maybe she's thinking of a red vitamin fluid. As you might think of maybe B 12 or B 6 vitamin, I think, if it is injected in a fluid form. It might be of a similar consistency, of something of that nature, like a vitamin fluid, but different.

D: I was wondering if you had an emergency and couldn't get the fluid, if there was anything on Earth you could substitute.

S: We would try to go back to the planet to get it. Or we would try to go to another craft that may have some extra, and get it that way. Usually there is another craft we can locate first before we would have to go back to the home planet.

D: Then it seems that the most important thing, as far as surviving, is the atmosphere within the craft.

S: Yes, it's important for our type of bodies.

D: This must remain constant?

S: As I said before, we can leave the craft for short periods of time. It's easier for us to leave it in energy form without taking the physical body with it. Do you understand? We can move an energy projection of ourselves more easily without being affected by atmospheric conditions, as another way of protecting ourselves.

This may be an explanation for reports in this book of wispy, non-solid beings.

D: *This way you're not endangering the physical form.*
S: Yes, we have to maintain a mental state when we go outside the craft, if in a physical form. We program ourselves so that we'll remain in a constant state of atmospheric condition, so not to be affected by it. But we cannot hold that mindset forever. We have to again change it. And that's why we prefer to do it only for a short period of time. Does that explanation help?
D: *Yes, I think I understand. If a human being was within the craft, could they breathe or live in the same atmosphere?*
S: We don't prefer to take beings onboard our craft in a full physical form. Unless they have some protection around *them*, and we are protected from that being, too, because they wouldn't be used to the atmosphere on our craft. We put them in a similar mindset before they're taken aboard. A trance type state. We protect their consciousness so it can handle a different type of atmosphere without causing physical harm. But, again, if an Earth being were on our craft for very long - usually they are immediately returned - they would have difficulty maintaining selves in that atmosphere. In fact, I think it could cause perhaps a health problem, other than just adjusting to us. But they might be in a state of mild shock to the whole experience. A combination of the two could damage that being's health. That's why these things are done for a very short period. Other beings sometimes do not return an Earth being. But that being probably would eventually expire after a short period of time. We prefer not to do that, because we are here to help. Some beings view human life in more animalistic terms, and treat a being as you would a cow. You know, perhaps dissect it for scientific reasons, just thinking of it as an unintelligent animal. Usually never to eat or anything

of that nature, and they probably would wait until the being did expire before any type of such experiments would take place. But we *honor* the life here. We have made a commitment, in the council, to help the beings here, even though we are more advanced. We see hope in these beings. And they are reaching out to us, too. They have honored us and we honor them. But some beings from other systems that are not a part of the council don't view the human life as a valuable thing, as we do.

D: *I'm glad you do. Because this way, we are in a similar mindset. I think we'll be able to communicate better that way, because we both feel the same way about life.*

S: There has been a being or two that has been transported to our planet and other planets. Other space beings have done similar things, but it's a very rare thing. The only way it is possible without that being expiring before it gets there, is to take it immediately onboard, and to *immediately* go to a home base planet. Because time is significant in its being able to survive the experience. It is not always a pleasant experience, yet some beings desire for this to occur. And that desire creates an opportunity for it to take place. But once they are there, sometimes they aren't as pleased as they think they would be, because they get lonely for beings of their same type. It's interesting for them for a while, and they feel honored to have been especially selected. But they yearn for a mate, as most beings.

D: *They would have to be kept in a special atmosphere there, wouldn't they?*

S: Yes. Like I said, human beings are wrapped up with their emotions. They can feel more obstacles, and because of that they experience what's called "loneliness." And it can affect a being so much that it does not want to live any longer. I don't understand the reason for this.

D: *Couldn't they be returned if they were experiencing things like that?*

S: (Sigh) Most of them would have difficulty surviving an experience like that twice without expiring. It is a great shock to the system. They're not used to traveling in those speeds, and usually they require immediate medical type of attention when they arrive there. Some of them don't survive the trip there even, because of this hurt on their system. Most of them desire just to have someone else, another being, transported there rather than to return.

D: *They think they want to do it, but whenever it happens they find out differently.*

S: If that being advances enough from our teaching, then they may be given an opportunity to go on a craft from that planet. Short distances to travel to learn how to control a space craft, but usually they would only be capable of going a short distance. It would be difficult for them to learn how to travel such a far distance, without a certain type of body made for that type of travel. Ours are. Our bodies can go at high velocities and speeds, such as light years etc., without causing physical harm to us. But a human body has limitations to it, you see. So it can't handle that type of travel as easily until it's more evolved. There are higher evolved beings that have a human form that do travel in space. But they *aren't* human, you see. They have a human appearance, but the cellular structure has been altered. They are more evolved. And that is why they can space travel, while other human beings would find it more difficult to maintain themselves without having a serious physical side effect from that type of travel.

D: *Then they look human but they're really not. Do these type of beings come to Earth also?*

S: Yes, they visit here, too.

D: *Then it would be deceiving, wouldn't it? We would think they were human.*

S: Yes. You see, there are some forms that can take on many forms. They use it as a tool, to study and observe the people more closely. Some of them aren't as affected by atmospheric conditions as our type are. Those type of beings that are capable of this are very advanced.

D: *You mean they form a body?*

S: It's just like being, what you would call, a "chameleon." It can change its form to blend in. They really basically are energy. If you saw them without taking on a form, it would be a liquidish type looking energy. Floating.

D: *Floating? Would it be solid?*

S: When it takes on a form it has a solidity to it. But if you saw them in their natural form, it would be more of a liquid fluid energy type of being. Like your spirit in your body is, without the body attached to it. It would look similar. But these beings are more advanced even in their so called original or normal condition. What we would call "spiritual form" is like a physical form for them, in a way.

D: *But they are capable of making a body.*

S: Yes, they do manifest things very easily, because they're very advanced.

D: *It seems there's much we don't know about.*

S: There are many forms. Just as on your planet alone there are many forms of living things. Many species, insects, animal species, plant life. You know, it's hard for one person to name all of the different type of species. So if you can look at it in that way, you'd see that in the universe there are many, many forms out there, too. And even on other planets there are many other types and forms of life. There are insect life, plant life, which are very different from your planet.

D: *You said when they do take a human being onboard they put them in a trance state. And this is to adjust them to the environment in addition to protecting their psyche. Would that be right?*

S: Consciousness.

D: *Their consciousness?*

S: Their psyche, too, yes.

D: *I always thought it was a kindness that sometimes people don't remember these experiences, so it wouldn't disrupt their normal life.*

S: It is to protect them from coming out of the experience in a full state of, what she would call, "shock." Our purpose is not to harm the individual, so we wouldn't want to incur such an experience on them.

D: *But it's also so they can adapt to the atmosphere.*

S: Yes, it is a combination.

D: *But they can only hold that trance state for so long, and then they would have to come out of it.*

S: Yes. That is why most of them are returned very quickly. Time is almost stopped, as you know it. These things can happen in the blinking of an eye. Time can be altered, and things can happen that are hard for man to comprehend at this stage of development. But that is why these different beings have the experience. Even as *this* channel had an experience. It was in almost the blinking of the eye that many things took place, because time was altered in the human being's mind. But in our mind it has not really altered. It's just natural. (Chuckle)

D: *It's natural to you anyway. I've often thought a type of hypnosis was used on the individual.*

S: It's a telepathic transmission sent to that individual's consciousness. Something they are capable of receiving. Also there are different points in the brain that can be stimulated. Like an opiate, she would call it, to produce that sort of effect. If the energy is *pushed* on to a certain part of the brain, it can produce a trance type state. This type of consciousness is similar to what is happening now. That is why you can do what you are doing now in a hypnotic state, as you call it. A certain part of the consciousness has been stimulated by a form of communication by a form of energy. It's similar, but this energy is a much higher velocity; it's stronger. That part of the being's brain would be much more strongly stimulated than it would in this type of trance state.

D: *Some people do have partial memories, and other people have flashbacks in dream state, and then others remember nothing at all after these experiences.*

S: The reason for this is because every being's brain is a little different. And it is going to react a little differently than another being's brain. The basic setup is similar, but these positions where the pressure points are in a person's head, are a little different in each person. Just slightly altered. The different cellular structure and the chemicals that go through a person's brain will be altered by what that person does. The drugs that person has ingested, the food that person takes. If somebody's hit their head there is a fluid in the brain that has to adjust to it. If there's a concussion, etc., etc. Medical conditions also affect the brain. Intoxicants taken into it affect the flowing of the fluids. All these are factors in how that person will react to that type of experience. That is why some have better recall than others. Because when that energy is pushed into that person's brain, some will adjust to it differently than another. That's why some will remember and have more recall and others won't. Also, it depends on the level of development of their consciousness. What they're willing to accept and deal with. While others are afraid of re coming into touch with an experience like that. They're more likely to hide that total experience from themselves, because they're afraid to face it.

D: So it's very individual.

S: Yes, it is.

D: But it's interesting that we're able to have access to these memories by the use of hypnosis.

S: It's stimulation of certain points and cells in the brain.

D: Memory banks or what? I've always been curious about how it works.

S: There are electrical transmissions. It's like electrical nerves are transmitted across different parts of the brain. There are parts of human beings' brains that store data, information. Other parts are used for creativity and manifesting ideas. But it's like an electrical current darting across to reach another end of a thread. I know that, physically speaking, that's what it would look like if you could see it.

D: When a person is put into a trance and taken on the ship, does this produce blocks within the mind?

S: Blocks of consciousness to protect that individual. An experience like that can be very upsetting to a being that's not used to having those type of experiences. So just as someone who has, say, a car injury, or has an accident. Their brain automatically protects itself from certain types of pain that person is going to experience. It automatically puts it into a different state of consciousness. That is why some people have an out-of-the-body experience. Their consciousness is trying to protect itself from the "horror" as you might call it, or the "fright" of that experience. It protects itself in a similar fashion as an out of the body experience.

D: That makes sense to me. But then hypnosis can go around these protective blocks.

S: They open these closed doors.

D: But I do know it only happens if the person is willing.

S: Yes, the will is what keeps the door slightly ajar.

D: If they don't want to remember or to experience ....

S: Then they close it. People that have these type of alien experiences have a connection with this or it usually does not occur. Their *desire* is there first for an experience like that to happen. They *want* to expand their consciousness. They may not admit it, but they're ready for that experience before it will happen.

D: *Yes, I believe that. - Well, I really appreciate everything you've been telling me. I would like permission to come again and speak to you. May I do that?*

S: Yes. I will be able to give you better description of things in time when she's more used to this type of transmission.

D: *I think you've done very well today.*

S: I'm just barely integrated in her energy field, just barely. We have already made an agreement to communicate through this vehicle. We want to be of assistance and help.

D: *And I thank you for allowing us to speak to you.*

S: Thank you.

I then brought Suzanne back to full consciousness. I was interested to find out what she experienced as the alien being spoke through her. I turned the tape recorder back on.

S: As soon as I woke up I remembered seeing a being with a white head, no hair at all. But I see big, dark eyes. It was staring at me. Really looking at me. It seemed to be communicating with me on other levels than I spoke about. And it was emitting certain things to me beyond what I could convey verbally. And I got a real sense of presence of his head, how it was peering at me, while I was becoming more conscious. There was a definite contact made with this particular being, and there was a very strong energy. I still feel part of that energy in my head right now.

D: *But it's a good feeling, isn't it?*

S: It's a comforting feeling, yeah, I mean it feels good. But it's very strong, almost trance like.

D: *And that's all you remember right now, was that he was staring at you?*

S: Right now.

She said this being seemed to be putting a lump of information into her head and "scanning" her brain. Much more was inserted than she told me. When asked how to contact him again, he showed her a symbol of a "triangle." She called it a pyramid and didn't seem to know the meaning it had for me. This symbol has been seen in many abduction experiences, usually onboard a craft or on an insignia. Suzanne was not frightened by this experience. She felt exhilarated and excited. She had the feeling it was not a matter of giving the information to the "wrong" people, but why bother giving it to someone who wouldn't know what to do with it. She felt something physical when he said he was scanning me. I felt a prickly scalp feeling, like when your scalp is falling asleep.

The next session with Suzanne was held at the first MUFON UFO Conference in Eureka Springs in March 1987. This was the only time the conference was sponsored by MUFON. The next year Lou Farish and Ed Mazur took it over, and have called it the Ozark UFO Conference ever since. The main presenters at this conference were retired military investigators in the original Blue Book and Grudge Projects, so it was geared toward skepticism, and official denial of the whole UFO phenomena. More interesting experiments were taking place away from the conference hall.

Lou was the only person I was sharing information with about my fledgling cases. As I took my first baby steps into this type of investigation I had to have someone I could trust to discuss these cases with, and to bounce theories off of. Lou proved to be that person, and he has never betrayed my trust in all the years we have worked together. He knew about the surprise twist of my regression session with Suzanne. Lou Farish said he would like to sit in on a session and ask questions, as he had in other meetings in Fayetteville and Mena. We thought this would be the best chance, at this conference, since everyone would be together in one place. Many other people also expressed interest. This would certainly be a change of pace from the hours of official denial we had endured at the conference.

Suzanne was naturally nervous about the session, because she had never done this in public before. This contributed to an uneasy situation as we went to the motel room after the conference had ended for the night. She became more nervous when she saw the crowd that was gathering. She asked several of them to leave. We tried to do this in a discreet way so they would not be offended. There were still about ten people present in the motel room. Most were investigators I had met at the other meetings, but one was John Johnson, a black psychologist who later worked with me on UFO cases. In the years that followed he became indispensable as I groped my way in a field where there were few experts in the 1980s. We were all learning from each other, and from our own mistakes.

John gave the impression of a quiet, reserved gentleman. He was not talkative, and sat quietly observing. Not knowing him, I was afraid that the idea of communicating to an alien through a girl in trance might be too far out for him. I was more concerned about what he would think than the others, because they had all been exposed to the type of work I do. But he surprised me by saying he believed in reincarnation, and understood what was going on. He was working with dying patients in the Veteran Hospitals, so he was definitely into the metaphysical way of thinking. I was pleasantly surprised and relaxed as we prepared for the session. I turned my attention to Suzanne. I was a little concerned about the results, since this was the first time she would be put into trance before so many people. I had no idea what would come forth.

She was apparently worried also, because she began breathing deeply in an attempt to relax. She needn't have worried, because I knew the keyword would do the job with little effort on her part. The lights in the room were disturbing her, so we turned them all off and opened the bathroom door to allow that light to shine in. Thus, everyone sat quietly in a semi darkened room, waiting for whatever was to occur. I used the keyword and counted her to the scene where we had spoken to the being, in hopes of finding him again. If we were successful, I intended to repeat some questions I had already asked, for the benefit of the investigators in the room.

D: *I will count to three and on the count of three we will be there, back at that scene. 1, 2, 3, we've gone back to that scene again. What are you doing and what do you see?*

I was surprised by a commanding tone of voice. "Be specific!" It was almost as though we had intruded or interrupted someone. I was taken off guard.

D: *Be specific? All right. The last time we spoke I was trying to find out more about you and your craft.*

The mood changed suddenly and the tone of voice was very soft. "What do you want to know?" Then louder and almost impatiently, "What information are you seeking?"

D: You told me the craft you're on now has only one room. Is that correct?

S: The one you referred to before?

D: Yes. Or where are we now?

S: I am inside a craft. I am not always on the same craft that we have spoken about before. I transfer occasionally. So some crafts are used for different purposes.

D: The one you are on at the present time, what is that used for?

S: What you might refer to as a "scouting craft." It is used to observe. I am trying to speak with her consciousness. It is a bit of adjustment for her. The energy is different, and she's trying to adjust.

D: Okay. But remember no harm to the vehicle.

S: No harm.

D: It takes a while to get used to it, doesn't it?

He apparently didn't want to beat around the bush and engage in small talk, but wanted to get down to business. "What do you want to know?"

D: All right. You said the craft is used for scouting? What type of function do you mean?

S: (Mechanically) To observe, to monitor beings. All types of life forms.

D: Why do you do this?

S: This data is sent many light years beyond this planet to a home base planet. It is then analyzed again by other beings there. I merely send it there. I get as much information as possible that I am capable of communicating. We have a communication device that makes it easy for us to send information long distances.

D: What type of device is this? How is it powered?

S: It is probably difficult for you to understand it completely. We are very telepathic type beings. We can mentally send information very far, but we also have a sound device. A vibrational sound is emitted and sent. Sound travels farther than you might have discovered. There are ways of sending it farther. We have a tube of a metallic, as you would call it, type substance. Vibrational sound is kind of pushed into it, and pushed out through it. It must be focused in a certain direction to a certain location, a certain vibratory spot, which we set our dials at. And it is immediately transferred there. There is, what you would call, a bit of a time lapse because of the distance. Sometimes a matter of what you would call "days" before it would actually reach there.

There was some disruption in the room as one of the people started coughing and got up and went into the adjoining room. My attention was distracted.

D: *And this is powered by this sound directed into it?*
S: And a message encoded into the sound. Like you have a Morse code, similar. Does that make sense to you?
D: *Yes, it does. Although we wouldn't understand the sound, I can understand the concept.*

This was the same concept Phil had presented in *Keepers of the Garden*, that some alien communication was sent over long distances by tones.

D: *I think you told me before there was a pole, an antenna like device on the other planet? Is that correct?*
S: It is a receiver for these messages. There is a sender type of pole and a receiving type of - what you would call a "flagpole." A very tall metallic cylinder. It's sent to that exact location, to the exact same vibratory position. That's why it will end up there and not be misplaced. As an antenna receives a radio transmission, this is used in a similar fashion, as a receptor tuned into that frequency.
D: *And you said the information was decoded at the other end, and put into your files? That you were keeping records on different life forms?*
S: Well, we don't keep files as you do. It is kept in our, what you might call, a memory bank. That information, once it's there, is never forgotten. It can be recalled very easily. We don't have to put it in a book. We do have places where we store different samples of things. They are kept in a certain location in, what you might call, an underground type of container, to protect it from the elements of our planet.
D: *Are all the records of Earth contained there?*

S: We are not concerned with all the records of Earth. We have what we want from Earth, and many other planetary systems. We just get what we're interested in. We don't need it all. We can figure out many of the life forms here already. It's very easy for us.

D: *Is it all right if other people ask you questions?*

S: I will try to answer them, too, to the best of my ability in this combined energy state.

I thought the people would want to question aloud, as they had at other sessions, but some began handing me notes. It was difficult to read them in the semi darkness.

I read the first question: *"How are you able to physically transverse these vast distances?"*

S: There are many different methods of transference of energies. Electromagnetic, thought, and others that all accomplish the same task. In many instances there is simply the transference from one dimensional reality to another. Also there is simply the mental adjustment that allows that energy in the control of those who are commanding this ship to simply do as is told. That is, as in thought transference. You need only place yourself mentally in one area to be there. As your awareness and understanding of your realities expands, you shall see that your mental power can have a direct influence on those physical objects around you. Such that when those objects are resonating at *your* identical mental frequency, then *you* have absolute control over that physical object. Your world, as it is now, is somewhat scattered in its frequencies such that there are no two resonating alike. However, when these materials are in resonance with that mental energy, then they too are transferred with this mental energy. They simply appear and disappear according to those thought commands which control them. You will be given that technology (for thought propulsion of craft) in short order. However the council at this point has no way of allowing you this technology until such time as you have progressed to a more responsible level. You have already jeopardized your entire planet's existence with your nuclear energy. You know not what you do, however you do it anyway. We would ask that you please not jeopardize the rest of the universe with it.

I read the next question: *"What type of information are you gathering about human beings on Earth?"*

S: Human beings are special and unique in many ways. That's why we are trying to assist them at this time. We also are interested in the planet itself, environmental changes occurring on it. The beings are *less* advanced, almost animalistic at times, but there is much hope for these beings. They are developing, advancing rapidly, with our assistance. We have been working with Earth beings for a long time. We influence telepathically, through dream states, to help man advance technologically, scientifically. To come to what men might call "emotional maturity." Emotions cause great havoc for man, until he learns how to master them, control them. He must learn how to propel himself with his positive energies, and how to transmute the negative energies. The negative energies are emotions: anger, jealousy, these type of emotions that you are familiar with. These are man's downfall. These hold man back from progressing. The positive emotions propel him into advancement. But this may take some time for the whole planet to come to this realization.

D: (Reading) *The type of being that you are, do you have emotions?*

S: Not as you do. There is a feeling of closeness between our beings when they want to, what you call "reproduce." A being will *bond* with another being for this purpose. But we are not hung up with these emotions, as you are. There is not the *attachment*. We are more detached, because these emotions can be an obstacle for advancement. It is not in our nature to let a *feeling* stop us from advancing. Some other space beings *are* fascinated by these emotions, just because they don't experience them in the same way. They are curious, but they see it as almost an obstacle. They think it can be helpful. It depends on how you want to use those, what you call, "feelings." If they're used in a positive way they can help the being advance. It's up to the individual.

D: *I was wondering if you understood emotions as we know them.*

S: We observe them in other beings. We understand enough for what we need to know. But we see men as energy channels, as an energy. There are spinning vortexes in a human body that channel all different types of energies surrounding him. Many beings aren't aware of this.

Was he referring to the chakras in the body? They are often spoken of as spinning, and they have to spin or function in harmony in order for the body to maintain a healthy balance.

S: But we think there is hope for man. He is a special being. If he can use his potential, his gifts, more fully, he can advance in many ways that will benefit himself and the whole universe.

D: *That sounds very good. Are you sexual beings then?*

S: We are androgynous. Either one of us could reproduce, in other words.

D: *I am curious about that. Do you mean you would take turns at the different sexes, or do you have both sexes in one body?*

S: Telepathically in our case. We mentally project an image of what is to *grow*. It's not growing as in "growing older." But there is a swelling in the, what we would call, "stomach" region. The younger being is formed in a very short period of time compared to what a human being would endure for this. And when the being comes out through the stomach type area, as you would call it, it immediately seals back again. There is no surgery necessary or incision. It is all done mentally. The beings come out a little smaller in size. And then they come to a stationary size and remain there, as long as atmospheric conditions are kept a certain way.

D: *Then you just decide when you want to reproduce. It's not an automatic thing.*

S: It's a mutual decision between two beings as to which one would want to. We can trade off, so to speak. It does not matter. But our beings are very advanced at a very young age. As soon as they can walk they are shown galaxy maps, and become immediate star travelers. That is our nature. We are very advanced in that area.

D: I guess I am curious about emotions. Do you have any type of feeling toward these young, these children?

S: Not in the same way you do.

D: *Do you have a nurturing?*

S: There is a nurturing, a *teaching* desire, but it's not emotional. It's just instinctual for us. The teaching instinct. To teach the young to maturity. And our young automatically learn what they need to. It is ingrained in their makeup, in my makeup. It's just what you need to know, and the evolvement just comes out. It's very easy. There's an instinct to teach, to advance. There is not the nurturing type instinct. It is not the same. Although if one of our beings is injured or harmed in any way, there is a type of feeling sent out. It's not really a sadness, as you would call it, but there is a vibration sent out. There is a yearning for that being to be complete again, but it is not sadness as you know it. And something, if possible, will be done to help repair that being, if that does happen.

D: *I'm trying to understand how you are alike and how you are different from us. You would never have any negative emotions, like anger? (No)*

I was handed another note: *"What is the most common type of being that is visiting our Earth at this time? A physical extraterrestrial being."*

S: The humanoid subgroup of ... I cannot find a translatable equivalent, however, there are subgroups of the general category of humanoid. There are many that are identical to your physical bodies. The seeding that was done on your planet was of this nature. And there are those that are distantly related, yet very unconventional by your standards. This type, the distant cousin, is the more prevalent of the visitation type. The androids, as you might call them, are simply workers who volunteered for this mission. They removed themselves from that area in which they were programmed, to volunteer their services in this "accomplishment." I hesitate to use the word "experiment," for the outcome is already predicted and known. However, not to say "mission," for the majority of the work ... I find I must discontinue this line of discourse. I am being told there is arising a misunderstanding of the intent of the direction taken. The information given has been misconstrued as aggressive and not of a helping nature. We would not wish to promote the idea that we come as conquerors, however as helpers.

D: You mentioned that the outcome was already known. Can you tell us what you mean by that?

S: The ultimate outcome, not the individual and personal outcomes, which each of you must create in your own fashion.

D: What is the ultimate outcome?

S: The raising of the human race to universal level of awareness. To be brothers of the star people, and not subjugates or subordinates.

D: What do these androids look like?

S: Those which you have described as gray in appearance and small in stature are typical. The eyes of course are the most prominent, simply because they are the communicative receptors.

D: Do their eyes function the same as human's eyes?

S: In a sense. They see, however they collect much more of what you call your visible light spectrum. Also including the infrared and ultraviolet regions.

D: Do their eyes have pupils and function in the same manner that ours do?

S: Not in the sense that they focus and capture light. In that sense they are different. They do receive, yet their method of reception is somewhat based on a different principle involved here.

D: Do their eyes have eyelids?

S: Not in the sense that they cover. Not as you would say yours do.

D: Do they have similar respiratory systems as we do?

S: They are similar only in the fact that they are used to analyze, not to digest or ventilate.

D: Is there a matter of sustenance for the body among these people?

S: Pure mental energy is sufficient. They need no physical sustenance to maintain. They are energy beings that can maintain on pure energy.

D: Then this is what we refer to as eternal life.

S: Not so, for the bodies are dissimulated after their use has expired.

D: Then they do not consume anything, like a human would?

S: Not in that gross physical sense.

D: What about osmosis? You said they were energy beings. Would they assimilate by osmosis?

S: There is the assimilation. Analyzing of compounds, and perhaps rectification of certain anomalies that may appear. However, as sustenance they derive energy more from energy sources than from digestive or respiratory functions.

D: *Do you mean like elements present in the atmosphere? Or what type of energy would they live on?*

S: Mental energy sustenance.

D: *Would they thrive on emotions?*

S: There is no emotional content here. These are called androids that are emotionless, yet responsive to mental energy.

D: *I mean, would they thrive on emotions thrown out by others?*

S: They would be affected, however, not sustained.

D: *Are these beings subject to any afflictions that limit their life terms?*

S: There are none that we could relate. However, there are those that in proper context could be debilitating.

The questions were being handed to me in groups, and I was trying to organize them in the dimly lit room.

D: *How are these creatures produced? Are they cloned, manufactured or what?*

S: There is a process in the central part of the ... to use an analogy, it is similar to the county or perhaps state in which your political system lies. A process assigned to that planet which holds the residence of those energies that are of the gubernatorial nature. The process is a blending of energies, both physical and mental in nature, such that this physical construction is then given mental responsiveness. Not to say mental identity, however a mental responsiveness that allows this physical creation to respond to mental stimulation. Those androids are responsive to your mental energies, but yet take orders or are subservient to those who are directing that particular operation in which one would find them. They are servants.

D: *Are they cloned, or manufactured in some way? Made by another individual?*

S: They are both, in the sense that the mental energy is given by life forces. However they are in a sense manufactured in that the process is more of assembly than growth. However, there is living or life force in these units, yet they are elements or machinery.

D: *Do the androids communicate with people on Earth?*

S: I wish to clarify that they communicate, not with Earthlings, but with those who are their superiors. A human would not direct the operation directly. However they do respond to human emotion, but not to the extent that they interact with the intellect.

D: *Who are their superiors?*

S: Those who are responsible for that particular mission, in which there is an interaction. However, there are elements of awareness far above and beyond even that. It is as if the masters of the universe are sending out those underlings who would then participate in whatever mission is desired and then report back. Much like your military structure.

D: *Do they understand human emotion?*

S: That is accurate. They are empathetic.

Another question: "Do these androids have the ability to reproduce other androids?"

S: That is not accurate. The androids would not be capable of procreation. They are not self-sustaining in nature. They are simply *creations* that are, through a bonding process, given a life force that reacts with and is empathetic *to* the life force with which they come in contact. They are not however procreative.

D: *Are there any other beings on these craft with these androids?*

S: Certainly. There are many, who are of many different forms, but they do not necessarily *have* to be.

D: *Are they more like us? Having to have sustenance and ....*

S: That is accurate.

D: *What do those type of beings look like? The most common ones that accompany these androids?*

S: They too are humanoid in appearance, and yet are oftentimes unobserved. They are perhaps, seeing but not being seen. They are not readily apparent to those who are taken aboard.

D: *They don't usually reveal themselves to the person, you mean?*

S: That is accurate.

D: *If they take sustenance, what type would that be?*

S: Those elements and minerals that would be necessary to their bodily functions are given in fluid form.

D: *This would not be in the form of solid food, as we know it?*

S: Not of the same type that you yourselves would sustain.

D: *Are there any elements or anything on Earth that these beings require? That they must get from Earth?*

S: There are elements of energy, not so much the physical compounds themselves. The energies that are prevalent on your planet. The spiritual aspects of electricity and water are examples.

D: *I was wondering if they needed anything like water.*

S: Not in the sense that they need the water, but the energy of which water is simply a translation of.

D: *Is this the reason they've been seen over power stations?*

S: Possibly, but not necessarily. There could be many reasons why they would be over power stations. Observations. Manipulations. Experimentations.

D: *Are there large numbers of the planet's inhabitants undergoing a form of contact or communication with these beings?*

S: We would say that, yes, there are many who have volunteered for this.

D: *Why are these beings taking people on board these crafts? What is the purpose behind that?*

S: You must understand that your residence on this planet was not, as some feel, accidental. Nor was it, as others feel, accurate according to that which is called your Bible. That is, that God created man in his own image, such as is understood from a somewhat fundamentalist viewpoint. We would ask that you understand that the human existence on this planet was given by those who are now returning to examine the fruits of their labor, as you might say.

People were trying to ask me questions in a whisper. It distracted me for a moment. The being heard this.

S: And the question is?

D: *You said you use your ship for scouting, do you also scout other planets?*

S: Other planetary systems, in this solar system and in other solar systems.

D: *Have you ever discovered any intelligent life within our solar system, besides Earth?*

S: Oh, yes. There are dimensional beings. Some beings vibrate very fast. You cannot see them with what you call "physical eyes," but they are there. Some of them can be very highly evolved. And some of them exist even on your planet, that you're not fully aware of. There's more going on, on some planets in life forms, that you can't see with the physical eyes. If you were in a similar dimensional range you'd be more aware of it. Like my vehicle is telling me, there was discussion tonight about the possibility of life on the planet, what you call "Mars."

D: *Is there life there?*

S: Yes, more than one type. There is intelligent life there. The life forms there that are advanced are in forms of light beings. There are different degrees of light reflecting in them. They come as flashes of light. That is why they are not always visible to, say, a being of your type. When they want to manifest in a more light form they can do it. If they do not want to be seen, that is also possible.

D: *Then they don't have a physical body like we do.*

S: No, but there is an animal form less advanced than them. That animal life is there for a purpose. It helps with the - Words - the substance that the planet is made of. Their bodies are made to adjust to the environmental conditions there without dying. They are not the advanced life form there though.

D: *Is this a carbon-based type life form?*

S: Yes, there is a carbon type of substance in what you would call the "atmosphere." It is a mixture of the atmospheric chemical type ... chemicals - Words.

D: *Yes, the words are always difficult. I've been told many times that this language is insufficient. - I have another question. Have the extraterrestrials ever tried to contact people in a position of power on Earth?*

S: Oh, yes, many times. They have negotiation that has been going on for many years.

D: *Who did they negotiate with?*

S: It was with the government leaders. It has always been with the governments.

D: *What did the extraterrestrials promise in return as a barter?*

S: Sometimes the governments bartered for information on energy, information on medicine, information on extraterrestrial activity, information on lost astronauts.

D: (Surprised) *Lost astronauts?*

S: Many have been lost.

D: *In our time, in our twentieth century?*

S: Since 1960 many have been lost.

D: *How were they lost?*

S: They were sent into space and because of failures in the mechanics of these primitive vehicles they were not able to return to Earth. Some died in the vehicle. Others floated aimlessly until they were picked up by other ships, and taken to different places for study. Sometimes these individuals were allowed to return to Earth through these negotiations.

D: *Were they alive at that time?* (Yes) *But we, the public, believe we have known everything about all the flights.*

S: No. There have been very secret flights, both in the United States and Russia. Other countries have experimented too: Japan, China, England, Canada. All the so called "advanced" people have sent vehicles.

D: *We thought it was only the major countries, like the United States and Russia. You mean these other countries also have space programs, and places they can launch space vehicles from?*

S: At one time or another they did experiment. Many have discontinued because of their losses, and fear of public repercussion.

D: *So they have space stations in these different countries?*

S: In their military installations, yes.

D: *But if some of the men were lost, I would think we would have known about it.*

S: No, because of the fear of being stopped. And many times they didn't know where these people were. They didn't know if they were alive.

D: *Wouldn't the men that were brought back tell people?*

S: No, because they don't remember.

D: *They don't remember the flight and being brought back by the aliens?*

S: No. It was agreed upon that, if they were to be returned, all knowledge would be kept safe by disrupting their memory bank.

D: *Was this disrupted by the aliens?*

S: Yes. It was felt that the people on this planet were not highly evolved enough to know where some of these planets are, and about the technology. We do not want unsolicited visitation at this time.

D: But you said the government officials knew about this. Part of the bargaining was to know what happened to the astronauts?

S: Yes. They were told that we had them, and that we would or we would not return them. That is the extent of their knowledge.

D: Then the aliens keep track of our space flights.

S: Most definitely.

D: And you said these negotiations and bargaining are continuing even now?

S: Most certainly.

D: Are the aliens getting anything in return?

S: We have access to natural materials that we need, that are common here, but are not found so easily on other planets. And ... sometimes we take people to study.

D: How do you obtain these people?

S: In negotiations with governments. They allow us to have some.

D: Do they tell you whom to take? (Yes) *Why would they have* decisions over that? Couldn't you just take whoever you wanted?

S: Oh, yes, but we are agreeable to take who they choose.

D: I wonder how they decide which ones should be taken.

S: At first it was undesirables, and we decided we had had enough of those.

D: What type are considered undesirables?

S: Military personnel who did not achieve what was expected, or discipline problem type people. This also caused us some areas of concern, so we don't take these individuals any longer. Now those going with us volunteer their services for a limited amount of time. The time is agreed upon before they are taken.

D: Do you mean the ones you called "undesirables" created discipline problems?

S: Yes. They weren't very agreeable.

D: Well, the ones that are going now as volunteers, are they all military personnel?

S: No. Some are from the medical field, some are from the scientific community who wish to learn and experiment also. However, they volunteer knowing fully that when they return, all knowledge must stay with us.

D: Then when they return they don't remember? (No) *Can they explain that length of time they are gone?*

S: Generally it is told they are going on sabbatical leave.

D: Doesn't it bother them that they can't account for it, in their own mind, when they come back?

S: Sometimes it does. However, they are counting on the fact that within the next twenty years they will remember.

D: Rather like a time release thing? (Yes) *Well, the "undesirable" ones that were taken, were they brought back also?*

S: Some were, some were not.

D: I was wondering about their families. If they suddenly disappeared, how would that be accounted for?

S: Most had no families, or were alienated already.

D: This is why they were chosen? (Yes) *But the ones that are going now are volunteers. They're not being taken against their will.*

S: That is correct.

D: I think that's important. But it is still in cooperation with the government? (Yes) *There's been talk about underground bases, especially some in the United States. Do you know anything about that?*

S: There are many bases, both underground and above ground, of which you know nothing.

D: I have been told that at some of these bases, the aliens work with the government.

S: That is correct. We are trying to network our efforts and be open with our knowledge, provided it is for the right purpose. Up to this time it has been kept very secret, because the government has felt the general population was not prepared to accept the reality of such networking. Within the next two, maybe three, decades, all of this will become common knowledge.

D: Can you tell me what they are mainly working on together in these bases?

S: Space travel, energy systems, medical technology. Food storage and preparation, manufacturing supplementation.

D: Those are all good things. You would think they wouldn't mind the public knowing about them. Are these people of the medical and scientific world that are going now voluntarily being supplied information, or are they supplying information to the aliens?

S: Both.

D: Both ways. It's also been rumored that in some of these underground bases genetic experiments were being performed.

S: Yes, by the medical community, and also by other beings. This has always been of interest to other life forms.

D: *Is it the governments that are mostly performing these experiments? Whose idea is it?*

S: It was initially from the aliens. The space beings have always had an interest in this field, because they have been involved with it for so long. The *human* race is only concerned with the development of a super human being. This is not always in conjunction with the goal of the space people.

D: *Is that why the government agreed to these experiments? They're trying to create a super race?*

S: Not totally. It's only one aspect.

D: *Well, what would be the purpose then for our government being involved with genetic experiments?*

S: Some hope to find answers to genetic problem areas. Why they occur, how to prevent them. And once they occur, if it could be changed.

D: *That is a good idea. What about this creation of a super race? Is it proceeding?*

S: Many would like to see it proceed. However, it hasn't been doing very well, because of the fear of many involved on this Earth, that it would get out-of-hand. Their focus at this time is mostly on genetic weaknesses, and how to eliminate them.

D: *That's the major concern of the aliens?*

S: No. They would like to produce higher realms of beings, capable of a variety of accomplishments.

D: *It seems a super race of people wouldn't have emotions, or am I understanding that correctly?*

S: Emotions are a mostly human trait, not relevant on other planets. This is one area of study for us.

D: *Then the aliens are mostly interested in developing a new type of species of human? You said a higher species of some kind, not necessarily a super race.*

S: That is correct.

D: *There has been talk about the underground bases, that they were creating monsters: very horrible hybrids or deviations. Do you know anything about that?*

S: Sometimes things happen, and what is horrible, to use your term, to one species is beauty to another. When you start combining species in genetic experiments you will always get variations.

D: *The idea to us sounds rather repellent. But would these different species have a soul, a spirit, as we know it?*

S: Some do, some do not. It depends on from whence they came. If they are genetic mutants, robotic in nature, they have no spirit. They are strictly genetically created. If their source, on the other hand, was spirit natured to begin with, then the result of this will have a spirit function.

D: *What about the intellect? Is this creating another worker race, or are they intelligent like humans?*

S: There again, there are very many species being experimented with. Some are robotic in nature, who do not have an intellect. And some are very high in intellectual accomplishment.

D: *What will eventually happen to these creatures or these different species that are being created?*

S: Some have already been taken away to other planets, who are more open to the nature of these things.

D: *Will any of them ever be put on Earth?* (No) *Then the government knows these purposes of the experiments?* (Yes) *So the government doctors and scientists are also cooperating with this?*

S: Some are. Not all. A chosen few.

D: *And this is one of the things the aliens have negotiated. To allow the government to gain the knowledge of these experiments, and in return the aliens are given the natural materials they need.*

S: Correct.

D: *It's amazing how the government can keep all of this secret from the people.*

S: It is very well hidden, and it has been understood in the past that only very few would have knowledge of these negotiations.

D: *What about the President of our country, the United States? Would he know about these things?*

S: Some do, some do not. It depends on their personalities.

D: *I was wondering how they could keep these bases hidden, with military personnel, without the President knowing about them and their functions.*

S: Sometimes the President is the last to know anything.

D: *Then the bases are guarded, and the military personnel and the money come from other budgets or something.*

S: That is correct.

D: *I'm assuming they're well guarded. Is that true?*

S: After a fashion. They are not guarded as you would think. There are no guns or missiles. They are guarded in other ways.

D: *Well, we have heard of one in Nevada that has many armed guards, military personnel, and no one is allowed to get near it. Is that one of these places? (I was thinking about the infamous Area 51.)*

S: No, that's something else. That's strictly a military operation.

D: *The aliens are not involved in that?* (No) *It seems that having military personnel and guards would attract attention. Is that what you mean?*

S: Yes, but we are not involved in military ventures.

D: *We were told there are military weapons, like the stealth bomber, that came from alien technology. It was given to us. Is that true?*

S: In part. The technology was mainly given for travel. It was not meant to be used as a military vehicle.

D: *I see. Can you see what the military experiment is on the base in Nevada, that has caused it to be so highly guarded?*

S: The military experiment is to advance the speed of travel of military transport. Also, its weaponry, and its ability to shield against attack by enemy warriors.

D: *Enemy what?*

S: Enemy personnel.

D: *But yet, at this time we are thinking we have no enemies to defend against. Why would there be a reason to continue military experimentation?*

S: There are always those in control who want power over other races and humans. And to this end they are devoted to the development of mechanisms that will make this possible.

D: *Does the present President know about this military base in Nevada?* (George Bush in 1987.)

S: Yes, he does.

D: *So if it has something to do with military defense, he would know about it.*

S: That is correct.

By 1998, when this book was written, Area 51 was quietly and stealthily closed. Was it because of all the unwanted attention by the public and the media?

D: *It seems that there are many things going on that the average person doesn't know about. Is it all right for me to tell people what you have told us today?*

S: It will be all right, because within the next three decades it will be common knowledge. It is hoped that an alliance *can* be formed with the people of this planet, so we may come and go as friends. - My vehicle is about ready to wrap up transmission. I am sensing some more have questions. But it must be wrapped up rather quickly. She is tiring.

D: *All right. We don't want to do anything to make her uncomfortable. - Someone wants to know, is there anywhere else except Earth that has human type beings, that you have found?*

S: I described them to you in our last session. Fluid life forms. Liquid fluid floating. Like a chameleon. Can take many forms. Highly advanced being. Can blend in to many planetary civilizations by making themselves appear as the beings that are present there. Can take human form, can take space brother form, can take many forms. That is the closest to a human type form I think you come into encounter with on this planet.

D: *What about other planets? Are there other human types on other planets, that you have found?*

S: There is another planet. It has a similar human form, but not quite as advanced, because of the environment there. It's taking a longer time for them to evolve. Similar human features, but their nature is different from the beings here.

D: *I believe there are only a few more questions. Do any of the beings and/or associated craft come from or travel through or inside the planet Earth?*

S: That is accurate. There is the area that is partially beneath your Mexican gulf coast, that is, at this time, inhabited by those of the Atlantean descent. There is also the area beneath your Antarctic circle, which is inhabited by those who are interdimensional in nature.

D: *Is the planet as our scientists perceive it to be on the inside?*

S: It is a solid core with a floating mantle. However, not a continuous solid mantle.

D: *Is the Earth hollow?*

S: That is not accurate.

D: *Are large areas inside the planet hollow, suitable of sustaining a large civilization?*

S: Yes. Although not large in terms of total Earth volume. Large in the sense of space as compared to your distances. Large enough to sustain a civilization.

D: *In those areas you mentioned?*

S: Yes. There are others. However these are major in the sense that they are, at this time, playing a more prominent part in your upheaval.

D: *Did you say the vehicle is becoming tired?*

S: Yes. I can be of assistance when called upon. I have come to communicate data to help with man's advancement. To solve unsolved questions man might have. This will not be forced upon anyone. If you desire more information you may call upon me. I will be of assistance and communicate information to you. Telepathically, if necessary, to help with your advancement.

D: *All right. I do appreciate it. And I'm going to pass it on to other people, and it will only be done for good, positive reasons.*

When Suzanne came out of trance her stomach area was bothering her. She said she didn't exactly feel nauseated, but as though a lot of energy was swirling around inside her. There was a healer present and he worked on her. At our other sessions when Suzanne came out of trance she always felt wonderful and even awoke laughing upon occasion. Since this was the first time this had happened, I tended to think it might have been related to the nervousness she felt before we started the session. There were many people in the room and she might have picked up on their energy since she was in a sensitive state. Also, we had used this being's energy twice within a week's time. It might have been too much to do so quickly. It might take more time for her to get used to channeling this type of energy. I really thought it was a combination of many factors.

Since Suzanne had been in a deep state of trance she was not aware that other things were going on in the room during the session. It was caused by some of the investigators who refused to take this type of investigation seriously. As a result of the attempts to ridicule by snide remarks (which have not been included here), I decided not to allow this type of questioning again. I thought it would be a method to gain information for research and study, but I soon realized that the investigators in 1987 were not ready for this. Some of them had not yet approached the subject from the metaphysical angle. I had come to realize that unless the investigator understands metaphysics, they would never begin to understand the complex nature of UFOs and extraterrestrials. It is all interrelated, and cannot be separated, although the "nuts and bolts" type persist. I suppose there is room for all types of investigators in this field. We all hold bits and pieces of the puzzle. We cannot assume that our one small bit is the entire puzzle. There are too many shadings and variations, thus we have to learn to all work together.

Most of the people left, but a few of us remained and talked until after one o'clock in the morning. Suzanne took a shower about that time and then called me in to look at her feet. When she came out of the bathroom she noticed they were covered with large red blotches. The discoloration was only on the feet and did not extend up past her ankles. It was already beginning to fade back to the normal color of her skin. No one really knew how to explain it, unless it had something to do with the alien energy. It could also have related to the nervousness she felt before beginning the session.

At that time I didn't know that in the following years I would have other cases where the body would be affected by some type of similar energy. I was soon to become aware that the human body is capable of doing many things that the body is not supposed to do, when working in the deepest states of trance. The most important tenet to remember when doing this type of work is, "Do no harm!" But you must constantly be prepared for the unexpected.

I did not have any more sessions with Suzanne. This had been interesting to her, but she treated it as a strange curiosity and did not want to encourage the channeling of aliens. She was attending business school and was more interested in finding a job. I always respect the wishes of my subject, so I did not pursue it any further with her. I did not have to worry, because now that direct contact had been established with beings from another world it was to continue. They had found a willing listener, and communication would continue through other means. I had opened the door to another adventure.

I think it is remarkable that all the cases reported in this first section (and cases I have not included) follow a recognizable pattern. The same characteristics are repeated all over the world. There is a redundancy that cannot be fantasized, especially because in many cases the subjects were not familiar with UFO literature. In the 1980s, when most of these were investigated, there were not many books published on the subject. And even those that were in print did not focus on the facets I have uncovered. Such as: similar types of beings seen most frequently, similar types of spacecraft, similar procedures performed by the aliens, similar motives, and the repeated story of the seeding of the planet. These similarities give the stories validity, because there was no possible collaboration between the subjects. Also, while other investigators and publications were reporting the alien agenda as negative and evil, my cases consistently reported a benevolent creature. Even science recognizes that when an experiment is repeated and the results are the same, this is the credible evidence they require to establish validity. Most importantly, the people in this book did not wish publicity or notoriety. The opposite was true, they sought anonymity, and to respect their wishes their names and occupations were changed so they could continue to live their lives in privacy.

SECTION

TWO

CHAPTER 8
CONTACT WITH A LITTLE GRAY BEING

I decided to put this entire portion of investigation into a separate section, because it was the continuous work with one subject, Janice S. The other cases supplied valuable information that led me from the simple cases in UFO investigation to the complex. My work with Janice took a different turn. It resulted from the direct communication with the aliens themselves. The information they supplied over a period of three years took me deeper and deeper into complex theories and explanations that would have been impossible for me to comprehend in the early days of my work. I have always known I will never be given more than I can handle at the time. If the information is too radical or too much a departure from the norm, then there is the tendency to ignore it or to push it aside as not making any sense. If the information is spoon fed or given in small doses then it is easier to develop a new line of thinking about this phenomenon. Then what earlier was impossible to understand gradually begins to make a strange kind of sense, even though it does bend the mind and makes us think in a totally new direction.

This is what happened with my work with Janice. In the beginning it was following the same direction as the other cases, although supplying new information. Then it began to flow into areas that were so complex that I decided not to include it all in this book. This book was already larger than most of the books I write. But when it came to choices of cutting material to reduce the size the choices became difficult. As an investigator I considered all the material valuable in adding new insight. But as the sessions with Janice continued they left the area of UFOs and entered the area of different dimensions and complex theories about time and parallel universes. I was already working on another book about these subjects, *Convoluted Universe*, so I made the decision to move some sessions to that book so the reader would not be completed confounded and overwhelmed. By the time the reader is ready for the next book maybe their mind will also be ready to comprehend the theories involved.

When I first came in contact with Janice in 1989, I had already been working on UFO and suspected abduction cases since 1987. In those early days I traveled long distances to work on cases, and I tried to work with anyone that requested a session. That is not possible now. My schedule is so hectic with lectures and traveling to conventions, seminars, etc., that I no longer have time to travel just to work with one person. I no longer have that luxury. I am still accumulating information, but not in the slow paced manner that I did in the early days of my work.

In the summer of 1989 my first book *Conversations With Nostradamus, Volume I,* was in print and I journeyed to Little Rock to give my first lectures on the subject of the Nostradamus prophecies. Many people requested sessions out of curiosity, and when they found out I was also doing hypnosis for abduction cases I was getting requests about that also. Since I knew Lou was interested, I tried to schedule as many UFO cases as possible when I made my trips to Little Rock. Janice was one of these, a woman who approached me after my first lecture, and said she would like to talk to me about troubling events in her life. When I returned to Little Rock in August 1989 she came to the house where I was staying, and we talked for two hours as she tried to make sense out of strange events that had occurred most of her life.

Janice was a woman in her forties who had never married, although she was attractive. She is unable to have children because of female problems since puberty. Her main concern was keeping her identity a secret, since she had a highly responsible position as a computer analyst for a large corporation. Her main fear was that she would lose her job if there was any hint of incompetency. Over the years she tried to talk to someone about her experiences, but was unable to do so. I was the first person she felt comfortable enough with to reveal all the strange incidents.

At this time I was staying with my friend, Patsy, when I drove the four hours to Little Rock. She had a large house, and gave me the privacy needed for discussion with the clients, and the hypnotic sessions. On this day we had the house to ourselves, and I set up my tape recorder on the dining room table to record Janice's remarks. She noticeably relaxed as the discussion proceeded, and the only time attention was brought to the recorder was when I changed the tapes. We talked at random and even digressed into other areas of her life, so I only transcribed the pertinent portions.

When she finally began to release all the pent up information it was coming in such a rush that I couldn't make sense of it. I was being overwhelmed, so I tried to organize it by asking her to start at her earliest memories.

These memories went back to the age of four when she would awaken screaming that "they" had come and gotten her. Her mother thought she was just having nightmares, but agreed to let her sleep with her light on. She remembered many times playing in her room, and looking around and seeing a face at the window. She knew "they" were coming to get her, and she would start running down the hall. But she never made it very far, because she would be stopped, paralyzed, and unable to move. She never knew how much time elapsed, but when she came back to herself, she would be standing in the hall, very cold, barely breathing, with her mother shaking her. This also occurred when she was playing in the yard with her brother. He would run into the house shouting, "Mother, it's happening to her again. She's gone again." All during this time as a child she had a foreboding fear that "they" were coming again, or "those people," as she started calling them. Although she never had any idea who "they" were.

I asked her to describe the face she saw at the window, and she said it was a little guy with big dark, dark eyes, but then it would change into a dog looking in the window. Naturally when she told this to her mother she wouldn't believe her, especially since the window of her room was very high off the ground. No normal dog could look in the window.

She tried to explain to her mother, after the paralyzed incident would occur, that she had been out somewhere. "I knew I had been outside myself, in a state other than we know how to do. You can call it 'out-of-the-body.' The only way I've come close to describing it is if you took your essence out and left the physical. I might be *physically* here, but the essence is on another plane or something." Often she would wake up in the morning knowing she hadn't really been in bed all night.

During childhood there were several occasions when she had serious illnesses that were life threatening. There was even one time when the doctors told her mother she would never walk again. In each of these cases she had a miraculous recovery, and the doctors could never explain what had happened to her.

As she grew older she had many episodes of missing time. She was not aware that anything unusual had happened. The missing time was only confirmed by others, which added to her confusion. Her mother remarked, "You're the only person I know who can go to the grocery store, and come back three days later." She had to fabricate and tell her she had met a friend and went to their house, when in reality she had no idea where she had been. She would have a faint memory of coming down through treetops, then going into the grocery store, getting the bread and going home. By that time she was a teenager in high school and her mother thought she was out partying, but Janice said she drinks very little and has never done drugs.

This sensation continued throughout her life. She would start to go somewhere and arrive late. She didn't know what happened to the time, and was afraid if she told anyone about this they would lock her up. She said, "I had a sensation, a little glimmer of knowing *something* had happened. And I would come back *moving fast*. I have now learned that my Earth time and *that* time have to adjust and get back in sync. It would be the feeling of *going fast*, and I would find myself back in my car driving. That would be a *big* adjustment."

She grew up feeling she had to hide somewhere so they couldn't find her. She worried it would start happening to her family, so she moved away from home when she was eighteen. She still had no idea what it was. "An unknown something was dealing with me. And I had nobody to tell. I was afraid to tell, because they wouldn't believe me."

The memories of an actual contact with unknown forces began to finally seep through around 1987. It usually happened unexpectedly, and at the most inopportune moments. An example was while she was at work teaching a girl in the office about super copying on the computer. "This is where you're in two documents at the same time. I was trying to explain it to the girl. I said, 'Actually it's like being in two places at the same time.' Instantly I had a telepathic flash, 'Yes, simultaneous time.' And it was like a movie in my head of simultaneous lifetimes. It was so overpowering I had to excuse myself and go to the ladies' room. I sat in there and all this knowledge kept coming in about teleportation, how it works mechanically, and how you can be in two places at the same time. And in my mind I saw my body dissolving, and ending up in California or some place I've never been. I felt a strange sensation in my head while this was happening. I wouldn't call it 'dizzy.' I don't know what you could call it actually, except that while I was in the toilet I was taught some complex stuff. And this has continued since 1987. Some kind of teaching."

Also in 1987 Janice had a strange experience that both awakened these old memories and made some pieces fall into place.

J: I was getting ready to go to a potluck dinner, standing in front of my bathroom mirror, when I got this funny little sensation in my head. I felt a little dizzy, and thought I ought to go sit down. It was not very far from the bathroom to my bed, but I never made it. I felt myself start to lift out.

D: *What do you mean?*

J: My spirit, my essence. I guess it could be called an Out of the body experience, but it vacuumed out my insides. It was like a "whoosh out." And I could look and see myself standing there. Three hours later I was still standing there, like I was when I was a child.

D: *This was from the other perspective.*

J: This is true. That's what put me in touch with the child thing. That's what got me thinking and remembering, "Now that happened when I was little."

D: *And you were sucked out, and you could see yourself.*

J: I was out, and I still could see the physical. And there was somebody there; maybe it was my guardian angel. I didn't even have to look. I felt it was somebody familiar. And he asked, "Do you want to go to your beginning?"

D: *Do you want to go to your beginning? That's interesting.*

J: I had been telling, saying, praying, sending; there's a level of intensity you get to when you want to do something, and you *do* it. And I had been saying for days and weeks, "I mean it. It's time for me to know my source. It's time for me to go to my beginning. It's time for me to unravel all this stuff I've been living with for forty something years. And I mean, now." So he said, "Are you ready to go?" And I said, "Yes, let's go." And I still had a physical me of sorts, even though I could look and see me standing there. Even though my hand went through my arm, I saw a physical me.

D: It looked like you, but it was not ... solid. (Yes) *But could you see* through your house, or where were you?

J: Yes, I could see through the house. I could look through my ceiling down, and there I was standing there. And I thought, "That's kind of neat." And I wasn't afraid. I have since figured this out. If I had been afraid, this would never have taken place.

D: Yeah, you would probably have been put right back in or whatever.

J: Yes. And we rose, and we went up through some levels. As if you had a layer cake and you went up through the layers, so to speak. And there was the baby soul level. Then we went up, and there was a level of - I don't know - some kind of spirit things. And I thought, Hmm, this doesn't feel good here. Then I looked over to the left, and there were demons and monsters and things over there. They were coming at me. And I said, "Stop! In the name of the Lord Jesus Christ. I'm not afraid of you." And whoosh. It was like a piece of Saran wrap came down, and they were soaking into it. And I said, "See, I told you I wasn't afraid." And as we continued going up, I could look over there and there was the 1800s. I could look over there and there was 1945. And I could look different directions and see different time periods. It was like tuning a television set. "Oooh, that's neat. That time period was right over here."

D: You could see it all by just looking around in a circle?

J: Well, it wasn't in a circle. It was sort of in a straight line actually.

D: Linear? But you could look in on anywhere?

J: I could tune in here and see what was going on. It's all going on.

D: It's still going on?

J: Oh, yes. It is all still there, and is presently now going on. (Laugh) So I said to this fellow, "Oh, that's so pretty. I want to go right over there." And he said, "You've been over there. You've done this. This is *time*. You can go over there any time you want. However, you wanted to go to your beginning. You'll have to do that another time." So we went past it. Then the next thing I came to was a point. And I thought, "Golly, I'm light, I'm light. Wow." As in light like a bulb light.

D: Made out of light, you mean?

J: Yeah. All of a sudden I was pure light.

D: You didn't have this resemblance of your physical form? You were light?

J: Yes, actually I was. I actually shot to a star. And I said, "Wow, I'm a star," and I wasn't Janice anymore. I was that star. And I looked around - as a star - and I saw this universe spread out. And I said, "All right! This is my point in the universe." I've since learned why that happened. A star or a particular portion of the heavens is the entry point for the soul essence energy into the physical. And it comes through a particular sector.

This sounded familiar to me, and I remembered the Near Death Experience that Meg reported in my book, *Between Death and Life.* In her experience she also went to a star and felt the totality of the universe.

D: *But you were essentially a light being made of light.*

J: Yeah, at that moment. I stayed there until I realized it. And then at the point of realization, whoosh. Each time, as soon as I realized it I went on to something else. So from that point, it was like the angel level. We went through colors, and I could feel and be each color. And when we got through the colors, I looked and said, "Wow, I'm just molecules. I'm just air." I knew this section was me. I had a beingness. I had a form.

D: *You still had a personality.*

J: I had anything. I was everything I ever was, except the physical. But if I wanted to be physical, all I had to do was think it, and I could see me. I could see Janice, me.

D: *So you knew you hadn't lost contact.*

J: I was still me if I wanted to be ... if I wanted to think and I could also think, "Oh, that energy. I would like to see." As soon as you think it, you can see it. They were telling me, "Well, this is your beginning." And I went, "Oh, wow, this is neat." And they said, "You've done this level." And I said, "Yeah." It was like you stayed there and exchanged energies in that level. And as soon as I thought, "But this is not my source," I went on. All the way past to the point where there is no time, to the point where there is a creation, past the point of creation, to a level where the All Knowledge and the Ancient Ones are. I passed the gods, goddess level, and I went straight to a big rose quartz essence. It has to be the most unconditional love I've ever known. I was just happy to be at my beginning. It was like I was revitalized, and I thought,

"Well, maybe I've died." (Chuckle) I was hanging around there, just basking in that warm, beautiful spirit of God. Oh, it was beautiful. Everything tingles when I think about it. And then I heard, "It's time to go back now, my child." I didn't want to go. I was crying, because I didn't want to come back. And I said, "I don't want to be alone. I've *always* been alone down here. And those people will come, and I don't want that." And as soon as I said that, whoosh, I was in a spaceship. Well, now that was a little much on top of what I'd just been through. I mean, I was freaked out now. I didn't know if I was physical or not physical at first, when I was in this metallic room. And I realized it was round, and it was a spaceship, and these beings were there. I was protesting, "Okay, this is it. I'm tired of this." And they started telling me they had been with me since my childhood. "We are here to protect you. We are here to help you. You are helping us. You agreed to this before you ever entered your physical life." And I shouted, "I *did not*." I was raising hell, right? Because I didn't know nothing about no space guys. (Laugh) And so they brought a paper out. I looked and said, "That's my name. That's my signature. I did do it, didn't I?"

D: *Did they tell you what you agreed to?*

J: They said I had lived my purpose as a helper. That many times in many situations energies come through me that transform this, that or the other, depending on the situation, to help people. That most of the time the people didn't know how they were helped, and I didn't know either. And they said it would be revealed to me. That I was to learn. And that I would never be alone.

D: *What did the spaceship look like?*

J: It was metallic, silver, clinical. It was so clean. I mean, it was just unreal how clean ... it was clinical. There were instruments. There was a round shaped room. It had dials. It had square ... I don't know what they were. Something like a screen. In the room where I was there was a table. I didn't look behind me, but there was a doorway into another room. And this room had like - you know how window seats look? It had curved seats all the way around. And people can lie down on them, or just rest in here. So we had a discussion in there, and there were more people, more energies. They were all around me, and I don't really know where I was. But anyway, I remember trying to see everything. They were talking to me, and telling me about my agreement, and that I didn't have to do it.

D: You could get out of it, you mean?

J: Sure. They said if you really do not want to continue, then you don't have to.

D: That's a good thing to know. Free will again, I suppose.

J: Yeah, we do have free will. And they showed me, at this point, a movie of life.

D: Was this on one of those screens?

J: It wasn't on a screen. It was like they were thinking to me. Telepathic is all I know. There were no real words. I was looking at the Earth, and I saw people all over. They were flowing into two separate lines. You make a choice which line you go in, and the choice is, either to higher consciousness or not. Not everybody's going into this line. You can see the other line of people, and you're in the white light body as you go into this line. That's what has to do with the raising of the vibrational rate of the people, in direct correspondence with the raising of their level of consciousness. And at a point, and I don't know what it is, the Earth will, as in Revelation, go up in flames. The possibility exists that it will. If and when that happens, they will take out the people in this line.

D: The UFO people will?

J: The UFO people. They will be taken out. I saw the Earth as it exploded. I saw it turn into a sun, and just disappear from the sky. It left a big hole, like the sky was suddenly all black. You know, if you look on the Earth and its blue green, then all of a sudden it turned orange red. It was the end of the world. Now when that Earth disappeared from that hole, I saw a new Earth roll in. There really is a new Earth. Whether it was symbology they were showing me, I don't know yet. I just know that a great part of their purpose, in what they were showing me in relation to me, is that I don't believe I'll go through that. I won't be staying. And they were trying to help, and I asked, "But what about this one and that one?" And they said, "Not everybody's going to choose this line. So you choose the line or you choose not." Then suddenly I came back to my apartment, and I'd lost three hours. I was protesting, "Space people! I don't do space guys. I don't know anything about that stuff." I was back in my bedroom. I was back into me. And I came back in through this section of my head.

D: *Your forehead.*

J: And honestly, when I got back into my body, I wanted to go to the bed. And I thought, okay, I'm going to the bed, but body didn't go to the bed. Body didn't move. Body stood there, and said, "Oooh, we're frustrated. We can't get to the bed. Oooh, how do we get to the bed?" The word was "walk." Walk? Walk? And I was having trouble with the word "walk." Up there in the spirit, when you wanted to go somewhere, you thought it and you *went.* I was having trouble making the body operate. And I was also having trouble knowing what things were. Like: car, drive. It was like I was a baby and having to learn, having to reintegrate. I actually learned I was reintegrating because I had experienced so much energy. It's like taking 120 volts and putting that back down into a 60 watt bulb. And so my body had not necessarily assimilated that, to be able to function back here. It took me a week.

D: *A week? This might be a good reason why people don't remember a lot of things that happen to them. They remember subconsciously, but not consciously.*

J: Yes. And there's been times since when I've been allowed to remember things, and times when I have not been. I was very uncomfortable with that at first. But now I've come to terms with the fact that I don't have the problem of "something freaky's happening." And the next sunrise was the Harmonic Convergence. I was supposed to go with some people to see the sun rise. But instead I got my little dog, and we went down to the lake. And the sun was coming up, and when the spark of the sun hit the dew on the grass, that same spark was the spark I was. They made me know that connection. That I am always connected. And I was crying, because I wanted to go. It was a very lonely feeling, like your relatives are leaving, going away. And I was sad that they had to leave. I wanted them to stay and help. And so, I looked up at the sky over the lake and said, "If I've really been connected with spacecraft, give me a sign. A physical sign. Show me. Because I can't believe this is happening." So as I was leaving this place, I said I wanted a physical sign, otherwise I'm having nothing else to do with this. This is ridiculous, bizarre, and I'm finished. That's it! So I was walking back to my car and started laughing, thinking they're not going to show me anything. And I looked and there was a spark down there on the ground. I thought, that's probably a piece of glass. I'm not going down there and get that, and I walked on past it. And I was physically backed up. I was walking to my car, and it was like "Stop! Back up!" And I went to get it. And you won't believe, out of this whole big place, what I found there on the ground.

Janice then rummaged in her purse and took out a small coin purse. She then pulled a small locket out of it. When she opened it there was a small object inside. She held it in the palm of her hand. It was a small metal star.

She explained, "I didn't want to lose it, so I put it in the locket. It was totally pink when I got it. Now it's turning silver."

I handled it carefully, trying to see what it was made of. "It doesn't feel like metal. It feels like really hard plastic. It's so small ... oh, not even a half inch."

J: When I picked it up I knew where the top point was. There's one particular point that's the top. And I can't put it in that locket any other way.

We were playing with it and laughing. As she was putting it back in the locket on a sudden impulse I examined it closer. It was then that I noticed it was similar to my ring. I have an unusual silver and turquoise ring that I came into possession of through mysterious circumstances. In the early 1980s before I became involved in any of these type of investigations a woman left the ring with one of my daughters with instructions to give it to me. The woman said she knew I did not charge for my services, and wanted me to have the ring in appreciation for the work I was doing. She knew if she gave it to me I would refuse it, but by giving it to my daughter I could not return it. She was right, I considered it too valuable to accept. But because I could not return it I kept it, and put it on the only finger it would fit on, my second finger. Although I normally do not wear jewelry I have never taken it off since, which also might seem strange. Many people have admired it and asked if I would sell it, or at least tell them where they can find another one like it. I think it may be one of a kind, because I have never seen or heard of another with the same design. There are seven silver balls placed around the edge: five along the bottom and two at the top separated by a silver bar. In the center is a five pointed turquoise star. Many people think there may be some sort of symbolism in the design. The only clue to the silversmith who made it is a U or horseshoe mark on the inside.

Janice placed her little star over the star on my ring and it matched exactly in size, as though it was a duplicate. Now I was impressed. Could this be a coincidence? I called Patsy from the other room so I could show it to her. We were all laughing, but it was a strange feeling that something unnatural was occurring. Patsy also thought it was unusual that it matched precisely. It was an *exact* match. Of course, Janice's star was silver colored and my stone was turquoise.

"Look at this," Janice said. "I have to store it in the heart locket so the top point is up. And that's the way you wear the ring, with the same point pointing outward."

Little did we know at that time the precise match of the stars was to be a type of omen. An indication that we would be doing important work together. Had our coming together been pure coincidence, or was there a higher motive or power behind this?

We had been sitting at Patsy's dining room table with my trusty tape recorder discussing Janice's experiences and memories for over two hours. It was now time to do the regression. The only problem was deciding which incident to cover first. We went up to the guest bedroom, and as I was preparing my equipment she told me about another very recent incident. It had occurred the month before in July 1987, so it was very fresh in Janice's mind.

When she awoke that morning she was coughing, and as she sat up big clots of blood came out of her mouth. This frightened her, but as she got up she noticed there was no blood on the bed. Instead there was something that appeared to be water over the lower part of her body, and on the bed underneath her. She had not wet the bed, and there was no odor associated with it. It was as if someone had poured water on her and the bed. The only discomfort was a burning sensation in her vagina area. She went into the bathroom and washed her mouth out, and the bleeding quit as suddenly as it had begun. Her little dog was behaving in a very excited manner, which Janice had come to associate with her returning home from work. The blood concerned her enough to cause her to go to the doctor that day, but he could not find anything to explain the clots.

I decided to focus on this incident since it was so recent. If there was nothing there, we had plenty of other material to explore. When she entered the hypnotic trance she dropped to a very deep state immediately. I then counted her back to the night before she awoke in the distressing state, to see what had caused it. I also suggested that she could watch it as an objective reporter if she wished, in order to eliminate any physical discomfort.

D: *I will count to three, and on the count of three we will be at the beginning of that evening when you're getting ready to go to bed. And you can tell me what's happening. 1, 2, 3, we've gone back to that night. What are you doing? What do you see?*

J: I'm watching my dog. He's looking around so strange, really strange. And I know he's looking at something I can't see yet. But I know it's there, because I *feel* it.

D: *What can you feel?*

J: It's them. It's them. I want him to go ... (Deep breath) with me, because I know they're coming.

D: *Has he ever done that?*

J: Yes, he's gone.

D: *Oh? I wonder how he likes that?*

J: (She was beginning to seem apprehensive.) I don't know.

D: *All right. Tell me what's happening.*

J: My energy's been real low. A lot of stress at work. They're telling me they need to do some work. (Apprehensive.) And I don't know where we're going. - And my head hurts.

I immediately gave suggestions that would take away any physical discomfort. In a few seconds her facial sensations indicated she was no longer under as much stress, and the headache had been eased.

D: *Where are they?*

J: They came through my window.

D: *What? Climbed through?*

J: Just through the wall. (It seemed to bother her.) Right through the wall.

The Custodians

D: *What do they look like?*

J: Not at tall as me, but almost. And I know them, but every time it happens it's a little bit scary. (Big breath)

D: *Oh, yes, I can understand that. It's only human. But you won't be afraid as you talk to me about it. Do you understand?* (Her breathing and bodily sensations indicated apprehension.) *You don't have to be afraid when you talk to me, because I'm here with you. And I'll stay with you. But how many are there?*

J: (Her voice trembled. She was close to tears.) Two.

D: *Do you want to tell me what they look like?*

J: (Her voice was still trembling.) They don't have any hair. And they have these big brown eyes. And they have skin, but it's not like ours. It's different. And you think they have clothes on, but you don't know if they have clothes on.

D: *How is their skin different?*

J: It's not like skin feeling. It feels dry. It feels kind of like paper, but more like crepe paper. (Her voice was still close to breaking up.)

D: *I understand what you mean.* (She began to cry. It was a fear cry.) *It's all right, I'm with you. What happened?*

J: (She was hard to understand at first, because of the sobbing.) They want me to go with them, but I ... I said I wanted to stay a little longer here. I wanted to keep my baby. (Sobbing)

This was a surprise. She had told me earlier during the interview that she could not get pregnant.

D: *What do you mean?*

J: It was time for them to take me, but yet I wanted to stay and keep it for a little while.

D: *Are you pregnant?*

J: I think so. I don't think they call it that. I don't know what they call it. They just say it's time to go.

D: *Then how do you leave the room?*

J: We go through the wall like they do.

D: *Do you feel yourself do that?*

J: Yes, I feel myself do it. They can fix it where you can do that. And you really do go through there. You're gone from your room.

D: *Then your real physical body just goes right through the wall?*

I wanted to clarify that it was not an Out of the Body Experience. The first time this occurred with John, I was surprised to discover that the actual physical body was capable of being taken through solid objects, like the walls or roof. Each time this has been reported since then I have tried to determine whether it was the physical body or a spiritual experience. The subject is always positive about what occurs. They are never vague or uncertain.

J: (Her voice was steadier.) It has to do with displacement of the molecules. They showed me how it happens. And it's a funny feeling when it starts to happen.

D: *How does it feel?*

J: Your body just feels a little numbness. And then you feel it melt. It just melts into like air. It would be air, but you're not air. It's like you're air, except you have a form in the air form. It makes you more of the consistency level of air. What happens is that it's speeded up to the point that your body's a different vibrational rate than the matter you're going through. Therefore you pass through the matter.

D: *That sounds like a very remarkable thing to do.*

J: It is strange.

D: *Then what happens after you've gone through the wall with them?*

J: It's dark and we're moving. I'm not sure how I'm moving.

D: *Are they still with you?*

J: Yes. They're on both sides, and I have my dog.

This has also been reported in other cases. Once the body is taken through the wall or ceiling there is an alien being on either side as the person is taken up to the ship. Maybe this is part of the mechanics of how they are transported. The beings have to be present around the human so it can move through the air to the ship.

D: *Then the dog went through the wall too. I wonder how he felt about that.*

J: He wasn't afraid.

D: *Can you see where you're going?*

J: (Breathing heavier again.) I just am in the ship. I'm on the table.

D: *How did you get in the ship?*

J: I don't know. It's blank. I just know I'm in there.

This is another repeatable detail. There often is a blank as they enter the craft while it is in the air. Maybe they also go through the outer shell in the same manner as they left their house. If so, it apparently causes a memory lapse. When the craft is on the ground they often remember walking or being taken up stairs or a ramp.

D: *Then what's happening?*
J: They make ... I lie down. And we're gonna do that again.
D: *Do what again?*
J: It's like you are at the gynecologist. I don't know how they do it, because I never get to stay awake. (Getting upset.) I wanted to know. And I begged them to let me know how they do it.

I discovered in my early days of investigation that it was possible to obtain answers even though the physical body was put to sleep. You can go directly to the subconscious, because that part never sleeps (even during surgery), and can supply objective and thorough answers.

D: *I think the way we're doing this now, maybe you can find out. Do you want to find out?*
J: (Sniffling) I think so.
D: *Do you want to stand back as an observer and watch with your mind, while your body is asleep there? Do you think that's possible to do that?*
J: I don't know. I feel like I'm there right now. I'm right there now. Right there. (She was sniffling.)
D: *Ask one of them if you can watch as an observer. And see what they say. (No) They say, no? Can we ask questions? (Yes).*

At this point her voice unexpectedly changed. With her answer, "Yes," the voice sounded more authoritarian, not frightened as before.

D: *All right. But the body is asleep? Is that how it is done?*
J: It is not a sleep state.

The voice that answered was definitely not Janice's. It was monotone, mechanical, almost robotic. It pronounced each syllable individually, not at all the way we speak by slurring sounds together. At times it sounded hollow, and had almost an echoing quality that was definitely not caused by the tape recorder or the microphone. This was the way I heard it coming from her, and I could not understand how she could naturally make it sound that way. It bore no resemblance to Janice at all. This voice with its unique tone and mannerism continued throughout the rest of the session, and did not change until the entity was told to leave at the end. I was not startled by the shift, because this has happened before. I took advantage of the opportunity to ask questions.

D: If it is not a sleep state, what is it?
J: It is a level of consciousness to which you are unaccustomed.
D: Why does she have to be in that state of consciousness?
J: So there will be no pain.
D: I think that's very good. We don't want her to experience any pain. What is happening that might cause pain?
J: Human birth is painful.
D: That's true. Is this a birth?
J: This is a birth.
D: Can you tell me what's happening?
J: The same thing that happens in your birth on the Earth.
D: But on Earth it happens naturally.
J: It is happening naturally.
D: On Earth when a birth occurs there are labor pains associated with it.
J: That is why you have the altered state. There is no pain felt by the mother.
D: But am I correct in assuming that the embryo couldn't be very large?
J: This is correct.
D: Then it should be able to be passed very easily.
J: There will be pain. This human has never had a child on your Earth, therefore the canal is different.
D: Does something happen to stimulate the process? Similar to birth pains, birth cramps?
J: I do not understand your question.
D: Is something done with instruments or machines to make the body go into labor?

J: It is time for it now in our realm. The nine-month time period which you consider ... termination ... culmination, is simply altered. It is a shorter time period, because of the kind of growth that takes place during the time the baby is carried by the mother. Therefore the organs and the various embryonic states of beingness are developed to a higher level than would be developed in a nine month time period in your Earth years.

D: *Then it is not the size of a nine month, or a full-term baby?*

J: This is correct.

D: *But it is fully developed according to your standards?*

J: This is correct. You do not yet understand our standards, in that our standards would mean that the baby is a nine-month baby although the physical size is not such as a nine-month baby.

D: *Does it have all the characteristics of a full-term baby?*

J: Yes, and so does its systems.

D: *In our way of thinking, a small embryo would have a very primitive type of development, and could not survive.*

J: It requires four months' time period if carried on your plane of existence. We maintenance the birth process during the time the mother is carrying the embryo. This particular maintenance causes the systems to develop at a different rate of speed than the normal birth process you humans carry out.

D: *What is the size of the fetus when it is born?*

J: It is a four-month child in physical size, in relation to your birth.

D: *In my understanding that's about the size that would fit in the palm of a hand.*

J: It is somewhat larger.

D: *Has she had this fetus inside of her for four months?* (Yes) *Was she aware?*

J: Not as aware as before. She has time periods when she is aware. It is not a constant awareness. She sensed she was pregnant. She has the same sort of phenomenon you Earth people have, in that the abdomen does expand, and she can tell by that what is taking place.

D: *Do the periods stop?*

J: She no longer has periods.

D: *That's not required for this?* (No) *All you need is the uterus?*

J: Even the uterus is not necessary. It has to do with the energy of the human body as opposed to hormonal secretions of the human body.

D: *I'm trying very hard to understand. In human terms there has to be that lining of the uterus and the hormones, so the placenta can attach and nourish the growing fetus.*

J: This fetus experiences life in a much different manner than your human baby that is carried by the mother, in that, as the mother goes about her daily activities, it experiences life on your planet to the fullest that the mother experiences life.

D: *Then this can be done with a woman of any age.*

J: Correct. But it has to do with a particular type of woman, in that there are certain conditions that need to exist for the participant in this project.

D: *Can you tell me what those requirements are?*

J: (Methodical, as though reciting.) Requirements are: dietary. Requirements are: maintaining a particular level of existence. Requirements are: purity. And there are some others which we can discuss later.

D: *This would seem to fit most women.*

J: Not most women.

D: *In what way wouldn't they be the same?*

J: Because of the involvement of most women in particular activities. Because of the concentration level of most women. Because there is an interaction with the brain of the woman at the time. Subjects are selected in a manner that relate to criteria of evolvement of the being, of evolvement of the mother. It is an intricate process.

D: *I think you will see I have many questions. I am very curious. Are you speaking about sexual activity?*

J: This is a contributing factor.

D: *Because that does affect hormones, emotions and everything else.*

J: It has more to do with the essence of the mother than it does with the hormonal physicalness of the mother. You might call this the spirituality level, in your Earth language terms.

D: *Then every woman isn't suitable.*

J: This is correct.

D: *Has this been done to her before?*

J: Correct.

D: In my work I have been told that reproduction is also done by cloning?

J: There is a project for cloning. It is separate and apart from this project. Some women participate in both, some only in one.

D: If you can have births in this way, why is the cloning process also needed?

J: Because there is a genetic difference that takes place in cloning, that is lacking in this other type of project.

D: Can you explain? I do understand something about cloning. That it is an exact duplicate.

J: Cloning is an exact, exact duplicate. The other method takes outside stimuli into the process, other than just the mother's essence. There are two separate and distinct types of individuals produced.

D: Then the clone is an exact duplicate. The other one has a different type of genetic makeup. Would that be true?

J: This is correct. For the other also contains all the extrasensory stimuli the mother receives during the time period of the embryonic state.

D: You mean the clone or the natural one?

J: The natural one.

D: Would this mean that the clone would be a colder, emotionless person?

J: Not unless the mother is of the same emotional makeup. The problem you are having understanding this, is that the clone *contains and is* everything the mother is. With the natural childbirth, as you would call it, the child contains and is everything the mother is, *plus* all that the mother has been exposed to during that time of carrying the embryo.

D: So there is a difference.

J: A definite difference. We are trying to explain to you, that as the embryo rests in the mother's womb so it lives her life with her.

D: Experiences what she is feeling.

J: Exactly!

D: And the clone does not do this. Well, can I ask you how this embryo was germinated? Was the father also human or what?

J: This will not be discussed at this time. The information will come to light. First we must know of a trust in you.

D: *That's perfectly all right with me. I just ask many questions, as long as that is not objectionable.*

J: We wish to see what you do with this information, and how it is used.

D: *I will do whatever you want me to do with it.*

J: It is not to be disseminated to the public until you have the entire picture.

D: *I'm willing to accept that. I don't want a half story anyway, a half truth.*

J: We must remind you to protect the individual.

D: *I have placed protection around her while we are working in this state. Is this what you mean?*

J: No. What we mean is that, with what you do with the information, there can be a direct effect upon this person's life.

D: *That's very true. Most of the people I work with don't want to be known. They want to be anonymous. This is very important because they don't want their life disrupted. And I try very hard to respect that.*

J: This is why we are talking to you. For the reason that you are a very responsible individual.

D: *And if it is within my power no one will know who she is. There are always things that are beyond my control. But with what I can control, her name would never be revealed. Is that what you mean?*

J: At this point in time it must remain so. There is other work we must do. She is a very highly evolved subject. She understands more than most subjects. Therefore we have a bigger project in mind for her, which we do not wish to be interrupted by curiosity.

D: *Yes, and there are many curious people. It seems as though I'm the one that will have the problems.*

J: Not if we can be allowed to protect you also.

D: *I would like that. Because I feel I'm going to be traveling into places where there is negativity.*

J: Exactly.

D: *And skepticism.*

J: Exactly.

D: *And I would welcome any protection you could give me.*

J: You will know through your ring that we are with you always.

This was my star turquoise ring that was mentioned earlier, that I had obtained in a strange manner, and which I have never taken off.

D: *I wondered about that ring. Can you tell me anything about it?*

J: You Earth people always think that the UFOs come from the stars. The star to you should be your symbol that you are connected to it. And that you are with us in thought always, for the work you have become involved in, helping to dispel the notion that we are bad and evil beings.

D: *Yes. Because the information I have obtained seems to be positive.*

J: It is positive. However, I must warn you there is and there does exist a force out of which can come the other side of the coin, as you speak in your Earth time.

D: *But I always believe you draw to you what you want, what you expect.*

J: This is correct.

D: *I have not expected to find that negativity.*

J: But you must know and be aware that it does exist. You must also know and be aware that in your work you will perhaps come in contact with that side of the beings. However, it is a choice each individual must make, as to what side they work on. There is a definite choice to be made.

D: *I have heard talk of this negativity. And I don't want to be involved in that side.*

J: If you have made your choice, then you do not have to fear, for you will not be involved in that side. It may rise about you. It may come around you, but you will be protected from *it* working with *you.*

D: *That is very good. I appreciate that, because all I want is information.*

J: And that is what we wish to share.

D: *All right. Can I know who or what I am speaking to?*

J: I do not understand your question.

D: *Well, I don't believe I am speaking to Janice's subconscious, am I?*

J: No, you are not.

D: *Who am I speaking to? It doesn't have to be a name. I'm just curious as to what.*

J: You look on the face of the book *Communion*, and you will see my picture. This is why the being, Janice, was affected by that cover in the manner in which she was. She is most familiar with us. She knows that in Earth perspective there are times when it seems we might cause pain, or it would be observed by someone from Earth that we are unkind and unfeeling beings. She has been allowed to know the story behind that. In that it is simply the perspective of the being. And she has been able to shift perspectives to the point of understanding the meaning behind what we do, and any kind of pain we might cause her. She knows this is incidental to any kind of problem she might have with accepting what she has agreed to. She is aware and has been most often reminded by us, that at any moment she can and is allowed to refuse. She also knows that from us there would be no ramifications in her nonparticipatory action at any time in which she feels too uncomfortable to continue. She knows and has been told that we help her in any manner in which she needs help at any time.

D: *Those are all very good things. You see, one of the theories people have is that your people are very cold and unfeeling, and cause pain and don't care about humans.*

J: By your standards that is correct. The problems people have is that they cannot come to *our* side, and see from our eyes. Individuals such as Janice, to whom you speak, are able to effectively become us and know our purpose and know our minds and know our beingness. Therefore they understand we are not involved in causing pain simply for the matter of causing pain. Because of the fact that we do not feel pain as you feel pain, it is sometimes hard for us to understand that we cause it.

D: *I see. Is this because your nervous system is different?*

J: Exactly.

D: *Then you have not developed in the same physical way that humans have?* (No) *Are you capable of emotions?*

J: We are capable of simulated emotions, but we do not have them built in as you humans carry them around.

D: *Are you more like a - I don't want to say a "machine" - like a manufactured person, than one that is genetically reproduced?*

J: Excuse. The question is unclear.

D: *I'm trying to think how to word it. I'm used to people being human and having emotions, unless they are machine like. Manufactured rather than reproduced in a genetic manner.*

J: We feel, but it does not mean the same thing.

D: Can you help me understand?

J: If you touch me, I feel it. It does not transmit to ... it does not mean that the same sensation will take place. In that, my mind knows you have touched me. I feel the touch, but not in the same manner as a human feels a touch. It is a process, a telepathic touching, as opposed to physicalness. In that we operate from a level of telepathy. Therefore our evolvement is to the state that our senses come through that way of knowing, as opposed to the more physical level of emotional touching that you would understand.

D: I'm thinking of the way people caress each other, especially when they caress a child.

J: We are learning. We wish to integrate the two different types of emotions, and understand them. In the integration process, what will take place is an evolvement of and an integration into the telepathic way of feeling and knowing, and sensory feeling and knowing.

D: I see. Then you also don't feel emotions such as love or hate?

J: We do not understand them, although we can feel them. It is different for us.

D: Then you can feel anger?

J: We can feel any emotion you can feel, but it is felt in our minds as opposed to affecting our physical bodies.

D: Then you're not totally cold people.

J: That is correct. We experience it, but it does not affect our physicalness as it does the human. Stress is a part of the human life. It breaks down the body. It affects the mind. It affects the molecular structure of your body.

D: And you are trying ....

J: I am trying to tell you that if stress is applied to us, it does not affect our body that way. However, we do experience it with our mind. We are not here to harm. We are not here to take over your planet. It is too bad that you cannot understand this.

D: I believe this.

J: Yes, you do. I was speaking collectively.

D: This lack of feeling, was that caused because your race developed in a different way?

J: It is simply caused by the fact that where we are from and where we developed, we developed differently. It is not because we didn't have it. We didn't know it. It was simply an unnecessary part of our existence.

D: *I thought maybe we all started out the same way, and you evolved into a different way.*

J: We began the way we are. That is why it is hard for us to understand Earth emotions, and some of the manners of existence in which you apply yourselves.

I paused to turn the tape over in the recorder.

D: *You're probably very aware that I am using a machine.*

J: We understand machines.

D: *This is a machine that captures the voice, and helps me to regain that voice at another time. The words.*

J: We retain the voice in our mind.

D: *We don't quite have that capability, so I have a little machine that the words go into. And when the time comes I can play them back, and hear and understand them again.*

J: You could retain them in your mind.

D: *But it's very difficult when you have so much information.*

J: It's a matter of self .... (She had difficulty finding the right word.) It's a matter of sorting the information and categorizing and filing.

D: *Well, I'm able to do that to a great degree.*

J: It's a matter of imaging and image tracing. Much as we fly. We can image your planet or a place, and then we do not have to physically fly there to go there.

D: *Are you in our atmosphere now?*

J: We are in your atmosphere.

D: *But you mean, where you come from originally? You would just image where you want to go?*

J: This is correct.

D: *And you don't need any type of power source for the ship or anything?*

J: We do not need a type of power source. Thought is our power source.

D: *This is enough to operate the entire ship?*

J: It can operate many ships.

D: *Is this collective thought, or the thought of just one individual like yourself?*

J: It can be one or it can be collective.

D: *Scientists in our day think you must have some type of power: mechanical, electrical or something similar?*

J: There are ships that run off many different sources. That is where you go astray. You humans think that all ships must use the same kind of energy. Is that correct?

D: *Or at least energy we can understand, combustible or different types.*

J: Do you understand light energy?

D: *Only in the way we use electricity.*

J: Well, there is a point just past light on which we travel. It's a light frequency. It's not visible to the naked eye.

D: *I'm thinking of laser.*

J: You are getting closer.

D: *Closer?* (Chuckle) *As much as I know of it, laser is a faster frequency, I believe. Isn't it?*

J: Yes. This frequency is faster than your light.

D: *I'm thinking of microwaves.*

J: That is a different thing altogether.

D: *Okay. Then you are able to travel with a physical ship on this frequency by using thought.* (Yes) *By using thought are you able to dematerialize and materialize in another place?*

J: Exactly.

D: *All right. Because we think of traveling at the speed of light.*

J: This is faster than the speed of light.

D: *Is this similar to the way she went through the walls?*

J: This is similar, but there is a different process used for travel. When you speak of passing through matter, you're talking about a different type of process than that on which we travel from our universe to your atmosphere.

D: *Just because it doesn't go through matter? It would be a different process.*

J: Exactly.

D: *But it is still a dematerializing in one place and rematerializing somewhere else. Is that correct? Because I'm trying so hard to understand.*

J: I am not able to explain it to you at this time. I can tell you that there are two separate processes of travel. Once the being came through her wall and began to travel, she traveled by the second process between her outside wall and the craft. This is why the human sometimes has trouble readapting to reentry into your time frame and vibrational rate. For vibrational frequencies change in this kind of travel. It takes a while to slow it down, depending upon the manner of reentry.

D: *It's traveling faster, then it has to slow down again.*

J: Exactly. It sometimes causes adjustment problems. It can cause some disorientation, which we try to alleviate as soon as possible when we become aware it is taking place in the individual.

D: *May I ask you, are your people sexual?* (Yes) *You have male and female?* (Yes) *And do you reproduce in the same way that humans do?*

J: We have a choice.

D: *Can you explain?*

J: We may reproduce in that manner. We may use several other methods.

D: *What other methods are available?*

J: I have explained two of them to you already.

D: *Cloning and this method with Janice?* (Yes) *I am curious about what will be done with this baby. I mean, why would you want to have a human combination?*

J: Because in the human combination you have all the physicalness of the human, as well as all the mental capacity of our race, integrated.

D: *But don't your own people have excellent physical capabilities?*

J: We think you are beautiful. We have physical capabilities, but they are unlike your physical capabilities.

D: *I thought you would be happy with your own, the way you were made, and you would not ....*

J: It is not a matter of unhappy. It is a big lesson for you humans to learn. Different *than.*

D: *What do you mean?*

J: Different *than* as opposed to dissatisfied *with.* It is not a matter of *better* than or *worse* than. It is just *different* than.

D: *That's what I was trying to understand. Why you would want to change the physical appearance of your race?*

J: It does not change the physical appearance of our race, as such. Because it is not *our* race, as such. Nor is it your race, as such.

D: *What do you mean?*

J: I mean it is not *either* race, but *a* race.

I did not understand that he was referring to the creation of a new, separate race.

D: *You mean everyone belongs to one race?*
J: Ultimately that will happen.
D: *Was that where it started?*
J: I do not understand that question.
D: *Did we all begin as one race?*
J: I have explained to you the differences in the manner in which we experience emotions, as compared to the manner in which humans experience emotions. The integration of these two types of experiences into one being creates a different being, but takes nothing away from either race. Nor does it change the fact that, that particular individual is composed of both races.
D: *So we all started out as different races. Then the goal is to integrate into one race that has the best parts of all of them. Is that right?*
J: This is one project, yes.
D: *There are other projects also?* (Yes) *Could you tell me about them?*
J: I cannot tell you at this time.
D: *Well, I have lots of patience, but I also have so many questions. I am trying to understand the purpose of this.*
J: A part of the essence that remains on the Earth can be transferred to the new human at a point in time when there evolves a new Earth.
D: *A new Earth? What do you mean? (Pause) I know a great deal about future prophecies. I'm trying to see if what you're saying fits in with that.*
J: I'm saying that the new being will be the kind of being that populates the new Earth.
D: *In our future or what?*
J: Yes, in your future. In all our futures. You might understand it better if I used the word "transfer."
D: *Transfer what?*
J: If you choose, depending on the outcome of your choices on your planet, the need exists for a race of humans to repopulate your

planet. The essence of the humans that already populate your planet exists in the new race. Therefore, should you choose the path to destruction, the repopulation will more than likely take place out of this race of humans. Therefore, you will truly have a new race to populate your new heaven and your new Earth. A new race with only the most positive qualities.

D: A more evolved race really. (Yes)

A similar concept was described in my book *Keepers of the Garden*, about a planet that was being prepared to receive a new (more perfect) species of humans in the event that we destroyed our planet Earth. This new human was being developed through the experimentation process conducted onboard these spaceships. I was told that the human genes must not die, but were being preserved in this way.

D: Well, this embryo ... I guess you could call it a baby. You said it was full term, and completely formed at the size of four months.

J: Four months.

D: Where is the baby taken?

J: We have facilities much as you have in your hospitals. We service and maintenance the child in the same manner. We have beings whose job is to maintenance the child. To serve as you would call "surrogate" mother to the child. The natural mother does visit with the child if she elects to do so, although she will often not retain the memory of doing so. The mother of the child also teaches these beings how to interact with the child. This is a part of our necessary learning.

D: Does the child grow at a different rate?

J: Yes, it grows at a different rate. It can be four years old in the span of two minutes of your Earth time.

D: That is very fast. Does it seem to be that fast in your time?

J: It can or cannot be that fast.

D: That way you could have an adult in a few days, couldn't you? (Yes) *I see. Are these new beings, this new race, going to be used anywhere else?*

J: They live and are being taught in a very different place. Much as the environment in which they will ultimately live.

D: But this place is away from Earth? (Yes) *And this is where they will become accustomed, so to speak. Climatized?* (Yes) *What about the clones? Will they ultimately come back to Earth?*

J: Yes. Some of them are already on Earth.

D: In what capacity?

J: As humans.

D: What was the reason for that?

J: Because we can clone a human and we can, in a matter of speaking, redesign its physicalness to a point where, if the need arises that the clone return to help its source, that can be done with an instant rapport with the source.

D: But the clone will have the memory of what has happened?

J: Not necessarily.

D: I was thinking, if the clone was raised in this other environment it would retain those memories.

J: We have the same capabilities in relation to time, as I previously explained to you, with a clone. In other words, we could very well have a human in a very short time span. This clone can be sent on a mission, or elect to go on a mission, to help one of you in need. Thereby retaining all of your essence, the rapport is integrated more fully, more instantaneously.

D: I was thinking that the clone would know it was not like the other humans.

J: Yes, some of them know. But a clone does not necessarily remain on your planet for any length of time.

D: It is just there for a certain task, a certain job, and then it goes somewhere else.

J: That is correct.

D: I think one of the problems people have accepting much of this - and I'm trying to clear up some of this misunderstanding - is they think you are interbreeding aliens and humans. Now these are their words, and they claim it's being done without our knowledge and our cooperation and against our will. And I think this is where the misunderstanding is coming in. They see it as a bad thing, because they don't have all the facts.

J: This is the same problem that I explained to you in relation to your perspective regarding pain that we have been accused of inflicting. It is the same misconception.

D: *They think this is doing something against the person's will. Forcibly taking them and performing tests and things on them.*

J: It is because that human cannot be fully awakened to the mission which they have undertaken. Anyone who has been abducted has previously agreed. Because of some problem in their molecular structure we cannot fully activate the cell that allows them to remember, as much as we can in other subjects. The subjects who have greater intestinal fortitude and inner strength are able to understand better the fullness of the purpose of the entire space program.

D: *I was wondering why some people remember and others don't.*

J: You remember what you can withstand. And as your growth rate develops you remember and are given more information.

D: *What some of these people remember is very frightening to them. They only have bits and pieces.*

J: It is frightening because it is very foreign. And some of the experiments *are* frightening to humans. But the experiments that frighten humans are the same experiments that humans perform. And it is the same fear that an animal feels as the human performs the experiment on the animal.

D: *Yes, that makes sense to me. On your craft, are there only your type of beings?*

J: At this moment?

D: *Well, as a rule, are you the only type of being that is on those craft?*

J: On this particular type of craft we are the beings. Other beings may enter this craft, depending on the subject.

D: *What type of craft is this? What does it look like physically on the outside?*

J: This is a round disk craft.

D: *Is it large?* (No) *Then there are other types of craft?* (Yes) *I'm curious about other types of beings that may go back and forth between the different craft. We've heard so many different descriptions.*

J: What do you wish?

D: *Can you tell me about some of the other types?*

J: Depending upon the human subject, depending upon the project, we are in cooperation with other beings. Therefore, it would depend upon the level of the project and the type, as to who is involved.

D: Do these other beings all come from the same place you came from? (No) *Because I think they all look differently, don't they?*

J: They look differently.

D: And I have the assumption that each one has a different type of job. Maybe I'm wrong there. Like an assignment that only they do.

J: It is complex, the projects that we work on. Some humans are involved in many of our projects.

D: Do you mean as a subject or as a participant?

J: Both. A human can be a subject in one project, a participant in another, an advisor in another, a teacher in another. So it depends if the human is multilevel. We look for multilevel humans. You are speaking to a multilevel human when you speak to Janice. She understands levels and dimensions, and can function at different levels and dimensions simultaneously. Therefore she is more suited to work with us, and therefore a highly valued participant, teacher, subject.

D: I was wondering if the other humans, that are involved in these multilevels, know what is going on?

J: Some know to different degrees. Some know more fully than Janice. Some know less fully. It depends on their degree of evolvement. It depends on their vibrational rate. It depends on the degree of molecular structure development. It depends on the degree of brain density. There are many elements that are taken into consideration. And we are most, to use your Earth term, "loving" in that regard. In that we do not wish to cause harm to anyone who has agreed to participate. At first the people of your Earth who agree to participate do not understand, do not know why, and cannot know initially all the things they later learn as they continue to participate. For oftentimes what can happen to them is that they become unbalanced, and they eventually are committed to your insane asylums. (She actually said: "asane asylums.")

D: Because they can't handle all of it?

J: They do not know how to integrate it into their daily life. Therefore the imbalance takes place, and they cannot find a point of equilibrium. We are sorry for this, and try to prevent it. And sometimes we have been fed misinformation by other human elements within your society for which we do have agreements. They supposedly supply us with individuals who have been examined to participate in them. We find that we have a better success rate by approaching the individuals on our own. Because there was some game playing in the role between certain of your .. There was some misinformation given us by members of your society, to which we agreed to participate. Therefore we found it necessary to work outside of the list provided us.

D: *Who provided this list that had misinformation in it?*

J: There is a group that supplies certain names of individuals to us, which they wish us to work with. We agreed and have done so. But we found deception in the purpose, and impurity as to the underlying source for wishing to interact with us. Therefore we could not participate on that level.

D: *Can you tell me what the group is composed of? I don't want names, but where the group is from.*

J: Not at this time I will not. I can tell you, but I will not. For at the moment I must not reveal that to you.

D: *Okay. In other words, they were tricking you.*

J: Somewhat.

D: *I would think with your higher mental capacity, you would have detected they were not telling you the truth.*

J: We did. We had hoped we were incorrect.

D: *Do you think this was a deliberate deception to harm your project?*

J: It was a deliberate deception in order to control our project. It was a manner of control, as opposed to sharing equally.

D: *They were supplying names of people they thought you should work with, so they could control the experiment.* (Yes) *I can't see how they could benefit from that, unless it would be controlling the results in some way.*

J: Controlling the results, and also gaining the knowledge and perhaps misusing it.

D: *Were you sharing the knowledge with this group?*

J: That was our intention. And we have done so.

D: *Are you still sharing it with them?*

J: To a much lesser degree.

D: *Because of this deception?*

J: Yes. They do not know that we realize they deceived us.

D: *I can understand why you wouldn't want to tell me who they are. They think you're still working with them.*

J: We are. It is just on a different level. And they chose that level.

D: *You're being more careful now.* (Yes) *Would I be allowed to have more information at another time?* (Yes) *I thought maybe you might want to check me out first.*

J: We already checked you out. It is just not time yet. The subject needs to develop and digest what has become available to her. We have slowed in our work with her, because there was much for her to digest.

D: *You also said there was something else she had to do at a future time.*

J: Yes. This individual works with energies other than the space energies. She works with energies that are much higher developed than we.

D: *You have other projects in mind then.*

J: It is not *we* who have the projects in mind. It is we who have been directed by a level that is more highly advanced than we are.

D: *But am I to understand she will always be protected and not harmed intentionally?*

J: There is a level of protection around this being that is impenetrable.

D: *That is very good, because that is what I always wish for anyone I work with. I don't ever want them harmed or uncomfortable, if possible.*

J: There will sometimes be discomfort.

D: *But you can do your best to make it minimal, can't you?*

J: That is our job.

D: *Then may I be allowed to come again and ask for more information?*

J: We would hope that you would come again. We would hope that you be most careful with what has been revealed here to you today. We would hope that you would wait, that you would digest before you even *think* about revealing it. We would ask you to come back to this state of beingness and receive a guidance. We ask to elicit an agreement with you, and that no printed word be given out by you at this time. There is more work to be done. If you feel you wish to participate, you may again address us or someone.

D: *Then I will keep it in secret at this time.*

J: Yes, that is correct. You will keep it in secret at this time.

D: *I don't know when we will be able to work again. I have to come a long distance.*

J: There will be a manner in which you will work again, and it will be facilitated.

D: *Then when I come again how can I contact you, the being am speaking to?*

J: We will contact you, and you will not have to worry to contact us. When this vehicle, Janice, goes into this state she contacts whomever she needs to work with at the time.

D: *I thought if I had a name I could ask ... or some instructions.*

J: You will know me by my voice. There are other voices you will come to know. Later we will give you methods of determining.

D: *Then should I take her to this altered state, and then take her to your craft? Or what kind of instructions can I have so that I can contact you?*

J: The instructions you may have for contacting us are very simple. The subject will enter a state of different reality.

D: *Like this?*

J: Like this. You will notice a change in her voice. Therefore you will realize a shift in energy has taken place within her. There is no code.

D: *I don't have to ask to speak to any one certain person.*

J: It will come whenever it is needed.

D: *All right, because I wanted to be sure that I could contact you again.*

J: You can contact me again if I am the one you need to speak with. You could perhaps contact other beings she works with. As I have told you, there are other energies other than space energies, with which she is identified.

D: *All right, but I only want positive energies.*

J: These are positive energies, for this is a pure light being. And other than positive energies are not allowed to enter. It is impossible.

D: *And I would like the same protection for myself, as you said earlier.*

J: You are a pure spirit. Pure in heart, pure in mind, pure in body, pure in soul. These are the things that it takes to raise your vibrational rate to such a level that you work with the energies you do. Otherwise you could not do the work you do. These are the same criteria contained in Janice, to whom you speak.

D: *I do appreciate it. And I hope that you will protect me as I go out in the world with these different messages I have to give.*

J: There is a feeling of, as you would say, "love" for the work you are doing. This is the reason we have brought the two of you together. So that you can feel kindred, so that there will be in one another, if you need a grounding of support.

D: *I thank you for speaking with me. I do appreciate it.*

J: We thank you for your work.

D: *Then I'm going to ask you to depart, with many thanks, and have the consciousness of Janice return to this vehicle.*

J: It is done.

D: *Then the consciousness is returning fully of Janice, and our good friend is departing. And I'm going to ask Janice to leave the scene she is watching.*

Janice let out a big breath, and I knew her personality had returned.

She had not moved at all during the entire session. The voice had such a strange mechanical resonate sound to it, but it seemed to take no effort on her part. After conditioning her with a keyword I brought her forward to full consciousness, but it was quite a while before she could even sit up on the bed, let alone try to get up and walk. She had no memory of the session, because she had gone into such a deep trance. When she sat up she seemed dizzy and disoriented. So I allowed her to sit quietly while we talked. I thought it best not to tell her too much about the session at that time, because I didn't want to frighten her. I told her I would send her a copy of the tape, and she could listen to it in privacy. It was a good fifteen minutes before she tried to stand up, and even then she was wobbly.

I definitely wanted to work with her again, but it meant I would have to schedule a special trip to Little Rock, or probably several trips because I anticipated this would evolve into a long term project. I did not know at the time that I would not encounter this little being again.

The being's remarks about the development of different galactic races caused me to think of our Earthly problems. Racial differences: colors, ethnic differences, religions, etc., are difficult enough for us to understand and come to terms with. Much violence has occurred because of the differences, and even wars have been fought because of supposed superiority or inferiority. If we cannot bring ourselves to understand, eliminate and reconcile these differences, how can we ever hope to understand space beings? Can we blame them for not wishing direct conscious contact? They have seen too many examples of the way we violently treat those who are different. Human beings are afraid of what they don't understand, and distrust anything they perceive as different.

WE ARE NOT FOUR RACES, WE ARE OLY ONE: THE HUMAN RACE. AND WE ARE ALSO PART OF THE GALACTIC RACE.

CHAPTER 9
TAKEN FROM THE FREEWAY

When I returned to Little Rock for a lecture in December 1989 I arranged to have a session with Janice. I was recovering from a cold and was not feeling well. The entire trip had been a drain, so I tried to schedule as light a workload as possible.

However, I definitely wanted to work with Janice again regardless of the way I felt physically. I was hoping to contact the same entity that spoke to me during the first session. That contact occurred spontaneously, so I was really unsure of how to proceed. We decided to explore a strange experience Janice had earlier that year. From there I could figure out how to contact the entity. On the day in question she left work and went to get lunch for several other employees. She remembered leaving the building, and while driving she saw a UFO over the highway. She tried to get people on the street to notice the object, but they kept walking by as though she was invisible. During this time there was also no noise, as though she had suddenly lost her hearing. The people ignored her completely. Afterwards she returned to work, and was astounded when her hearing returned and the sound came back in a loud rush. She discovered that now the people around her on the steps of the building could hear and see her. When she entered her work place the workers were irritated, because she was gone several hours instead of the short time she thought had passed. They no longer wanted the lunch she gave them. We decided to try to find out what occurred on that day.

Janice could not bring herself to listen to the tape of the last session. Although it is difficult for others to understand, this is common among the people I work with. They often avoid the tape recording like the plague. Maybe hearing their own voice say these things gives it more reality, and consciously that is what they are trying to avoid. There is bliss in ignorance. It doesn't matter, because the therapy and healing occurs on the subconscious level anyway.

As we prepared for the session, Janice was concerned she might not go into trance again, because it had been several months since the first session. I knew there would be no problem, because the keyword suggestion always works when it is given in such a deep state of trance. I used her keyword and counted her back to the day the incident occurred. I knew if I could zero in on it fairly accurately that the subconscious could locate it with no trouble, even though we were not sure of the date.

At the end of the count she had returned to her office on the day of the event. She was apprehensive because she was hearing a strange noise in her head. "It's that funny noise that I hear, that lets me know when they're around. I was at my desk and I heard it, and I felt a little sensation in my head. I thought it was them, and then I thought, no, I'm imagining it. And I was busy. I didn't have time to stop and think about it. It's a good noise. It doesn't hurt or anything. Sometimes it's very high pitched, but it can also sound like a hum. Except it's inside your head, and your ear pressure can change. When it comes you sort of feel your ears pop or something."

D: *And you don't realize that's what it is?*
J: Well, I do now. But you're not thinking about it, so when it happens it's kind of a surprise. I thought they were just letting me know they were there, and it was okay. That's not the first time they were at my desk. Sometimes they do that, and they work the energy through you. You don't have to do anything, because it's energy work for the planet. Sometimes you don't have to go anywhere.
D: *But this time you felt you had to go somewhere?*
J: I didn't plan on going anywhere. I wasn't going to get lunch, and then I was surprised when I said I *was* going to get lunch. Then I thought, "Oh! Did I say that?" (Chuckle) And I realized *they* wanted me to leave, because I had not planned on leaving. Then I thought, "Oh, well, they must be going to do work or something, so I needed to leave." It bothered me, because I'm usually at home when it happens, not in the middle of the day at work. Then when I went downstairs in the elevator it made my stomach feel funny, so I knew it was starting to happen. It does that sometimes when the time changes.
D: *The time changes?*
J: (Her voice was slowing down, becoming softer.) Yeah. You move into a different time.

D: What do you mean?

J: Things get different. You stop being on this time, and you go ... when I got on the elevator I realized the time was getting different. But it was okay. I know what it is now. And I wasn't afraid. And then when the elevator started to move ....

She began to breathe heavier as though with effort, or maybe from nausea. I gave comforting suggestions. After more heavy breathing I wanted to remove her from the elevator.

D: Then did you go to your car or what?

J: Yeah, I was feeling like in a dream state then. Whew! (More labored breathing.) That's when I realized they were really, really here. And that I was really, really not quite in this dimension. That I was in it, but I was out of it. I was moving through it physically, but it was ... (More sensations.) And I got to my car, and I was just trying to maintain this dimension. And I thought, "Well, I'm going to drive. I said I'd go get lunch for the girls in the office, and I'm going."

D: And you have to be able to drive.

J: Yeah. (She seemed confused.) And I started the car, and I realized that ... whew! I was feeling funny. It's like: speeded up and slowed down, speeded up and slowed down, speeded up and slowed down.

D: Boy, that would be confusing.

J: Well, it's not confusion. It's not even that. It's the molecular... you can feel your body doing it. And you know it's happening, and you know you're doing it, and you know it's... (Big breath) It's starting to move, starting to move. (Confusion) It's not bad. It's not a bad thing.

D: But we're just remembering at this point, and it won't really bother you in any way.

J: It's not a bother. It's an excitement. (Big breath) You know that you're here on this Earth, and yet, whew! It's like going over a culvert. Whew!

D: All right. Let's move ahead until that feeling has passed.

J: Well, it won't pass.

D: But you'll be able to ignore the feeling as you talk to me. So it won't interfere with your communication.

J: (A whisper) I'm sorry.

D: *That's all right. Because I don't want you to experience anything at all that would be of any discomfort to you.*

J: Oh, it's not discomfort. It's a wonderful feeling. It's good.

D: *But you can put it aside as you talk to me, so you can communicate clearly that way. Now, what happened as you drove your car down that street?*

J: (The sensation was apparently not bothering her now. Her voice was steady and clear.) Well, I got in the car and started to drive toward the edge of the parking lot. And I was supposed to turn to the left, get on the freeway, and go to Andy's and get lunch. (Surprised) But when I got to the edge of the parking lot I didn't turn left, I turned right. And as soon as I made the turn right, I thought, "Oh! this is really strange, because I should have gone to the left." That's crazy to turn right. And I thought, "Oh, well, the Post Office is down here. Since I'm going this way I'll just get my mail at the Post Office." So I turned and went down Seventh. And I turned on Woodlawn in front of the Capitol. And as I started going down toward the Capitol, that sensation started again. Then I turned to the right to go down Fourth Street. As soon as I turned the corner then I ...(her voice dropped softer) I lost it. (Confusion, garbled half sentences.)

D: *What do you mean, you lost it? You didn't know what happened then or what?*

J: I don't know. I seemed to have gone somewhere, and then I was "swish" back in my car. And it was, "Where am I?" Because I was back ... I mean, I was back. And I was going fast, but the car wasn't going fast. And I thought, "Oh, oh, oh, where am I going? What city am I in?" For a minute I didn't know where I was. Then I thought, "Oh, should I stop the car?" But then ... it was fine. I was fine. And I wasn't afraid. It wasn't fear. It was just a surprise and then, where was I? And I tried to look around and see where I was. It looked unfamiliar. And then all of a sudden I was at the Post Office, and there was no place to park the car. So I went around and around the Post Office. And while I was driving, I felt the strong urge to look up. And there they were right up there. Three of them and just beautiful.

D: *What did they look like?*

J: They were silver and round, and making a humming sound. There were three of them, and they moved in a pattern, like they were dancing. It was for me. It was like a thank you. I knew what it was, but I wanted people to know. I wanted them to see what I was seeing. They were pretty, really pretty. I knew I'd just got back from there. As soon as I looked, as soon as I saw them, I knew.

D: *Did anybody else see it?*

J: I tried. I wanted them to see it. I rolled down all my windows, and I was yelling. And I couldn't hear any noise. Cars were going down the street, and I couldn't hear them. I couldn't hear the people talking. They were standing right in front of me talking, and I couldn't hear what they were saying. I was getting exasperated, because I wanted them to look up there. I was pointing and yelling, "Hey! Don't you see it? Look! Look!" And I was trying to show everybody but they wouldn't look. I didn't understand why they weren't looking, and then I realized, oooh, I can't hear them. Ooooh! I must be invisible. Maybe they can't see me or something. I thought, "Where am I?" Because if they can't see me and I'm right here, where am I? I was having these thoughts. I didn't understand it, but it was kind of fun. And I asked the ships, "What's happening here?" And they mentally told me that I wanted to see them. So they wanted to give me that, like a present. I know I've been there, but I don't remember that part.

D: *Then did things return to normal after that?*

J: Not right away. I parked the car. And after I got out I was walking and I spoke to this guy, and he didn't even hear me. (Chuckle) That was a little unnerving. And I thought, "Okay. I'm just going to act normal." Then as I started up the steps I could feel my body again. And I saw somebody coming out of the building, and I yelled at him. I was so close it startled him. (Laugh) As soon as he said, "Hi!", then I could hear.

D: *The sounds came back?*

J: Uh huh. And I could hear people talking. I couldn't hear anybody talking till that man said, "Hi!" He looked familiar, and I knew that I knew him. But he jumped, he was startled.

D: *But that brought you back to normal. Well, I would like to explore that part where you think you went somewhere. When the time was speeded up, before you came back. We will see what happened during that time. I was told the last time we worked that if I took you to this state I could communicate with people on the ship. He said I didn't have to give any other instructions than that. Would it be possible for one of them to come and explain what happened during that time?*

While I was asking these questions and trying to reestablish contact something unusual happened within my own body. I had the strong sensation of heat up around my crown chakra, which is located on the top of the head. I felt heat and tingling all around the top of my head. It was a strange feeling, but it didn't interfere with my ability to concentrate and ask questions. I had never felt it before, and it was distracting. I glanced around the room trying to figure out where it was coming from. And I waved my hand over my head, like shooing away flies, even though I knew it was not being caused by anything physical in the room.

Janice made some vocal grunting noises as though it was difficult to get started. The voice that finally came through was different from the last time. This time instead of the mechanical, robot type, it sounded more human. However, it had an authoritarian sound. Janice's lighter, somewhat apprehensive, definitely female, voice with an Arkansas accent was gone.

J: You can know some of it. But you will not be allowed the fullness, because it is uncompleted.

D: *What do you mean, it's uncompleted?*

J: There is more to come from this incident. And it cannot be revealed at this time. Before we begin I would like to apologize for any discomfort I may have just caused you. We were scanning to be sure you were the same person that worked with Janice last time. We had to be sure that your thought processes were properly connected, and your intentions were still the same as they were in the beginning.

D: *That was causing the feeling of heat?*

J: Yes. It was merely a scanning device. It caused no harm.

D: *When I was scanned before it was a tingling feeling throughout my body (reported in Chapter 7), rather than heat.*

J: Different crafts have different devices, but they serve the same purpose. You cannot deceive us. We know your motives better than you know them yourself. If your motives were not still pure and clear, then you would not be allowed to have this communication. You may now proceed with your questions.

This entity had a masculine feel, and I felt confident with his explanation. I instinctively knew that this being would not harm me or Janice. I could feel protection in his voice. If he had wanted to hurt me he could have done it during the scanning, and I could have done nothing to prevent it. But I have never felt fear when working with these beings, only curiosity.

D: *I'm trying to understand what happened to Janice during this incident. Was she really driving down the street?*
J: She was driving down the street. But she transcended your dimension, and her car was not on your plane nor was she.
D: *Then where did they go?*
J: They went into our ship.
D: *It is possible to take a car too? A large object like that?*
J: It is possible to take any object.
D: *Does this mean that she disappeared off the street?*
J: Correct.
D: *If someone had been watching, would they have seen anything happen?*
J: They would not have known what they saw, because it is much as when you turn the light out. That quick the change takes place from light to dark. You don't remember the light, because you have the dark.
D: *So the people on the street wouldn't have seen the car disappear?*
J: They would have seen it, but they wouldn't remember they saw it.

This sounded very similar to other cases reported in this book, where the people who are not involved in the incident retain no knowledge of seeing anything.

D: *I'm trying to understand what happens in that process.*
J: They know ... they thought, but it is replaced with a memory that causes them not to know they saw it.

D: Because it would be confusing. Then why couldn't she be taken by herself? Why did the car have to be taken?

J: There was no purpose in removing her, for this was a trip for *her*. And further, if anyone had discovered her empty car, then there would have been a problem for the time period that she should have been gone. Police would have come. And when we returned *her*, there would have been a *big* problem for her to explain.

The voice also had a reverberating quality that seemed to affect the microphone.

D: Then you saw this as a possibility.

J: A very real possibility. More than a possibility, a reality.

D: Then what happened when she was taken onboard?

J: Interaction, much needed by the individual in order to continue the work. A refueling, if you wish, or a granting of desires by the individual to know certain things that, in a sense, could help her in assimilating and being able to function in the reality in which she lives. So in an effort to help her continue with this work, it is sometimes necessary to provide the individual with - if you will grant me the slang, to use your terminology - a warm fuzzy for them to feel and understand that they are appreciated, and not taken for granted. (He may have used slang, but it was said in such a way that it was awkward and definitely unfamiliar to him.) For this individual is of the importance to us that if she has a need or desire, we will see it satisfied within her or without in her everyday life. For the work she is doing and has done has been of great value to this planet. And therefore her desires will be satisfied.

I got the impression that the voice was coming from an older man. The words were very carefully enunciated and at times clipped.

D: I think that's very good. So when she and the car were taken, it just passed through a dimension? (Yes) *I'm always thinking of physically, I guess, how something that heavy could be transported through the air or whatever.*

J: It has to do with the speeding up or the slowing down of the molecules within the form, as she understands it.

D: It does no harm to the person or the car? (No) *Then when it came back, what was occurring there, with the absence of sound and the feeling of being invisible?*

J: It was in order for her to continue to experience the gift. It was not for the eyes of the others, and it needed to be in her consciousness that it was a real experience. It was a method for allowing her to know the value we place on her wishes. It was a method for us to say to her, "We agree. We agree." Maybe to put this in your frame of reference, it could be explained in the manner of saying, this is our way of communicating to the individual the importance we value them. If they wish to see us in the daylight, as she had been desiring, then that will happen, because it is important for them to know we trust them, and they can trust us. And in that trust the work can continue and flow. As to the sound, as to the state in which she found herself unable to communicate, that was necessary for assimilation back into this dimension. In that it is sometimes (He had difficulty with the word:) incongruent, and also because of the time reference frame, impossible to immediately pick up. In that there is a lag, because of the speed in the other dimension. You have to reassimilate back into this one. Therefore sometimes it is necessary to provide invisibility to the individual until they can assimilate back.

D: Then the other people really couldn't see her?
J: Correct.
D: Then she was between the dimensions. And this was ....

Janice began to experience signs of discomfort. She seemed to be heating up, and pulled the cover off. I gave suggestions for well being, and she seemed to be cooling down and becoming more comfortable. I then continued with my questioning, "The lack of sound was because of not being quite back?"

She seemed uncomfortable again. Then a sudden switch, as though the entity was back in control. Was it his energy that was causing the feeling of heat?

J: It can be explained in this manner. This individual can operate in more than one dimension at the same time. This was also a manner of showing her she is able to do this. An introduction, if you will, to that space and that time, of being able to transcend

306

one dimension into another. Perhaps the third dimension. There are times when she operates in more than one dimension, and she knows that.

D: Then as she came back she and the car really were invisible to the people until she parked it and got out?

J: Correct. There was a point in time at which her complete reassimilation would take place. Until that point in your time frame reference was reached, she could not return.

D: So as far as the other people on the street were concerned, she did not exist.

J: Correct.

D: When she saw the three ships in the sky, were they visible to anyone else?

J: No. Because she had the sight of more than one dimension, she could see them. The others did not have the sight.

D: Then as she was coming back the ships were still in the other dimension.

J: They were in the other dimension. But she could see them, for she could see in both dimensions simultaneously.

D: I've had other people also speak of experiences like this, where there was no sound and they were trying to get attention from other people. And I was wondering what was happening at those times.

J: It could be the same thing.

D: And sometimes there seems to be a lack of activity altogether, on the streets or wherever, as though everything had stopped.

J: That happens. That is a different thing.

D: What is happening in those cases?

J: Time stops.

D: For the individual or the outside world or what?

J: It can happen for both.

D: I'm very curious. I'm always trying to understand these many different things. When her energy was being adjusted, as you said on the ship, is this done with machines of some kind?

J: No, it's done with thought.

D: And she had to be there in physical form to do this?

J: She didn't have to be, but it took place faster that way. This individual can work from anywhere. There are times when it is necessary to commune directly. Necessary for the individual more so than for us.

D: May I ask, is this the same entity being I was talking to the last time? (No) *I thought the voice seemed different. And I was told that whoever was not busy, I guess, would be the one to speak to me. Is that correct?*

J: This is the individual with whom she is presently working.

D: All right. The other time the voice sounded more mechanical. And I am trying to understand how that communication took place. Was it telepathy, telepathic, or by some kind of mechanical means?

J: I do not understand your question.

D: The other voice seemed to be more mechanical, or similar to a robot type, I guess I should say.

J: That was a different level of communication.

D: How is this communication taking place, between me and you?

J: It is taking place through a method of transference into the brain cells of your subject, and then her vocal cords are being used to convey the sound to you. It could be done directly to you.

D: But then it would still have to come through something, wouldn't it?

J: It does not have to.

D: Where you are from, are you a being that uses speech?

J: We can or we cannot.

D: I didn't know if you had the vocal equipment to use speech.

J: We can simulate your speech. That's what I am doing.

D: That's why I thought maybe you were using some kind of mechanical device.

J: There are different levels of workers. You were simply speaking with a level of worker with which she was working at the time. There has been a stepping up. There have been many other meetings, and there is a different level of work going on, as was communicated to you before. I know that you remember. We told you we had many projects. The more that the being is willing and wishes to handle, as she progresses. This will become more and more a part of the reality to the point that there will be a time when you won't perhaps notice that much difference at all.

D: But you said you could speak to me directly. I prefer this method myself. I'd rather not be contacted directly at this time.

J: If those are your wishes.

D: *I think it would help the credibility of my work to remain the objective reporter at this time.*

J: We would not hinder your work ever, because it is a great service that you are doing to your planet. You are a pioneer.

D: *This is why I would rather do it in this way. I think if it came the other way, I might be frightened or startled to where I wouldn't want to do any more experiments.*

J: There is something that needs to be explained to you. That is: this method we are using or that is being communicated to you. Since your last meeting with this individual much work has taken place. And assimilation integration work has taken place to the point where we now work with this individual at an energy level state in which there is a difference of functionality. The individual has advanced past the point of working with the being she was working with. It is now at a different level.

D: *I knew there was a difference in the personality. May I ask what you look like?*

J: I look similar to your people on the Earth.

D: *Because the other one said he appeared more like the small ones with the large eyes.*

J: Correct. We know them. And we understand their work. However, they are subject to us.

D: *And you look more like we consider humans to appear.*

J: We can look like what we want to look like.

D: *How can you do that?*

J: It is a method that we learn from birth. It is thought.

D: *You will find I ask many, many questions. So be patient with me.*

J: You are a curious woman.

D: *I sure am. Then do you have any form that is your original form, or your main condition?*

J: We have.

D: What is that form like?

J: Pure energy.

D: *Then you don't necessarily need a physical body?*

J: Correct.

D: *But you manifest a physical body for different reasons. Can I know why?*

J: If we want to walk on your planet, if it is necessary to save a subject, if it is necessary to work in an area where we physically need a presence.

D: *Don't you feel rather inhibited that way though, if you're pure energy?*

J: It is very heavy to do this.

D: *I think it would be, because you're used to being so free.*

J: It is a little confining, yes. Do you understand that you're speaking to a level that is in containment of your small being, in that .... (Sigh) There is a point at which an individual reaches. The ability exists to work in the energy state, and that individual learns to do so. That is what Janice has been doing most recently. And she is aware of it.

D: *Well, are you onboard a craft?*

J: We are presently onboard a craft.

D: *I find that curious. Your normal state is pure energy, but yet you still need a craft to travel in?*

J: In certain dimensions we do. The closer we come to the Earth the more necessary it is for us to do this, because of the harmful aspects of your ozone layer and the various other pollutants in your planetary system. In order for the pureness of the energy to be maintained there is a need for sealing it in, in such a manner so that the teleportation of it is not hindered in any manner, or interrupted. Whenever you want to work on this plane of existence, it can be done in several different methods, depending upon the project. Now, what I want to tell you is that in relation to the energy state, you do not need *anything* to work. However, depending upon the purpose or the mission, that is what determines the method used. Light, your light, your pure light, pure thought, this we can work with from anywhere with no form, no shape. But when it is necessary to come into this dimension, be *here*, because of the existing planetary conditions we must protect that energy state, in order for it to be properly used. For energy can be affected by what it touches, molecularly. Therefore, if we came in the pure energy state that energy which we are bringing to your planet - which is so necessary at this time - would be changed molecularly. Even one molecule of change would make a difference, and would not affect the necessary change. Is that an explanation you understand?

D: I'm trying to. This is why you would manifest a body?

J: This is why you would manifest a body. This is why you would come in a ship. Because inside that containment the molecules of your atmosphere will affect the physicalness, but it won't touch the pureness of the internal energy. If you come in an energy state, you will interact with the molecules in the air. Therefore, the existing negativity will interact with the pureness of the energy being brought, therefore changing that pure essence state. It is necessary to maintain the pure essence state. That is also another reason for Janice to be taken upon the ship, to have her vehicle taken upon the ship. The essence she returns to Earth with could be transferred to *her from* where we are. But in order for containment thereof to be fully realized, that must be done in her physicalness, because she is to return and live in her physicalness.

D: Yes, she has to be in a physical body on this Earth at this time.

J: That's right. But the energy within her is not of the physicalness of this world that you live in.

D: Would that be because she is really one of you?

J: She has been one of us. She has passed us.

D: Then in past lives, as we consider linear past lives - that's the only way I can understand it - she was one of you at another time?

J: She is still one of us, but she is more than that. She is past us. She condescends to work with us. We feel honored to have her in our presence.

D: That's very good. When most people see you beings, are you manifesting whatever form you think they should see?

J: I do not understand your question.

D: Okay. When other people say they have seen aliens, as we call them, or beings from outer space, they see them in different forms.

J: Because there are different aliens.

D: I was wondering if all these forms were just being manifested.

J: They exist. They're not being ... (Sigh) They exist. They exist just as you exist. The difference in them is the same as the difference between you and someone who is Chinese.

D: That's what I've believed. But your type is different.

J: We are an integration. Because of our development we are able to do the things that the others do. That is not our main purpose. The experiments are something they are highly involved in.

D: And you're not involved in that.

J: Not in the medical experiments. We are working at levels much
past there.

Janice was breathing heavier, experiencing heat. I gave
suggestions that she would become cooler. The heat seemed to be an
energy build up that fluctuated.

D: *I know my questions must seem very simple, but that is the only
way I can learn. So I hope you will be patient with me.*

J: Words are getting in the way of our explanations to you.

D: *That's the only way I can understand though.*

J: We understand. But to fully explain a process in words in your
human terms is sometimes difficult. And the miscommunication
of the intent or meaning is not fully realized, because of the
limitations of your language.

D: *I've heard that many times from other people.*

J: We find it very interesting as to why you write your sentences out.
I will use the word "comical." It seems comical to us as to why
you have to write out every little tiny word. In our communication
we use one symbol, and that symbol can convey paragraphs and
paragraphs of information. We use symbols to describe or give
information, either in mental communication or in writing. Instead
of writing a name for an individual on the craft, one symbol could
tell what he does, what he has been doing, what his purpose is here
on the Earth project, and where he comes from, what type of
environment. His history and function is in that one symbol.
Other symbols describe the planet and star system the individual
comes from.

D: *That's a lot of information enclosed in one.*

J: Some of these symbols are on the walls of the craft, and also in our
books.

D: *Oh, there are books?*

J: Yes, Janice was shown a book with this type of writing. And
although she insisted she didn't understand what it said, she was
told that she *did* understand. But only in a certain state of mind
would she be able to interpret. This may help you to understand
the difficulty we have attempting to communicate with you in the
archaic and tediously slow method of spoken words. Especially

when there are often no words for the concepts we are trying to explain.

The entity then gave an example of mental communication through symbols. He said we do the same thing without realizing it, but we have not developed it to the point they have. For example, the symbol "Xmas" contains and brings to mind thousands of images: Christmas trees, decorations, presents, baby Jesus, Nativity, Santa Claus, the colors red and green, bells, and on and on. The pictures and also the feelings that one symbol brings to our minds could fill pages and pages of writing. I had no trouble bringing other such symbols to mind. The analogy was a good one. It explained the reasoning for communicating in symbols and incorporating whole concepts in such a simple device. It is no wonder they have problems with, and often a lack of patience with, our tedious methods of communicating in written and spoken language. I returned to the question I had asked before he began his lecture.

D: *Then when these other people have experiences with aliens, they are not all seeing manifested forms. These are definite physical breeds, so to say, species?* (Yes) *I tried to put these aliens I've been told about into different categories as to jobs they do. Now I don't know if that is possible or not, but I would like to ask some questions about that. For instance, the type of beings that we call the "little grays." You said they are mostly involved with the medical experiments?*

J: At their level they are involved and they are helpers. Many people have misunderstood them. They have been blamed for many things. There may be those of them who would do that sort of experiments that you hear people talk of. However, there are also the beings working in the area of helping the human begin to withstand certain levels of energy. Because of the changes that must take place internally in an individual, in order for them to operate in the realms of energy to which the person you are speaking to, Janice, operates, there must be physical changes within her body. Otherwise it would disintegrate, and it would not be able to return to your dimension. Therefore the grays and those of our brothers who are engaged in that level of work, would be considered much as your doctors are considered. In that they fix, reconstruct, maintain and do the sort of work *mechanically*. They are not involved in energy work as we are involved. The energy work they are involved in is simply to accomplish the mechanical changes within an individual. And actually when it is time for the change to take place .... (She was showing signs of discomfort again.)

D: *Are you getting cold now?*

It seemed to be the opposite of the heat build-up. I pulled the cover over her again, and gave suggestions.

D: *Then they are the ones involved with the testing and these different types of things.*

J: Yes. (Big breath.)

D: *I've also been told of another one that resembles the grays, but they are very tall with long fingers and long limbs. Are you aware of the ones I'm talking about?*

J: There are several breeds like that. I'm not sure which one you're speaking of.

D: *Well, I've been told they are very tall beings. And they wear robes, I believe. And have very long fingers, and long arms and legs.*

J: And what color, and what physical shape do you have of the face? Because there is a race of beings who are pure extraterrestrial beings, however they are tall and unassuming people. And if you saw them you would think they look like giant versions of your people on Earth. However, they are not, they are extraterrestrials.

D: *I believe these others had different facial characteristics. And they have been seen mostly on the large ships. What we call the "mother" ships.*

J: Yes. If you are speaking of the beings on the mother ships, then I am understanding you. But when you say they are tall, there are several tall races. Many of these are the teachers. When the individual is working with a mother ship, there is a great teaching. They are past the level of the grays. They have moved up, in your language.

D: *Some people have observed them doing laboratory experiments, on a larger scale.*

J: Well, my familiarity with it is they are doing experiments in other areas. Areas of ... when you get to the physics level.

D: I have classified them as being more intelligent.

J: Exactly. That's what I'm telling you. I said you have moved up the ladder, in your terminology. You would consider that as if you had graduated to another level.

D: And there's another type that people have told me about. They appear to be more of an insect type, as we understand insect facial characteristics and limbs. Of course, this always disturbs the person whenever they see this type.

J: If you will look at your planet you will see the same thing you are talking about. Go outside on your Earth and you look at your ants. Then you look at your grasshopper. Then you look at your worm. Then you look at your bird. Then you look at your bear. Then you look at ... anything. I could go on for endless, endless, endless. It is engaging in the same principle. The same life forces that operate on your planet operate here. In all these images that these beings come from, they are the same. It's the same ... (He had difficulty) the word is ... the language is .... (Sigh)

D: What? Molecular structure or what?

J: No. Comparatively speaking, what you are observing and what people on the Earth plane are observing are the different levels of the beings that are at work. Or that exist, simply existing.

D: But it seems to disturb the humans more when they see these insect type.

J: Well, do you think that it does not disturb an ant when it sees you?

D: (Chuckle) I hadn't thought of that. Of course, we're much larger.

J: Oh, ho! Oh, ho! Oh, you're very different from an ant. Physically you look rather strange to an ant. And you inspire fear in his heart when he sees your foot coming toward his head. (I laughed) So you have the same principle. I'm trying to tell you the same principle is in operation. Exactly the same principle.

D: But I've tried to classify them as to the work they do. And in my way of understanding, the insect types are more of a servant type being. Maybe I'm wrong.

J: No, you're not wrong.

D: In the way people have seen them, they more or less do as they are told. They didn't seem to have any initiative of their own.

J: They are considered to be the workers.

D: And other types seem to be presenting themselves one way, when they actually look like another.

J: They can present themselves as anything they want to be. If they want to be a cat, they are a cat. And individual humans that work with us come to know this, and therefore there is a very different manner of interacting, because of the fact that individuals come to recognize when this is taking place. So they honor each other. In that if it is necessary or needed that one of us come down and be a cat, then that's what we do.

D: *Would this explain ... some people call these "screen memories." They think they're seeing something, and it's actually not there.*

J: That is one of the purposes, but that is not the entire purpose. Sometimes, as in Janice's case, because of the high level at which she operates, and some of the projects in which she engages, in order to help with her reentry, it is necessary to bring a physical object to her. And in her interaction with it she becomes grounded to your planet.

D: *This is why she takes her dog or her car?*

J: No, no, not at all. It has nothing to do with taking anything. You see .... (Sigh) The physical body returning to your physical world must reintegrate. Reintegration is sometimes necessary to provide help to the individual. (He again had difficulty with the words.) Because of the energy level at which that individual has been operating prior to reintegration, it is sometimes difficult to step that energy back down into the physicalness of your world. Therefore, in order to do that it is sometimes necessary for that individual to interact with a special object provided by us. Therefore it could be in the form of an animal. It could be in the form of a rock that the person is attracted to. When they begin to touch that, we, through that reintegrate them into their physical reality. You should very well understand this. You bring people out of hypnosis all the time. It's much the similar principle in operation.

D: *I see. Try to be patient with me. I think as we continue to talk I will understand more. But in the beginning I am full of many questions that might seem very naive to you.*

J: You are a very wise woman, and I apologize for being abrupt. It's just that at this point I will have some place to be, and I want to get your questions answered. So I'm in ....

D: *A little impatient then. Abrupt. All right. I'll learn your personality too.* (Chuckle) *I do have some questions I would like to ask you. And we can get on to them.*

J: If it is time for you to gain this knowledge it will be given. But please understand that anything that is not answered will not be because we have any disrespect for your work or your questions. It will simply be due to the fact that, in our manner of being ... you must understand time, not *your* time, not *our* time, but *all* time. Because we are from a place that is past any time. Therefore, in order for us to come into and *through* the *different* times, it is very precise. Very precise actions, very precise moments - as you would consider them - moments of time. It can only sometimes take place at that one particular moment. If that second is one too soon, or one too late, everything has been changed.

D: *That's why you can't give me any information that I'm not ready for.*

J: It is important that you understand that. It is important that you know that some of this information will come. But it must come *specifically*, and it must come at a *specific* point in time. A specific point, not only in your time, but through time from where I'm operating to where you are.

D: *So I can only ask the question, and see if I can get the answer. These are some questions that my friend who is involved in UFO research asked me to present to you.* (I was speaking of Lou Farish.) *We will just see if you can answer. He wants to know how does genetic experimentation relate to cattle mutilations?*

J: Holographically. Cattle mutilations are a subject of much concern to us.

D: *Because they are perceived negatively here.*

J: They are perceived negatively on your planet. However, what you need to know is that: you may go out in Little Rock to your medical center, and you will see the same experiments taking place. And *you* are doing it *to* yourselves. So why should you be so alarmed that, for research purposes, you do the same thing to a cat and a dog, but yet when it is done at the level of cattle, then it - excuse me - freaks you out? Now these are not done for fun. (He had difficulty finding the words.) From an organ certain races are experimenting to reproduce things on their planet. Genetically a cell from the cow's liver could be mixed with that of a chicken's liver. And from that combination there can be a completely different sort of lifeform. Cattle mutilations have been lumped into one grouping. This is incorrect. Incorrect. Not all your cattle mutilations have been done by the space brothers. Some of them have been done by highly developed individuals on your own planet, for purposes that are less than honorable.

Janice displayed signs of discomfort again. She threw the cover off. She seemed to be trying to keep the temperature steady in her body.

D: *Well, the people that are doing this experimentation with the cattle, are they a specific group of aliens?*
J: It is all in one *whole.* See, it is much as you are always saying, "We are *one.*" Aliens are all one, but we are all different, in the same manner. And we develop much the same as you develop individually.

She began to experience heat again. I gave cooling suggestions.

D: *I know this is difficult for you, but it won't be much longer.*

Apparently it was only Janice's body reacting, because it was not affecting the entity speaking through her. He continued as though there had been no interruption.

J: In the same manner that you develop individually at a different pace, so do the aliens. Therefore at what point they are in their evolvement, they are being allowed to do their experiments, just as you are. Because of the interaction between the groupings of them, we all fit into the whole. There is a definite - and this is an improper term for it, but you will understand it - hierarchy. It is an evolutionary process with them just as it is for the people on your planet, and as it has been from the beginning of your planet. So! So we have evolution, alien evolution.
D: *One thing people have asked is why they have to kill so many cattle?*
J: They did not kill them all. That's what I'm trying to tell you. All that has happened here is that it has been sensationalized to the

point where the people who want to do this on your own planet can get away with it and blame the aliens. Much of it has been blamed on the aliens that the aliens did not commit. We do not come to harm.

D: *I can believe that, but still they want me to ask these questions. All right. In the last session the other being was talking about a deal, I suppose you would say, that had been made with the government. Do you know anything about that? Because he said the government ended up betraying them.*

J: This is correct.

D: *Can I know a little more about how that came about?*

J: (Sigh, and then reluctantly.) Well ... there was an agreement. There was a point in your time where your government, because of - what they called - our "power," (Sigh) had fear that we could or would or wanted to overtake and completely control your world. Now, we chose that time and capitalized upon that fear, however we did not mean to inspire the fear. That does not mean that we are not here to use *every and any* means that are available to us, in order to cause mankind to *stop* it. Stop it! *Stop* it, mankind. Do you not realize what you're doing to your universe? *So* what I'm trying to explain to you is that your government became afraid of us. We saw that as an opportunity to make a deal with them. However, we had no intention of overthrowing your planet, but we got their attention. And once we had their attention, of course, some things happened. Some accidents took place that gave rise to this whole scenario, in that we did have some accidents. And your government does have some information that some people are correct in assuming, with regards to the Roswell incident. You are familiar?

D: *Yes, I know about that.*

J: So meetings took place, and there was contact made that caused a truce in something that there never was a war to have a truce in. But we allowed that to take place. And we kept our part of the agreement. However, your government did not keep their part of the agreement.

D: *That figures.*

J: What happened is that the more information and the more technology we shared with them, the more greedy they became. So that we saw the heart of man again. The worm turns, and we realized what we were dealing with. And our hearts became very full and sad, because we realized. Then it forced us to become subversive again, and that is not what we need in order to perpetrate peace on your planet. But it's the only way you understand. You cannot seem to deal with "heads up," so to speak.

D: *With honesty.*

J: Correct.

D: *Then your people had contact with those in the government, and there are people in the government that know you exist?*

J: Very well.

D: *And communicate with you?*

J: Very well. There are people in your government much as Janice.

D: *What type of information was shared?*

J: Your stealth bomber is a result of it.

D: *Oh? Were there any others?*

J: There were others.

D: *I've heard it said that computers were a result of communication with aliens. Is that true?*

J: (Big sigh.) There were people who were already working on the computers. It was just a matter of speeding up. So we didn't necessarily give you the technology. You had already bought the idea of it from us. You bought the *idea* of it from us. The work had *begun* on it. So a sharing took place that speeded it up. The government was not involved to that end. That was not a part of what we were speaking of, the "deal."

D: *I was thinking of a deal to give information. It seems to me that a bomber would be for a negative purpose.*

J: Well, you humans have the attention span of an ant sometimes. You know, the bomber does not have to be for a destructive purpose. If you would take the technology and apply it, you could use that as a springboard to learn how to do what we do. Until you know what you do with a bomber, how do you know what you're going to do with a spaceship? (She sounded aggravated.)

D: *I see. Then you feel the government betrayed you?*

J: (She calmed down.) Yes. They betrayed the agreement. Because ... (Sigh) your government has supplied arms to countries all over the world. But the bomber was not for other countries. The technology was for *this* country, because this country was dedicated to peace. The technology of your atomic bomb was shared. Of course, your government is not totally to blame, because the technology was stolen and given to the wrong hands. That was our concern, that the wrong people would come into possession of this technology. And that has happened. So yes, we were betrayed. I'm not saying, of course, that your government was totally at fault. But when you make an agreement from where we are, there are no deviations.

Maybe this was the reason why the aliens could not renege on their portion of the agreement, even though they saw it was being misused. But it would not keep them from being selective in future provisions of the agreement, once they discovered our deceit.

D: *As a result of this are you still sharing information with them?*
J: To a degree. Not to the degree that we could. It is impossible. (Softly) If they do this with us ... (Sigh) then I don't see any justice. We are very sad to see the state of affairs.
D: *Then you have not stopped giving them all information. You're just not giving them as much as you were, or a different type.*
J: Selectively. There have been certain people, like Tesla, who could be trusted with what he knew. There are certain individuals, like Janice, who can be trusted to do what is proper with the information she has. It is a matter of trust. So as far as the sharing of technology, we will not stop that. Because we are here to *help*, not to even make deals. It's you that want the deals. It's not us that wants the deals.
D: *But you still are not going to share the technology you could, because of this.*
J: Exactly. Do I go and teach President Bush how to use the speed of light to transport himself? (Forced chuckle) I will teach Janice. She knows. She can do it.
D: (Chuckle) *But he couldn't be trusted with it.*
J: That's correct.
D: *Oh, I agree. But the man I am working with on this, he wanted to know more about that. He said that sounded more rational.*
J: What? I ... I?
D: *The man that I work with on this type of information. There is one man that I share things with, and he has never ....*

J: We know, we know him, we know this man.

D: *And he is the one who wrote these questions.*

J: What sounds rational to you?

D: *It's been said that the government was not the one who reneged on the deal. That it was the aliens. And he said, "That doesn't make sense."*

J: Your government made it appear .... You know, they are very good at this. It's as much as if you are very heavy and you want to eat two tons of ice cream. You will find a way to make that okay. So if you want to misuse our technology, you are going to blame us for your misuse. Because you're not going to sit and say, "Oh, I was bad. I did that." It is worse in America, really.

D: *That's what he said, "How dumb can they be to think they can fool people who can read their minds."*

He laughed, but it was forced, not natural.

J: This is correct. We were laughing, but it is no laughing matter. It saddens us. And we become very, very selective of the individuals that we share information with. To come to interact with the level you're talking to now, it takes a purity of the individual, the vehicle through which we're speaking. Do you understand that I am talking about energy?

D: *Yes, I can understand.*

J: If you reduced her to her energy state, you would find not one molecule amiss. That is from her own doing. And from her own life, the way she has devoted herself and lived. Now, in also knowing that, you must understand that this being is past where we are, energy wise. Past here. Do you grasp what I am saying to you?

D: *I think so. Because I've worked with people who said in other lives they were at a higher energy level. And sometimes they come back to this world.*

J: This person is not of your world. But yet she is operating in your world and in other worlds simultaneously.

D: *And that takes a very advanced spirit to do that.*

J: She is coming to more fully understand her totalitness. That is not the word.

D: *Totalness.*

J: No, that is not the word. The *totality* of her energy line as it transcends dimensions. Forget dimensions, we are not talking dimensions. The connection is past dimensions. There are no dimensions where she is from. She is very connected in her soul to her essence. The beginning divine spark of divinity. Within her she carries it all the time. Ah! This is to us an awe-inspiring thing to see that in a human. So we appreciate. And *that* is why we come when she bids to see us in the daytime.

D: *I can appreciate that. Let me ask one more short question, and then I will let you go. He also wanted to know: we have been told that "abductees" - I don't like that term, but that is the term being used - when people are abducted they are implanted with monitors or monitoring devices. And they are monitored throughout their life.*

J: (Hesitation, as though it is not correct.) Well ....

D: *Or kept track of.*

J: And you do the same thing.

D: *Well, he wanted to know: people like us who are UFO investigators, are we also monitored and kept track of?*

J: Of course you are.

D: *He said he suspected it, but he wanted to find out.*

J: Do you understand why? It is really important that you understand why.

D: *Yes, I would like to know. I think he would too.*

J: It is for your protection. It is not for any subversiveness. You are already trusted. You wouldn't be talking to Janice right now if you weren't trusted, because she has not submitted to anything like your investigation before now. And this has been well in her consciousness for three years. She has kept the integrity of all this to herself. And that takes a great strength of character within, to go through the experiences at the human level. Because she does it at the human level at the same time she's doing it on the other levels. So therefore it takes a great strength of character. Mortals don't do this that often in the humanness of it, because the humanness will *shatter.* They either become crazy, or they can't function, or they sit under a tree and stare in space, or .... But she functions, because of her highly developed nature. And because of the mechanics at which her brain and her every being operates, molecularly. The particular design of the energy pattern from her source energy allows her to do this. Now, back to your question.

D: Yes, of the investigators.

J: The investigators. You, your friend, are valued. For us, we value that. You know, you're like our personnel people. What do you call them? You're the PR (forced chuckle). We look to that and we appreciate that. But as far as into your level of understanding, some of you may become frightened, but that is not the intent as far as monitoring. Now, to your original question. The devices that are implanted, most of the time - and I do say, most of the time, because there are different purposes for different devices ....
(Signs of discomfort. Heating up again. Suggestions given.)

D: You said the devices are implanted in the investigators also?

J: No, this is not what I said. You said that.

D: Okay. You were speaking of the devices that were implanted.

J: I said ... Okay. You're back to your original question. Your original question, you said the abductees have these devices implanted and then they are followed for the rest of their entire life. Well, that is the same thing as the cattle mutilations. There are misconceptions and misunderstandings as to: Number one: the purposes thereof. Number two: who they are implanted into. And number three: that they maintain those for the rest of their life. Okay. Devices. (Sigh) Let's take the word "novice." Novice. What is a novice?

D: It's a beginner.

J: Oh! A beginner. (The tone was one of disdain.)

D: That's what I think. A beginner in learning.

J: You are correct. So would you take a child and put that child in the ten foot end of the swimming pool? Would you take a baby and throw it in there with no life preserver on? Would you do that?

D: No, I wouldn't.

J: Nor would we. You know, depending upon the level of work of the "abductee" - which is not what we consider these people to be, from our point of reference.

D: I don't either.

J: We simply consider them to be workers of the light, just as we are. If you take all the beings that we touch, that touch us, you could collectively call them simply and very truly "light workers." And you have heard this. Now, in the beginning when a light worker is becoming awakened, *or* in the grand plan it is *time* for that light worker to become familiar with .... Oh, boy! This could take hours to tell you.

D: *All right. Do you think we should ....*

J: No, no. You must understand this device business. Because it has been, as the cattle mutilations, misconstrued. It is a scary thing for humans to think that they have a device in them. It is unnerving because they think they are not in control. That they are being made into robots to be controlled.

D: *That is a conception.*

J: Yes. And it's a very real concern from the human ideological standpoint. However, that is not really the purpose of a device. The device is much like a seed. You have your time released vitamins. Okay. There are two main purposes of devices. One: to be able to (clapped her hands) ... that quick, connect with that individual. Because, the same way if you throw the baby into the ten foot end of the swimming pool. It is possible for the individual to come into situations in which it would be very necessary to very quickly connect with that person. So that no harm could come to them physically, because of the energy in which they are interacting. There are various other mental processes that the awakening individual goes through. And we're saying awakening, although it's not really. But the mental processes that sometimes begin to take place when a person knows they have been abducted, are *very fear* inspiring in that individual sometimes. We do not wish to cause fear. So these are monitoring devices, and these are also manners in which adjustments may be made. A source of contact that is highly ....

She was having difficulty explaining, and I was concerned because we were coming to the end of the tape.

D: *I think we're going to run out of time. I think we're going to have to continue this at another time.*

J: Certainly.

D: *I hate to stop it at this point, but that was the main question, whether the investigators were also being monitored and watched?*

J: They are being monitored and watched, but not for purposes of mistrust. For their own protection.

D: *Well, I think that's all we're going to have time for today. And it seems as though this energy is affecting the vehicle anyway, with her heat fluctuations. Would it be all right if I come again and speak to you?*

J: We are sorry to see you go, because we have not fully explained to you this device business. But you very well can know it at a future time. It is important to you to know about it, because you will encounter someone who is very fearful. You will begin to encounter more people who have misunderstood the concepts.

D: *All right. But now we are running out of time. And I don't want any information that's not on my little machine. I can start with that topic the next time. We will allow plenty of time to fully explain it then. Will that be all right?*

J: Of course.

The tape ran out. There was so much information I had really cut it close this time. Before I could start the instructions for orienting Janice back to consciousness the entity had a few parting words that I did not record. It sounded like a foreign language: "Alokei. (Phonetic: Ah-low-key-I or Ah-low-key-a)." When I asked him what it meant, he said it was similar to "farewell." So I told him I bid him farewell, too. He then said he would leave so I could bring her back. But he cautioned me to not bring her back too fast, to do it very slowly and gently. The shift was then immediate. I could tell when the entity left and Janice returned. At that point she began to cry, and emotionally said she did not want to leave. I had to give her calming suggestions and convince her that we could return again, before she cooperated and relaxed.

Janice was then brought forward to full consciousness. She again was groggy, and it was awhile before she was able to get off the bed. At least the heat fluctuations were no longer bothering her. That seemed to be related to the energy of the entity, and dissipated when it left and she returned to consciousness. She remembered very little of the session. She was interested when I explained portions, but she listened as if hearing new information. She pronounced the strange word with me, but said it had absolutely no meaning for her. She was confused because she could see she had been crying, and couldn't understand why contact with this being had made her so emotional. She was in total disbelief.

CHAPTER 10
THE ALIEN BASE INSIDE THE MOUNTAIN

During the time I was working with Janice I also found another interesting case in Little Rock. A woman named Linda was supplying information of a different type, which will be included in my book *Convoluted Universe*. I hoped to work with both these women. So a month later, January 1990, I made the trip to Little Rock for the sole purpose of working with Linda and Janice on their continuing stories. I again stayed with my friend Patsy. I did not schedule any lectures and hoped to come into Little Rock unnoticed so I could devote all the time to working with them. Of course, it didn't work out like that. I received a call from a man, who had been to my December lecture, who had a problem and needed therapy. So I scheduled him for Friday night after the long four hour drive. I scheduled three sessions with Linda on Saturday and three with Janice on Sunday. By reserving one day for each woman I felt I could have continuity. I had never done this before. I thought if I could continue to do this on a regular basis I could cram a month's work into one day. I didn't anticipate any problems, because I expected the women would only feel as though they had taken several naps during the day. I thought it would bother me more, because I was the one doing the work and would be tired. If it turned out to be too much on either of us, then I would not schedule such a hectic program again. But I was trying to get as much work done as possible in a few days.

The sessions with Linda on Saturday proved successful even though we did not finish until late that night. My first session with Janice on Sunday began around ten o'clock in the morning. My friend Patsy went somewhere so we would have the house to ourselves. I was a little tired from the long day with Linda the day before, and staying up late talking to drop in visitors. But now my focus was on attempting to locate the entity which had spoken through Janice during the December visit.

I used her keyword and she went into trance very easily. Since I was not given any explicit instructions on how to contact the entities I had spoken to, I had to devise some way to locate them. I instructed Janice to journey to wherever we could have access to the entity we spoke to before, or whoever we were supposed to talk with, so we could continue our conversation. I knew her subconscious could take her to the proper location, so I counted her there and asked what she was seeing.

J: I don't see anything.
D: *What do you feel?*
J: Greetings and welcome.
D: *Do you have any sense of where you are?*
J: No. It's just kind of a blank place.

In retrospect this sounded similar to Nostradamus' special place, which was gray and without form and substance.

J: (The voice unexpectedly changed.) Greetings and welcome. You've come to continue our conversation? So what is it you wish to know?
D: *Am I in contact with the same person I spoke to before?*
J: You are.
D: *I thought you might be busy, and you might send someone else. All right. The last time we were discussing the implants, the little devices that are placed in the heads or the bodies of some human beings. It was getting into a very involved conversation when I had to leave. You said there was much more you wanted to tell me, so we would understand the purpose of these devices. Would you want to continue along that line?*
J: Actually I believe we finished our discussion with regard to the implant devices. However, there was another point of information you were concerned with at the time. That being reassimilation. We know you have some knowledge of how this works.
D: *Go ahead and enlighten me, and maybe I'll understand what it is.*
J: It is to us a very simple process of speeding up the molecules to a point where, as they reach the speed of light in their velocity, then it is very easy for transference to occur bilocationally. If it is a

matter of bilocation or a matter of singular location, either process may be accomplished.

D: Let me see if I understand what you mean. Are you talking about when a person is taken onboard a craft from Earth?

J: Well, it does take place in that manner.

D: What other ways is this used?

J: To transfer energy from one point on your planet to another.

D: What would be the purpose of that?

J: Balancing the energy of the planet.

D: Where does the energy come from that is used?

J: The energy comes from the source of - your word would be "power" - but it is actually the universal flow of the cosmic energy that is throughout all the universes. So it is just harnessed to be used in a manner of balancing for the planet. Some of it is brought via ships, some of it is not.

D: Why would this energy have to be transferred? You said for balance, but why would it have to be balanced?

J: Because you are precariously perched on the edge of destruction.

D: I don't know if the human species is aware of that. We know there are many Earth changes beginning to happen. Is that what you mean?

J: Yes, that's what I mean. For the last three years (1986 1989) you have been perched on the edge of destruction. So you have had help in maintaining balance through different systems on your planet, because of the strategic location of your planet with regard to the universe and other universes. I'm sure it is very hard for you to understand how one small planet Earth could be so important to other universes, but it is a matter of the whole picture. With the folding in of the planet Earth would come destruction to other planets and universes, because of their atomic structure. Therefore at another level the planet Earth is vital, and so is its non-destruction.

D: You called it "the folding in of the planet Earth." What do you mean?

J: (She kept clearing her throat.) It is necessary for adjustments to take place within the physical form to whom you are speaking. At this point in time we are not quite able to adjust to her physicalness. So you will bear with us for a moment while we are tuned in and reassimilated. (After a pause.) Folding in of your planet means: if you took the center point in the core of your Earth, and considered that the Earth could go inside itself, you would see what we call a folding in. Now, in that folding in would come the destruction of your planet. Because as the circumference of the Earth folds into the center of the planet, there would be an explosion to the point of destruction. Therefore, destroyed by fire, as described in your book of Revelation, would be what you humans would consider to be happening. However, it would really be at the level of physics, because in the area of folding in, the space within the center of the core of the Earth would expand to the point where the explosion would take place. And that would cause a rippling effect into space and to universes and other galaxies. Similar to what has happened before in other galaxies. You are simply repeating history in your galaxy.

D: *I was thinking of folding in as a way of collapsing.*

J: You can use that word. We see it as different. The surface of your planet would in effect be collapsing, as is happening presently. That is why we are working with certain individuals at certain locations on your planet. To minimize the effect of the earthquakes regarding what is presently happening on the surface of your planet.

D: *Is it collapsing?*

J: That is a symptom.

D: *I know there are tectonic plates, and that these plates are shifting and moving.*

J: Shifting and moving and folding in.

D: *I keep thinking that is causing some of these earthquakes. And they haven't got to the drastic point yet.*

J: The folding in is what is causing the shifting.

D: *It seems this is something very difficult to stop. (She gave a big sigh.) Or to control. Let's put it that way.*

J: Actually, because of the type of electro-magnetic field that is occurring, we work through that electro-magnetic field in order to rebalance the energies. Energies having to do with the disassimilation of particular land masses. And i.e., that these land masses are eroding, as you would commonly understand it.

D: *Then you can't stop the earthquakes. All you can do is try to minimize their damage? Is that what you're trying to do?*

J: That is what we *are* doing. There is a progression of man that will take place. As far as *stopping* the earthquakes, we are not in the position to step in and do that. Although it is possible that this could happen.

D: *But with your transference of energy and balancing, I thought you were trying to keep them from happening.*

J: Minimize.

D: *Minimizing their effects?*

J: Part of their effects. It places much of the work we are doing in what you would term "a double bind," in order to get mankind's attention focused where it needs to be focused. Apparently the only thing that causes that to happen is cataclysmic events of such magnitude that it shakes his foundation, realizing that his planet is not indestructible. Therefore, to stop them would be defeating the purpose of refocusing mankind's consciousness. So we do not stop them, but we have helped to minimize the effects. Now, what you must understand is the strategic location of your planet. And that *if a* part of these things that are taking place ... it has also to do with the vibrational rate of mankind's consciousness. I realize this is a concept that is foreign to you, in relation to consciousness affecting the physicalness of your planet. However, there is a direct relation. It does not necessarily mean that because the consciousness of an area is at such a low level or is a misdirected state of affairs, that that is what is causing that event to take place at that physical location. It could be something that is happening on the other side of your planet, totally disassociated with the area in which the cataclysmic event takes place.

D: *We're not used to thinking of our consciousness influencing anything.*

J: This is why your consciousness is influencing everything.

D: *Because it's misdirected. Well, I've been hearing that all of these quakes, and the volcanic activity are a prelude to an actual Earth shift.*

J: I see that as unavoidable.

D: *That it will happen?*

J: I personally at this point believe it will happen, yes. What we are involved in is a matter of trying to allow mankind the time. Because you see, your events and pole shifts do not have to take place. However, due to the nature of man on your planet, it's as though you were driving down a dead end street, and you will not turn around and go back. You are heading toward the end, and the end is a brick wall. So therefore, all we are doing is slowing the speed.

D: *Do you think it could have already happened by now?*

J: Very well.

D: *But there is no way of keeping it from happening altogether.*

J: There is a way of keeping it from happening. However, we do not believe mankind will choose that path.

D: *Can you see what will happen, or do you have access to that knowledge?*

J: I have told you what will happen.

D: *I mean when the actual shift takes place.*

I was interested in this because, at the time, I was writing the trilogy *Conversations With Nostradamus*, and the possible shift of the Earth was an integral part of those books.

J: You are speaking of the pole shift as opposed to the destruction of your planet?

D: *Yes. Those are two separate scenarios, aren't they, or possibilities? (Yes) Isn't the pole shift the lesser of the two?*

J: The pole shift is just a point on the road map. It will not alter the course of ....

D: *Of what? (No answer) Do you mean the other is ultimate or what?*

J: At this point in your time it is ultimate.

D: *I've been told these are two possibilities. And the explosion of the Earth, or implosion, however you want to say it, would be the more drastic scenario, and didn't have to happen.*

J: Neither has to happen. But they will. (Sigh)

D: *But the pole shift wouldn't affect the other planets, would it?*

J: The gravitational flow will change to some effect. The ley lines will be totally reversed. Therefore it cannot help but affect the other planets.

D: *When the pole shift takes place, do you know the mechanics? I'm interested in the physical changes of the Earth. What would happen at that time to man?*

J: When you say, "What will happen to man?" What are you asking?

D: I guess I'm interested in the physical changes of the surface of the Earth, and how that will affect the people on the Earth.

I always took advantage of every opportunity to verify Nostradamus' visions of this probable event.

J: You are seeing presently some of the preliminary effects of the pole shift. You can no longer tell your winter from your summer. There are various other things taking place on your planet that should cause you to look about you and know that the pole shift has already started to actually take place. Or do you know that?

D: I've been told that. I know the weather is acting strangely.

J: That is why you have your, what you call, "freaks of nature."

D: But I'm curious about what will happen to the continents.

J: It will depend on what is happening with regard to the vibrational rate of the planet at the time when the actual pole shift occurs. Now, depending upon what other cataclysmic events are taking place, the whole of your planet could be unimaginably changed into completely different countries. The oceans could close and you would perhaps have your geography rearranged, and Asia wouldn't be Asia any more.

D: I assume that the poles would melt, which would create more water.

J: There will be more water, and the water will flow down through Europe, down through the countries and divide them. Along with the earthquakes and the various other things that are taking place. That's why I'm telling you that your world as you know it now will not be your world as you know it now. The United States could totally become a part of Europe. I mean there will be no .... Throw your maps away. You will have a new Columbus. You will be setting sail to discover new worlds. So you will begin to replay your history again.

D: What will happen to civilization as we know it?

J: Much of civilization could revert, because of the technology that will be lost, you will be starting over in some points.

D: But will that be everywhere on the Earth, or just certain places?

J: It will be much as your lost continents of Lemuria and Atlantis. When the technology was lost in those places the same thing happened. So you can take a clue from what you know of these planetary changes, in relation to knowing about these lost continents. Because continents will become lost, and so will all the technology that they contained.

D: *I think that's what bothers me the most, to think that we would lose everything and have to start all over again.*

J: That is the only way man learns.

D: *That's why I was thinking there might be portions that would retain their technology.*

J: There were portions that retained their technology when Atlantis was lost. But the degree and level of development of that technology was nothing like what was lost. So therefore it was in a sense starting over.

D: *Then there will be some parts that will retain this. I hate to think of it all being lost. I guess that's the human part of me.*

J: As I am telling you, you human beings do not seem to learn any other way but to lose it all. You go to Las Vegas and you gamble all your savings, and you learn.

D: (Laugh) *That's true. I have been hearing so much lately about this shift, that's why I was asking so many questions.*

J: There will be changes to the point that the rivers will no longer be rivers. Is this the kind of thing you want to know?

D: *Yes. I want to know what would actually happen.*

J: If you look at your globe and close up your Mississippi River, you will no longer have a line where the Mississippi River was, so that it is one land mass. And then, depending upon how it becomes divided at the time, you will have totally different continents. Therefore rivers won't exist where they exist now. Is this the kind of thing you're asking?

D: *Yes. The topography would completely change then. (Yes) I suppose there will be a great loss of life. (Yes) Can you see how this will happen?*

J: This will happen much in the same manner as it is happening presently. There will be some loss of land mass. You have cities along rivers and rivers overflow, therefore along the rivers entire cities could be lost. And also when it takes place, there will be many earthquakes. You're getting preliminary warnings of what is to occur. The results of your earthquakes are simply a point of .... (Long pause)

D: *What?*

There was a long pause, then a deep sigh. It was soft and unclear, but it sounded like she said, "Why are you interrupting?"

D: What? (A long pause.) *What did you say?* (A long pause and no answer.) *Is something happening on your side?*

The entity was gone, and Janice was back, and confused, "Something happened."

D: Was it something with you or with the one who was speaking or what?
J: With him. I don't know where he ... where did he go? Something happened.
D: All right. Let's see if we can get him back. Maybe he was called away or something. Maybe it was a break in the communication there.
J: I don't know what happened. It was as if I saw a wire, and it just ... snapped.
D: Let's see if we can get it back. Maybe they can adjust on another frequency or however it's done.

I gave suggestions to try to locate him or another entity on another frequency, because apparently the connection had been broken somehow.

J: I can see a meeting and ... I can't hear what they're saying, but I see them. They're away from me. They're over on the other side, over there. (Hand motions.) And there are more people talking to this one, and he's nodding, but he's saying.... I can't hear what they're saying. But there are six others besides him.
D: What do they look like?
J: They have robes on. Kind of regal looking sort of robes, except they're not like kings. They don't have crowns or anything. I don't know how to describe them. Loose, but there's a big wide band that goes down the front, and each side. The material is very pretty. I'm watching the meeting.
D: What do they look like physically?
J: (Surprised) They look like humans. But they look old.

D: Wrinkled or what?

J: Yeah, some wrinkles. But they look old. Real old.

D: Do you know which one was speaking to us?

J: Yeah, he's standing with his back to me. And they're in sort of a circle.

D: Where are you?

J: I'm in a large room. It's really white, clinical looking. But I hear a hum.

D: Is there anything else in the room, furnishings or objects or anything?

J: Yeah, but it doesn't look like our furniture. It's more like the seats are built on the walls. I mean, they're not chairs. They're part of the wall, and they're curved.

D: Like a bench of some kind?

J: Yeah, more like a bench, but I don't think they call it that.

D: Is there anything else in the room?

J: There are some screens ... over there. (She pointed to her right.) Big TV screens. Huge.

D: Are they turned on?

J: No. (Pause) Now somebody's coming in. There's a door. (She pointed to her right.)

D: Does he look like the others?

J: Yeah. Except that he has long ... it kind of looks like hair, but I don't know if it is hair. They all look kind. They don't look like those guys with the big eyes. They're all stopping and turning toward him, and each side made a line. Now he's walking to the front, facing them. And they're doing this. (Made motions.)

D: Put their hand over their heart?

J: Uh huh. And he does that. And they nod. Oh, now they're going to a table.

D: Can you get in a position to know what they're talking about?

J: It's like the sound is turned off. And I can see their mouths moving.

D: But you can still hear the hum?

J: It's like it's in my head. Now they're sitting around the table. He's at one end, and they're down each side. They're passing some papers. Well, it's not really papers. It's something. (Suddenly) Oh! Oh!

D: What?

J: Okay. Now they're turning that screen on. (A big breath.) Different things are flashing. They're going fast on the screen. There's water. Lots and lots of water. It's like a movie going really, really fast. (Pause) Oh! That looks like ... that's a mountain. I know what that is. Where is that? There's a mountain picture on there. (Pause as though watching.) They're talking about .... (Softly) Wait a minute. It just stopped on this mountain, this big mountain. It's a pretty mountain. The one at the head of the table is standing up now, and he's pointing toward one of them. Not the guy who was talking to me, but the one that's one, two, down from him on the left side of the table. He's pointing to the screen, and he's saying .... What is he saying? Gosh! I'm getting exasperated because I can't hear it. I think they're talking about inside that mountain. They have a base inside that. That must be it. (Pause) He's sending this guy to the mountain. The guy's leaving the room. I guess he's going to that mountain.

D: *The mountain was all it showed? It didn't show what was inside?*

J: I know what's inside.

D: *Are you picking it up from them?*

J: I think I've been in there. There's a whole world in there.

D: *Can you pick anything up from them?*

J: There's some kind of problem inside that mountain. And this guy's supposed to go and take care of it.

D: *You said you know that mountain?*

J: Yeah, I've seen it a hundred million times. I know that mountain, but I don't know where it is. But I know that inside it they have a whole city, in different divisions, just like we have a city. Except you go in with a little ship, and then you get out under there, and you go through these different rows and channels and things. And then you get on a thing that's like our elevator, and you go to different levels in the mountain. There's a green area, a blue area, different colored areas.

D: *Why are they different colors?*

J: Different things go on at them. Different kinds of training.

D: *Why were you there?*

J: Because one of the areas is where I went to classes. You sit in this room and people will talk and you know stuff. You go to different levels of the colors.

D: *When did this happen?*

J: Well, it doesn't stop happening.

D: *You mean you're still going there?*

J: Oh, yes. It's a wonderful place. It's like a city. And it's not necessarily clinical like some of the ships you're on. I mean, they're very, very clinical. But inside this mountain it's not that way.

D: *When you go there, do you go in your physical body?*

J: Yeah, sometimes. It depends on what the purpose is.

D: *Why are you not conscious of doing this?*

J: Well, I do know when I see the mountain that I've been there.

D: *I was wondering why you didn't remember.*

It was somewhere around here that the new entity came in. It was a few moments before I noticed it, because this entity was female and the voice was not dramatically different at this point.

J: Because of what takes place in some instances. When you're learning the kind of materials that they teach there, it would interfere with your everyday life if you brought it back to your consciousness as you went about your business. Then you wouldn't be able to function in your normal way, within the perimeters of your life. There are different points in time at which assimilations take place. So you do remember. It's not as if it's foreign to you when you know it. But as far as your everyday consciousness goes, it comes like a thought so you don't freak out over it. And then it becomes a natural part of you. It's more like, "Oh, I knew that all the time." When you really didn't know it, but you know where you learned it.

D: *When you go in your physical body, wouldn't someone miss you?*

J: No, because my lifestyle is such that I'm alone a lot. And another thing is that: in mankind's time what we'd count as a minute ... you could spend eight hours *there* in a minute, because the time doesn't work the same way.

D: *But that mountain is on Earth, and time can be fluctuated like that?*

This was probably when the other entity fully entered, because the information was not Janice's and was presented by someone who was very knowledgeable.

J: Yes, because there's a juncture of time there. That's why so many of your phenomena take place, is because you're at a juncture in time. The dimensions that come to a point at a juncture in time on the Earth planet and Earth time, cause a twisting and turning so man's perception is altered in such a way that he doesn't really know what happened. He just knows it happened.

D: *Is that why they put that base there, because it was at one of these junctures.*

J: Yes. You see, you have your physical ley lines of energy, but you also have time junctures which ... mankind doesn't know anything about time junctures. I mean, he knows about time junctures, but he doesn't understand the principles involved.

D: *Then is it possible for someone to go into a time juncture by accident?*

J: Oh, very, very real. These things happen all the time.

D: *How would the human perceive it when it happens?*

J: The human would perceive it as a memory lapse. "Oh, I must have forgotten that. Oh, what was I doing? Oh, wait a minute. Now let me think about that." That's how the human perceives it. Now, more *developed* humans will know there was more than just that thought of "What happened?" They will have a *sense*, because of the highly developed nature of their other senses. Depending on their level of development and the level of classes they have been to, or where they're at in their evolution, they will know more than just those thoughts. Because there is a whole other set of informational transfer in these kind of humans. Their consciousness and electro-magnetic force field and all the vibrational energies they are in tune with, gives them a whole other set of ways of knowing, and another way of learning.

D: *Well, it sounds as though you crossed these time junctures intentionally, if you were taken there.*

J: It's part of what I've agreed to do. And it's not something I can assimilate back into my daily life. Because of the fact that I wanted to serve mankind I have been taught different ways of assimilating that I'm not consciously familiar with.

D: *I thought if the average person happened to come across one of these junctures, it would be by accident, and there would be no purpose to it. Would that be right?*

J: There's always a purpose to it. However, when the average person comes across it they will experience exactly what I told you.

D: *And it would not necessarily mean they were taken by anyone.*

J: Exactly. It means that at a point in time they were at a physical location at which certain energies and time junctured.

D: *Well, you said this was a base. Who is in control of this base?* (Pause) *I mean, it's not humans, or is it?*

J: No, no, it is not humans. The humans are really unaware of this base.

D: *Who is running it, or who put it there?*

J: It was placed inside this mountain for us to be able to go out among the humans when we need to. And for humans to be able to come to this mountain. And for the kind of work to take place which we are involved in.

D: *Then the only humans that know about it are the ones that are taken there?*

J: This is correct. And many of them are not aware that is what has taken place. They know they've been somewhere, but they do not necessarily realize this is the case.

D: *I was wondering if the government knows about it.*

J: No, not this one.

D: *They know about others?*

J: They think they know.

D: *Has it been there a long time?*

J: Yes, it has. This particular mountain has been there ... in your Earth years? You're asking in your Earth years?

D: *Well, I'm asking how long the base has been in the mountain. I know the mountain would have been there forever.*

J: Well, so has the base.

D: *That long?* (Yes) *Am I speaking to an entity again?*

J: Yes, you are.

I can only describe this voice as sweet and extremely feminine. This quality was what made me realize I was no longer speaking to Janice. That and the degree of knowledge that had begun to come through.

D: *I thought I was. I thought it was too much information to come from Janice.*

J: (Her laughter had a lyrical quality.) Well, we do not mean to trick you. It's a sort of a shifting that takes place sometimes.

D: *I thought I could tell the difference. What happened a while ago?*

J: Well, it was necessary for Alyathan (phonetic: A-lie-a-than.) to go to a meeting. He was given a mission and will not be able to return to speak with you now.

D: *I thought this sounded like a different being. What was his name?*

She repeated it slowly, "Aleeathen." This time it sounded more like: A-lee-a-thin.

D: *Aleeathin. I didn't have a name to summon him by when I was trying to contact someone.*

J: We do not hold to names anyway.

D: *That's what I thought. But do you have time to communicate with me?*

J: I will be able to.

D: *Janice had the impression something was wrong in the base, and that was why the meeting was called.*

J: There was a need for a level of expertise at this point in time, that was not available there. And so in order for some... actually I really cannot discuss it. Other than to tell you there are certain levels of expertise that were not present, that are being sent there.

D: *I'm just curious. I ask many questions. And if you can't answer some of them, just let me know. I would like to know about the history of that base. You said it's been there forever. That intrigues me.*

J: Well, many things have been on your planet forever that you are not totally aware of.

D: *Can you tell me some of these things?*

J: Well, I can tell you of a source of communication that most humans are not able to - to use your slang word – "tap into." The only word that is the equivalent in your language is "vibrationally," although that does not adequately describe what I am discussing. There are particular human beings who have reached a level of evolvement that know of the communication processes, other than with words as humans communicate. And I am not necessarily speaking of telepathy. I am talking about a combination actually of sounds, currents, much as your study you have been conducting for some time with the dolphins and the humpback whales. You see, this is a totally foreign - although quite similar - method of communicating that man does not fully understand. He always looks for a language. And in his need to label things, labels everything or categorizes all things as a language. We are not disagreeing that all things have a language. They do. But the wind carries messages. That is something that is in your different mythologies. You will hear the children speak of talking to the wind, but you will never hear adults speak of talking to the wind. And yet it is a very real source of communication.

D: It sounds like some of the Indian stories.

J: The Indians were very in tune with nature. And where do you think the Indians obtained the knowledge? They were all very in tune with the UFO and space energy. It was around then. That's why I tell you it has been around forever.

D: That's interesting. But can you tell me about the base, and why it was constructed there in the beginning?

J: The base was constructed there in the beginning because of the fact that ... actually the mountain could be considered the center of the universe. You know, we are sticklers for balance. And actually, relating to the rotational axis of your planet, to construct at the point we did, you would logically think we would put it at the North Pole. But that is not the actual center of gravatational rotation of the axis of your planet.

D: But there have been many changes since it was built.

J: There have been changes, but the center will not change.

D: I thought the Earth had moved many times.

J: The Earth has moved. But in relation to how dimensionally this works, this particular center will not change.

D: Would you be allowed to at least tell me what continent it is on?

J: No, I can't at this time.

D: Is that because you think someone may find out about it?

J: It would not be a good time.

D: I was thinking the wrong people could find it.

J: It is just not to be discussed at this point.

D: But why was it built that long ago?

J: It was in the beginning just as this Earth was in the beginning. So as in your Bible you say, "In the beginning." It is not something that came evolutionarily, as your planet has evolved.

D: I always think everything has a purpose, a reason.

J: It does have a reason. Actually there are several reasons. One of the reasons is: a place for individuals in mankind, like Janice, who have attained a particular level, and who have agreed to serve in the capacity in which she serves. It is a safe place. It is also a place to develop further the talents of the individual. Much as you consider your college and university. It is actually a self-contained world within a world.

D: But if it was constructed that long ago there weren't any humans on Earth at that time, were there?

J: That is correct.

D: That is why I was questioning the reason for putting it there, if there were no humans at that time.

J: That doesn't have anything to do with its relation to the other dimensions, galaxies, planets, and further out.

D: I see. You have to have patience with me. I have many questions, and some of them probably sound very naive at times.

J: We understand that.

D: That's the way I learn. Something is going around in my mind: Have I ever been there?

J: Actually you have been there, but it was not in this lifetime.

D: Hmmm. During one of my past lives then.

J: Yes. Why do you think you are involved in the work you are doing now?

D: I just think because of my curiosity.

J: Ah ha! Well, that is not entirely correct.

D: Do you know the reason?

J: You have already lived through much of this before. So therefore that is why you're attracted to it now, you see. Because much of what the people you are dealing with are going through, you have actually been through yourself. That's why some of it sounds so familiar to you.

D: You mean the information I'm receiving?

J: Yes. It doesn't startle you.

D: No, it doesn't. That's surprising to many people.

J: Does it surprise you?

D: It arouses my curiosity, and I always want to know more.

J: You want to remember more. You don't want to know more. You already know. (She had a teasing quality to her voice.)

D: (Laugh) *But it is surprising that it doesn't frighten me.*

J: It would be interesting if someone would regress you.

D: *I've been regressed, but not to anything like that. The main thing is, I think it would frighten me if I were to tap into something that was negative.*

J: Why do you bring the word "negative" into this conversation? Whenever we have spoken nothing of anything negative? Do you consider it negative?

D: *No, I don't. I said that's why it doesn't frighten me. I said I think the only thing that probably would, would be if I were to tap into something that was negative.*

J: Life in *any* dimension is not all smooth, because you must have "the good with the bad," as you so well know on your planet. Because through this kind of thing comes progress.

D: *Do you think this is why I have this drive to search.*

J: I certainly do.

D: *I seem to want to find and replace lost information.*

J: Yes. Because how do you think you realize it's lost? Could you perhaps have been around when it became lost? Earlier your concern over the loss of the technology is what awakened me to come to talk with you.

D: *Oh? Because to me those things are tragedies to lose.*

J: They are tragedies. But only a soul such as yours is of the character to have concern for that. And it is a great work that you do in trying to reconstruct it.

D: *That all seems to make sense. But anyway, when I was there I was in the physical?*

J: You were in physical because it was one of your lifetimes.

D: *I am glad the government doesn't know about it, because I think they have caused some problems, haven't they?*

J: Yes. That's why they will never learn of this base.

D: *Could you tell me of some of the other bases they have found out about?*

J: I really cannot.

D: *I was wondering about the consequences, if they caused problems.*

J: There have been problems. And so what happens is that we simply move.

D: *The entire base?* (Yes) *I'm working with some people in the UFO study, and they think the government and alien beings are working together within a base. And that there are many things going on there we would not want to hear about. I don't know how much of this is true.*

J: It wouldn't be from our group of beings.

D: *I think they said the government had an underground base, and the aliens were there also.*

J: The aliens have been to the government's underground base, but it was not the aliens' underground base.

D: *Then the government has one also.* (Yes) *Were they invited there?*

J: Yes. They wanted us to participate in some experiments. They wanted us to show them some of our technology, but then they misused it. Of course the misuse would naturally be blamed upon the aliens. Would the humans take the responsibility for misuse of technology that perhaps should have never been given to them in the first place, as we now in retrospect know?

D: *I can see humans not wanting to take responsibility. What kind of technology was it?*

J: Different medical procedures. There was some genetic sharing. And some of the advances that have taken place in your medicine have come through this sharing. The first human heart transplant with your Doctor ... was it Christian Barnard?

D: *I think so.*

J: Yes. Well, where do you think he learned his procedure?

D: *Consciously?*

J: Subconsciously, but it came into his consciousness, and he never realized that actually he was not the inventor of it.

D: *But that was a positive thing.*

J: There have been many positive good things that have come from the sharing. But there is also, in your slang, the "down side" of the experience. Certain things have happened that are not too pleasant.

D: *Can you tell me what they are?*

J: I can tell you that there have been some experiments that were *improvised* on by the humans. Thinking that because they had the methods from us, they would improve upon them, when they were unimprovable. And therefore accidents took place. And they wanted us to come and straighten out the mess. But ... Ha!

D: *What kind of accidents?*

J: There have been some lives lost, I will tell you that. But past that I will not discuss what happened, other than to say there was some of your human life lost. So therefore you know some of the disappearances that have taken place were ... in any process there can be accidents. And so if procedures are not followed precisely, sometimes these happen. So in the beginning, when there is a disagreement regarding how to perform something, and the human continues, we do nothing but step back and wait, because we know the outcome. And when he doesn't listen, then there are accidents. So perhaps there's only one way for the human to learn, and this is a tragedy. I will tell you, it is a tragedy.

D: *Did these take place at the base?*

J: They took place at the base of the humans.

D: *You also talked about genetic experiments. Is that what you mean, or is that something else?*

J: That's something else.

D: *Can you tell me anything about that?*

J: I can tell you the end result of one of the experiments. But I cannot go into full detail on some of the others.

D: *That's all right. I take anything I can get.*

J: I can tell you that the in vitro fertilization method was produced at this base.

D: *But that is a good thing.*

J: There are many good things. And I hesitate to speak to you of the other types of things, because of the subject I am coming through. This particular person, Janice, would, because of her sensitivity level, perhaps experience those. If she did not experience in the physical, the pictures that would come into her mind would be in her consciousness, because of the fact of the way communication with her takes place. And we have already worked to erase some of those, because she has been present and has seen that.

D: *Many people I work with have this same problem. They are too sensitive, and when they view some scenes they also get emotions from them.*

J: Yes. Because as I discussed with you earlier, the particular kind of kinetic sense of communication - for example, Janice *is* able to talk to the leaves and the wind and the sun and the elements. Therefore, being that sensitive, being that in tune, being able to become something like that, causes at a cellular and soulular level ... you realize what I said here.

D: Solar, the sun?

J: No. Soulular.

D: The soul. Do you mean the internal soul?

J: I'm talking about in the purest energy essence state molecularly. Those molecules and particular interactions imprint in such a manner that it is not easily disassembled. Disassembled is not the proper word I want to use to explain to you. What I'm trying to say is that once she does experience that, because of the type of individual she is, that particular experience will never ever be gone. All that can happen is a retuning, to cause that to go into another point in consciousness, where it does not affect her, because she is so affected.

D: This sounds very familiar. There is one young man I work with who thought he could view these things as though viewing television. But they carried too many other residual effects with them.

I was speaking of Phil, the subject of my book *Keepers of the Garden*. When I used him to contact Nostradamus in Volume III of *Conversations With Nostradamus*, he had great emotional problems with viewing the scenes he was shown. Thus I had to discontinue working with him on that project.

J: The residual effects are something the individual must become familiar with in order to know how to handle them. And it is a process. It can be done, it just cannot initially be done.

D: He seems to be very sensitive, and he doesn't want to look at anything that is negative.

J: There will come a point in time in his development where ... it's much as a child learns. They learn to crawl, and then they learn to walk. In the process of viewing these incidents he can reach a level where he can do that and be unaffected. But at this point in his evolvement he is not able to do it. Nor, with regard to the experiments I am discussing with you. At this point in time Janice cannot do that, because of her sensitivity level. We have observed this, because we have placed her in situations that resulted in our ability to gauge her level in regard to experiencing these things.

Now, your next question is, "How?" Or how are we able to know that?

D: *What the individual can handle.*

J: Yes. How are we able to know what the individual can handle? For example, Janice's friend watches horror movies. She cannot.

D: *I cannot either.*

J: Janice's been in situations where she is driving down the road, and there is an animal on the road that has been run over, or something has happened to kill that animal. She cannot look. That tells us that she cannot look. So every waking moment, every moment of an individual's life that is in tune with us is very important to *us*, with regard to that person's level or ability of development. These are our so called "tests." In your schools you have tests to find out what level the individual has reached. We don't perform the same kind of tests necessarily, where a person sits down with a piece of paper. Our test of Janice driving to Fort Smith and seeing that particular incident, tells us she is not at a point yet where she could discuss this. We would not hesitate to discuss with you these experiences and experiments that she has been present at. However, because of her residual damage - and I don't use the word "damage" in the context you humans would use it. But because of the residual remnants of the experience that would remain too close to her everyday consciousness, I cannot discuss them with you at this time.

D: *And I wouldn't want to do anything that would cause her any harm or discomfort.*

J: She is a very strong person. But when it comes to some matters, she is not yet ready to deal with them.

D: *I don't watch horror movies or things like that either. But if there are some things here that the world needs to know, I'm willing to write about them. Even though I don't like them.*

J: Yes, you're evolving also. And each one of these sessions that you do places you more likely to develop that sense of being able to deal with the more ... I don't have a word for a description of what I'm ....

D: *I keep thinking of "negative." These things are negative.*

J: In your frame of reference that would be correct. However, at this particular time we would say to you that the focus you need is not in relation to the negativity, for the American government is doing

348

enough in that area to promote the aliens in an unfavorable light. Therefore the work you are doing is simply designed, and by your own design, an effort to present the alien in the true light that we came to be presented in. That's actually why we're working with you.

D: *Yes, because I don't believe all the horror stories I've heard.*

J: There are horror stories. I will not tell you there are not.

D: *I have the feeling I am speaking to a female entity. Is that correct?*

J: Yes, you are.

D: There's a different sound to the voice, and a different presence, it seems like.

J: Janice had been wanting to contact me, so I came. I am the entity who is sometimes with her after some of her adjustments.

D: *The first entity I spoke to seemed to be rather mechanical or robot type.* (I am speaking of the little gray being.)

J: Actually he was simply having to participate in two events at the same time. And that's why the transmission was cut very short there. He was unable to adequately maintain and participate with you and participate in the other event at the same time.

D: *That was the second one I've spoken to. When I spoke to him, he had a very authoritarian ....*

J: No, his authoritarian side was at another event.

D: *But the very first contact I had through this vehicle was a mechanical type, very robot like.*

J: And what is your question?

D: *It seems as though they're all different.*

J: That is because Janice works with more than one type of energy.

D: *The first one didn't understand many of my questions. It was more like a robot.*

J: The first one was *not* a robot. But in your sense of the word "robot," that could be true. It's just a different type of a being.

D: *He seemed to be ... well, not human, is the only way I can explain it.*

J: In your sense of the word "human," that is correct. But in my sense of the word "human," he is very human.

D: *But wasn't he a different type?*

J: Yes, very much so. And that is the level that needed to come to you in order for you to know, first of all, that you were in contact with the space energies. Otherwise, there are times when you perhaps would not recognize it, because the voices can become so similar to what you'd call "human" level voices. You consider yourself talking to a human type of being now, although you are not.

D: *I'm not?* (No) *I have a very good feeling about you.*

J: Well, I'm a very good being. And so was the little person that you considered to be a robot. He was a good being. He was just totally foreign from what you consider human.

D: *Can you tell me what kind of a being you are?*

J: I'm a being of the same energy pattern that you spoke to in your last session. I am a counterpart.

D: *What does that mean?*

J: That means I am the female side of the energy you talked to before.

D: *Do you have a physical body?*

J: Yes, I do.

D: *What does that body look like?*

J: In what respect? Do you want to know my description of myself to you in human terms, or my description of myself to you in terms of how I live?

D: *Well, I don't think I'm going to have enough time right now to go into all of that. I was just wondering how your physical body appeared. Maybe we can go into the other at the next session.*

J: Well, my physical body appears very much as a (She seemed to be amused.) I have a face, I have all the counterparts that a human would have. If I came to Earth you would not know the difference.

D: *But yet you said you were not human.*

J: I am human, but I am more than human.

D: *Do you mean more highly evolved?*

J: More highly evolved in an energy state, and also more physically highly evolved.

D: *Can you elaborate on that?*

J: I have eyes that look ... Hmm, I don't know whether you would say "oriental," for they are not oriental. It is hard to compare from my frame of reference of where I was when you asked the question. So I will have to reassimilate for a moment, and tell you physically that I am not a tall person. My skin is creamy colored. I have a clear luminescent type of look to my complexion. My hands are

... I do have hands of a human. I look like a human. I am simply not. My eyes will give me away.

D: Do you have hair?

J: Yes, I do. It is auburn ... it is dark. In your terms it would not be considered black. It's between a dark brown and black with some red highlights.

D: If I come again, is there any way I can speak with you?

J: If it is my turn to come, I will be here. You see, when you work with Janice, there are other beings you will be discussing things with. So it is dependent upon what point you come, at what time you come, and what is necessary for the information to be given at that time. So in speaking to me, if it is my time to come I will simply ... be here.

D: Well, I do want to ask one more question. I am attempting to have several sessions with Janice in one day, because of the distance I had to travel. Would this be physically all right for her?

J: Yes, it will be. And I can answer that because of the fact that my area of expertise has to do with physicalness. It has to do with the area of the - you would perhaps say "medicinal" - psychological. You could say in your frame of reference that I am a doctor, although that term would not be sufficient to describe all that I am. Because my area of expertise does not necessarily relate to just the physicalness of the human, but also to the planet.

D: I didn't want to attempt anything that would tire her in any way or harm her.

J: She will not be tired. I would say to you that you will be told through us if that occurs, so therefore do not place the responsibility upon yourself. For we will help you to determine that by telling you.

D: Then I want to awaken her in a few minutes, and have a few hours off, and then return. I've never attempted having several sessions in one day before, and I didn't want to tire her out.

J: She has a reservoir that is amazingly refillable and her rejuvenative powers are very, very strong.

D: Then I will return in a few hours of our time here, and contact you or whoever is available. Would that be permissible?

J: Yes. May I say to you, "Peace be with you"?

D: And I really enjoyed being in your presence.

J: And so have I. We will meet again.

I then requested the entity to leave, and asked for the total personality of Janice to return to her body. When Janice gave indications that she was back, I then brought her forward to full consciousness.

Janice retained an image of the doctor in her mind after she awakened, and wanted to describe her. She was very beautiful, with long dark hair that was pulled back and gathered with a metal band. Janice preferred the word "auburn" as a description of the color of her hair. With a "haunting" appearance, her eyes were definitely her most distinguishing feature. They were deep dark green, and the shape was not exactly Oriental. They reminded Janice of the ancient drawings on the walls in Egypt of people whose eyes were outlined with a dark substance. In the drawings kohl had been applied to outline the eyes with makeup lines that slanted upward from the corners of the eyes. Except, in the case of the doctor, that was the actual shape and appearance of the eyes; it was not done with makeup. This made me wonder where the ancient Egyptians got the idea of making up their eyes in this manner. Could they have actually seen these beings and wanted to imitate their beauty and unique appearance?

We then went out to get a hamburger, and turned our conversation to the mundane things in our lives, so we could orient back to the outside world for a while before having another session.

CHAPTER 11
THE ENERGY DOCTOR

After we ate lunch and rested for a couple of hours, we started another session at approximately 3:00 p.m. I used Janice's keyword and she again entered deep trance very easily. Then I gave instructions to try to locate the same entity again. This time when I finished counting Janice did not find herself onboard a craft. Instead she was floating in space, unsure of where she was going, or what she was trying to find. After more instructions she saw a light. "There's a focused light. It's a huge area like a pupil of an eye, except its light. And I'm not through it yet. I'm either in it, or it's over my face. Something's happening to me." Whatever it was, it was creating obvious physical sensations as she lay on the bed. "The light changed colors. My head's feeling funny." Of course, her well-being was my first concern, and I gave suggestions to take away any physical sensations. I continued to ask if there was anyone around who could talk to us and explain the purpose of the light.

Janice seemed frozen, and unable to do anything except focus on the light. "I can't see past it. I think there is someone here, but I can't stop looking at it." She was taking big breaths. "It's doing something. It's a really strong light. It's waiting for something. I'm not sure what." This went on for several seconds, and in spite of my suggestions to do so, she was unable to move past it. "It's like I'm on hold or something. I need to go through it."

D: *Do you want to?*
J: I think so. It's right over my face.
D: *I only want you to do what feels comfortable to you. What does it feel like if you go into it?*
J: A cloud. Like steam. It's making my body feel funny. It's not tingling, but it's like when your foot comes back from being asleep. You know, that funny feeling. My whole body feels that way right now. And sometimes the light has an edge around it. It's concentrated in a center and then out from it there's a dark area,

and it moves, it comes toward me. It's pretty too. It was colors, and now it looks like steam, but not the color of steam. It's dark but it's not like evil, and it's not bad, it feels good.

D: *Did you go through the light?*

J: I don't know if I did or not. I don't see it, or else I'm in it. My body doesn't feel funny now. It was feeling really strange. I think I've done this before. I know now what it was. That's the first stage. It's like you dissolve. (Chuckle) It was just for a second there I felt like a yo-yo. You know, bonnngg! (Chuckle)

D: *Well, you're all back in one piece anyway. All right. Let's find somebody around who can answer our questions.* (Pause) *Is anybody there?*

After all this searching, it surprised me when the entity answered. Janice was definitely gone, because this voice was soft and sweet and gentle.

J: What is it that you want to know?

D: *Well, the first question: what was the purpose of that light?*

J: It is a source of contact.

The female entity was definitely back. It was easy to recognize that lyrical, sweet voice.

D: *It was bothering Janice a little, because it made her body feel so strange.*

J: It does make the physical body feel strange, but it is very soothing to the mental state of the being. It is also a preliminary step in bilocation travel.

D: *Are you the same being I spoke to a while ago?*

J: Yes, I am.

D: *I said we would return in just a short while.*

J: But I am not located where you left me, therefore there was a difference in finding me.

D: *Oh? Is that why it was harder this time?*

J: It was not a matter of hard or easy. It was just a matter of changing relative relational points in time and space.

D: *Then our time here is not the same as the time you are experiencing?*

J: That is correct. And this is part of what Janice was experiencing. That shifting, because as she stated to you, she does go through a physical feeling of change as well as a shifting in time and space. That cannot be accomplished without *some* sensation in the physical. It is much as you would consider, in your terminology, suspended animation. Is that a term you understand?

D: *Yes. That seems to be where time stops, I believe.*

J: That is similar to what must take place for the shift to occur. So therefore the effect on the physical body is sometimes rather a strange feeling in that shifting transference of consciousness.

D: *Well, just out of curiosity, in the short time that passed for me, has it been a long period of time for you?*

J: Pardon me?

D: *Since I talked to you a while ago.*

J: Oh, yes. You are speaking in relation to the fact that it has been, in your time, approximately an hour or two hours. (Yes) In my time I have accomplished a year's work. So you see, there is a definite shift that takes place.

D: *When I said I would come back in a few hours, I didn't realize you would have to wait that long.*

J: Yes, I was continuing my life, just as you continued yours.

D: *That's a little hard for me to understand. Well, when I was last speaking to you, you were describing yourself and you asked if I wanted to know how you lived? And I was afraid the answer would take too long at that time. Could you tell me something about that now?*

J: Do you have any specific questions, or do you wish a general synopsis of what I participate in, or do you wish to know about my childhood? Where do you? Just find a starting point that would be satisfactory.

D: *Just generalize it first, and then I can ask questions.*

J: In my daily activity I participate in various missions to your planet. My work is very involved in some of the experiments that take place that Janice has participated in. She is familiar with me, because on more than one occasion we have participated. I know much about Earth science. As I told you earlier, in your frame of reference I could be considered a doctor of medicine. But at the same time in our culture the doctor of medicine is more than just medicinal. We incorporate into our teachings and our professions the entire whole of the being as opposed to just generalized, specialized medicine. Much as if you would go to a kidney specialist, because we are a systems specialist. That includes all systems, meaning physical, mental, molecular structure. I could go on and on. Earth science structures, communication structures systems, and various facets of those systems as they interrelate inter-dimensionally.

D: *That sounds very complicated. You must be very intelligent.*

J: (Modestly) Well, I am considered to be accomplished.

D: *Do you live on the ship, or do you go back and forth to your home?*

J: I go back and forth to my home, but there are times when I live totally on the ship. There are times when my mission has me assigned to a base, much as Aleathin was assigned to a base earlier. That is why I am now speaking with you, because I am a part of the group of space energies that work with Janice.

D: *Do you also work with other people?*

J: I do work with others. We do have people on your planet that are our responsibility, so to speak.

D: *I'm curious about where your home is.*

J: My home is not in your galaxy.

D: *But you said you could go back and forth? How is that accomplished?*

J: It is accomplished past the speed of light.

D: *We are used to thinking that the speed of light is the limit.*

J: That is why inter-dimensional travel is unavailable to you.

D: *Because of our limitations.*

J: Exactly.

D: *Is your home a physical planet?*

J: It is a physical planet as such, yes.

D: *Do you eat food?*

J: We have different types of food. Actually in your Earth gardens you label everything, where we don't necessarily do that. In that we don't call an orange vegetable a "carrot."

D: *But do you consume food the same way we do?*

J: We do consume food. Our food is different, in that the structure of it is different. In other words, we do not have animals there that we eat. But there are different states of our beings. Much as your baby would grow up on milk, there is a time when as a child we eat one thing. Then as we ascend to adulthood we learn to exist on ... we would not eat what would be called in Earth terms "conventional" food.

D: But you do consume it like we do and have a digestive tract?

J: Our digestive tract is nothing like yours, although we do have a digestive tract.

D: Do you have a respiratory system?

J: Yes, we do.

D: Circulatory?

J: Yes, we do, but in the conventional sense of the word only.

D: What do you mean?

J: I mean that when we are in our galaxy and in our own element, these systems do not function as they function when we come to your Earth. So there is a definite difference, in that, bi structurally, bi systemically, in whatever environment we are in, these systems function differently. Comparing them to your systems, your digestive tract has one function and it functions that way only. Ours do not.

D: You mean yours adjust to wherever you find yourself? (Yes) *Would you also adjust to whatever elements in the air or in the food or whatever?*

J: Yes. That's why we can come to Earth and live on Earth undetected.

D: You mean, live in the base?

J: Or among you.

D: Didn't you say you would be noticeable?

J: Well, only to the individual who is aware of this kind of difference in being.

D: You said your eyes might give you away.

J: Not to the average individual.

D: Then you must have a great deal of adaptability.

J: Yes, we do. What I'm describing to you is but a fleeting type of recognition. Meaning that, you might be on the street, in a restaurant or somewhere, and pass by one of us. And in one second of contact, your system of knowing - and individuals like Janice recognize that - it's as if there's a family recognition. Much as a mother would recognize her child without being able to see it. So it's that kind of recognition. And the Earth individual could pass on with that fleeting moment in time taking place, and yet not necessarily connect it. It would be as if to say, "I know that person. There was something there."

D: *I've felt those feelings.*

J: But individuals who are more highly sensitive, and who have participated in recognition classes, are able to do that and pass on without it affecting them. Because they accept the fact that it is a reality. And it is also the blending of two realities. Because of the fact that *they* also interact inter-dimensionally at the time they are on your Earth plane. It is easier for them to accept that, you see. The average individual would never even think of participating in but one reality.

D: *That's true. Then the other space beings do not have this adaptability?*

J: Some of them don't. There are all kinds of space beings, different kinds of races with different kinds of systems, much as there are all kinds of races on your planet. So what is peculiar to one race is not to another. The mechanical being that you spoke of earlier, was totally different from anything we experience or have on our planet.

D: *His systems and everything?*

J: Yes. He does not function as we do, in that, he does not consume food.

D: *What does he live on? What is his sustenance?*

J: He does not need food to live.

D: *He must have something that he uses for energy?*

J: (Big sigh) In an effort to try and explain to you. The mechanical being functions mechanically, so that in him is a.... Words! There are words to translate. (Pause) Perhaps if I explain to you, in your mechanical devices you insert a battery and they function. So when this type of individual comes to interact with your planet, he is fueled. It would be explained as if it were a particular, more of an electro type of energy, you see.

D: *Then he is more like a machine.* (Yes) *Does that mean he was created by other beings, instead of ... I'm thinking of how we create each other biologically. Was he created like a machine by other people?*

J: He was not created as a machine, because he is not a machine. He is a being. He is just a different being. And where he comes from, that is the kind of being that exists.

D: How do they procreate? Duplicate each other?

J: It has much to do with the electricity of their area. "Electricity" is not the word, for it is from an energy state.

D: Do they need to duplicate themselves?

J: They don't *need* to. They duplicate themselves just as we or you do, because sex to them is not sex to you.

D: That's what I was wondering. If something was machine like - I know that's probably not the right analogy. I was thinking maybe they would never die. And they would not have to create more.

J: They die.

D: Then they are mortal in that respect.

J: In that respect. In their own space of mortality, yes, they are.

D: So there would be a need to replace themselves, but it is done in a different way. Well, may I ask how your type procreate?

J: There are two ways we can procreate. (Pause) Well, I do not feel I should discuss this at this point. But I will tell you that one of the ways we procreate is as you procreate.

D: Why do you have two different ways?

J: Because of the type of being that is produced by each process.

D: I've also heard that some beings are androgynous.

J: They are.

D: I'm always curious about these many different things. (It was difficult and awkward to ask questions about a subject that she was obviously reluctant to discuss.) But if you don't want to discuss it, that's all right.

J: It's not a matter of not wanting to discuss it. It is more a matter of not being at liberty to discuss it.

D: All right. Any time I ask a question that you can't answer, I just want to know, that's all. I had many questions I made notes of, that I wanted to ask. I don't know if you can give me the information or not. One thing I wanted to know about, was the other planets in our solar system. Do you have that information? Or you're in a different field, aren't you?

J: I will have some of your information. I can tell you that there has been on the planet of Mars life as you now know it.

D: There was?

J: There was at a point in time.

D: Was that before there was life on Earth?

J: That was before there was the kind of life on Earth that exists now, yes.

D: *How advanced were these civilizations?*

J: These civilizations were very advanced. At one point in time Mars was - before the atmospheric changes - a planet much like your planet. However a great change took place during a cataclysmic event. So that life, as was currently known, became extinct on that planet. That is not to say there is not life there now. It's just not visible to you.

D: *What was this cataclysmic event?*

J: There was a juncture at which two planets collided. And the fallout from that collision changed the atmosphere of Mars.

D: *They couldn't live because of that?*

J: They couldn't live because they burnt.

D: *What type of beings lived there?*

J: A type of being similar to you.

D: *A humanoid type?*

J: Yes. They had more advanced systems than you do, physically, physiologically. Their society was more advanced than yours. The interactions of their people were more advanced. They didn't have the wars and murders and things that go on on your planet. So it was a more peaceful state of being, because their consciousness was at a different level. They were not at fault for what happened to their planet, as you are for what is happening to yours.

D: *They had cities?*

J: Yes, they had cities, the remnants of which you could probably see.

D: *There is a phenomenon that people say they can see on Mars. It's called the "Face on Mars." Do you know anything about that?*

J: Yes. It is a symbol to tell you that your face has been there, meaning: humanity's face. A being similar to yourself.

D: *How was that produced?*

J: I can't tell you that. I don't know how.

D: *But it was done by the race of people that lived there?*

J: No, it was not.

D: *Then it was formed later?* (Yes) *But you don't know who put it there or ....*

J: No, I do not. It is symbolic.

D: *It is also said there appear to be pyramids near this.*

The Custodians

J: As I am telling you, civilization much like your own existed on that planet. Your planet could become the second Mars in this solar system if it is not careful. (Sigh) A very delicate situation exists now. That's why some of the experiments and projects are taking place now.

D: *They think it could happen here?* (Yes) *But you said there is life on Mars that is not visible to us?*

J: That is correct.

D: *Can you tell me about that?*

J: I can tell you about that, but I'm .... (She hesitated as though we were encroaching upon forbidden ground.)

D: *There are many scientists who would like to know these things.*

J: Yes. Well .... (Pause and then hesitation.) I must get directions on whether I can discuss this, because I do not feel at liberty to do that without permission.

D: *I don't want to get you in any kind of trouble. If you can find out, I was just curious.*

J: I will tell you that there is civilization on Mars.

D: *Oh? I was thinking of rudimentary life, very elemental, basic. It's more advanced than that?*

J: There is civilization, in that there are colonies. There are projects taking place. If I told you there is an accountant from your planet and his family living on Mars, would you believe it?

D: *I believe anything is possible. He would need the right type of atmosphere and conditions.*

J: That is correct.

D: *I am assuming Mars has no atmosphere that we could live with.*

J: Not with the present level of development of your systems. There is no way possible you could live on the surface of Mars as you live on the Earth's surface.

D: *Then the cities are not on the surface. Is that correct?*

J: That is correct.

D: *Are these remnants of the other civilization that was there when it was burnt by the cataclysm?*

J: Some are, some aren't.

D: *Then some did survive?*

J: Some did.

D: *Were the other cities built by other beings that came there to colonize.*

The Custodians

J: That is correct.

D: *Well, the accountant, did he wish to go?*

J: (Emphatic) Yes!

D: *I think it would be quite an adventure, but he would have to leave everything behind.*

J: And so he did.

D: *I've been told that sometimes it's difficult for a human to adjust, because it would be so different.*

J: Not in an environmentally controlled atmosphere.

D: *That's interesting. You know we are planning on sending ... we already did shoot something off, didn't we? It was going to be a probe? And we've taken pictures.*

J: You Americans are going in all kinds of different directions in space. Perhaps you should concentrate on one project until you have accomplished it, and then go to another.

D: *I believe the Americans are thinking of putting a base on Mars, aren't they?*

J: They are thinking of putting a base on Mars, and they have also considerations for other planets. They are thinking of putting a base on the moon.

D: *I have heard they want to send a manned mission to Mars.*

J: That will be a cooperative venture. I do not believe the Americans will do that singularly.

D: *Do you think it will happen?*

J: Oh, yes, I do believe it will happen.

D: *Do you think it will happen in the foreseeable future of the people alive on Earth now?*

J: Yes, I think it will happen.

D: *I wonder what would happen if they got there and discovered there were other beings.*

J: They won't see them. They haven't seen them. They couldn't. Not for quite some time will they ever know. The beings of Mars will know, but the Americans and the French and the Russians won't know.

D: *I think it would be a shock to them if they landed and found there were other beings.*

J: Well, we can't land in your country without being shocking, so by the same token, you can't land in other places without being

362

shocked. Because your consciousness cannot advance past ... the shift point. Limitations of the mind.

D: *Well, is there any life on the surface of Mars?*

J: Life, but not as you know it. As far as you are concerned there is only one way to look at vegetation: vegetation has leaves, vegetation is green. So therefore, because of the type of vegetation that exists on the surface of Mars, it is not recognizable to the human eye. You only see vegetation in one frame of reference, but other beings can go to Mars and experience that, because they see it in a different frame of reference.

D: *Would we know this once we examined it?*

J: No, because it is different. The structure would not be comparable to your vegetation, so therefore you would not call it that.

D: *I think the photographs have only shown rocks.*

J: Yes, because you recognize it only as a rock. Differences in rocks exist. It's knowing the differences that we are able to perceive as opposed to what you can.

D: *What about any other type of life?*

J: I think I have discussed with you the types of life.

D: *I'm thinking of, on the surface of Mars, like animal, insect or ....*

J: No. There is vegetation, but there are no animals living on the surface of Mars.

D: *They're beneath the surface?* (Yes) *Is there anything I could identify with?*

J: Yes. I have said to you there is an environmentally controlled atmosphere that an accountant from your planet could live in. If an accountant could live on Mars, would you not think he would have the same kind of atmosphere, habitat, created for him, in order to do that?

D: *Yes, but I'm thinking of something that would be native, indigenous to the planet, or had been there since the cataclysm. Something that would not have an artificially created atmosphere below the surface.*

J: There are areas of the interior of the planet that are still native, just as your forests in certain areas of your country are still native. However, developments have taken place, so the entire intersurface of the planet is not left in its virgin state.

D: *Then there are native animal or insect life still surviving?*

J: In the naturally created environments.

D: *I thought if beings came from somewhere else, they might have brought life in different forms. Is there any type of animal or insect life that I might be familiar with?* (No) *Well, what about the other planets in our solar system? Did they ever have life on them?*

J: Other planets have had life on them, yes.

D: *Which ones?*

J: Jupiter, Venus.

D: *What about Mercury?*

J: Mercury, I'm not that familiar with.

D: *Well, can we talk about Venus?*

J: Venus has had life. I am really explaining things to you that I should not be discussing. However, I am continuing because I have received no information not to discuss it. Therefore ....

D: *Do you think someone would stop you if you were?*

J: I believe that is the case, yes.

D: *Because we've long been curious if life did exist. Let's see, Venus is covered with clouds, I believe. I'm trying to go with what I know, which isn't much. When was there life there?*

J: (Pause, then hesitation.) I think perhaps we will need to change the subject matter.

D: *All right. One thing I did want to ask you about was the Red Spot on Jupiter. Can you tell me anything about that, or is it not allowed?*

J: Jupiter is a very serious planet for Earth to consider exploring. And at this point in time I'm being .... If you will excuse me for a moment.

D: *All right. I don't want to get you in any kind of trouble. Maybe there's someone there who has more answers along this line, if it's allowed.*

J: There are others who have much better knowledge. That is more their area of expertise than it is mine. However ... I should not discuss this further with you at this point.

D: *Do you think someone that has more knowledge could discuss it with me?*

J: Not at this point.

D: *All right. Maybe we can come back to it at another time.*

J: Yes. Let me tell you that .... One moment.

She appeared to be speaking with someone else, and she murmured, "Yes ... Okay." It then sounded like another language. It was soft and difficult to hear, but the tape recorder caught it: Vashusha. (?? phonetic: Va-shu-sha or Ra-shu-sha. No accents.) It still sounded as though she was speaking to someone else, because the sounds were soft, and obviously not directed at me. Then the language again. This time it sounded like several words: Temtem tensesavene (?? phonetic: tem tem tense sa ve ne ??) Spoken very fast, the words slurred together. The syllables could be incorrect.

Her voice was louder. She was speaking to me again: "I am to tell you that, in the chain of planets Earth is the most strategically located. In the chain to cause...." There was a pause as her attention was diverted again. She whispered, "What?" Then she was back to me again. "What happens on Earth will affect every other planet in your solar system. Therefore it is *vital* that the existence of Earth continue."

D: Is someone else telling you what to say?
J: Yes. I cannot continue to say other than what I am told.
D: Is it all right if I ask about the Red Spot, or do you want me to stop talking about the planets?
J: It will be discussed with you from another area of our development.
D: Okay. Somebody else who has the information?
J: Yes, because the information that will come to you is vital in understanding Jupiter and its relation to the Earth plane.
D: And that will come later? (Yes)

Since this topic had been closed off, I decided to switch to a different subject.

D: I discussed with the other entities the implants that are put into people's bodies on Earth. And they gave me some information about those.
J: What do you wish to know?
D: Are these put into everyone's body?
J: No, they are not.
D: Just certain people?
J: That is correct.
D: How are these people selected, if they are selected?
J: It's not as much a matter of selection, as it is a matter of agreement.

D: I'm trying to understand the purpose. It's a monitoring device, I believe.

J: It is, in some cases, a monitoring device. In some cases.

D: What could it be in other cases?

J: Let me explain to you one thing I'm thinking of that you can relate to. You have patches that you put on after surgery, and even after the post operative period, that automatically release certain amounts of necessary medicine to the individual. So therefore implants have two purposes. They have more than two, but two of the purposes that I can discuss with you are: they are considered to be, and understood by you to be, simply a monitoring device. They are also, in some cases, devices by which particular systems of the individual are, analogy wise, post operatively, being serviced.

D: Then you mean the individual is operated on? There is surgery performed?

J: In some cases.

D: Since this is your line of work, can you tell me about some of this surgery and the reasons for it?

J: We have discussed systems, and humanly there are all kinds of systems within the human body. From circulatory to respiratory to digestive to nervous, and I could go on. So it depends on the type of necessary evolvement to advance that person to a point where the individual can handle different amounts of either, a: information, b: vibrational rate, or c: atmospheric conditions, as we discussed briefly earlier. So you see, they're not strictly monitoring devices. It depends on the type.

D: But what is the purpose of having them adjust?

J: Just as your time release vitamin does.

D: So they can adjust to the conditions of the world or what?

J: They can adjust to inter-dimensional travel. They can adjust to molecular reconstruction at a faster rate. There are various reasons for the devices, so the human at the human level, can assimilate things properly, in order for the human to continue in the program that human has chosen to be a part of.

D: Do these devices ever cause problems?

J: Sometimes, although these are not life-threatening problems. When you say "problems," define for me what you would consider.

D: *Well, any problems that would interfere with the functioning of the body. Anything they would notice.*

J: The individual does from time to time notice a problem. And it is not a life-threatening type of a problem. I'm trying to think of a parable I can relate to you, that would be the equivalent in your own environment or your own culture. (Thinking) It's much as if you give a child castor oil, and it makes the child feel sick when it takes it, but it cures the ailment. So in relation to a problem, depending upon the system that is being effected, there can be connective problems in conjunction with the functionality of the implant.

D: *Can you tell me what some of those problems would be, so they could be recognized?*

J: The person may experience a feeling of restlessness sometimes. There can be actual physical symptoms take place. In that the body can feel as though it has been on a hundred-mile hike, when it's not used to exercise. There are various things that can happen digestively. As the individual adjusts to higher and higher frequencies, so must they adjust their food intake. So that the higher vibrational rates can pass through this individual. You will find that certain individuals have changed their dietary intake. So that could be considered by some to be a problem. If you love to eat meat, and you love to smoke, and you love to do things like that, then you can have a period of adjustment. Much like a person at the human level who would diet and have to give up their sweets. So the human will go through physiological, physical changes.

D: *Are these caused when the implant is first put in the body?*

J: Not necessarily. It can occur when the implant is put into the body. However it can occur slowly over a period of time, i.e. your timed released implant.

D: *Then it doesn't have to be adjusted?*

J: Yes, from time to time there are adjustments made.

D: *Does it have to be done onboard the craft?*

J: In most cases, if it is done on the physical body.

D: *I'm wondering about the digestive problems. Does that mean upset stomachs or flu type symptoms or what?*

J: Well, the body is going through changes. Perhaps like a person whose diet had been primarily that of meat. When that person changes to fruit and vegetables, there will be a physical symptom digestively. And there will be a cleansing process that takes place. Therefore in order for that to occur there could be some instances of diarrhea, if that is what you speak of. So it does have to do with purification of the systems.

D: *So it is not necessarily caused by change in diet, it is caused by the functioning of these implants.*

J: The implants help to affect the change in diet. So it is a combination of the two. It is not strictly one or the other.

D: *I see. The common belief is that these implants are bad. People think their body is being invaded when they find there are implants in their body.*

J: That is because their consciousness is not yet at the level of understanding what they are participating in. They also have the option not to participate.

D: *If they don't want to do it anymore?*

J: That is correct.

D: *Because some of these people feel very angry as though their body has been invaded without their permission.*

J: It is perhaps understandable they would feel that way, because what has happened is an imbalance. Many people agree to participate in something, and then find out, "Oh! I don't want to do that." Now, if they're not willing to grow in certain ways, or their mental ability is not present to make advancements in the area of higher levels of activity, they will respond in this manner. Now, different things can happen by the choices the individual makes, but it is their choice.

D: *This is not a conscious choice, is it?*

J: No, it isn't.

D: *But it can be conscious if they discover this. At what age are the implants normally put in the body?*

J: There is no particular age.

D: *It doesn't have to happen when they are a child?*

J: It does not have to happen when they are a child. It can happen at any age, depending upon the individual.

D: *I suppose I have the idea they are monitored throughout their entire life.*

J: Not necessarily. There are individuals who are. Now we have come to know that the individuals who have been monitored throughout their life, in most cases are the individuals that, through their participation throughout their life, are able to transition and work with the higher levels of energy. It is not necessarily from the conditioning, as much as from a developmental point of view.

D: *What are the most common sites of the body where these implants are put?*

J: There are various parts of the body. In actuality there are many tests performed before the level of implants is reached. (She displayed frustration.) How can I tell you? Implants are used as monitoring devices for some key individuals. The dual purpose of the implant is to aid that individual in the work they have chosen to do. The individuals who feel invaded or violated by these implants have not developed their consciousness to a point of being able to know, or being trusted enough to know, the fullness of the entire project. And they will go through a feeling of rage. If they continue in that rage, then they are not the - and I hesitate to use the word "quality," but I can't at the moment think of a better word to describe the fact that either they stay in that rage or they transcend that rage. If they stay in that rage they are dropped from the project, because that rage is a part of their choice.

D: *Or if they become angry enough to say, "I don't want you to do this."*

J: Then it will not happen. That rage is a transition period too, because there's a dropping away of the old individual. In consciousness raising many times _ you have heard the saying, "Discontent breeds progress." So the individual who is not working in the consciousness level will sometimes begin to *want* to know. When they begin to want to know, we know they are able and ready to handle the next step. Is that understandable?

D: *Yes, I can understand that.*

J: We do not like this time period, just as a person who has surgery does not enjoy the feeling of the incision as it heals.

D: *Yes, the recuperation afterwards.*

J: But that is the only thing I can think at the moment that would be the equivalent. And I'm having a bit of difficulty in translating my thought processes to your frame of reference, if you will forgive the hesitation.

D: That's all right. I think it is important for people to know this is not a violation, and they shouldn't feel this anger.

J: They cannot feel anything other than that anger, for at their level of consciousness they could not handle knowing the truth.

D: They just think that something very bad has been done to them.

J: Yes. And they only see it in that light, because they are affected a great deal by the media on your planet. A person in the state of being that is living totally for themselves, will feel violated, very violated. Because of the fact they are so into their humanness, the only one they are thinking of is themselves.

D: Yes. But you said there are many tests performed before the area of the body was chosen to put these implants?

J: Well, it will depend upon the system. And it will depend upon the system that is being affected: neurologically or circulatorally.

D: Are there any sites that are common?

J: Yes, there are common sites. One of the monitoring devices is placed in the nostril. That is because it can be placed through a space that is closest to a nerve leading to the optic nerve and to the brain.

D: What is that type of device used for?

J: There are two purposes for that. One is to record what the person is seeing. And the other is for monitoring purposes, because the brain transmits the thoughts of where the person is at any given moment. We can use it as a communicative device also.

D: What is another common site?

J: Another common site is in the rectum.

D: (That surprised me.) Oh? Pardon me, but I was thinking, wouldn't that come out?

J: No, it would not come out, because it is placed in the skin. Another common site is behind the ear. Another common site is at the base of the head or on the scalp. Another common site is - or not so common site actually - would be at joints.

D: Joints like the elbows and knees?

J: Yes. And wrists and ankles.

D: What is the purpose of the one in the rectum?

J: I cannot discuss it.

D: That's one you can't talk about? Well, what about the one behind the ears?

J: There are pressure points throughout the meridians in the body. And the devices are located in relation to pressure points. You are familiar with acupressure?

D: *I've heard of it.*

J: Along the meridians there are central points - as we have already discussed the junctures in time, there are meridian junctures. So electrically, depending upon what project the person is involved in, it dictates where the devices are placed.

D: *What about the one at the base of the skull?*

J: It is a monitoring device. It is also part of a neurological project.

D: *Would it be influencing the person?*

J: It is not necessarily influencing. Some of the devices are used, as I have told you, for communication purposes. There are different types of communication that take place between an individual and ... (hesitated) the space energies. In that ....

Her voice hesitated as though listening, then became softer. The same thing that occurred when she was interfered with while telling me about the planets.

D: *Is someone telling you something?*

J: Yes. I am being communicated with by a very high-pitched noise in my left ear at this moment.

That side of Janice's head faced the table on which the tape recorder was sitting. But I could see no connection as the room was very quiet.

J: It's a manner of communicating from a distance to me.

D: *Oh. Because it's not in the room where I am.*

J: No, you do not hear it, because you are not where I am. It is a manner of communication of my people one to another. As I talk to you I am receiving information, although I do not have to know the content of the information.

D: *It will be automatically inserted into your mind, you mean?*

J: It will come to me via the high-pitched noise, and either I will tell you what it is or I will receive instructions. As we talk there are two processes taking place. I am communicating with *you* and I am being communicated with. But I don't have to focus on the communication taking place between.

D: *Is it anything that I need to know, or is it just strictly for you?*

J: If it is, we will discuss it. I don't know at this point in time what it is.

D: *All right. I was curious about the implant at the base of the brain ....*

J: (Interrupted) Yes, I was discussing with you .... (Big breath.) In order to discuss the different purposes for implants as I tell you they are not all used in each individual in the same manner. So that the implant at the base of the skull on Janice would not necessarily be used as an implant at the base of the skull on someone named John or George or whomever. So, therefore some of them are simply tuning devices. By tuning I mean a way of tuning in to where that individual needs to be focused. And it is a source of contact radiologically for us.

D: *I'm always very thorough. That's why I ask so many questions. And sometimes that becomes irritating, I think.*

J: It is not a source of irritation to me. I only have to be careful, because I have been told I am not at liberty to discuss everything I would like to discuss with you.

D: *Well, what about some of the other implants? You said there were some in the joints in the body.*

J: Yes. If you will think of the meridians of the body. If you will think of the ley lines of the planet. If you will think of the person as being located on a ley line with the meridians in the body corresponding to the ley lines of the planet. Then you will understand one of the projects in energy transference that I am involved in. I can discuss portions of it with you. However, I will not be able to release intimate details. I can tell you that particular devices are more necessary at a particular stage of involvement with the space program. Now, if the person determines they wish to continue, it is not as necessary to have the implants.

D: They don't need them?

J: From time to time they will be necessary, simply when systems evolve and vibrational adjustments need to be effected on the physicalness of the human.

My curiosity took over.

D: Are you allowed to tell me if I have any implants in my body? Or can you tell?

J: (Pause) I am not finding one, but that does not mean you do not have one.

D: I didn't know if you had a method that you could ....

J: (Interrupted) I have a method. I can perhaps scan your body, if I have your permission.

D: Yes, as long as it wouldn't cause any discomfort. (Embarrassed chuckle) *I'm just curious if there are any.*

J: (Long pause) I'm not finding an implant.

D: You're not? All right. Because sometimes I've had discomfort at the base of the skull, and I wondered if that could be one.

J: I do not believe it is an implant. I do believe there are molecular changes going on within your cranium.

D: Anything I need to know about?

J: You are such a curious woman.

D: (Laugh) I certainly am. Maybe that was why I was chosen for this. (Laugh)

J: I can tell you that the energies you are working with ... in order to be able to do what you are doing, you cannot work with them and not be, in some manner, affected. Now, any adjustments that are taking place within your cranium are happening so you will be able to continue the work you are doing. Because it will perhaps become a bit more intense.

D: It occurred to me that maybe there were implants, and that was what was causing discomfort.

J: (Interrupted) What kind of discomfort?

D: Oh, sometimes ... not like pain, but an aching there, like when your neck and muscles are sore. Sometimes a sharp pain, but it doesn't last. So I was wondering about that.

J: Perhaps the top of your head should be examined.

There was a long pause while she did something. What happened next was unexpected. When scanning has been performed on me by other entities my body would tingle, and I could always dismiss it later as perhaps my imagination, because the feeling could have been caused by my focusing upon what was occurring. In other sessions with Janice I felt a slight feeling of heat or vibration on the top of my head, but it was brief and not uncomfortable. This time I was expecting the sensation would be similar, but this was more intense. The top of my head suddenly felt hot as though a heat lamp or a similar heat source had been applied directly to the area. It could not have been my imagination. The feeling lasted several seconds. I exclaimed, "Ooooh! I feel the heat!"

I laughed nervously because, although it was hot, it was not uncomfortable and I felt this entity would not harm me.

D: (A long pause) *Anything there?*

J: If you have had an implant, you do not presently have one. And whatever the implant's purpose was has been accomplished, for there is an increase in the activity in your brain.

D: *Then you think it's possible at one time there may have been something?*

J: There may have been. It was not I who placed it there. That does not mean it ....

D: *Why was there such heat when you did that?*

J: I was looking inside.

D: *Oh. Then I do have a brain in there anyway.* (Laugh) *It was a strange feeling.*

J: (Sweetly) I had your permission, you know.

She was correct. I could not complain about the sensation of heat when I had given her permission to look. I just didn't know what it would feel like. My attention was now drawn to the clock.

D: *I think I will have to leave again for a little while. I want to try to have one more session today, since I have to travel a long distance.*

J: Yes, I know. And this is a good thing that you are doing. It's good to have the continuity. There are many important subjects that can be discussed with you through this entity. And we wish there was a way it could take place on a more convenient ....

D: *Where I could see her more often.* (Yes) *But when I come, if I can have several in one day, that will really help.*

J: You will gain a continuity.

D: *As long as I'm not draining the energy, or doing anything to the vehicle that would cause discomfort or harm.*

J: That cannot take place, because she is fully protected, as you have been told before. I feel there are other more important subjects to be discussed.

D: *I'm trying to think of some. I will come back in a couple of hours, my time, and maybe you can think of some we can discuss.* (Yes) *All I need is a topic, and I can find the questions.* (Laugh)

J: I may not be the person ....

D: *(I didn't hear her.) Maybe I can make notes and see if I can come up with some questions. Then when I return I will see if we can contact you again. And I do appreciate you speaking with me. It's been very enlightening and very important. I think we're making progress.*

J: Peace be with you.

D: *Thank you.*

I then brought Janice back to full consciousness.

After this session we went downstairs and ate supper with Patsy. During the meal I noticed that Janice's palms seemed discolored, but it was not really noticeable. It looked like a stain as when you handle a newspaper and the ink comes off on your hands. It was not enough to even comment about, but I was wondering where it came from, because she had no opportunity to even pick up a paper or anything similar after coming downstairs. After eating and visiting for a few hours we decided to have the last session. She seemed to be holding up fine. I was the one who was becoming tired, but I was determined to see this through. I could always sleep later in the morning so I would be rested for my trip back home. We had discussed questions and made a list. One that Janice was interested in was: She often had the distinct feeling when she awakened in the morning that while she was asleep she journeyed somewhere or was involved in some type of work. Her question was, "What am I doing at night when I am asleep? Or am I doing anything?"

The next session began around 7:30 or 8:00 that night. We finished the day's work after 10:00. Even then we sat around and talked afterwards before Janice left for home. It had been a long day, and if you include the day before when I had the same grueling schedule with Linda, it had been a long hard-working weekend. But the information that had been gained made it all worthwhile.

CHAPTER 12
JANICE MEETS HER REAL FATHER

After eating supper and resting for a few hours we began our last session at approximately 7:30 or 8:00 that night. We had a list of questions we might possibly ask, but it ended up that we didn't get to them. I used her keyword and gave instructions. Janice immediately found herself in a beautiful but strange place. She was sitting in a large room that resembled an auditorium with tiers going up the curved walls. The walls were a pale green, and there were archways decorated with pastel colors of green, blue and peach. It was a beautiful peaceful place, but there was no one else there. The tiers went down to a sunken hollow in the center of the room. She was then startled to see the bottom of the room open and something resembling a table come up out of the floor. When that occurred she felt the urge to walk down the tiers to that portion of the room. There was still no one else there, but now beautiful music flooded the room. She could not identify what instruments were making the music. It was like nothing she had ever heard before.

Sometimes the subject can become so immersed in describing their surroundings that the session will move very slowly. It is the job of the hypnotist to move the scene forward. I kept trying to do this, by having Janice move forward until someone came in. She was in no hurry, but was enjoying the music and peaceful environment. She seemed to be waiting for something or someone.

J: There's a door over there, and it seems like I'm waiting. (Big breath) Oh, my! There are some people coming in. (Apparently said to someone else:) And to you, too.
D: *What?*
J: There was someone saying, "Welcome, and peace be with you." And I said, "And to you, too." Now he's moving.
D: *Did many people come in?*

J: Yeah, there are some in the front. And I'm not afraid or anything. It's just that I don't know what's going to happen. There are others up on that level that I was first at. It's sort of like being in an auditorium, or maybe a theater that has a balcony. And they went around up there, and there are a few down here where I'm at. They seem to be talking to each other. I don't understand it.

D: *What do they look like?*

J: There are just different ones. I mean, there's one that looks .... (Hesitancy, a little uncomfortable.) Looks like those strange ones. And there are others that have those robes on, and then .... (She seemed a little upset.) I'm not afraid, but they're talking to each other, and I wish I could understand them.

D: *But they're all different types?*

J: Yeah, there are some different types. There's a short guy up there on that second level. There's a man in a robe down here. But they're kind. They're just talking. I've not been in this room. I don't know what takes place here.

D: *Are you the only one like yourself?* (Yeah) *How do you perceive yourself?*

J: I'm just me. I'm just here. I'm just waiting for them to tell me what I'm supposed to do.

D: *I was wondering if you were in a physical body?*

J: I can see myself. I can see me.

D: *The way you look when you're in the physical?*

J: (Pause) I'm not exactly that way. But I know it's me. I'd like to know what I'm here for.

D: *Can you mentally ask them?*

J: I'll try to. (Long pause) They're going to ask me some questions.

D: *Oh, they're going to ask you questions. That'll be interesting. We've been doing all the asking. How do you feel about answering questions?*

J: It's okay. They seem to be waiting for somebody to come. (Pause) I wish they would just do it.

D: *You have the ability to move ahead. Instead of waiting we can speed time up until whoever they're waiting for comes in. (Pause) Has the person come in now?*

J: No. (A pause of a few seconds.) He's coming in now. He's very nice. He's touching my head. It feels cool.

D: *Is he anyone you have seen before?* (She nodded.) *Who is he?*

J: That man who used to visit me when I was little.
D: Someone used to visit you when you were a little girl?

Janice began to cry. She very emotionally sobbed the word, "Yes."

D: Why are you crying? Is it upsetting you?
J: No. I'm glad he's here. It's like your father came.

I tried to talk her past the emotional reaction, but she was still crying openly. You could tell it was an emotional reunion.

D: You said he used to visit you when you were little?

I had to get her talking in order to stop the crying.

J: Yes, he takes care of me. He's ... (She broke down again.)... like my father.
D: There's that type of feeling toward him?
J: Yes, he is my father.
D: Your real father? (Yes) How do you know that?
J: Because I know how I feel about him. Do you know what he calls me?
D: What?
J: (Emotional) Daughter.
D: Do you think he is your real biological father? (Yes) And not the man who was in your home when you were growing up, your other so-called father?
J: No, it's not him. They're two different people.
D: All right. Is he going to ask you the questions?
J: Uh huh. He comes and asks me questions.
D: I can't hear them. Will you repeat the question to me before you give the answer?
J: (Still crying.) If he lets me.
D: Ask him if it's all right.

The change was so sudden it was like pushing a switch. She had been crying and having difficulty voicing the answers because of the emotion. When the next voice came through the change was immediate. There was no emotion, the tears stopped, and the voice was obviously male. While the first male entity that spoke through Janice sounded like an old man with an authoritarian tone, this one also sounded old but with a tone of sophistication, a little more regal.

J: The questions can be repeated if they are properly placed.

D: *All right. Because I can't hear unless you tell me the questions. And I have only her welfare at heart.*

J: And so have I.

D: *She was very emotional about seeing you again.*

J: This is understandable. For I am emotional about seeing her.

D: *I wondered if you had emotions.*

J: We have emotions as you have emotions. Especially for one of our own.

D: *That's very good. Then will you ask her the question so I can hear it?*

J: Some of the questions will be internally placed, and we will not be allowed to discuss them with you. We are at a crucial stage in Janice's - as you know her - development in her work. It is an important stage we find ourselves at. Many are learning from her *here.* So some of the questions we ask her would be mundane to you.

D: *So this is going to be taking place on two levels?*

J: That is correct, in that we have gathered representatives for this - what you might term - a meeting. There are times in Janice's lifetime, *Earth* lifetime, that she does need to experience what we term "communion." Communion being interaction with her sources. So it is not merely a question and answer, as you would think of questions and answers, but there will be an *exchange* of energies and a reinforcement of whatever she feels she needs.

D: *So if you do it on two levels, you can ask her the internal questions silently, and then ask the other ones so I can hear them. Would that be all right?*

J: That will be all right. I'm not quite sure how this will work out, for this is the first attempt we have ever made to allow another human to be present at any one of these gatherings. We consider it important, or you would not be contacted in this manner, for this is not a normal process.

D: I appreciate that. If I can help with the questions and answers I'll be glad to do that, with my limited knowledge.

J: Sometimes an individual just needs a reinforcement of strength.

D: Do you want to begin the questions?

J: You will understand that the benefit of the answer will not be necessarily for you, as much as it is for the others gathered here.

D: That's all right. I'm interested in what they are interested in.

J: They are interested in: what does chocolate milk taste like?

D: (What a strange question? I was amused.) *What does chocolate milk taste like? That's a good question.*

J: For in her answers some of them can experience that. - She is answering presently.

D: Can I hear what she is saying, or can we do it that way?

J: I don't think it is possible to do it that way. There is an exchange taking place between her and the members gathered here. It is a way of exchanging information, and it is a part of her service. And it has been a part of her service throughout her lifetime. I have been with her through her lifetime, and am familiar in that sense, as her father. I cannot stay for long periods of time, or do not come to interact with her on a very frequent schedule. In that, what it causes to happen is the emotional reaction that you experienced, in the feeling of separateness from me. It is a very emotional experience for Janice.

D: Did her mother take part in a breeding experiment?

J: Her birth was somewhat different from the ordinary sense of conception.

D: In what way?

J: I'm not at liberty to tell you that.

D: I respect that. But I was thinking if you were the biological father, it might have been done in a different way. That's why I asked.

J: It *was* done in a different way during the act of sexual intercourse.

D: With you or with the father that she calls father?

J: With the father that she calls father.

D: So it can be done that way?

J: There is a point at which it can take place, in a manner of speaking.

D: I thought it had to be done under laboratory conditions.

J: Not necessarily.

D: You people have many talents that I'm unaware of. Then you were with her from time to time as she was growing up? (Yes) *And she knew this subconsciously?*
J: Yes, she has always known it. But it was not in her true day-to-day consciousness. There were times when she experienced feelings much as you saw, but they were not in relation to her Earth father. They were in relation to a visitation that had taken place, and an interaction with me. It became so traumatic that I stopped coming as often.

This type of childhood experience with a "real" father also occurred with Fran in Chapter 5.

D: Yes, this could be very confusing, especially to a child.
J: It was somewhat confusing, but it made her sense of aloneness and longing to go home more intense.
D: So it was better if you didn't come as often.
J: Yes, I have come at different crucial points in her life.
D: That way you were there for reinforcement.
J: Exactly.
D: Well, as she explains what chocolate milk tastes like, do they pick up the taste and smell and everything? (Yes) *That way they can experience it.*
J: That is true.
D: Very good. Do they have any other questions?
J: They have many questions. There are things they do not understand. And they will ask again and again the same questions, hoping for a different answer.
D: Or one that they can understand. (Yes) *What are some of those questions?*
J: We will explain to you how certain ones gathered here perceive your Earth planet. They do not understand violence. Therefore their questions to her will be in relation to trying to understand violence. This is a part of their growth, and it's also an educational experience, if you understand where they are evolutionarily. Because of their environment, and due to certain missions they performed on your planet, certain things they came in contact with caused them a great deal of confusion. That confusion being: they

don't understand violence. They don't understand the pain. How can man continue in that cycle?

D: *I think it's important to tell them that some humans don't understand this either.*

J: I know this. But it helps to hear it from an inter-dimensional being, rather than to have me or someone stand and lecture to them.

D: *They should hear it from someone who has experienced it.*

J: Inter-dimensionally.

D: *Don't they have any violence where they come from?* (No) *Did they ever have?* (No) *I thought maybe they had in the past and then evolved above that.*

J: This has never taken place. They don't even know the word, what it is called, to understand it.

D: *Do they experience pain?*

J: They experience pain when they see someone kill another human being. For they cannot ... it's out of the realm of their conception, to see that and know what is taking place in the life form state of being. Because they could not do that to another of their own kind, they don't understand man doing that to man. There is no possible way I can explain it and have them accept it, for they realize I have not experienced nor necessarily lived in that type of environment myself.

D: *But it's even difficult for those that do live in the environment. Do they know what pain feels like?*

J: Not in the same sense.

D: *I wondered if their bodies were able to feel it.*

J: It is a mental concept that they understand, but physically it is not felt.

D: *Have they ever hurt themselves?*

J: Not physically. Everything takes place at the mental state.

D: *Then it would be difficult for them to even understand what pain feels like to the body. And also suffering.*

J: Yes. They do not have that. Where they come from that does not take place.

D: *Do you think Earth is unique in this way?*

J: No. Earth is just more highly developed in those types of activities.

D: *I would hate to think we were the only one that had sunk so low, if I want to use those terms. Then there are other planets that do experience violence?*

J: There have been other planets that experience violence, yes.

D: *But these representatives have had no experience with them.*

J: Not intergalactically.

D: *Is she having any success trying to explain this to them?*

J: There is much communication taking place. We are past that now.

D: *I imagine they take things from her mind that she has seen and experienced.*

J: That is correct. They can relive particular experiences she has participated in. They begin to understand emotionally and in a sensory way what takes place at the physical level, because they can experience physical. It's just a matter of being able to experience it through another person.

D: *Then they have to sense it through her own mind.*

J: And sensibilities.

D: *And they can relive it that way.*

J: Yes. Understand now that not everyone gathered here is doing that. There are others like me who fully understand the range of human emotions, as well as the physicalness.

D: *It is a teaching for those who have not experienced it.*

J: Yes. For them to continue in the work in the project they are presently undertaking, this is like a school.

D: *These are interesting questions. I am getting much insight into the way you feel. - What is the next subject they're interested in?*

J: They are talking about the atomic bomb.

D: *Ooooh, that is a big one. What are they asking about that?*

J: They want to know if she understands why you used the atomic bomb on each other.

D: *There are arguments pro and con on that within our own civilization. Can they understand these are not things everyone on Earth does?*

J: They do understand that not everyone on Earth is a participant in that activity. However, they feel confusion because of the fact that on their planet each of them is responsible. They have a responsibility not to participate, or to allow a thing to take place. They feel each and every one of us has that same responsibility. They are having difficulty understanding why Janice cannot do something to change that. They know she has the capability of influencing various aspects of your atmosphere. So they are asking her why she is allowing that to be. They don't understand she is not the totality of what it takes to annihilate that.

D: *No. She's just like one little speck.*

J: But they do not understand that yet.

D: *And at the time it happened she would have just been a child, or maybe she had not been born yet?*

J: Was not born. Part of the reason for her birth. Janice was actually borned *(actual pronunciation)* as the war ended. Therefore the energy she brings to the planet helped to serve to balance out the years after that war. There was a time when .... Well, it is not to be discussed now. I will tell you that part of her purpose of being born *on* the planet, has to do with energy work of the planet.

D: *Maybe they can understand that she could not influence the dropping of the bomb, because she was not alive at that time on our planet. So she had nothing to do with that.*

J: That is correct. It is not a matter that she has nothing to do with the dropping of the bomb. What it is a matter of is that the bomb still exists, and she is there.

D: *I see. And they think the bomb should not exist?* (Yes) *Do they know that some atomic power has been used for good?*

J: Yes. That's part of the problem they are having with understanding. That it could be allowed to be used for bad. Or that it could exist in a state of readiness to be used for bad.

D: *These are difficult questions. I hope she is helping in some way. Has she answered that one?*

J: There can be no more information given at this time with regard to that question. There is an interaction taking place between them.

D: *Are they having a discussion?*

J: Yes. (The voice dropped to a low level.) So, Janice, I would like to say, daughter, that I am very proud of you. (Louder) When they are having discussion, I can have discussion with her, because it is a waste of time for us to participate. And we will have an opportunity later to talk. I wanted you to experience this meeting so you will understand a part of her function.

D: *This was a question she had. She wanted to know what her work was.*

J: There is more than one kind of work that she does.

D: *She wondered what she was doing when she feels she is in this energy state. She felt as though she was working, maybe with other energies or something.*

J: That is a completely different project from this one.

D: *She wanted to know: when she is doing this type of work in the energy state, are these other energies she feels around her anyone she knows in the physical?*

J: These energies she is presently with are not people she knows in the physical. But at other times on the other project, there are some that she knows, and some that she will know.

D: *She felt there was a familiarity, but that was all she knew.*

J: There is.

D: *Can you tell her anything about the other project, or is that allowed?*

J: I can discuss it. That is part of why I've come. When she does not understand things, I help her to do that. That is what a father does, in this sense of the word. So at different points throughout her evolvement I have come to help her understand complicated concepts. Or to understand things that were troubling her in relation to the work she has undertaken. So this is my responsibility.

D: *She wanted to know about the work she was doing, that she's not conscious of.*

J: She does have some knowledge of it, and is aware that in her energy state there is a holding on, so to speak. A sense of holding something, helping something, healing something. By the *holding of* something, the healing takes place. It is a very gradual thing. I will tell you that the holding is of a frequency.

D: *What purpose does this serve?*

J: The holding of the frequency serves to balance the atmospheric conditions outside the planet, which directly affect things that go on, on the planet Earth. That is the part I can tell you that is taking place. Now, what you must understand is that it is a very complicated situation to discuss. But I can tell you that others are involved with her in the project, and they .... (Pause) Well, it is a great service. For it is very ... it is ....

He hesitated. Was it because he was not supposed to tell me these things, or was he trying to decide how much he could reveal?

I saw the tape was getting ready to run out, so I took advantage of his hesitation. I turned the tape over and continued.

D: But you said this is a great service?
J: It is a great service to mankind, for it is keeping your planet from self-destructing.
D: I think of frequencies as radio frequencies. It's different than that?
(Yes) And how are they affecting our Earth?
J: They are affecting your Earth. And some would say we in this project cause various earthquakes, and the volcanic action, and the different levels of activity climatically that are taking place on your planet. They would like to blame it on us. However it is the opposite. Were it not for our participating in this project, the disasters would be much worse. And the destruction would be coming toward Earth in a very fast rate of speed.
D: Then you are causing a release?
J: What we are saying is that we are helping to maintain a balance at whatever point of the globe needs balance. A balance of energy in the flow as these events take place. There could be much worse earthquakes at various locations were we not involved in the work in this project. So perhaps you could look at it as a maintenance project or a maintaining. Meaning that it lessens the severity of the catastrophe climatically.
D: There's no way you could keep it from happening altogether?
J: We could keep it from happening altogether, but there is a point past which we cannot, at this time, go, in relation to disasters.
D: Because of what has to happen to the planet? (Yes) *And you cannot interfere in the ultimate destiny.*
J: At this moment.
D: So you are only allowed to do certain things.
J: That is correct.
D: Is there anyone or anything that determines these rules?
J: The rules are universal. They have been known for, as you would term, centuries, throughout time, throughout past time. It is written, it has always been written. They do not change.
D: What are some of these rules?
J: There is a law of noninterference. Now, much as your politicians work within the framework of the laws that have been set up by them, so we work within the same framework. However,

remember perceptually, interference does not necessarily mean the same thing to us as it means to you.

D: *In other words, you're able to bend the rules a little, to where you can help.*

J: We can help. We can assist. We can instruct. We can interact. We can convey.

D: *But you can't take direct interfering action.* (She sighed.) *I'm trying to make a distinction.*

J: In certain cases we can and do directly interact to the point you might describe as interference. If it has to do with one of our own, then we definitely will interfere, because that is not interference in that sense of the word.

D: *No. That would be protection, I would think.*

J: That is correct, but it is perceived as interference.

D: *Is there ever a point when you would interfere in the history or the changes of Earth?*

J: No. Not unless we are directed by the source.

D: *That's what I was wondering, if there was some central figure or part where all these rules came from.*

J: There is a source.

D: *How do you describe the source?*

J: Unlimited energy in the purest essence state.

D: *Are you able to see it?*

J: We are able to experience it. As you do, at particular points in your lifetimes.

D: *This is probably what we call God, in a very limited term.*

J: It is the same. We just use different terms.

D: *You said the rule of noninterference was one of the rules. Are there any others?*

J: We do not perform violent acts. We are not involved in the negativity of your planet, nor can we become so. It is a law that anything having to do with that negativity be canceled by the opposite of negativity. From within us we cannot send that. It is impossible.

D: *If the rules are set down and come from the source, how are they sent to you? How do you know about them?*

J: The same way you know about them: through our history.

D: *I suppose I have in my mind a figure writing down laws or telling people this is the way it is.*

J: Excuse me?

D: *What happened?*

J: What was your question?

D: *You jerked your head. I was wondering if something was happening there.*

J: Yes. I was looking to see what was appearing to happen here.

D: *I don't want to keep you from anything there.*

J: They are leaving.

D: *They didn't want to ask anything else?*

J: They've already asked their questions.

D: *Did they ask any other questions that I can know about?* (No) *The others were for her?* (Yes) *All right. I was saying, in my own mind I perceive something like a man or a figure writing the laws or telling them to someone.* (Physical reactions indicated something was going on.) *What's the matter?*

J: Quiet! (A long pause.)

D: *What were you doing?*

J: We were talking.

D: *All right. Will she remember what you said?*

J: Later she will remember. Perhaps tomorrow.

D: *That's one advantage of having it in my black box, because she can hear it in her conscious state.*

J: It is more important that she learn it another way in her conscious state, for this is how it has always taken place. From childhood and in her adulthood, this is how our communication has taken place. She is not that familiar with my voice.

D: *Then she will remember what you have said.*

J: Yes, but it will not happen all at once. For it is, in your terminology, an emotional and traumatic experience to interact with me. That's why the communication takes place as it does. Were she to hear what I have to say and play it over and over on a tape, that would only cause the reinforcement of that kind of emotion.

D: *I can understand these things. Is it all right if I ask a few more questions?*

J: I would like to tell you on your box that - for Janice. The times you have sensed me being with you, you are correct. It is important for you to know when you sense my presence, I am truly there with you. This I want you to have and to carry with you as you go about the days to come.

D: If she needs help can she call upon you?

J: Yes. It is difficult for both of us. For we experience love for our children in the same manner that you do.

D: This is something humans don't understand. They think of aliens as not having any feelings, or any emotions. I think it is important for them to know you do have feelings.

J: We do, from our galaxy, have the same kind of emotions, especially for our family, that you do for yours. That is one of the reasons we are here. To help the others to understand those emotions, as they see us interact with our own.

D: These others don't have these emotions?

J: Some of them have them, some of them don't have them. In the days to come there will be trials, as your Bible says, and tribulations. And it is hard for me to know that one of my own will perhaps experience or witness some of these things taking place. For already she is affected by the Earth changes. I will tell you that at this present time she cannot hear me. It would be too much for her to hear what is being said, and to facilitate my voice at the same time.

D: But she will hear it when she plays the tape back.

J: (Emotional) Yes. And ....

D: It may help her. (This seemed to be disturbing the entity, so I thought we should get off the subject.) *Can I ask you? She wanted to know ....* (She was displaying signs of emotion.) *It's all right, it's all right. I appreciate it that you are sharing your emotions with me. I feel honored that you're letting me participate.*

J: This is very difficult.

D: Maybe you can continue the communication while she's asleep tonight. Is that possible?

J: Oh, I do that quite often.

D: She had a question. It seems as though she's been having sick feelings just before a catastrophe occurs.

J: That is correct. That is another reason I have come. I know what she has been experiencing. And it must be so, for it is being instilled in her, and is happening for different reasons. One is to allow her a reference for knowing what is coming, so she will be able to protect herself. The other is that, a part of the project and the work she is involved in, is to reduce oneself to that energy state from whence one came, and act with other energies of the same source as a blanket of protection to the planet. And from that state of being, energy is transferred through different ley lines throughout the globe. So one is totally interconnected with the planet in the energy state. When the energy returns to the physical state it is not disconnected. Therefore the being is affected by these events in a physical manner.

D: *She said it has a different feeling, according to whether it is an earthquake or a general disaster like a plane crash or something like that.*

J: That is correct.

D: *Will she be able to tell the difference?*

J: She is already able to tell some of the difference. You must understand this is a part of her - for lack of a better term - schooling. It's a matter of learning as well as participating in a project at the same time. She is learning to protect her humanness, but at the same time she is participating in a project that is helping the planet every moment she wakes, sleeps, feeds, breathes, on it.

D: *But she can't really do anything to stop these catastrophes, because at the time she is feeling this, it is the time it is occurring.*

J: No. It is not the time it is occurring. It is before it occurs, it is during when it occurs, and it is after it occurs.

D: *But in that way she can't do anything to warn anyone.*

J: It's not a matter of warning.

D: *She can't stop it in any way.*

J: It's a matter of energy. It is not a matter of stopping it. It is a matter of lessening the effects of, because of the conduit that she is, because of the receiver that she is, and because the energy flows through her as it does. Then what happens is that planetarily the level of severity is affected by that energy. Because it does not matter if she is in the energy state at that point in time or not.

D: *Are there other people who have come to Earth, so that they can act in this energy type of way?*

J: Yes. There are people all over your planet that have come to act in this same way.

D: *Like Janice, they're not aware of what they're doing, consciously?*

J: They, *like* Janice, are aware, and they have some knowledge consciously. It is just not time for them to know the fullness of the entire project. In the same manner in which you do not wish to preaffect your subject's answers to questions that you ask them. We do not allow the fullness to be known, so as not to affect the outcome, or the interference by the human level individual in the project. For sometimes when the emotional state of the human is affected, the same results cannot be obtained.

D: *The other beings that have come to help, are they Earth energies, or have they come from somewhere else?*

J: They have come from somewhere else.

D: *I am working with a young man I think is the same type.*

I was thinking about Phil, my subject in *Keepers of the Garden*.

J: Yes, he is.

D: *He has been affected very much by the things he has seen on Earth too. It has been very difficult for him.*

J: It is very traumatic, physically, mentally, for them. Every cell is involved in it. When these individuals are reduced to a cellular, molecular state, it is as if every atom was infused with these events. Therefore when they experience them back in this state of matter, the human being state, then every atom within their body re-experiences those events to a point of sensitivity that is more highly developed than the average human's. Therefore they are so severely affected, some are beyond being able to get out of bed.

D: *He did at one point in his life try to commit suicide.*

J: And many do.

D: *Because he just couldn't understand. He didn't want to be here.*

J: Janice has experienced the same traumas, because she does not understand herself why this must take place. Because she is and has a soulular memory of another way of being.

D: *That was what he kept saying. This wasn't home.*

J: It is not home. It is *home* in the truest sense of the word. Their frustration is that they know the potential of the home it could be. That is the sense of frustration.

D: *It seems to me these are spirits that have essentially never lived on Earth before.*

J: Some of them have lived on Earth before, and some of them have not.

D: *And they have volunteered to come to participate in this project.*

J: This is correct. But you must understand that not all of the energies are the same, although they are participating in the project. It does not mean they are one and the same energy, or even from the same source of energy.

D: *When I first started working with Janice I was told there was a negative side to the space beings. I thought they were all like you are. I wondered how a negative side could be allowed to exist. I was thinking, I guess, that you had all evolved to a perfect state.*

J: Well, not all of us are as evolved as my state is. Just as not all of the humans are as evolved as you are. So therefore you must understand that there are different energies in space beings, just as there are different energies in your lives.

D: *I was curious about this negative side. I wanted to have a little more information about them, without affecting her in any way. Do they also have craft and operate in the same way that you do?*

J: I am not able to discuss this with you through her. I would not subject her to it. Perhaps at a later time, at a different point in time, but not now. For right now there is a need for interaction as we are doing. There are certain times when you on your planet have family reunions. Sometimes we do too.

D: *What about the other members of Janice's family? I think she has brothers.*

J: She does have brothers. They are all very special. They are like she is. They do not know it.

D: *Are you their father also?* (Yes) *But they are not as sensitive, are they?*

J: They are sensitive in a different way.

D: *Do you have a family elsewhere?*

J: I have a family elsewhere.

D: *I have the feeling you must have many children.*

J: I do.

D: *On Earth as well as somewhere else.* (Yes) *Is a father picked for a certain reason, biologically or whatever.* (Pause) *Do you understand what I mean?*

J: No. I'm not sure I understand what you mean.

D: *For instance, were you chosen to be the father of many children on Earth, because you were special in some way, or had special traits?*

J: Yes, I do have the traits you see personified in Janice. You see, not all our children - as your children - turn out to be the same. For when they come to Earth they have the choices they can make.

D: *That all goes back to the soul, the essence.* (Yes) *What are your traits that are present in her?*

J: We have a purity of intention. We have a dedication, honesty, straightforwardness. And we have a pure sense of love, and understand what it means to love unconditionally.

D: *Those are all very wonderful traits. So not all the children you have fathered have these traits.*

J: They have them. They are either latent or they have rejected them.

D: *I can see why you're justly proud of her.*

J: I am very proud.

D: *But can you tell me where you come from? Where is your home?*

J: I can only tell you that it's outside your galaxy.

D: *Which is always hard for us to comprehend.*

J: I am sure.

D: *Is it a physical planet?*

J: It is a physical planet.

D: *Do you go back there at different times?*

J: Yes. I came from there.

D: *Just now?* (Yes) *I'm a Navy wife, as it is called. My husband was many years away from his home traveling, and I sometimes traveled with him. I guess I think of you being assigned to that craft, if that's where we are.*

J: It doesn't matter what craft I'm on.

D: *I think of you as maybe being assigned and being away from your home for many years.*

J: Not necessarily, because interdimensions and intergalactic travel doesn't go according to the time of years as you think of it.

D: *Then how do you travel?*

J: I travel by thought.

D: *Some of these answers I have heard, but I'm always looking for more verification. What is your occupation where you live?*

J: I am the ruler of the planet.

D: *Oh, then that is a great honor. Is that why you were chosen for the seeding, if I can use that word?*

J: If you want to consider it a choice. It is strictly a way of life for us, in that we do not think of ourselves as chosen.

D: Then you are not the only one that has fathered children on our planet? (No) *Is it a big responsibility being a ruler?*

J: It is a big responsibility. But we do not have the problems you have, so therefore I do not have to deal with the type of activity that occupies the time of most rulers on your planet. Can you imagine a planet where the flowers are as big as the house you're in?

D: No, I can't even conceive of that. Is that what it's like there?

J: That is part of it, yes. It is very beautiful there.

D: Do you have seasons like we do?

J: Actually we do not have the kind of winter that you have.

D: That's a blessing. (Chuckle)

J: And we do not think of them as seasonal types of seasons, as you call it here. It's more a matter of entertainment, than it is a way of life. For we do not participate in your seasonal growing, harvest, that sort of thing that you equate so with the seasons on your planet.

D: Do you consume food?

J: We consume light. However, understand that if we wish to experience food, we can experience food.

D: Because you have a digestive system?

J: Not as you think of digestion.

D: Through the senses? (Yes) *The way she was telling them about the chocolate milk?*

J: That is one concept, yes.

D: Then when you are on the craft, do you have trouble getting the type of light you need?

J: No, because I am that.

D: I thought maybe it had to be replenished.

J: No. Not for my existence.

D: Well, on your home planet, are you sexual creatures?

J: Oh, yes.

D: Do you have two sexes like we do? (Yes) *But do your children grow like ours do, from a baby?*

J: They do not have to learn to experience tying their shoes.

This was said soberly, but I sensed he was trying to joke with me. They probably didn't even have shoes.

J: The mechanics of their life are inbuilt, so they don't need to learn to eat when it's time to learn to eat ... with silverware, if that would take place. And I am not speaking of learning to eat. I'm trying to give you a way that you can reference what I am talking about when I say "inbuilt." Meaning they don't sit at a table and necessarily *eat* with silverware. But if they came to your planet they would not have to *learn* to do that.

D: *It's something that would be automatic.* (Yes) *But do they start out as a baby?* (Yes) *And they do develop in the same way that we develop to an adult.*

J: They develop at a different rate, but they do develop, yes.

D: *Do the people on your planet experience death?* (No) *What happens to the body eventually?*

J: The body does not die.

D: *You mean it is capable of living forever?*

J: It is capable of living forever. There are transition states, but we do not think of them as death.

D: *I am comparing to our planet, the body grows old, deteriorates, and it has to ....*

J: There is an "old."

D: *But the body doesn't have to die because it just runs down, so to speak, or ages?*

J: It doesn't age.

D: *I guess I've always thought if someone couldn't die, that would be the ideal state. That's the way humans think.*

J: Humans think that, yes. It's not a matter *of can't* die. It's a matter of choice of transition.

D: *Then what happens when you decide you don't want that body anymore?*

J: You return to the source.

D: *What happens to the body?*

J: The body is molecularly reabsorbed.

D: *This is done when you are tired of it or what?*

J: There are different reasons. (She began to display discomfort.)

D: *I think we have just about run out of time. I can see she is getting hot and uncomfortable. I want to tell you I have really enjoyed speaking with you. It has been an honor.*

J: Thank you very much for coming to talk with me. And I appreciate your patience. For I have not truly been concentrating totally on you and your questions. I have been selfish in that I wanted to interact with Janice for her needs of knowing that I am here.

D: *That's all right. I feel selfish that I have distracted you.*

J: No matter. It was important that she see I still exist at this time.

D: *Maybe another time we may speak again.*

J: We certainly will speak again. I thank you very much, and appreciate you and the work you are doing with my daughter.

D: *I will always take care of her as best I can.*

J: (Authority) Yes, you most certainly will!

D: *I'm very protective when I do this work.*

J: I know that. I do not mean to speak harshly to you. I'm just very protective also.

I was preparing to integrate Janice so I could awaken her, but he stopped me.

J: I need to speak with her.

D: *Will you do it now or when she's asleep tonight?*

J: It must be done now.

D: *All right. Go ahead, while we still have a little time. Do you want to do it aloud or internally?*

J: I will do it both ways. - (He spoke with great tenderness.) My daughter, my child, know that I am always with you. I have promised you that you will never be alone. And so you must always know in the coming days that I will never leave your side. You may experience me whenever you wish. Any time you need the strength to fulfill your mission, and any time you need to speak with me, you know the method to use. And you know the place from which to do it. Do not forget that I love you, that I am always with you, and we will always be as one. We are a part of each other. We cannot cease to exist. Although we are now residing in different dimensions, you know you can come to me at any time. I will help you. I will take care of you. It is important for you to remember this, and that is why I am speaking it to you now. In the days to come there will be times when you may forget, as you have most recently forgotten, that I am here for you. This is a reminder to you. Take me seriously. You will need me and I will be here. In love, I bid you Alokeia.

D: Alokeia. Thank you very much. It is time, we must leave. Janice must awaken so she can return to her home. I am now asking all of the consciousness and personality to once again return to the body of Janice, and the other personality to depart and go back where it has to go.

I gave instructions for reorienting. As I was bringing Janice back up to consciousness she resisted and began to cry. It was as though she didn't want to leave the entity. I comforted her, but still insisted on orientation. *"No, you have to, you have to. You have to come back."*

I spent time talking with her and comforting her before awakening. I assured her we could return to find that entity any time we wanted to. We had found the way, so it was not a permanent departure. When she awakened she did not remember, and was surprised to find she had been crying.

After she awakened and was sitting up in bed, I noticed the palms of her hands. They were not visible to me while the session was going on, because she had lain perfectly still with her hands palm down. This time the discoloration was so dark it was almost black. She also noticed it and wondered what caused it. She shook her hands and massaged them. There was no discomfort, it was just puzzling. As she did this the black color began to recede and normal coloration slowly returned. I turned the recorder back on to mention this.

D: The thumb and the big muscle below the thumb, and all the fingers on both hands were so blue they were almost purple. It looked as if you had gotten printer's ink on them from handling a dirty newspaper.

J: But I haven't handled a newspaper. (Besides when she rubbed them the color would not come off. It was definitely internal, coming from inside the skin.) And I washed my hands when I went to the bathroom before I came in here.

I remarked that when we stopped for supper I had noticed a slight discoloration, but this now was much darker, almost black in color, and more widespread. After she got up and began moving around the color started to fade, and her hands were returning to normal. I didn't think it was caused by lack of circulation, because it is common for the subject to move very little when they are in the somnambulistic state of trance. Since it seemed to not be producing any discomfort, we decided to merely treat it as a curiosity.

Later I asked my friend, Harriet about this, and she had the feeling it might have been caused by energy, possibly caused by the different entities speaking through her. She suggested that next time I look at the soles of her feet when she awakened, and possibly the back of her neck. These were energy exit points. She didn't know where these ideas were coming from. They just popped into her head, and she didn't know if they had any validity or not.

Someone else said the skin does not do that unless the person is dead. I mentioned this to Julia, my daughter who is a nurse. Julia said the person who said that had obviously never spent much time in Intensive Care. She had observed this phenomenon in certain heart surgery patients, but it was only under extreme conditions. In those cases the discoloration was not confined to the palms, but was present in other parts of the body as well, and had to be alleviated by medication. I consulted my medical expert who has helped me on other books when I had medical questions. Dr. Bill knows of my work and is used to my strange requests, so I didn't have to explain why I wanted the information. He gave me the medical terms for the cause of the discoloration: Venous obstruction while arterial inflow remained intact. In layman's terms: the blood flow out of the extremities (arms, legs) would have to be constricted, inhibited, blocked, to create the phenomenon I described. It could be caused by a tourniquet or something similar restricting the blood flow, and under those conditions could result in nerve damage if the constriction continued long enough. He couldn't think of anything else that could create a similar discoloration. But Janice's hands were not being constricted in any way. They were resting palms-down on her abdomen during the entire session. He said that under those conditions it was definitely not normal, and was possibly caused by something supernatural that we don't understand. It was obviously not a normal thing for a healthy person to experience.

When I spoke to Janice months later, while trying to arrange another session, she said the condition had never returned. She also said she had never been able to listen to any of the tapes. Every time she started to something would stop her. I had wondered about her reaction to this tape, because of its emotional content. So the father entity didn't have to worry about her reaction to hearing his voice. The message had been inserted into Janice's subconscious, just as he wished.

The phenomenon of the discoloration of Janice's hands could have been a variation of what occurred with Suzanne in Chapter 7. That had been my first encounter with an alien speaking through one of my subjects, and when she awakened in the motel she had huge red blotches all over her feet and lower legs. In 1997 when I first regressed Clara (Chapter 3) in Hollywood she discovered a red mark on the back of her neck at the hairline after an alien being spoke through her in the session. Maybe these physical manifestations are the result of the different energy interacting through a physical body. Although the results were startling, they appeared to be temporary and caused no lasting physical effects.

When I called Janice in 1998 for permission to use these sessions, she had still never listened to the tapes. She didn't even remember where she had packed them away.

CHAPTER 13
THE ULTIMATE EXPERIENCE

It was six months later in July 1990 before I was able to journey again to Little Rock to work with Janice. I wanted to attempt several sessions in one day. The last time this was done it appeared that three sessions in one day were too much for both of us. On this trip we would see how many would be sufficient without overtaxing either one of us. During this visit the sessions took a new turn into more uncharted territory. We definitely drifted away from UFO experiences and were communicating more with beings in other dimensions. Some of these beings were composed of light, and referred to themselves as pure energy beings. It appeared that the more Janice worked with these energies the more complex her training became. The concepts that were presented were so complicated that I knew they could not be presented in this book. These will be reported in detail in my book *Convoluted Universe*. That will be a book directed toward those who are ready and able to comprehend concepts and theories that make my poor brain feel like mush. I thought it would be better to combine these into one book for those who enjoy being challenged. Since this book deals with mostly UFO experiences and hints that there is much more behind them, I wanted to keep it focused in that direction.

One thing I do want to include here pertained to the purple discoloration of Janice's hands after the three sessions in January. The answer came from the energy doctor I had spoken to before.

D: *The last time I worked with Janice she had a definite physical change in the skin on the palms of her hands. Can you explain why that occurred?*

J: It occurred because the physical body had not adapted properly to the energy level at which she was operating. This was a circulatory system problem.

D: *The skin was so dark it was almost purple in certain areas on her hands.*

J: Yes, she was at a very, very high energy level.

D: *It was caused by the being speaking through her?* (Yes) *I was afraid maybe I had done too many sessions that day, and it caused something to happen.*

J: No, it would have happened anyway. Part of the problem was that her physical peak condition was not present. Actually it had to do with the interaction of the energy that was flowing through the veins, in relation to the system of energy to which she was connected.

D: *Was there any way it could have caused harm, with the discoloration of the skin?*

J: We would not have allowed it. The being is too important. It will not occur again. She is at a different level of development now.

This type of discoloration never occurred again while I worked with Janice. Also, in the later sessions she did not experience the heat fluctuations that had caused me concern in the earlier sessions. It appeared she had adjusted to working with these higher energies speaking through her body. Apparently this type of communication does have a noticeable physical effect on the body in some cases, but it also apparently does not cause permanent harm. It is a transitional phenomenon.

Another strange curiosity connected with this case occurred during this time. I always make copies of the tapes and send one to Lou and one to the subject, so there will always be other copies in existence. Normally I transcribe tapes that I intend to use within a few weeks after the session, so I will have a paper copy. I transcribed the first sessions that were conducted in 1989 and 1990. There were three more sessions in 1990 and one a year later in 1991. I always put the tapes I intend to transcribe in one place in my office, so they won't get mixed up with miscellaneous tapes. However, I couldn't find these last four tapes to transcribe them. I searched for them throughout my office each time I thought about them. I even asked Janice and Lou to send me their copies. Janice had never listened to any of her tapes and had misplaced them. And Lou said it would be quite a job to find his, since his office is very disorganized. I kept remembering the alien admonishing me that I would not be allowed to print any of this story until I had the complete picture. Did they have something to do with this? I was not ready to print it yet, I only wanted to transcribe the tapes.

Mysteriously the tapes remained missing for five years while I was busy with other books and projects. They suddenly appeared in an obvious place on my desk in early 1996. It was a place where they were in plain sight, and could not possibly have been overlooked. At that time I had begun to compile the information from my files for this book. When the tapes mysteriously reappeared I knew it was time for the information to come out. I had kept my promise and eight years had passed since they asked for my silence in 1989.

I will now include information from the last session I had with Janice in September 1991, which I call the "Ultimate Experience." At the time I thought she went to a spacecraft, but after going over the transcripts of our sessions I wonder if she instead was at the underground base inside the mountain. Wherever it was it is the location of schools that provide learning without parallel anywhere in the universe.

I returned to Little Rock in September 1991 to have sessions with two cases of suspected UFO abduction. Lou and Jerry drove me to these and were witnesses. While there I also worked with Janice. At the time I did not suspect this would be the last time I would have a session with her. It was held at my friend Patsy's house again. Janice wanted to explore a strange event that had happened very recently in July 1991.

At this time Janice was very happy because a man she had known several years before had come back into her life, and she was romantically involved with him. She felt as though she had finally found a kindred soul. Not wanting to frighten him away, she had not told him anything about the strange experiences that had plagued her. He was a military man, and she had gone to the town next to the military base to spend the weekend with him. They were in a motel and Ken had to get up very early the next morning to go back to the base. After he left Janice fell back into a very deep sleep. A few hours later she was awakened by the maid knocking on the door, but she couldn't rouse herself enough to answer it. The next thing she knew the maid had let herself into the room, and was screaming hysterically. This startled Janice awake, and she lay there watching all the lights in the room flashing erratically off and on until some of them exploded. This was what frightened the maid, and she ran screaming from the room. Thus, during this session we wanted to discover what had happened that night.

I used Janice's keyword, and it worked perfectly even though we hadn't had any sessions for a year. I then counted her back to the night of the incident. When I transcribed this tape I heard a strange sound effect that was not audible at the time of the session. When I finished counting I heard something that sounded like a car ignition starting up, or more correctly, like a motor boat accelerating. It was loud, so it was not coming from outside. It sounded like it was right next to the microphone. It was obvious from the tape that I had not heard a real noise in the room, because I continued my instructions without interruption.

Janice recounted the pleasant memories of that night. Then they both had fallen into a very deep sleep.

D: Did you sleep through the entire night?
J: No, it was like I woke up. He woke up too, and we were talking. And we said, "What happened?" It was like I just got there. And he said, "Wow, it feels like we've been out of this world." We knew we were there in the physical, but we knew we were somewhere else in another way, because we could touch that other place somehow. It was really strange. I knew something had happened during the night, but I didn't know what. He had to get up because he had to leave at 4:30 in the morning to go back to the base, and he had difficulty getting awake. I was worried, because I knew he wasn't really back. And I thought, "Oh, my God! He has to go out and drive." Then when he went out the door, out in back of the motel there was this *huge* open field, and it was covered with fog. It wasn't anywhere else. It was really weird, because it was July and there was fog out there. I asked him how could he drive in that fog and he said there wasn't any fog. He didn't see it. After he left I went back to bed and fell asleep immediately. It was like I knew I wasn't really going to sleep; I was going somewhere. And I was gone. Then it was morning, the maid opened the door, and she was yelling and yelling. I could hear her, but I couldn't move. I couldn't get my eyes open. She just stood there screaming. I was trying so hard to open my eyes, and it wouldn't work. When I finally opened them, all the lights were flashing ... oh, really fast. And I was so

dizzy. The maid kept screaming. She didn't know what to do. (Softly) It's okay. It's okay. And they kept flashing, until some of them exploded. And then they quit.

D: *Let's go back to the night before, and you will find out what happened. Did the experience happen while Ken was there?*

J: Some of it happened while Ken was there.

D: *Let's go over that part. Tell me when it began. Were you asleep?*

J: (Smiling) We weren't asleep actually. It was right before being asleep. And we left together.

D: *What do you mean?*

J: I mean we left the motel. We went out to the ships.

D: *How did you do that?*

J: I don't know. We were just on 'em. It was really fast.

D: *Did you go in your physical body?*

J: It seemed like we did. I could see his physical body.

D: *So you both left the room?* (Uh huh) *Where was the ship?*

J: I don't know. We were just drifting, and then we were on it. Just swoosh! Really fast.

D: *All right. Tell me what you see.*

J: Oh, we're happy we're there. We're not at all afraid. We went into the sacred room.

D: *What is the sacred room?*

J: (Pause) I'm not sure I can tell you that.

D: *You mean you're not allowed or what?*

J: (A reverent tone.) It's the highest room on the ship. You can't go into that room unless you're a spiritual teacher. It's a very special place. Not everybody goes there.

D: *Did you two go there?*

J: Yes. And we sat on special chairs. It's an awesome room.

D: *Why is it awesome?*

J: Because it's a ....

There was a long pause, then the voice changed. Someone else was speaking. Janice had been in awe, and this voice was unemotional.

J: It's a replication of the future.

D: *Of the future?*

J: Yes, many things happen in this room that affect the spirituality of galaxies and planetary systems, not just the Earth's planetary systems. So it's an awesome place to be. And it's a very sacred place.

D: *Is it on every ship?*

J: No, just this one.

D: *Is this a special type of ship because of that?*

J: Yes. It's not like any of the others.

D: *Is this ship located in a special place?*

J: This ship is every place. It goes to all the galaxies, and all the universes. It's awesome. And different people come here.

D: *What is different about the people that come there?*

J: They have to have reached a certain level of development, or they don't ever come here. They must have a common purpose. Even though they have multi purposes, there is one that brings them to this ship. And it's the ship of union.

D: *What else is different about the ship?*

J: The shape of the rooms. They're not square rooms. They're not like any rooms you've ever been in. They're many sided, with eight sides.

D: *Is there a reason for having eight sides?*

J: I don't know.

D: *Are all the rooms in the ship the same way?*

J: There are four rooms that are the inner chambers, the interior, the center core of the ship, that have eight sides. And there are exterior rooms where people are taught. The exterior rooms are curved. They don't have sides.

D: *Is this a large ship?*

J: Oh, it's huge. It is ... oh, God, it is huge.

D: *Are there many people on there?*

J: Yes. There are many people, but they're not all there for the same purpose. And they don't go to the same rooms.

D: *What other purposes would they come for?*

J: Some come for integration work.

D: *What does that mean?*

J: It means it's time for a change in their developmental level. And there has to be integration of physical, spiritual, emotional, mental, causal, astral. All the bodies. There is sometimes molecular reconstruction. Some people have fusion. Some people just go to class. Some people come to teach. Some people come to participate in other activities.

D: *What type of things are taught there?*

J: The mechanics of sound. The mechanics of light. The mechanics of energy. The mechanics of molecular reconstruction. The mechanics of dematerialization. The mechanics of bilocation. The mechanics of parallel universes. The mechanics of time. The mechanics of space in relation to particle matter and energy. The mechanics of movement through time and space, and travel with relation to the light ... past light, past the speed of light. There are many more subjects that I can tell you.

D: *Are the people in their physical bodies when they come to this place?*

J: Some are, some are not. But you see, if you are in your physical body that can change even after you're here, so it doesn't matter actually. If the students come in their physical body, most of them stay in their physical body. But the teachers and the avatars can change into energy, and they, in a sense, refuel. They revitalize and do much interaction and work that has to do with energy, and understanding how to bring it back into the physical and transmit it. To continue their work once they return.

D: *Then even Earth people do this?*

J: Well, very few Earth people are actually Earth people. "Earth" people are taken to other ships, but there are Earth people who are not actually totally Earth people. They are Earth people, but have mastered areas and levels of development that cause them to function within themselves at the physical level, and at the same time function on multidimensional levels. They are not, in their Earth form, always necessarily aware of this in the beginning. But once they reach the interior rooms they are aware of functioning within different molecular structures, and also inter-dimensional and interplanetary service. So it's past the normal UFO phenomenon when you are here. You're past that.

D: *Then when they bring this knowledge from the classes back to Earth, do they use it?*

J: It's used, in a manner of speaking, it becomes functional within them to carry a vibrational rate. And one of their most important missions is to maintain the vibrational rate they attain here or are exposed to here. That is integrated into their being when they return to Earth. They will use it at the proper time, and it will serve them in many ways in the future, as we go forward to the next century.

D: *These people don't remember this consciously, do they?*

J: There is a possibility it can be recalled into the conscious state, depending upon the structure of the being's brain. There are beings who can function in the physical and maintain a level of development that causes a reconfiguration to the point that functioning in the physical becomes so normal it's not apparent. When .... (She broke off unexpectedly. Something appeared to be happening.)

D: *What's the matter?*

J: (Janice was back.) I think we're moving some place. We're going now to some other room. It's not exactly a corridor. There are four rooms and they have eight sides, and you have to go through all four rooms.

D: *Do you walk from one room to the next?*

J: No. We didn't walk, but we're holding hands and we're moving. By thought we moved.

D: *What's in the next room?*

J: Actually the next room is a different sort of place. It's metallic, and we're going to be working in a different manner now in here. (A sharp intake of breath.) Oh, my goodness! (Heavy breathing.)

D: *What is it?*

J: We're just ... air! We just dematerialized right here.

D: *But you were solid in the other room. Is that what you mean?*

J: Oh, Yeah! (She was excited. It apparently was unexpected.)

D: *And this room is for dematerialization? Would that be right?*

J: That's what happened.

D: *What's the purpose of that?*

J: I don't know. Well, now we're not separate people any more.(Heavy breathing) We're not separate people any more. (Excited laughter) Oh, my goodness!

D: *Can you explain what you mean?*

J: (Stumbling and mumbling. She had difficulty even forming words.) Whew! Oh, God! I'm so hot! (I gave suggestions to cool her down.) I'm burning up!

D: *What did you mean, that you were not separate people anymore? Did something happen in that room?*

J: Yeah, we entered, and then swoosh! We were just not separate people any more.

D: *What were you?*

J: I don't know. You're just not people. (Excited laugh) I knew as in: this part is mine, this part is yours, this part's mine, and this part's yours. But yet we're not separate people any more.

D: *What do you mean? Parts all over the room?*

J: (Laugh) No, no, no, no. There are no parts, they're no ....

D: *You were pointing. (Chuckle)*

J: Oh, I'm sorry. I mean, we're not separate people. It's: he is here, I am here, we're both here, but we're one people ... we're not even physical. We're not even solid ... you can't touch. You can touch, but you can't touch. (Chuckle) We're not separate people any more.

D: *You mean you have fused together or what?*

J: Apparently we are. It's pure energy. There's no physical form here, but yet there is a form. There is a form, but there's not a physical form. But I know I'm me, and he knows he's him, but we know we're not.

D: *Will you maintain your personalities?*

J: Well, we are, but we're not. We're different. We are each other, but we are the same ... blended.

During this sentence there was a low roaring on the tape, like a motor, which caused vibration in the microphone. A strange sound. Maybe energy?

J: It's like: this molecule's his, this molecule's mine, this molecule's his, this molecule's mine, etc. I know that, he knows that, but in totality they're not ours.

D: *So you think "blended" might be a better word. But the way you were smiling, it seems to feel all right.*

J: Oh, it's wonderful! It's really outstanding. It's just the most total harmony. That's what this is. Just pure .... Oh! They're telling me now. It's an essence energy.

D: *Essence energy?*

Note: Essence energy: Does this refer to the purest form? The earliest or original type? The God energy?

J: It's energy. It's our energy. It's in their purest forms as they began. And this molecule's mine, this molecule's his, this molecule's mine, this molecule's his, but they're all our molecules. And they're light. They're spinning, and they're moving so fast it looks like a miniature galaxy.

D: *You said it was like air, but now you can see it as little points of light?*

J: Yeah. Exactly. It just feels so good.

D: *But you still know that you're you.*

J: Yeah, I know I'm me. And I know he's right here, and I'm me and he's him, but we're not separate.

D: *Is that the purpose of this room? To show you how this is done, and what this feels like?*

J: Yeah, because then you can move as one entity through space from here to other galaxies. Past any known galaxies. Past any known universes. You could move from this room in this state of being to anything, *into* anything, and never lose what you are as an essence. Because you could become anything you can conceive, at the same time.

During this last sentence the strange noise of a motor again caused vibration and some distortion on the tape.

D: *What would be the purpose of that?*

J: To change certain structural energy patterns of solid materials. If the necessity arose to call forth that particular action, then when you return to the physical you have the capability of doing that at a physical state, *to* a physical state. Within a physical state. Within a living or nonliving object.

D: *Then you don't require that room again to make it happen?*

J: Not necessarily. You don't have to be in this room for it to happen, once you've experienced it.

D: *Once you've experienced it you know how to do it? Is that what you mean?*

J: You know how to do it. That's not to say that you won't come back and re-experience this room. Because experiencing this room restructures the totality of the essence energy. Because it can become fractured in the physical. It never will dissipate, but it can be reconfigured, because of interactions with different physicalness - the word. That's not a word. It's something like that. That's not quite the word.

D: Then do you go to another room after that?

J: I don't know. Right now it's just spinning. It's actually as if you were out in space, and you *are* a galaxy spinning.

D: And you're able to perceive the entirety of it all. Would that be right?

J: Exactly right.

D: You would be unlimited then.

J: Oh, totally. There just aren't any limitations. You don't even know what that is.

D: No restrictions.

J: None in any form.

Would this be similar to the "body" of God? In that He is everywhere at once? It has been said that we are molecules or cells of the body of God. And our final goal is to be reassembled or reintegrated into the total body or entity of our Creator. It was said that in the beginning we splintered off. Was it done by the same kind of process? Thus explaining to Janice how we are individual and yet One. Maybe this is as close as we can come to understanding the totality or complexity of God, and our role in His universe.

D: Is this the way the space people operate?

J: These space people do.

D: But not all of them?

J: Not all space people, but these space people.

D: So different ones have different abilities?

J: Exactly.

D: Well, let's move ahead till that experience is over. And we can see what happens after that.

J: (A deep sigh, then an interjection.) Ooooh! My! Whew! Well, it feels funny. (Laugh) Oh, goodness! It's just so ... going back into your ... it's like it's a .... (Confusion) Just a movement. Just very fast. Just collecting your molecules. They move very fast.

D: You mean you have to collect them back?

J: Well, it happens automatically, but it seems like that's the terminology. Collecting *your* molecules. No, collecting is not the word. Reassembling is the word. It's not collecting, but they come back together.

D: *Do you think this room is like a machine or something?*

J: No. It has to do with the energy inside it. It has a vibrational rate that's maintained in it, so when you walk into it, it happens. It doesn't have to be a machine. It's because of the energy that you carry in relation to the energy that's in the room. The transformation takes place automatically without machines. Machines are only used at levels other than this. This is the highest level of this type of work.

D: *Then when you're ready, the molecules automatically come back together?*

J: It depends on the purpose of the visit to the room. There are many different purposes for which you come to this room.

D: *What would happen if somebody of a different vibration were to enter that room? Would it have the same effect?*

J: (She didn't understand.) What? Different in what?

D: *You were saying that when you enter the room, your vibrational rate matches with the room's vibrational rate, and it causes this to happen automatically.*

Somewhere in here the voice became authoritative again, and it was obvious I was speaking to someone other than Janice, an entity who would be able to supply more detailed information.

J: The room has multifaceted purposes. And people of vibrational rates that are different from Janice and Ken enter this room. So therefore you must understand that: if another vibrational rate would enter the room at the present vibrational rate, the body would disintegrate into nothingness. And never be recomposed. So you must understand that: a student could not enter at this vibrational rate. So the vibrational rate of the room would be adjusted before a student entered this room. Now in the case of Janice and Ken, you must understand that: they are at the master level. And they entered the room for a different purpose than a student enters the room.

D: *That's what I was wondering, if a person could dissipate and not get back together again.*

J: A very real question on your part, and a very intelligent question, I might add.

D: *Thank you. I'm always wanting to learn. But I wondered what would happen if the wrong type of person went in there. But they wouldn't even be allowed on the craft, would they? The wrong vibrational rate?*

J: Wrong as in ....

D: *Negative or discordant.*

J: I think you do not realize where you are. Negativity is not even in the realm of possibilities within this ship.

D: *It didn't sound like it. But it is still a possibility of someone entering the room, and being ....*

J: There is no possibility of that, because we are very much in control of the vibrational rate of this room. And not only that, the master level students are the only students that enter this room. Now we have master level students, and then we have masters.

D: *I see. Who am I speaking to?*

J: You are speaking to the person in charge of this room.

D: *I thank you for answering my questions, even though they do sound a little naive.*

J: They're very intelligent questions.

D: *Are you in charge of all four rooms, or ....?*

J: No. I am in charge of this room. I've been to school for many years to become adept at the vibrational rate adjustment. It is my ultimate job. I teach in this room. It is a purpose for which I am on this ship.

D: *It would take a lot of training and a lot of responsibility to make sure everything worked right.*

J: Actually, from where I come there is no training required, because we are, as you would use the word, born knowing these things. So it takes no training, and I actually was not "trained" to do this work. I was selected to be in charge of this room because of my abilities.

D: *Are you male or female, or do you have any sex?*

J: I am basically male, but I have female characteristics also.

D: *Can you tell me where you come from originally?*

J: I come from Zylar. (She spelled it out to be sure it was correct.) It is in an undiscovered galaxy your people are not aware of at this moment.

D: *We wouldn't be able to see it with our telescopes? (No) Are you humanoid?*

J: Yes, I am. In a sense. We consider Earth people to be humanoids, so therefore in relation to that, I could answer, "No." But, "Yes," in relation to how physically I would \appear, or could appear to be if I wished to be.

D: *Do you have one normal state or appearance that you maintain most of the time?*

J: Well, my normal state is pure energy. So it would not be necessary to become physical, because of .... The necessity to be physical is .... Why would I want to?

D: *You don't need it, in other words.* (No) *This is why you can function as a teacher and a maintainer of that room then, because you mostly operate in the energy state. Is that right?*

J: That is correct.

D: *But you did say you were mostly male with female characteristics.*

J: Well, I mean I have female energy. I am a total balance of male and female energy.

D: *I was associating that with physicalness.*

J: No. I understand you would speak mostly of the physical, and I would be relating to mostly the energy. So therefore we have a difference of communication.

D: *I have spoken to other beings who said they operated in the energy level, and they could manifest anything they wanted or needed. Would that be correct, or is this a different type of thing?*

J: No, that is correct.

D: *I have been told there are whole cities and whole planets and everything that operated on energy.*

J: Totally. But you must understand there is more than my planet from which beings will come that operate similarly.

D: *There are many in the different galaxies?* (Yes) *But is the planet a physical planet?*

J: It is a physical planet.

D: *But the people are not physical?*

J: The people are whichever they wish to be. They have a choice, and it doesn't mean they must stay in the physical state because they become a physical state. They can be physical today, non-physical tomorrow. Physical this minute, and non-physical the next. It depends on what desires, or what interaction at what level they wish to participate. So it's a matter of actually learning to manipulate energy in such a manner that physical is a diversion. It is interesting to move from level to level. And there are reasons why you would operate in the physical, as opposed to an energy state. There are things that take place in the physical that cause you to want to be that way.

D: But you can manipulate it back and forth either way you want to. You're not trapped, so to speak. (No)

Although these concepts sounded like Science Fiction in the early 1990s, they have been popularized in new TV series and movies. Through this type of fiction they are now being presented in ways that people can understand. The energy beings, especially the flowing liquid types mentioned earlier, are permanent characters in Deep Space Nine. They are also called "Shape shifters." Alternate realities and parallel dimensional worlds are presented in TV shows like Star Trek, Sliders, and Stargate SG 1. What was Science Fiction is becoming more and more science fact, as our minds become capable of comprehending complicated theories.

D: Can you tell me of other planets that you know of?

J: I am not allowed to at this moment, but I will in the future discuss with you. And perhaps I am not the teacher who will be speaking to you of other planets. For my field is energy, and if you wish to know of energy I will teach and tell you. But I will not necessarily discuss with you other areas, for that is someone else's expertise. And I respect that from them.

D: I was just curious, because I don't know the rules.

J: There are no rules, as such, other than whoever is at the highest level of expertise is whom you should be discussing this with. For that is the area of development at which you are operating at this time.

D: To me at this point it's all confusing. It seems to be beyond my mental capabilities, but I always want to learn. Then if I want to ask questions dealing with energy of any kind, and their properties and their uses, I should talk to you?

J: I will be answering your energy questions, yes.

D: How will I know who to contact?

J: You will come to this room. I will be here. I am always here.

414

D: I will call you the guardian.

J: You could call me the guardian, if you wish.

D: Of the metal room, the metal energy room.

J: Just call it the energy room, because, although it appears to be, it is actually not metallic.

D: Can you tell me, have I ever visited this craft?

J: I do not believe you have, no. There is one craft away from here that you have visited, as far as development.

D: Then you go to different ones for different developments. And this happens when you're sleeping, and you don't know about it?

J: It can happen in many states. It can happen in the sleep state, or in a conscious state. In a split second, in the blink of an eye, you could have been here and back. That's how energy works, you know.

D: And you would never know it consciously.

J: You might think, "I started to go to the other room to get a pencil. *But* ... what was I going to get? Oh! I was going to the other room to get a pencil." And in that particular span of time you've already been to the ship and back. It was just a little lapse for you.

D: And you learned something while you were there.

J: Exactly.

D: Why would it have been necessary for me to go to one of those craft?

J: Actually you wanted to. Even though in your conscious mind you do not realize or think you want to. Because of your work it will help you relate better to your subjects. If you understand energy, your energy is interacting at all times with your subject. And there is sometimes a bit of shift that takes place in you, to be able to tune in to your subject. You are unaware consciously that you do know how to do this, but you do know how to do this.

D: Is this why I am able to get the results I do?

J: It most certainly is a part of why. It is only a part of why you are able to get the results. You are able to get the results because *you have a pure essence energy.* And your intentions for gathering the knowledge are pure intentions. You have no ulterior motive and will not misuse the information. For when we tell you it is not time to disseminate information, you don't.

D: That's right.

J: And I respect you.

D: *Thank you. I usually don't know what I'm after. But at least I ask questions and try to accumulate the information.*

J: Yes, but you have advanced in a very short time period. Perhaps in your conscious mind you are not really aware, and yet you yourself know that you have begun to grasp concepts at a faster rate than you were able to when you began this work. Is that not true?

D: *Yes. In the beginning even simple concepts seemed strange.*

J: Everything was strange in the beginning. But now not very much will shock you. That was part of why you came to the ships. Because there was some adjustment, and adjustment time period which could only take place at a ship level. You were agreeable, although you perhaps would not say so. And it did not disturb your life. In order to continue your work it was necessary.

D: *Then it is better to do these things without the consciousness knowing about them.*

J: It would depend upon your wishes. And your wishes are not consciously known at this time. You may change that at any moment. You may change and wish to know. If you wish to know we will find the appropriate time and method, and allow that to begin to take place at a very slow pace.

D: *I always feel it is better if I just act as a reporter, and accumulate the knowledge.*

J: That is entirely your choice. You can come here at any time. If it is the proper frame of time for you to know, these energy questions will be answered. If it is not the proper time frame for you to know, then I will most assuredly decline to answer. However, you will be doing work with energy, for there is a possibility you will begin to explain some complicated theories in the future.

D: *I don't understand that type of thing. In order for me to explain them, they would have to be explained to me in a way that I could understand.*

J: That's part of why you are connected to Janice. And a part of her expertise is that she is able to, as you have been told before, bring complicated information to the practical level, and explain it in a practical manner. That is part of her training on the Earth. She has been involved for the past twelve years in doing, at an Earth level, exactly the same thing she does at a spiritual and an energy level.

D: *Why is it important for people to learn these things, and bring them back to Earth? Is there a purpose for this on our planet? Knowing about these energies so we can manipulate them?*

J: It depends upon the project in which you are involved. It will also become more common amongst people who are, not necessarily involved in a project, but who have dedicated their lives to balancing the energy of your planet. They must know these things. And whenever there is time for integration work, or there is time for an advancement, or there is time for different purposes, they come to this room for adjustments in some of their physicalness. Because when they come to this room, once the dematerialization and configuration have taken place, they will never be the same.

D: *You mean they change after they have been broken apart into molecules?*

J: They don't necessarily change in a physical manner. There can be physical changes, but in some instances there are physical ramifications in that, if the physical body is operating ... it becomes very complicated. And I will explain it to you if you wish. But the physical body can change and be affected. However, normally it is not.

D: *Janice has awakened many times with bruises on her body. Does that have anything to do with your department?*

J: (A smirk and a chuckle.) I am sorry this happens, but that is one of the side effects of which I speak, of doing this kind of work when you come to this room. I have explained this to her in a nonconscious state. And she is subconsciously aware of this taking place, but there is no way around this happening necessarily.

D: *I'm just guessing. When the molecules are reassembled something happens that causes the bruising?*

J: It depends upon the cause or the manner in which reassembly takes place. Sometimes things happen at the Earth level that ... well, time. It has to do with time, you see, depending upon when these molecules reassemble and how it takes place. If something happens to interrupt before the time is up, there can be damage.

D: *Does this occur in your room, or as they are coming back?*

J: It occurs mostly on the return into the physical vibrational rate of the Earth, and to the physical rate at which the body was vibrating before it left the Earth. Because the vibrational rate that it carried at the time it left the Earth is not what it will return with.

D: *When it comes back, is that a more fragile condition after being taken apart and put back together again?*

J: It is actually in a stronger condition internally. But physically the actual structure, because of the fragility of the physical structure of human beings, this is the highest energy at which you can work. And it is a great feat to return with that. Having been to this energy level, it is amazing to be able to return to physical form. Only certain people can do this work. It is not done by everybody.

D: *I was thinking that was why the bruising occurred, because the body was fragile in the sense of being put back together, and going through cohesion.*

J: That is correct. The energy enters the physical body and begins to dissipate through the physical body. If there are places in the physical body that are not exactly ... well, perhaps it doesn't pass through at the proper rate. Or if the body moves at all; if there is any movement in the physical body. *Any.* I said *any.* That includes breathing.

D: *During reentry?* (Yes) *But wouldn't the body suffer by not breathing?*

J: The body is maintained. It does not have to breathe in the energy state.

D: *And if there is any movement at all, this could cause the bruising.*

J: Sometimes the physical body tries to take over the energy. Because it is aware of its physicalness at the same time it is aware of its energiness. When the physical body wants to become the owner of the energy before it's time to own the energy, that's when the problem occurs.

D: *She also has something wrong with her right knee. Do you know anything about that? Did that occur on one of these trips?*

J: No, it occurred on the Earth. She was falling, and she twisted her knee in the process. We did not have time for her to have this injury, because of the need for her work to continue. So we medically fixed it, and if she had not removed the device then the knee would have been totally healed. But she did remove it, so
....

Janice had told me before the session about discovering a small lump just beneath the skin of her knee. She was able to extract a tiny black piece, and she could not understand how it became embedded under her skin. She treated it as a curiosity.

D: She was curious. She didn't know what it was.

J: We understand, and we are not upset that this took place. It's simply being done in another manner now, from a distance.

D: Then her knee was repaired on one of these trips when this device was implanted?

J: Yes, but do not confuse this device with an implant, because she no longer requires implants.

D: She has gone past that stage. What was the purpose of the little device? She said it was very tiny and black.

J: It was very tiny. It was black. And it is similar to when you have a tooth pulled and the dentist puts something in the hole to dissipate medicine to the affected tooth cavity. The device was releasing a particular healing energy through the knee.

D: Then when she took it out it interfered with the process.

J: Yes. It was not imperative that it remain. It was for her comfort that it was placed there.

D: But it is now being worked on from a distance. (Yes) Well, I thank you for giving me all this information. When I want to ask questions again I most certainly will call on you, with your permission.

J: You are most welcome, because I have much more to tell you.

D: I will have to plan my questions, because I was caught off guard. Then can I have Janice back? I want to ask her what else happens onboard the craft.

J: She is not in this room any longer.

D: Can I locate her? Which room did she go to next?

J: She actually is between the rooms, and waiting for you to get tired of me.

D: (Laugh) All right. Let me catch up with her then.

J: Thank you for coming, and I've enjoyed our visit.

The voice then suddenly changed. It sounded softer, more feminine.

J: First before you catch up with Janice, I wish to have a word with you. You have spoken with me before, I believe you know.

D: *Well, I've spoken to many people.*

J: You have commonly called me the doctor, although that is not exactly what you would want to call me.

D: *I thought you were in a different part of the craft when I spoke to you the last time.*

J: Well, I don't stay there. I can go to different locations on this craft, you know. But what I want to explain to you is that I am in care of Janice's health over all. And you commonly call me the doctor?

D: *You did tell me you were a doctor, although not the type of doctor we are familiar with, because you are also involved with energies.*

J: That is correct. I work with the entity to whom you just spoke. We work very closely together. That's why I wanted to speak with you, and let you know there is a co reordination of effort on our parts. And we have the utmost concern for the welfare of Janice and Ken. They are wonderful energies.

D: *Then the one I was speaking to in the room was a different entity than you are?*

J: Oh, yes!

D: *Then you just caught me on the way out?*

J: Well, I was here. I didn't want to speak and interrupt.

D: *I thought it sounded like a different person. I do recognize your voice.*

J: That is nice. You have been a long time away.

D: *Oh, there are many things going on in my life. I couldn't journey to where Janice lives for a long time now.*

J: Well, we have been waiting and hoping that you would come.

D: *I had many questions I wanted to ask you. I don't know if now is the time though.*

J: That is entirely your prerogative.

D: *Well, we were curious about what was happening with Janice. That's why I asked the questions about her knee, and about the bruises. And we were given the answers about those. So if I have medical questions, could I come to you?*

J: Yes. If you have medical questions, psychological questions, sociological questions. I am involved with every aspect of the well-being of Janice and Ken, in their functionality. You see, actually we serve them. We serve *them*. They don't serve us. That is one thing I wanted to clarify. And that is why I spoke to you, because you have never asked that question, nor would you perhaps have thought of it.

D: *I probably wouldn't have.*

J: But you see, both Janice and Ken are very high caliber, and operate much above where we are. In actuality, it is important for you to realize that we serve them. Let me see if I can give you an explanation. They are directors of many projects, you see. They are not totally working with one energy, or one group of beings, or one particular purpose. They have many different projects, and they control many different projects.

D: *But they're not consciously aware of this.*

J: In a sense Janice is becoming somewhat aware, because she has integrated to the point where she can know at a physical level, and be taught in a way in which Ken has yet to be able to remember. It is simply a matter of actually being able to... (Sigh) there's not a real word for what I want to convey to you, other than .... (Confused and frustrated.) Oh, my!

D: *Can you find a concept or anything close?*

J: (Confused) Perhaps ... let me see. No, maybe I can't describe it. There must be balance. For beings such as Janice and Ken to operate and continue to be functional in all the areas and the many galaxies in which they function, there must be a point to which they return from time to time to reestablish that balance. So the purpose for them being in this particular ship is to cause that particular balance to be reestablished. Now, at a physical level they have come together, because their work requires them now to be in a physical state together. Through the years that was not the case. And it had to evolve to a point where it was time for a physical connection as well as a connection at the other levels.

D: *That's what I was going to ask. Why did they get together after so many years of not seeing each other?*

J: They have work to do in the physical. They will come to know in the physical that these projects will evolve in their consciousness in the physical. And thereby they will be able to affect greater change planetarily.

D: *The other entity said there are other people working in this same way.*

J: There are other people working in this same way, but you will discover they are not connected in the same manner, perhaps, as Janice and Ken are connected. There are very few instances where a connection is as it is with these two.

D: *It would seem that would make the energies they are working with more compatible.*

J: Well, it is as your question to the energy guardian, of negativity. It is not even relevant. Their energy interaction is past any compatibility factor that Earth people even know.

D: *I think it's wonderful that they've come back together after all this time.*

J: Oh, it was just simply a matter of time. This would have taken place in the past had they made different choices. And plus, you must understand that the history of your planet is at such a crucial point it is necessary for them to come together in a physical state, because in the physical state the same thing happens to them that happened in the energy room. It happens in a much more subtle way in the physical state, but it happens nonetheless. And they will be noticed, but people will not understand what they see.

D: *That's the way human beings are. Can you tell me what these other rooms are used for?*

J: I'm not at liberty to discuss that with you. You will experience it, but perhaps not on this visit. I'm not sure where you will be directed next. I wish to discuss any information with the council before you put it into a book. As I understand it, the information that comes through Janice to you will be passed on by the council before you could put it into a book. Because, as I understand, if you even attempt to put it into a book it will not come to fruition, unless permission has been given. What you don't realize at this point is that everything interacts. In some of your work you realize the value of timing. And so if information of this caliber is disseminated prior to certain events in historical time, it can intensify the negativity level if it falls into hands other than the proper disseminators, or the proper translators, or the proper forms of energy transmutation. i.e.: into the negativity side of your planetary balance. Then there could be a more intense negativity level created through the mechanics of understanding the positive side of the energy. So what I'm trying to say, in short and in an uncomplicated manner is: don't disseminate the information until you have gained the permission, not only of Janice but of a council who will pass upon it. Because you see, there are certain events that will take place. And in your other books you have discussed these events. It is very important that certain energy information not be disseminated prior to certain historical events. I don't know if you have gathered the event of which I speak. If you have not, then I need to inform you.

D: *I won't do anything right now. At this point I'm just collecting information, and I will abide by your instructions.*

J: But there is an important event which ... in actuality I really am being told to tell you this. It is important that this information that you learn, the mechanics of certain elements *not* be disseminated. And my council is becoming most excited. They're speaking very rapidly, and I'm simply not able to keep up with the torrent of words to tell you. But I must tell you simply that you cannot disseminate the information prior to the proper juncture in time. Certain of it cannot be at a physical level of exposure prior to that time. It simply cannot.

D: *Then I'll be very careful.*

J: (Sigh) Too many people talking. Too many people talking. (She began to breathe heavily and showed signs of discomfort.)

D: *It's all right. Calm down, because I'm not going to use it without anybody's permission. I'll be very, very careful.* (She was calming down.) *If I'm disturbing you we can change the subject. I just hope I'm not getting you into trouble.*

J: No, it's not a matter of trouble. It's just that there was such an infusion of vibration that my own vibration was raised to a level that I'm not accustomed to operating at. And I'm having a bit of .... (Deep sigh) But you must hear this, so you must give me a moment to adjust to .... I am being dictated to at my own level of energy. (Big sigh)

D: *All right. You go ahead and assimilate there. I have something to do on my level.*

I took the tape out and put another one in.

D: *Are you feeling better now?*
J: (Confusion) There's just a total .... (Heavy breathing.)

D: I certainly hope what I was asking you wasn't causing you problems.

J: It did not cause *me* a problem. It caused problems at a higher level, at a much higher level.

D: Because I don't want to cause anyone any problems.

J: No, it was a matter of your misunderstanding what you could and couldn't disseminate, you see. I was speaking to you with relation to vibrational adjustment of energy infusion. And I was being dictated to by the members of the sacred room. And I was not aware of the power of that energy in that room. (She was still feeling the effects. This was what caused the confusion, and the inability to communicate.) I do not enter that room. I am speaking to you from the energy room, at which I am accustomed to operating. And Janice and Ken are in another state of being in another place. I am in this place, and they are in that place. And this place and their place and the physical place. So you must see it becomes complicated in some moments to discuss with you, and have it come through a physical being.

D: It seems as though the council are the ones in the sacred room that are picking up on what we're talking about. And apparently they thought you ....

J: (Interrupted) They are always aware, and they monitor what is being discussed with you. However, there was a very powerful something that came through me.

D: I was thinking they thought you might have been revealing things to me that it was not time for yet.

J: It was time for you to have *some* of this information. (Heavy breathing and confusion.) You will excuse me please. I am not functioning properly at this time. But if you will bear with me, I am returning to some semblance of myself.

D: I'm sorry if I caused you any discomfort.

J: Ohhh! It wasn't discomfort in the sense of discomfort. It was simply .... Oooh! I was taken to .... Thank you very much for .... It was, oh, an overwhelming experience for me. You see, I am not allowed in that ... it is not a matter of allowances. It is just that I don't go to that room, for .... Whew! I'm a little disoriented. (Confusion again.)

D: The main thing I wanted to clarify is what they don't want me to do.

J: Yes. I am being held at this rate. It is important for you to know that I am functioning at a different vibrational rate from my own. And that may change. You may speak directly to one of the sacred elders if you ... I'm not sure what's going to happen here.

She was taking deep breaths trying to adjust. This was why the outburst of a loud and different voice surprised me and took me off guard. "Dolores!" The voice had authority and commanded attention.

D: *Yes.*
J: (The breathing was now calm.) Dolores!
D: *Yes, I hear you.*
J: Can you relate to me?
D: *Yes, I can hear you very well.*
J: Can you hear me with other than your physical ears? Can you hear me inside your head ... yet?
D: *Well ... I don't know ....*
J: Can you hear me in a sense of a light? Can you hear the light?
D: *I don't know what it feels like, but I'm feeling something.*
J: That is enough for you to know then. It is of no harm to you, but I cannot communicate in the same fashion as you are accustomed. I will try. I am simulating a voice, and it is not my way. But I must tell you some things, because you have entered an area that it was not expected for you to enter.
D: *Is there any problem with that?*
J: Not in the sense of the word a problem, as we would relate to a problem. But you need to adjust Janice in her physicalness, for I am using her voice in a manner, but yet I am not using her voice. And she is not suffering any physical discomfort, other than that ... (Sigh) you need to give her instructions to adjust herself. Adjust herself.
D: *To the energy or what?*
J: You need to give Janice's physical self ... hurry and give physical self an instruction to adjust. Just simply do that, and say to her physicalness to adjust. (Emphatic) Say to her physicalness to adjust!
D: *All right. I am speaking to Janice's physicalness. I want it to adjust. I want it to relax.* (Her breathing was slowing down again.) *And be calm. This is only a different energy that's*

speaking through you. Adjust and relax. No physical problems whatsoever. A very good feeling. A very relaxed feeling. It is just something different that is happening. But the physical body is very capable of handling this. All right. Is she making the adjustment?

J: (A sweet and feminine voice.) She is making the adjustments, yes, she is making the adjustments.

D: *All right. But you said I have entered an area you weren't expecting me to.*

J: (The authority voice again.) Allow the adjustments! This is very important. For you must understand, you have crossed many energy levels here. And we cannot allow any harm to come to the physical. We have Janice operating in four energy states at the present time. You do not realize that. And you must bear with us, because there was a bit of a ... shift. A very rapid shift that she was, at those four levels, not able to adjust to properly in the physicalness.

D: *Yes, and I wish her no harm at all.*

J: No, but you are working in the highest of energy states at this moment. And we must tell you that sometimes this will happen. We will direct you. Do not be afraid that you won't know what to do. For, as you can see, we reach a point of allowance and non-allowance with relation to certain physicalness. With relation to certain sacred space. With relation to certain energy space. With relation to certain holding pattern space. So we have all four of those states in being. And what you must understand is that, at each of these levels there is constant molecular motion. Motion. And when you are transcending time, and when you are moving through different types of time at a rate of speed that is faster than light, to even attain this level of energy, certain *rapid* changes cause pattern changes all the way to the physical structure. And it is very important to maintain the balance. We will never allow imbalance in this being or in Ken. There *cannot* be imbalance in these beings. It is the reason for their still being able to function in the physicalness. Ken, at this moment, is at a rate of imbalance in his physicalness. And we are working with him to bring his life into a point of balance. He is experiencing difficulties, and we are working with him. Although he is not conscious, and cannot be brought to consciousness. And he will be brought to consciousness through Janice. It is important to *know* that Ken is also with Janice at the moment in a different state of being, although he is also asleep in his bed in Oklahoma. So you must know these things. And it is important for *you* to be aware of what you are relating to, because you are not always aware. And this is not a shortcoming. Please understand that we do not look at this as any shortcoming of yours. You must understand that these are simply methods of which you are unfamiliar, because you have not worked at this level. You *truly* have not worked at *this* level. You have been close to this level, but not at this level before. And that is the reason for your connection with Janice. The reason for some of your interactions with other energies at certain other levels, is because there must be also within you a willingness to come to this level. For you too truly will, in a sense, although it will not change in any manner of being in your physical life or in any manner of being in your energy. You will be feeling a bit of difference. It will be a good difference. Now, what you must understand is that you had a willingness to come to this level, or you could not have come with Janice to this level.

D: *It would have been blocked, in other words.*

J: It would have been not allowed. So you were ready to come here. Now what you should know is that, in a sense, some things will become easier for you. It will be a natural transition for you. Do not misunderstand when I say the word "adjustment," because adjustment does not mean the same at this energy level as it means to you in your state of being. What happens is that, only your highest good is held in our highest regard. For the work you are doing, you must know that we have a deep admiration for your willingness to pass beyond the point of your own physicalness, which you do. You do that. You actually push yourself past the point at which your true physicalness is developed. Because what you are sensing is, when you asked for a *method*, that was our key to know you were ready. (I did not consciously remember asking for anything, but apparently it had occurred on a subconscious level.) It was the point when you were scanned. After that time you were exposed to that very method which we gave you tonight. However, in the beginning you did not accept it. You heard it, but you did not take it. And we knew you were not ready to come to this level. So that is why different people came to you through

Janice before. She was always at this level. But she had to come down to bring you to a point of being willing to come here. And to develop to a point that you could go past your fear of being changed as an individual, because you will not change. But you had a fear of being out of control. In a sense, you had a fear within you of any source of exposure of *past* something beyond where you were comfortable. You felt you were not able to handle this particular point. And you were not.

D: *That's a very human trait.*

J: It is a very human trait.

D: *But I don't remember being given a method. There was nothing on the tapes of those earlier sessions.*

J: It was not on the tape. It occurred in a discussion after the tape. It was not given on the tape, because it was not meant to be on the tape. Many of your discussions with Janice, we will tell you at this point, have been to - if you will forgive us. We ask prior forgiveness from you, but we have tested you in a conscious state, with simple discussions in which Janice discussed concepts after your session. This was exposure through things she would say to you. That, if you had reacted one way, we would have known of your level of development with relation to being *willing*, and being *ready* to be exposed to this level of energy and mode of operation. You have touched on this through other people. You have touched a session of classes. You have touched a studentlevel of being, but you have not touched a master level of being before. That is what you have done here tonight. You have touched a master level of energy interaction. For that is where, as I have told you before, Janice and also Ken operate through UFO energy. But they operate outside that energy also. Even at a higher vibrational rate than is understood by UFO beings to which you have been exposed.

D: *I was concerned because there were physical reactions to Janice's body. I thought maybe she couldn't take that energy. The other being seemed to think I had progressed into a level of energy that I wasn't ready for.*

J: No, you misunderstand. You were speaking with the doctor. I am not the doctor. I am a mediator. I am a balancer. That is what I do. You are not speaking with the doctor. The doctor's energy field was disturbed. But you must understand. I need to explain to you some things that are important for you to know, because this will occur again. In that *you* did not realize that when you took Janice to actually when Janice and Ken entered the sacred room, they were living again the sacred room in *their physicalness.* And they moved from the sacred room. But they did not move from the sacred room, because *they are* in the sacred room, even as we speak. And they moved to the energy room in a different state of being. Although they are also in the physical, and in the energy, at a different *kind* of energy in the sacred room. It is complicated, but it is important for you to understand this, because you must understand the mechanics of these shifts. And further, it is important for you to know you have spoken with the energy guardian, which you very correctly labeled him in your own terminology. He *is* the energy guardian of that room. However, the doctor is also, and does have the freedom to come in and operate within that room. She knew you would be there. She heard you ask earlier tonight to speak with her, or that you wished to contact her. She came and she was there. And you did not ask to contact her, so she did not speak to you. However, you were moving from the room, and she felt that because she wanted to grant your wishes she spoke to *you.* That was well, because you are moving into another area. You *are* a recorder, but you are more than a recorder. And if you do not wish to be, you have only to tell us now. There was a reason you were not allowed to begin this session at the time you wanted to. And I am at liberty to discuss that reason with you. You were anxious to begin the session, but you were not allowed to begin the session until the absolute correct time. It had to be the absolute correct minute in order for you to enter this energy state. The phone call was meant to occur at that time, so you could not begin the session. And you desired to conduct the discussion in relation to certain knowledge you have come to be comfortable with.

That was true. I had longed to return to areas of exploration that I could understand on a physical, earthly, level. Instead, the information had continued to become more complicated and convoluted.

J: And you *do* know there is always a choice. You believe that. There was a point at which you were not really sure. Was there a choice? *Could* that happen? You had a fear that it could happen that you would not have a choice. And that something very bad might come, and you would not have a choice. That was a deep fear in you. Maybe you only touched it. Maybe it never seized you as such, except for perhaps once. But that was an exposure to which you were exposed in another fashion other than UFO energy. (I believe he was referring to the exposure to the Anti-Christ energy in Volume II of *Conversations With Nostradamus*.) But energy is working in all manners other than UFOs. We are balancers, in a sense. And that is one of the main purposes for *why* we come to your planet. There is such an intricacy of design, of interaction of elementals - and I do not speak of little fairies when I'm talking about elementals. Elementals, different forms of structures, timing - but I'm getting away from the point. And the point I'm being brought back to by the council in the sacred room, is that I must explain to you the mechanics of what happened tonight. So that when you sense it is happening again you will realize that you need to slow down. What happened is that you were speaking to the doctor. And then you got into an area where you were single mindedly on one subject. But actually they were wanting to speak to you with regard ... they did speak to you with regard to the information that was coming - see, I am being dictated to and I am speaking rapidly again, because these words are in a torrent, and they are coming very fast. And I'm bringing them through four energy levels to bring them to you. So what you must know is that, you were speaking to the doctor and you did not understand when she told you about giving the information in book form. You thought she was simply speaking to the information of the light energy. She was speaking about the information that comes, because the type you receive here is not to be mixed with your investigation cases, because there is a different purpose involved here. And what you must know is that this purpose has to do with events in Earth time that cannot be disturbed by disseminating information in book form before they have passed their time in Earth time. It cannot happen. And it was felt by the sacred .... (Searching for the proper word.) There's no Earth word for it. It's not a council. It's past a council. It's past elders. But you would not understand the word, because it is not in English translation. I cannot even bring it to my own consciousness, because *I* am not of that level. And when you did not understand, it had to come through the doctor. All that energy from that sacredness was trying to come in through her energy, and also through where the holding pattern energy of Janice was, back to the physical, back to you. And it was such a rapid shift ... it was disturbed. So there was an imbalance, and that's why you had to make the adjustment. It is important to know that there will be a book of this magnitude, which will be an expansion of any concepts you have been exposed to so far. But you have to understand that before you place the information you gather from Janice in book form, we must agree.

D: *I do understand that. I was a little concerned when Janice had these physical sensations. But when that heavy voice came through, you said it was apparently coming directly from the sacred room.* (Yes) *He did indicate perhaps I had gone into an area I was not expected to go into.*

J: At this time.

D: *Would it be better if I backed off?*

J: It's the fact that you may be exposed. You may go into the area. It's just that you did not hear what he told you, or perhaps maybe it was that you didn't quite understand the rate of where you are in relation to just disseminating information. There is an emphasis on your planet at this time, and an urgency for dissemination of information. And we wish to contact every being on your planet, so there can become a change with regard to vibrational rate. However, certain *kinds* of information, if it is disseminated, as I have said, prior to historical events that are set in time, it will intensify the ability of the negative energies to use those mechanics in their own negative way. And we are most concerned with that.

D: *Then you don't have to worry. I won't do anything until I'm told to do it.*

J: I will say to you, that certain parts of the information that you gain will be used *after* the time of the Anti-Christ.

D: *I was wondering if I would be around to write it, and to disseminate it.*

J: You will be around.

D: I will survive into that time frame?

J: I think, yes, you will.

D: And I'll still be writing and gathering information?

J: You will be gathering, and you will be writing.

D: I figured I would be very old by that time. (Chuckle) But I will still be able to do this even though I grow very old? I'll be able to write my books, and ....

J: Yes, because your age will be different.

D: You mean it will be changed as we go into this other time period? This other frequency?

J: Yes. You see, nothing stays the same. You've heard this throughout your life. You are very comfortable as you are. You don't really want change as such. And yet internally there is a glimmer within you that knows that it takes place in a tiny, tiny, tiny way within *you*. As you grow through your work it will be a naturalness, and it is not a manufactured change. It is what you came to do. It is your purpose unfolding. So embrace that change. It is your purpose.

D: Then I will still be alive, even though I'm very old. And be an observer of all these events that take place.

J: I'm being told that the thing that is important for you to know is that, you will continue to do this work. And you will be here.

D: On the Earth. (Yes) All right. I have so much I want to do. I just want to remain healthy and have energy so I can do these things.

J: You will develop. As you do the work you will understand more and more of those things which complicate your mind, because it is simply a matter of wanting within you. And only at the point where you *want*, will you receive. For we will never seek to overwhelm you. You see, Janice and Ken are in a common project in which you are also involved, and so are some of your colleagues. You have traveled this past year because of that project.

In 1991 when this session was occurring, I had just begun my traveling to speak at conferences in the States. In the years to follow I would travel all over the world several times. But on this evening I had no knowledge of what my future would hold.

J: It was in service to us and in service to your planet, unbeknownst to you, that you traveled. It will be in that same service that you go to London, and you *will* go to London. And what you need to know is why. And what do I speak of when I tell you, you are involved in a project?

D: *Yes, that's what I can't understand. I thought I was writing these books to get information out. But is it beyond that?*

J: It is much beyond that. And the work is most important. Not everyone on your planet is involved in this project.

D: *Can you tell me what the project is?*

J: Yes, it is time for you to know. So you will be more comfortable with things you don't necessarily understand why you're doing. This is a most important project. It would take a while to explain to you the mechanics of the interrelated energy flows that take place in human beings. And to discuss with you particles and their intermingling, i.e.: merging and sub dividing. However, the simplest form to tell you is that, we speak of human ley lines of the planet, and you are very connected in this way. Although you are unaware in most instances of energy fields and energy sources, you do on occasions relate to them. You have become more interested and will become more interested in knowing. Because your vibrational rate was necessary in Denver. It was necessary in California. It was necessary in the different cities to which you have traveled this past year. It will be necessary in the cities and countries that you will travel to in your future time. You never lose your connection to those you have touched. It is the same as drawing a line from you to them at all moments, because everything that is, never ceases to be. The energy you have at this moment will also stay in this room when you leave. It will never totally leave this room. You will never *know* that it does not leave this room, because you will not feel a *lack*. Only in great instances and expenditures of energy will you feel a lack. That is the time when it is important for you to learn how to replenish. You will need to know how to do that at a quicker rate of speed. Now, what I am trying to say to you is that people will talk to you about ley lines on the planet. They view these lines as existing within the Earth, which is true. The project I am talking to you about has to do with human ley lines, human connections. If you can visualize certain people at certain points and locations on the planet at a specific point in Earth time and inter-dimensional time. And there cannot be any second's difference. It must be coordinated to the letter. It has to do with the balance of the energy of the ley lines within the Earth. It is a hologram of ley lines. (There was a sudden burst of strange static on the tape recording that sounded electrical. It did not obliterate any words. It was very quick.) i.e.: Your connection to Janice. Your connection to other people in your life, form to you and form a triangle. It is the Triangle Project. It is vital to this planet. It is most important that you try and understand that your vibrational rate, when you were in Denver, caused a change on the other side of the planet. Because of your connection to different people in your life. Because that connection is never broken.

D: *Even these new people that I'm meeting all the time?*

J: Yes, yes. But there are people who are in the project. Not everyone that you work with or meet will be in the project. You have a friend that you talk with, and he is in the project. You are in the project. Janice is in the project.

There was much discussion about different people I had met, and their possible connection with my work, and my future. I was concerned about much of this at that time in 1991, because I had not yet formed my own company.

J: What you need to know is that you have protection. So you can be involved with anyone, you can be involved with whomever. And it doesn't really matter, because you're going to get to the same place. So if you feel as though you are having a struggle, what you need to understand is what I began to talk to you about initially. And that was junctures in time. Because you can beat your head against all the walls, but until such time when it is congruent universally, that opportune moment where mankind's time, inter-dimensional time come together - come *together* - it will not take place. Because the work you are doing is a planetary work, and it is for the advancement of mankind. You must understand your purpose here. You must understand that you have a very heavy responsibility, and you have asked to have that responsibility. Although you do not necessarily in your work look at it as that kind of a responsibility, because you are busy living your purpose. You don't have to discover what it is.

D: I keep feeling I'm going to find even more information.

J: Oh, you are. That's what you came here to do. You are a translator, and your job is to help mankind come to know concepts that have been forgotten. Concepts that, by the turn of the screw, will change planetary history.

D: Hmm, that's a heavy responsibility.

J: Yes, it is. And I came to talk to you tonight.

D: I appreciate that. I feel Janice needs information, but I do appreciate you talking with me. Because I sometimes wonder if I'm doing what I should be doing.

J: You know you are. You do not wonder.

D: It's as though everything has taken so long, in our time.

J: That's why I'm trying to explain time to you. You have to understand *time*. And that is *your job*, because that is what you are dealing with in your books. You are dealing with inter-dimensional time.

D: And also with very complicated concepts.

J: Complicated concepts that it is your job to simplify, so the man on the street can read it and go, "Oh!" So people will begin to learn to live *lifetimes* at the same time. Understanding that everything they do here in the physical on this planet affects *every other lifetime*. Their line goes all the way. That trail of energy from where we are now, what we are saying *now*, what you are saying from where you are to where I am, will always stay. The difference is only as you move from dimension to dimension.

D: I keep thinking I'm being led to lost knowledge, to lost information.

J: It is lost.

D: I feel I have to get it back.

J: That is my point. That is what I am telling you. How do you feel, in relation to what I have spoken to you about your own being? I was told to ask you that.

D: How do I feel about it? Well, it feels comfortable with me. I want to continue my work. The main thing is that I remain healthy, then I can do the work in a better way. And have energy to do the work and to travel. As long as I can do that I know I can do the work. Is that what you mean?

J: That is what I mean. You realize that when you feel a problem, do you know what you need to do?

D: *Ask you for help?*

J: Yes. If you are willing. As you tell your subjects, "If you are willing."

D: (Chuckle) *Then do I ask the doctor, or you, the mediator?*

J: You will only have to ask, and you will be connected to the proper place, to the proper energy. And, yes, I would say that it would perhaps be the doctor.

D: *To help with any discomforts or any problems I might have in the physical body.*

J: Discomforts are problems. And, yes, I will come and I will help you.

D: *All right. Because I'm going to need that in order to keep functioning.*

J: You are feeling very tired?

D: *Well, we've been at this a long time. And I think we're going to have to end the session now.*

J: Because you are feeling very tired.

D: *Well, it's not only that. It's that Janice has to go to work in the morning. We do have our physical lives to live. And we've been at this longer than any other session we've ever had.*

J: Well, the point you must understand is that, it is one year later since you last worked. And Janice has developed beyond your initial methods of gaining information. To the point where her physicalness is totally different, as you should have sensed. And she is able to function with absolutely no sleep at all.

D: *But I wouldn't want to do that to her.*

J: Well, no, it's not a matter of that. But it is one of those things we have taught, and can be used if the necessity arises. This is a very important time you are in now, and it is a very important location you are in now. And I'm not sure when you will be allowed back here.

D: *Well, I do think we have been here long enough.*

J: It is entirely up to you.

D: *Because we are functioning in Earth time. But I do appreciate you speaking to me, and giving me instructions.*

J: You are welcome. I wasn't expected to contact you tonight, for I was not expected to be asked to intervene.

D: *But the next time we do this, I will allow more of our Earth time, because I'll know these sessions can go longer.*

J: You should do so, for when you reach this level there is much information that needs to be gathered and brought back. It will become important, because it is the kind of information that will be used to function after certain events in history take place. It is that kind of energy. (The voice changed and was different again. Louder. I was trying to end the session, and this voice had authority again.) There is something I would like to tell you before you go. I wish to explain one thing to you. And that is that no harm can come to you as you do this work. We will explain many complicated processes to you. And you are being entrusted with a level of knowledge to which in actuality you have not been exposed. And it is important for me to impress upon you that we appreciate your work. And we want you to know that everything will be done to aid you. And we want to thank you for being, in a sense, a type of facilitator for Janice. So you can perhaps help her to integrate by what you are doing. This work, in a sense, is a great service to your planet, although, it will take place without your work. As in the last year you have not worked with Janice, but she has surpassed certain types of communication. So I just wanted you to know that I, personally, am in agreement with how you conduct yourself.

D: *I thank you.*

J: You are most welcome. And I bid you peace and love and light.

D: *Thank you again, whoever you are.* (Janice was making hand motions.) *That's a very beautiful gesture.* (Janice then took a deep breath and I knew the other entity was gone.) *All right then. I bid all of them farewell. I want them all to recede. And I want the consciousness of Janice to once again return totally to this body.*

J: (She interrupted.) The lights are flashing!

D: *Why are they flashing?* (She seemed confused.) *Is it the energy? (No answer, as though she was watching.) Is it caused by the energy?*

J: (Softly) Yeah. Because the maid interrupted. (Sadly) She interrupted.

D: *She didn't know.*

J: She is banging on the door. She ruined it. (Almost crying.)

In my opinion the flashing lights may have been caused by the maid's intrusion before Janice had fully integrated back into the physical. The energy was so strong that, when it was interrupted, it was dispersed into the electrical connections. It was such a frequency overload that it caused them to explode. It was not anticipated that the maid would cause a disruption before Janice could be returned totally. This could have caused physical damage, as they said, if the reentry was interrupted, even by breathing. Instead the entities sent the overload into the electrical circuit.

At that time my journey was just beginning, and I could not have believed that my first baby steps would lead me all over the world. I did travel to London the first time in the next year 1992, and have journeyed to Europe at least twice a year ever since. I investigated the Crop Circles and visited the sacred sites: Stonehenge, Avebury, Glastonbury, giving lectures and spreading the information I have discovered in my work. I was the first American author and past life hypnotherapist to go into Bulgaria after it broke away from Communist control, and I was in the Balkans directly across the border from where the fighting was occurring in Yugoslavia. I have spoken at every major city in Australia. In 1997 I climbed the Andes in Peru to see the ancient Inca ruins at Machu Picchu. I travel all over the United States now, and am often in a different city or state each day. We are now making plans to travel to Hong Kong, Singapore, and South Africa in 1999. It appears that soon I will have touched foot on all the continents in the world.

Have I left my energy in all of these places, as they said? If I have then I have also not noticed any lack, as they said. In fact, if anything my energy has increased as my work has spread. The books are now translated into many different languages, and thus the energy is being spread to places I would never have been able to travel, through the power of the written word. If this has occurred so unexpectedly to me, then every human being has the same responsibility. Each person spreads his energy unknowingly for either good or ill. The object should be to allow that energy to influence people in a positive way to allow our planet to grow into a higher spiritual plane of existence.

CHAPTER 14
INVESTIGATING THE INVESTIGATOR

It appeared that once the aliens found a way to communicate with me through my subjects (or maybe it was the other way around, and I had discovered the method), they continued to supply information at every opportunity. The communication and influx of information is still continuing, and much of the more complicated parts will be included in *The Convoluted Universe*.

This case shows that not even UFO hypnotherapists and investigators are immune. They can be having experiences without their conscious knowledge. I do not think this has happened to me, but I would not discount the possibility. However, I prefer my method of investigating. This way I can remain the observer, the objective reporter, and not experience the complicated emotions involved with active participation.

The hypnotherapist in this case prefers to remain anonymous, because she has an active practice and does not want this information released prematurely. She is also planning to write her own book dealing with the information she has uncovered in her work. At that time she will refer to this case and the connection between us will be revealed. Thus, I will call her Bonnie. I have known her for several years and we have had contact professionally and on the lecture circuit. In June 1997 we were both speakers at a conference at a University in Wyoming. After it ended we held this session in the dormitory where we were staying. We were both extremely tired and I would be leaving the next morning, but we wanted to take advantage of the rare opportunity to be together and have the session. There were two men present who had asked Bonnie's permission. One of them operated Bonnie's tape recorder, while I monitored mine.

Before the session she told us about a strange incident that had occurred a month before in May 1997. She had the vague uneasy feeling that there was more to it, and she knew more details could be uncovered through hypnosis. She had been to a dinner meeting with several UFO researchers at a restaurant north of Santa Barbara in California. It had been very interesting and stimulating, so she did not leave until almost midnight. She knew the exact time she left the restaurant because she was estimating it would take her approximately two and a half hours to drive home.

She said, "I noticed it was 11:35 as I pulled out of the parking lot of the restaurant, and got on the freeway heading south. This was Highway 101 along the Pacific Coast. It was a very, very black night. Sometimes I really like to be in complete blackness, and this night was kind of velvety, elegant. And I was happy I was going to be driving home alone, so I could think about the wonderful evening visiting with all the other investigators. It was like meditation time, free thought time, driving by myself on that very, very black night. It was so black that I couldn't see where the shore on my right side ended and the ocean began. In past years when I drove that highway at night I would be aware of reflections of oil rigs or boats. You had a sense of where the water was, or the moon might be out and casting a reflection on the water. But this was one of those nights when there were no stars, and it was so black you couldn't distinguish the difference between the land and the ocean. After a while I remembered seeing a little sign 'Seacliff'. I had not remembered a town by that name on that highway, because it's a long stretch of coastline without any towns or any lights. I had been driving for quite a distance when I realized there were no other headlights and taillights on either side of the highway. At one point I thought it was kind of curious that I was the only car on the road. But it was all right, because I was very comfortable. Maybe that was why the next events were so unexpected, because I had no feeling of apprehension."

Bonnie was driving through this long empty stretch when she was startled by a big round flash of light to her right down along the coast. It was white with a greenish tinge, and only lasted a second. And then nothing, no sound. It wasn't fireworks or flares. She simply thought it was odd and kept driving. There were big hills on the left side of the highway in this area of Hwy. 101. And as she drove through this uninhabited stretch of road she noticed an incredibly bright glow of light shining from behind those hills. It covered a large area, had a round arc to it, and was not moving. It was very bright and had the same color as the flash: white with a slightly greenish tinge. She didn't think it could have been the same thing because she had not driven that far yet. They were two separate lights. The light behind the hills covered such a distance that it took her several minutes to go past it. She studied it trying to see what was creating it, when unexpectedly something else drew her attention back to the road. There was something parked on her side of the highway. It looked like the back end of a very large truck, a big tractor trailer or semi. But there were no cones or reflector lights or flares so it could be noticed by oncoming motorists. It wasn't all the way off the road on the shoulder, but was sitting partly on the highway. There was still plenty of room to pass it, but it created a dangerous situation, because her headlights didn't pick it up until she was very close to it. It was just suddenly there on her side of the road. As she approached it she saw some people (maybe four or five) walking around the back end of the truck and onto the freeway. Again this was a dangerous situation, because they could have been hit.

"These were impressions, because it was all so fast. I was driving probably 70 miles an hour or more, because I was all alone on the freeway. I noticed this vehicle had some sort of dim light shining on it from the road, like maybe a flashlight had been put in the road, and was shining up on the back end. And just as I was about to pass it I saw big black writing at the top of the back of the vehicle. My impression was that it said, in big black squarish letters: 'Emergency Vehicle.' And I thought, that's odd. I've never seen an emergency vehicle like that. It wasn't a fire truck or a police vehicle or an ambulance. You wouldn't normally think of a semi-truck being an emergency vehicle. My impression was that it was quite a long truck. Anyway, I thought the series of events were odd: the light down the coast, the light behind the hills, this big truck, emergency vehicle, people walking by, but no flares. And the thought flashed through my head that maybe this truck had just arrived, and maybe they were about to put out flares, and maybe it had something to do with the light behind the hills. It definitely wasn't a fire, but maybe this truck was investigating it or something. But all of this was just impressions, because it happened so quickly. These were just oddities, and I was feeling perfectly comfortable, no fear or anything."

"Then a second or two later the weirdest thing of all happened. I don't know if I had driven all the way past that truck or was still in the area of the truck. But suddenly right in front of me the whole windshield area of my car was completely dazzling with the brightest light. I didn't see myself approaching a light or any light coming to me. It was as if a switch had been turned on, and suddenly the whole area right in front of me was blazing with light. All I could see through the windshield was this complete dazzling light. It was probably the brightest light I have ever seen, yet it was very beautiful too, kind of yellowy white. It was blinding. It was very strange, but even more so, in the middle of the light, it looked like a *strip* of something. I could see this for only a fraction of a second before I hit it. It was either colorless or white, but it was *in* this light. It looked like a ribbon or maybe a tape stretched taut across the windshield and slightly at an angle, slanted down to my left. The first impression I would normally think of might be a wire, but it was wider than that, like a tape. This was very odd, because this was after this dark, dark, dark night. Everything black ahead, and then suddenly the windshield was completely filled with this dazzling light, and this *thing* stretched across, which obviously I was going to hit. And it made a tremendous *smack*! Almost like a *crack*, a crack smack sound. It seemed to reverberate all the way around me and through me. It was so startling. And I thought, 'What on Earth was that?' Then I noticed, right after the smack, that now there was a great big crack on my windshield. A big spider web crack on the driver's side, with big tendrils reaching half way across the windshield. And then it seemed I was out of that light, and driving along with the regular lights of the headlights. The crack was not really blocking my field of vision, but I could see there wasn't any *hole* in it like a bullet or a rock would make. But even if it had been something like that, why would there have been all that blazing light? So I was really *stunned*."

"I kept driving, although one of my impulses was to slow down, pull over, back up and ask those men back by the truck if they had seen anything. But what I call the 'big voice of my soul' was *booming* through to me so vehemently, *'No!* Get out of here! Keep going! Don't stop! Don't go back! Get out of here! Keep going! Keep going all the way home!' And so I did keep going all the way home for another two hours, worrying the entire way whether the windshield might shatter. I got home a little bit after two o'clock, which was the right amount of time, especially without traffic."

Of course Bonnie was filled with unanswered questions when she arrived home. She was relieved to find there was no missing time, but she could not account for the incredible light, and the strip stretched across the freeway that had cracked her windshield. She had thought about pulling off the highway and finding a pay phone to call the highway patrol, but it was late and she was a woman alone, so she kept going until she arrived home. Her husband said he was glad she didn't stop. Sometimes people set up situations where they can trap people and rob them or steal their car, so it was very wise to keep going. At least whatever cracked the windshield didn't cause an accident.

I agreed with Bonnie that this didn't sound like a normal incident. It had too many unusual components. I knew that under hypnosis we could get more details than the conscious mind could supply. Bonnie was an excellent subject and went into a deep state of trance immediately. Sometimes a fellow hypnotist can offer resistance, because they are aware of procedure and are consciously trying to analyze the technique being used. But I had no problem with Bonnie. She felt confident with me and relaxed and returned immediately to the scene on that night in May 1997. The only problem was that she was filling it with too much detail. She remembered the names of everyone present at the dinner, where they sat at the table, what they were eating and what they were discussing. I knew I would have to move the scene forward to the portion we wished to explore. She went through much detail as she left the restaurant, got into her car, noticed the exact time, and drove out of the parking lot. This is always a good sign. A subject that is reliving a true incident will supply more extreme detail than asked for (often considerably more than necessary), and will often volunteer seemingly irrelevant bits of information. This seems to be the subconscious' method of being extremely accurate. Thus I knew we were off to a good start.

She was reliving driving south on Highway 101.

D: *So as you're driving, it's just a normal drive?*
B: Well, it's normal except I am surprised there aren't any other cars ahead of me or behind me. And it seems strange there aren't any coming the other way either.
D: *Is there normally traffic there?*
B: Well, I don't usually drive home this late from Santa Barbara. But I would think on a Friday night around midnight there'd be some

traffic. But it's very nice in the sense that I don't have any glare coming into my eyes from the oncoming traffic.

Bonnie remarked about the blackness of the night and the inability to distinguish the land from the ocean. She then drove past the little sign "Seacliff." Immediately afterwards she saw the big flash of a perfect circle of light down by the coast. A little further along she saw the big glow of a light shining behind the craggy mountains to her left. The light covered quite a distance, because it took her a while to drive past the reaches of it. So far she was reliving the evening just as her conscious mind had reported it, except she was continuing to supply information about the meeting at the restaurant, and her plans for the coming weekend.

B: It's like a corona of light from something. And I don't see what the something is, because the hills are in the way. But the arc of this corona of light is like the top of a great big perfect curve, or circle. And it has a lot of definition to it. You know, some light is diffused and glowing at the edges, and just gradually fades into the darkness. But this one isn't that way. There's more like an edge to this light. It's so big and so bright, and I can't see where it's coming from. It's like that other thing that flashed. That's so interesting, because there was that flash on the right side, and now there's this big light shining on the left side. What could it be? There's no town over there or anything. I'm going at a really fast pace too, but it's so big it's taking me a while to go past it. And by the way, it's not moving around or anything. It's just staying there static. And now though, on the right side, I'm seeing this big thing. It looks like the big back end of a very tall truck. So I'm thinking of maybe a trailer truck or ... I mean, it would have to be a really big vehicle to be that tall. I'm not seeing along the side of it or anything, or the front of it, 'cause I'm approaching it from behind, from the rear. And I'm thinking it's odd that I didn't see it until just right here. And I'm wondering why it's parked there. I'm assuming it might have something to do with that weird light over there, across the freeway, past the hills on the left. There's some kind of glow shining up at it from below. It must be from something on the highway, I guess. It's sort of a soft light. And

I'm seeing the silhouettes of some people walking. And I'm not sure ....

D: Are you afraid you might hit them?

B: Well, I see there's enough room. I wonder if we could sort of freeze ....

D: I was going to suggest that, to freeze the scene so we can examine it.

B: Because I'm driving so fast. It happens so quickly.

D: You can slow the whole scene down frame by frame.

B: I need to do that.

D: All right. As you come up onto the back, you can see it very distinctly, and you can report it. Because as you slow it down you can see it in great detail. Tell me what you see as it is slowed down.

B: Well, these people are very spindly. They're very thin, with long legs. They're all in motion. Some of them are walking past the back of this thing, this truck. They're all walking in different directions. Some of them are walking toward the front of the truck right on the freeway side. One or two are rounding the corner toward the back from the side. They're moving quickly, but smoothly.

D: Can you make out any other details about them?

B: They're different heights. (She showed signs of discomfort.) They have big heads. (Becoming upset.)

D: Remember you can look at it objectively if you want to, as a reporter.

B: (Almost sobbing.) Well, they're not really people.

D: Why do you say that?

B: Because they're much thinner than people. And they have these long necks, and big heads. If they're people, they're very weird looking people. I thought they were human, men road crew people or something.

D: Why does that bother you?

B: Well, it's just a surprise. I didn't expect this. (Still upset.) It's not that it's bad. But it's a surprise.

D: Naturally. As this is slowed down frame by frame, can you make out more details about the object at the side of the road? You can see it clearly now. (Her facial signs indicated something.) What do you see?

B: I see these big letters up there. Well, I thought they said, "Emergency Vehicle." But it's more like a pattern, I think. It's kind of like ... (Pause as she examined it.) I want to say "triangles," but not exactly. Like parts of triangles, angular shapes. Like if you put them together in a certain way they'd form triangles, but they're not forming triangles. I wouldn't say they're letters like we have letters. And the corners are not sharp now.

D: *Do you think later you could draw it?*

B: I can draw part of it. I'm still going fast, very fast.

D: *I want you to fix that design, those letters, in your mind, so you will be able to draw them as best you can later. Can you do that for me? (She mumbled something.) Just remember what it looks like.*

B: And the glow of that light down there. I thought there was some sort of light on the road, but there isn't. You know what it is? It's something about that big vehicle that's just glowing from underneath. It's not that there's something shining on it like I thought. I don't think it's as long as I assumed it was either. And where there was a sharp edge, or a corner, between the side and the back, it's more of a curve.

D: *But you're moving past it. Tell me what happens, because you can know now. You can see all the details.*

B: Suddenly there's this tremendous light in front of my windshield.

D: *What is it?*

B: (In wonder.) I don't know!

D: *Yes, you do.*

B: It's just dazzling. It's so incredibly bright and dazzling that it's startling. I mean, I can't see anything else. I can't see anything through it, except I see in it.

D: *But your mind knows what it is. Trust it. Where is it coming from?*

B: It's coming somehow from them.

D: *These people?*

B: Yeah. And that sort of silvery thing with the light radiating out from under it, out the back of it. It's not even that same color light, but it has something to do with them. I know they're doing it.

D: *Then what happens?*

B: And then I'm ... that's funny, I thought I just kept driving. But I'm not. I mean, I'm driving, but I'm ... I'm driving up. Upward. That's so weird. (Unbelieving.) I'm still holding onto the steering wheel, and I'm driving up. And I'm still in all this light. I thought that light just lasted a second, but I'm still in it. Now it's all around the car, and it's all in the car. It's really a beautiful, beautiful light.

D: Can you see where it's coming from?

B: No. I'm not driving forward, but upward, as if on a big ramp or a hill. Up, heading up.

D: Like at an angle?

B: Uh huh. But I also sense I can't be on the road anymore, because the road doesn't go up there. And there's also a feeling of lightness and effortlessness. I think the car motor isn't even on, but I'm still holding on to the steering wheel.

D: Can you hear the motor sounds?

B: No, I don't hear anything. Now instead of moving forward, it's like it's floating upwards. But I feel very protected, because I'm in a big oval bubble of bright, bright light. I can't see where the light stops. I just know that I'm in it.

There was lots of distraction for me from noises going on outside. We were in a dormitory on a college campus. Earlier there had been busloads of young people arriving for a tennis tournament. They looked like high school kids. Now as it was getting dark, they seemed to be gathering on the street below the window. A lot of squealing, screaming and laughing was going on. I tried to ignore it. I hoped it would not interfere with the session. But normally the subject is so concentrated on what they are seeing that even loud noises do not disturb them at all. I got up and closed the window, even though it made the room hot.

B: This light is really beautiful. And it's all around the car, and it's even *through* the car. It's like I'm just sitting in this tremendous bubble of dazzling light. I don't hear anything, but everything's okay. I'm still hanging onto the steering wheel. That feels good. ... Okay, now it's as if me and my car have come up into something. It feels like the car is being set onto something, like a floor or a ground or something. And that light is beginning to fade.

D: Can you see where you are?

B: It's a great big room. All around me, a circular room with hallways and doors going off it. And there's a lot of light too, but not as bright as the light I was just sitting in.

D: How do you feel about this?

B: Oh, it's okay. It's a surprise. (Pause) But now there's a whole swarm of - I want to say "people," but they're not really people. They're all around the car. It's so funny. They must be up on the hood of the car looking in. And they're all around the windows. I turn around and look out the back, and they're there too. (She found this amusing.)

D: What do they look like?

B: (Chuckle) Oh, they look really nice, but they're certainly not human beings. They've got these big liquidy eyes, and bald heads. I mean, they're not threatening at all. They're curious and childlike and friendly. And they're just peering in, and tilting their heads now to get a better look.

D: At you or at the car?

B: I think both. I think mostly at me, it feels like. And then they open both doors for some reason. And that's weird, because I had the doors locked. I always drive in the dark with the doors locked. They just opened them. Two of them ... (Loud laugh) two of them are getting in the passenger seat to my right. My purse is there, and little candies I have out to eat in case I get sleepy. And they're pushing those off. And the second one is sort of pushing, nudging with his hip as the first one is in the seat. Like little kids, sort of. (High pitched, imitating kid's voice:) "I got to let her get in there first." And there are three or four by my door. And they're just reaching in, and they're ... it's weird; it's weird, because I have a seat belt on and the door locked. But that doesn't seem to bother them. I'm not aware of anybody reaching over and unhitching my seat belt, but they're sort of dragging me out by my left arm. And then they grab me ... not grab me, but touch me on my right arm, and close the door. Now there's some on either side of me, and one or two right in back of me. And they're like shuffling on.

D: Well, can you see what their hands look like, as they're touching your arms?

B: Yeah. They have real skinny fingers. These guys are sort of ... (Pause as she examines them.) I want to say "blue," but they're really much lighter. More of a gray with a bluey tint. And their eyes are very pretty. They're very big and liquidy and bluey too. Bluey-blacky.

D: Can you see how many fingers they have?

B: Well, the one who has its hand on my right forearm, I can just see three fingers and then there's a funny thing trying to wrap around my forearm. It doesn't look really like a thumb, but it's sort of doing the job, more or less.

D: *So they have three fingers and this funny looking one.*

B: Yeah, and they are very thin. I guess we would call them sort of bony.

D: *Where are they taking you?*

B: Well, they're walking me along. I said shuffling. It isn't really shuffling. I'm not even walking the way I walk. I mean, it seems like I started to, but then I don't have to. Because we're kind of gliding along. It's real smooth. They're smooth and I'm smooth. And every once in a while (Laugh) I stick down a foot, you know, as if to take a step. And that sort of slows us down. It gets in the way. So they're taking me across this big ... I think it's really more of an oval shape than a round shape. I seem to be the only car and the only person. Oh, gosh, it's got a very high ceiling. There isn't really anything *in* it, but there are some doors. We're going across one end of the oval, in this floating kind of way. Not up in the air really. I think we're pretty near the floor. And I want to look around and see my car, and see what's happening to it. But I have a feeling they're really in there looking it over.

D: (Chuckle) *Just like little kids. They want to see it.*

B: Yeah. And I'm wondering what they'll think about my candy wrappers, and my purse, and my notebook, and my tapes. There are audio tapes.

D: *Well, they may not bother anything.*

B: Yeah, I don't think they would want them. I just had the thought, "I wonder what they think." Especially of the tapes that have to do with UFO things. (Chuckle) And I'm wondering if they'd like to know what's on them. But anyway, we're coming to a door, and we're going into another room. And in the middle of the room there's a chair that has arms. It has a headrest, and a foot place, like a .... Well, they're putting me in it, and it's like a recliner chair, but it doesn't have the part for my legs to rest on. But it does have sort of a diagonal footrest thing, and I put my feet on it. It's got corrugations on it, ridges, so my feet don't slide off, because it's on a slant. And they put my arms on the arms of this chair. Let's see, what does it remind me of? Kind of like a dentist chair. And a little bit like a beauty parlor chair, with arms that have some padding on them. And they put my arms there with my wrists hanging over the ends. This is kind of like a beauty parlor, in a way, because you know in the beauty parlor they have this heating hair dryer type of apparatus? *(Yes)* So they're putting something over my head from behind, that is part of this chair thing. It must be adjustable, and it fits right around my head. And there are some beings, one on each side, adjusting it. And this is a smaller room. It's not round.

D: *What do you think they're doing with that?*

B: (Wondering) I don't know. If they didn't look nice, I think I'd be really terrified. But I'm *not* terrified.

D: *Can you see how it fits over your head?*

B: No, because they put it on from behind. As I was approaching the chair I noticed it was almost like a beehive shaped thing, and it's smaller than the dryer at a beauty parlor. Anyway, here I am, and I'm sitting upright in this thing. They're pressing it in pretty firmly, and they seem to be adjusting it on my temples. I hope they're not going to make it too tight, because that's a tender area. It doesn't come down over my face, it's just on my head. Now I guess they've got it about as snug as they're going to get it. And the ones at the side are looking at me. (Laugh) They're really kind of cute. I mean, they still have that open curious look. And they're looking at my face and my head, and the temple area. They're touching it with their little bony fingers, and sort of nodding. And I'm just amazed that I'm not terrified. I'm curious, and so are they. And I'm thinking, "Wow! I'm really here. I'm really having this experience. These beings are really here, doing things here with me." They're starting up something right now. I can't say that I hear anything, but I feel a hum without hearing it. I guess that means feeling the vibration, but a very, very soft one. It's coming right through my head from all directions. And it's like they're telling me to "just relax your neck." And relax into this thing around my head.

D: *Are they telling you this by talking to you?*

B: No. I just know that's their thoughts, because they're not *my* thoughts. But since I'm going to be in this thing anyway, I'd like to relax my head and my neck too. And there is a neck support there. It's kind of hard, but at least it's something to sort of lean back into. It has a little padding on it just like the arms.

D: And then what happens?

B: I'm just sitting there wondering about it. And there are all these knobs, and other ones are coming over. Suddenly this small room has a lot of them in it. They're different heights too, like down on the road.

D: Do they look alike?

B: No, there's a taller one. It seems like a "he." He has a very, very bony white head, and different eyes.

D: What's different about them?

B: Well, they're really, really big. They're much bigger than the other ones, and a different shape. But you know, the neat thing is that *all* of these seem to have expression in their eyes. And I feel great interest, like an honoring. I mean, it's more than curiosity. It's like they're *intently* interested in what's happening, and I'm also feeling a great sense of approval. I mean, they're not moving around with excitement or clapping or anything. But I'm getting the feeling they're really happy they found this one. (Chuckle) Me. Because this one has a lot of information that they want. And it seems like they haven't had *this* one before, meaning me. I feel like I'm a new one, like a new subject, so they're *especially* interested. So I'm just sitting here. And they're all watching, and new ones come in. Nobody who comes in goes out, so pretty soon this little space is pretty crowded with different people. Some of them are even pushing past each other. (Laugh) Like those two little ones in the car.

D: You said you felt this vibration. (Yeah) *Where was the vibration?*

B: In my head. It feels like a hum, but I can't say I hear any sound. There's something, like a current, but it doesn't hurt or anything. It's very soothing, in fact. It's very relaxing.

D: But you don't know what's happening?

B: No. I just know they're very interested. It seems like they might be wanting to know what's in my brain.

D: Can you ask any of them to tell you?

B: Yeah, okay. I can't move my mouth, but I guess I can think it.

D: Yes. Tell them you're curious.

B: Well, there are two or three layers deep of these ... (Laugh) beings around. But I'm asking that taller one, who's kind of in the third row in front of me. The big tall one with the *huge* eyes, and the very bony white head. And it's amazing that I like him. I mean, normally if you saw something like that, you'd get the absolute creeps. But he seems to be really neat, so I'm just looking at him. And it's actually hard to look in both of his eyes, because they're wide spread, so that my eyes looking straight ahead don't quite match his. So I have to look at one or the other. My eyes are much closer together. (Chuckle) But still I can look at one eye and then the other. So I'm asking, "What are you doing? What's going on here?" And *he* is beaming back, "You are our treasured one." (Bonnie became emotional and started to cry.) "We need to learn from you, just like you learn from us. And now we're meeting face to face." (She was now openly crying.) "And we can know what you know about us." (Her crying obscured the words.) "And it's very good." (Crying) Feeling completely honored ... and happy. These are tears of happiness.

D: *Then they're not tears of sadness or fear?*

B: Oh, no! (Crying) I'm feeling profoundly honored all the way through.

D: *That's very good.* (I tried to make her objective again, so she could stop the emotions.) *And how are they learning from you?*

B: (Regaining her composure.) He says, we're downloading information from your mind. And you know what that means now, Bonnie. Good for you! You're learning your computer, and you understand this now. We're just taking all that you know from all those people you've worked with who've had episodes - interesting they call that "episodes" - with ones like us. And we want to know how these people experience *our* interactions with them. We want to know how we affect them, and how they experience it, and what it means to them. And you know all that, Bonnie, from many people. And you've seen them change. You've seen them go from terrible fear and trauma, as you call it on Earth, to acceptance and peace. And in many cases wanting to know us better. As you too have been wanting to know us. As you have had some awareness of. And now you can. So this experience is for you too. You've been with us before. You just haven't thought so. And I'm thinking, "Yes, I have met with these bluish ones before, way back in 1742."

D: (That was a surprise.) *1742? That is a long time ago.*

B: When I was a castle guard back in Wales. They picked me up bodily and brought me way, way, way, way, way, way, way out in space to where these silvery bluish, beautiful ones with the liquidy eyes and radiating good will, greeted me. It was wonderful.

D: *So you've known them a long time?*

B: A long time. And I experienced being part of their group mind, which is really, really different.

D: *But have you known them since that time?*

B: I'm not aware of that.

D: *So they knew who you were, that's what you mean. All right. But you are on the ship experiencing this downloading. What happens after that?*

B: This doesn't even go on for very long, probably just a few minutes. It's hard to say. And I'm so dazzled by them. You see, the innermost ring of these beings are these beautiful silvery bluey ones. They all look just like each other. And they exude a lovely gentleness and interest, curiosity. The tall one in the back is exuding really good will too. He's the one who's been talking to me.

D: *Well, what happens when they finish this?*

B: The hum feeling is stopping. And they're around the sides now where my temples are, opening something. I don't know if it's hinges or plates or something. And they're taking this apparatus off my head. I'm still sitting in the same position with my head upright. And the big tall one says, "Thank you. We appreciate your information. And we appreciate the work you're doing with people whom we work with. We honor you very much, and you will be absolutely fine. We're not taking away *your* memories. They're all perfectly intact. And we're very happy to have you share anything you want with people on Earth. Because it's important that they become very accustomed to the idea that we all exist. And that we interact with many, many of you."

I had become so engrossed that I forgot to watch my tape recorder. Bonnie's recorder shut off, and that caused me to look at mine. It had almost reached the end of the tape. So while the man changed her tape, I took mine out, put a new one in, and continued.

D: They're allowing us to have this information?

B: He is saying, "Please do! Use any opportunity you can to share. Any group that you're in, any individuals you meet, any people you talk to. And you *must* begin acquainting your own family with this."

D: What would he say to someone who thinks it's wrong to take their personal information?

B: He says in the universal scheme of things it's not wrong. And someday, even though *we* - meaning them. This is him saying this. - Even though *we* are the ones learning much more about *you* at this time, you human beings, you Earth people, will have your turn eventually, learning more about us. And many of us *want* you Earth people to learn more about us. There are some that don't, but we do, because we're interacting for the common good. We are really working very hard through many Earth individuals to keep improving the quality of life on Earth. And it is very, very important for other people to know that part of it. There is needed a very large balancing and off setting of the disaster modes that are so often presented to your societies. And you, Bonnie, just inherently, always in your life anyway, are looking for balance, and mutual understanding. That is why you are one of the people we are working with. We even sometimes send people to you to work with. It may not seem like it to you, because they say they heard you speak, or they were referred by somebody whom you know. But we often are the ones impressing them and leading them to the lecture where they'll hear you, and learn where they can reach you. And they'll come and work with you, because you are one of the ones who's open for the balance, open for the good that many of us are trying so earnestly to achieve. It's very sad for us to see so many of the things going on amongst Earth people. And very sad for us to see the close ness of mind to other beings in the universes. So when we find one like you, and others like you, you have no idea how much we honor you all. We honor that you learn and inquire and read, and you're open always to all the other inputs. And you share that with other people. The work that you're doing with other people to help them in this life to open up and accept the interactions with us, has a far greater affect on their souls than you realize. It's way beyond just this lifetime, for each of those people begins to integrate it and accept that they are interacting with us. So this has far longer effect, or far reaching effect than you can possibly know at this time.

D: Then would I be allowed to work with Bonnie again at another time?

B: Oh, absolutely. We're very pleased that she's becoming aware of this.

D: Then if I work with her again we would be allowed to have more information?

B: Oh, yes. We would be pleased. We're making this experience very easy for her. We very much appreciate the fact that she is on her way home. And from her Earth perspective it's late at night, and it's a dark night, and she has many things to do. I want you to know that when we, as you might say, pick people up and take them for experiences, we choose very well the time in their lives that we do this. We do not pick them up when they're sick. We do not pick them up if they're about to have surgery. We do not pick them up if they're going through a marital crisis. Or if they've lost somebody very close to them through what you term "death." We choose oftentimes when they're not in the middle of anything exceedingly demanding or important of their time, attention or emotions. That's one of the reasons we tend to work so often with people when they're sleeping. To not interrupt their work day or their family life. We often meet with them and take them when they're on a vacation where they have leisure time. A friend of yours, Bonnie, has been taken often on camping trips. Far more than he knows. And that is as it should be, because he's not stressed, and he doesn't have to function alertly the next day. So we try to be considerate. And with you yourself, you have a very busy time ahead. But here is a lovely window of time, driving home at night, late. And yes, you have a busy day tomorrow, but we're not leaving you with any traumatic effects or any body effects. We will just gently put you down, and you will continue on your way. And barely even know that anything happened, until you're ready to know.

D: Can I ask, what was the object by the side of the road?

B: Oh! that object, that was one of our little scouting vehicles. We just simply made it look like something familiar to Earth people, like a big truck. And it was some of our beings that she saw walking around it.

D: What was the glow behind the hills?

B: That's another one of our ships. Actually there was quite a fleet of ours out here this night. And one of them was off behind the hill. There are some people who live off in the distant hillsides. There are many, many miles of just hills and valleys over there. Occasionally there's a dirt road and a house. And some of those are our people. Sometimes Earth people wonder why people continue to live in remote areas, if they're having these experiences.

D: You mean the people living in the house are your people? (Yes) *They're living on Earth, you mean?*

B: I'm referring to the people we visit and take with us.

D: I see. I thought you meant people like yourself.

B: No. We don't live on the Earth.

D: These are people in isolated areas that you work with, in other words.

B: Yes. Behind those hills where Bonnie was driving, there was one of our crafts. And some of them emit great amounts of light. And that particular craft was visiting somebody in a house. It's, oh, a series back there, of isolated rural homes, that you don't see from the highway.

D: Then it was not the craft she is on now.

B: No, no, no. It was another one. And, as a matter of fact, there was another one, from her perspective, down the coast. What she experienced as a bright sudden round flash without any sound, was simply *that* craft just *popping* right into *her* dimension. It only takes a moment, and once it gets into that third density, then it sort of evens out. It's only the collision point that causes the flash.

D: The collision of the dimensions, you mean?

B: Yes. The collision of the craft coming in from another dimension into the third dimension of reality. It often will make a flash. We do this a lot in the daytime, but people don't tend to see the flashes, because the sky is light from the Earth point of view.

D: So once it enters the dimension then the light fades.

B: Yes. It goes through an immediate adjustment to being.... I know it's hard for Earth people to understand, but it becomes more dense itself. The craft and those on it. And so they very rapidly enter *and* almost immediately adjust to being enough in the third dimension that, oddly enough, third dimension doesn't see it usually. They *can* see it, but they're usually not looking. You'd be amazed at how many of our craft fly around without anybody ever seeing us.

D: (Chuckle) *I wouldn't be amazed. I know it can happen.*

B: And there is another thing. When we put her back again on to the road, we'll make every effort to put her back at pretty much where we took her. Which should be easy, because our craft is still down there. Sometimes we don't know exactly. But when we do *she too* will have to enter back into that third density.

D: *While she is on this craft she is in another density?*

B: Right here on the craft sitting in this chair she's not in as dense a form as she is when she's back on Earth in a third density.

D: *So you have to adjust the density as the car comes back down.*

B: Yes. Plus the fact that at that very second when she reenters there will be a flash of light. And it will be very startling to her.

D: *This is because of the two dimensions interacting again?*

B: Yes, because she's coming in from a lighter density to the denser third density. Just like there was that flash of light down the coast. There will be a flash of light right there on the freeway. And she will see it. She will be in her car. We'll put her back in her car here, and then we'll lower her down. She won't know any of that. And then suddenly there'll be this flash of light. And she'll be back on the road, motor running, driving again.

D: *But when this experience first began, she saw a flash across the windshield.*

B: Right. That's because she was starting, right then and there, with our help, of course, to enter into our dimension.

D: *So it created a flash also.*

B: Right. So as Earth people, Earth vehicles, Earth animals - for that matter, Earth lifeforms of all kinds - leave the third dimension and come into our lighter higher vibration density dimension at which there is a type of physicality, but not as "solid" - although you don't even have that either. At that point there can be, and often is, this flash of light. Now, again, in the daytime most people don't see this; or if they're asleep at night they may not see this. Or they may experience just being in the *beam* of light, and not so much that flash. But sometimes when it happens very quickly, as it happened very quickly to her, there is this big flash. Now, many times we do it a different way when somebody is driving along the road. We will surround them with light, and render their car motor inoperable. Their car motor stops, their lights go out. We try to make sure they get over to the side of the road first, or off the road. We know what can happen there. It would be disadvantageous to all. But it's a slower process, and the person in the car is aware that the motor is going off. So there's not such a sharp sudden transition into our dimension. You see what I mean? The light pans around the car, the motor stops, the person's off the road. We show up, we take them through the car door, or open the door, as we did for her. And usually we'll bring them up in a beam of light. So in that case there's no flash. You see, it's a more gradual transition.

D: *So it can happen in two different ways. (*Yes, yes.*) All right. We are running out of time in our place here.*

B: I understand that.

D: *So I would like to ask a few more questions. She said she saw something like a strip of light in the bright light. What was that?*

B: That's one of our laser effects. It's a very thin beam. And it actually came from our vehicle that was down there on the road. Actually that vehicle is still there. It's not actually on the road. It's just above the road. We don't really ever put any of our craft right on the earth.

D: *Why?*

B: It would be very harmful to our craft, because of the energy effects radiating around the craft, and under the craft, of course. Over the whole surface there is a radiating energy effect that helps us propel and fly. It would be interrupted if the bottom of the craft were to sit on the earth. So it has to hover, or sometimes put down legs. In this case it's just hovering. But it's quite close to the ground, so it appeared to her that it was.

D: *What was this laser effect you were talking about?*

B: It's just something we have on that small craft. We have them on all of our craft actually. They're instantaneous and very powerful. It's a beam of light. A certain quality, a certain frequency of light that has definite - I won't say "physical, physicality" - but it has a strength. It's very dense and compacted and concentrated in its frequencies, in its beam. It's really quite a narrow beam. Nowadays you have a little sense of this, when you people give lectures and show slides. You have a laser pointer. And you push a little button, and then over on the screen you see the red dot. Well, actually in between the gadget and the red dot there is a beam, a certain frequency. It's very narrow, and to the human eye, usually it's not seen. To *our* eye it's seen all the time. We see different frequencies. So this little beam of light was shot out to get her attention. And to let her know, especially later on, that something unusual *did* happen. But we don't want to do anything that will really frighten her, or traumatize her too much tonight, because we appreciate that she has the long drive home. And she has definite responsibilities this weekend, and needs to be refreshed and rested to do them.

D: *She said that the windshield cracked. What caused that?*

B: That was the beam of light.

D: *The beam of light hit the windshield?*

B: Yes. It had so much strength.

D: *Was this intentional?*

B: Yes, it was. And the reason why it was on an angle is because it came from slightly higher up in the craft. Remember I said the craft was hovering. It wasn't entirely down at ground level, as she was driving by in the car. So it came *down* slightly from above across her windshield. Because it's not physical we knew it would do two things. We knew it would make an impact, and make a mark on her windshield. We also knew it was not *of such* a density that it would cause her to swerve and have an accident.

D: Did this hit the windshield before she was taken up into your craft, or after she was put back down?

B: No. Actually we haven't even done that yet. What happened before was the intense bright light, and actually *seeing* the strip. We do have quite amazing ways, I imagine, from your point of view. (Chuckle) But we had her see the light. And then she drove *up* in it - she was right - on an angle. Then we lifted her the rest of the way to another craft overhead, while the other little one stayed down by the road. And when we put her *down* again, as I said, it will be as close as possible to *exactly* where we took her. If we can, we will take her down to that exact moment when she saw what she thought was a strip of something in that dazzling light. And then we will let the experience proceed. She will be impacted by that laser beam, and it will affect her windshield. So at this moment in time that hasn't happened yet. But time is so relative it's almost as if it has happened, because it will happen.

D: *All right. Well, as I said, we are under time constraints in our dimension here.* (Yes) *I would like to really thank you for communicating with me.*

B: I'm very glad to. Many of my fellows have communicated with you, Dolores.

D: (Laugh) *I didn't know if it was the same group or not.*

B: Well, you work with many groups. But I'm one of the groups, we are one of a number of groups. So I'm familiar with you.

D: *Then you know I'm always curious.*

B: Oh, and it's *wonderful* what you're doing worldwide. We are so pleased. We *couldn't* be more pleased.

D: *Then it's okay if I continue to work with ....*

B: (Interrupted) Absolutely! And to share. We honor your writing and we honor your lecturing. And we honor your traveling. It's absolutely *magnificent.* You have a wonderful quality of being such a good human being that your fellow humans *accept* you. And they *believe* you. They open to what you are saying. You are a down home regular person, who's actually far more outstanding than that. But that's what people have the impression of. You're a good motherly person they can trust. And that's tremendously important on the Earth today. That people hear this from likable, credible people.

D: *Then I have permission to contact you through Bonnie and we can obtain more information?*

B: Absolutely. Please do. We're delighted. And I would like to say before we finish, that the little ones around her are the very same kind that really did work with her long, long, long ago in another life.

D: *Because they live longer.*

B: Yes, we all live as long as we want to live, or need to live, to do the jobs we're doing. It's just as easy as that. An *thank* you for facilitating this experience. Thank you for helping Bonnie with this.

D: *And you know I protect her and I always have her welfare at heart.*

B: I am sure you do. And she is sure of that too.

D: *Then can I ask you to depart?* (Yes) *And have her personality and consciousness once again return ....*

B: (Interrupted) We do need to return her however. And it won't take very long.

I had forgotten that we were out of their time sequence, but the taller being had not. We apparently had to go with his schedule before Bonnie could be brought back to consciousness, and our present reality.

B: The little ones are putting her back in the car. And the little curious ones are backing away. And they're opening up the bottom of this big craft. She's been lowered down in light. By the way, there's still no one on that freeway. We have influenced anyone who was going to go north or south on the 101 freeway at this particular time - which is actually a very, very *short* period of Earth clock time - to just not drive. So you'd be surprised at the people who are pulling off the road, and just being inspired to look at the ocean, or to have a little nap. There are many people out there who were heading north and south, just having little naps. Just for a little while. Just a little snooze. We do this because we don't want them to see all this light effect.

D: *I'm sure it's not for them.*

B: Then we'll put her down on the road. She's going down now. She's down on the road. Whoops! There's the crack! Laser beam. Perfect timing! Absolutely perfect. We're very proud of that maneuver actually. (I laughed) And she's driving on. She's tempted to stop. But we are beaming through to her - not the big voice of her soul necessarily - but we are beaming to her, "Keep going! Don't stop! Keep going! Get out of here! Get home!" And that's what she's following. We had to get her on her way, because we have to open up the freeway again.

D: *Good. And she knows it all now. And it's perfectly all right for her to know it.*

B: Yes, that's wonderful.

D: *All right. Now she's in the car going home. And you are departing with much love and much thanks.* (Yes) *And I will see you again some time.*

B: Thank you, my very dear.

I then gave instructions for the integration of Bonnie's consciousness and personality back into her body, and instructions for orientation back to this time frame. She then awakened, and began to ask questions about the session.

Bonnie's drawing of the symbols on the back of the "truck."

One of the men who was observing said he was amazed at the way the entity kept talking and was so fluent. Bonnie said this is what happens when she works with her subjects also. She is apparently using the same type of technique to get past the conscious mind emotional state to where the real information is.

Bonnie was full of questions, but I knew there was no time to answer them all. I had to get up at 3:00 a.m. to catch a bus back to Denver in order to catch my plane (a four-hour drive). And Bonnie and the two men were driving back to Colorado, a 2 1/2-hour drive. One of the men said he would drive, because I knew Bonnie would be incapable after such a deep session. Bonnie later said they played the tape in the car during the drive, and she was quite amazed at the information coming through her.

A few months later in September 1997 I had to do a series of lectures in California, and I was in Los Angeles for only one day. Bonnie came to my hotel to have another session. She had prepared a list of questions she wanted to ask if we located the same entity as last time.

I used her keyword and she went immediately into a deep trance. I returned her to the scene onboard the craft, and she again saw herself surrounded by the cute, childlike beings.

B: I'm sitting in the chair. And all the little ones are crowded around me. They're still very curious. And vying for position, elbowing each other out of the way, shouldering each other out of the way. Just peering at me, it's very sweet really. I don't mind it. They're so lively with their interest. It's complimentary really, to have so many who are so interested.

D: *Maybe they don't get to see very many like you up close.*

B: *I don't know. I never get to see them. That's for sure.* You know, I'd like to pause and take another look at these little bluish gray ones.

D: *You want to see them clearer, you mean?* (Yeah.) (There was a pause as she examined them.) *Do they look different, or are they all alike?*

B: Well, all these smaller ones look like each other. But this time I wanted to notice their skin texture, and more details. Before I had the impression that their skin was very smooth. But it has a fine grain ... slightly bumpy texture, like little tiny bumps on their skin. And when I say "bumpy," those little bumps are so subtle and small; it would be almost like... the nearest thing I could liken it to would be when we have goose pimples. Maybe a little more rounded than that. And there's something about their eyes. More like a sort of ridge over their eyes. You know how with human eyes you see an eyelid, but then it sort of recedes back in over the rounded part of the eye. *(Yeah)* Well, it's sort of like that, except I don't see any *eyelid* that closes down over the eye, or any eyelashes. I'm looking at one who is very close to me, by my right hand. (She had difficulty explaining what she was seeing.) It's not flat, there's kind of a sculptural shape around the eyes. Sort of denting in a little on both the eyes. And almost an eyebrow, but no hair.

D: *You mentioned a ridge. Is that what you mean?*

B: Kind of arching over the eyes, the shape. It's hard to describe it, but I can see it. And there's even a suggestion of a cheekbone shape. Very slight. And just a *tiny* sense of shaping for a nose, but they don't stick out like ours do.

D: *Are there openings there?*

B: Yeah, I guess you'd call them nostrils. They're not round. They're a little oblong, with an up and down, vertical direction.

D: *Is there any kind of mouth?*

B: No. Just a very, very slight, very small ... I don't really see lips. I'm trying to get a sense of measurement. Mouths are maybe an inch wide. Maybe a little more, an inch and a quarter.

D: *That would be small. Can you see any ears?*

B: No, there's nothing that sticks out. But there seems to be - wonder what you call it - looking from the front of our face, we have a little bump or flange that sort of protects the opening of the ear. There is something like that, but there's no outer flap. Behind that little flange there might be an opening, but it's so subtle. I can't really see in the opening, like looking in the ear hole or anything. There is something there, but it's ever so slight.

D: *Can you see their hands?*

B: Yeah. They're quite different from ours. They're very thin. If you look at the back of the hand, it is very narrow compared to ours, and there aren't as many fingers. There are three fingers, then there's an extra thing which would be equivalent, I think, to a thumb. But it's a little more lined up with the other fingers. It's not quite in the position, but it seems to have more sideways movement than the other fingers.

D: *Are these beings wearing any clothes?*

B: That's really hard to say, because it's all the same color. I'm trying to see if there's any difference in texture. I think there might be a suit of some sort, although I don't really see an edge to it. That's what's strange. But it seems to be smoother over the body part.

Bonnie was doing an exceptional job as an objective reporter. In many of the other cases I have investigated the subject was repelled by the strange looking creatures, and did not want to look at them any longer than they had to. In some cases their subconscious would only allow them to see a blurred image, or (as in the case in *Legacy From the Stars*) only see them from the back. Bonnie was as curious as I am, and she requested the scene be slowed down so she could study the creatures and see them in great detail. By doing so she also displayed no fear, but scientific curiosity. And by becoming completely objective more information can be brought forth.

D: *Is the other being there? The one that answered our questions?*

B: Yeah, he's standing behind the ones that are in front of me. He's almost directly straight in front of me, slightly to my left.

D: Can we ask questions again?

B: Yeah. (Softly, not directed at me.) I would like to talk with you further, and ask some questions. I need to let him come more fully into focus. He's saying, "Get more clear. Get more clear."

D: Do you know what he means?

B: Yeah. To let myself see him. (Sigh) Maybe I can describe him and then I can see him more clearly.

D: He doesn't bother you either, does he?

B: No, he doesn't. Okay. He's very tall, and very thin. And he's very, very white.

D: The skin is a different color?

B: Yeah, he's very different from these other little ones, because they're more of a darker blue gray, and he's pure white. Not white like we're white, but white white like white paper.

D: That would be very white. Is his face different?

B: Oh, yeah. He doesn't have nearly such a rounded head as they do, but he has a longer, thinner head and face. It looks rounded on the top, except that it has a minor indentation in the middle of the top, rather than being completely rounded. And I don't see any ears. It almost has a skull look, in the sense that I don't see anything that really looks like flesh.

This description sounded so different that it would normally seem to be frightening to a human viewing a creature like this. But amazingly, Bonnie described the being with no apprehension at all, only a sense of well-being and of feeling comfortable with him. This would seem to be contradictory, given our human emotions, but it was also the way she felt toward the little beings: a feeling of almost love and compatibility. In the first session she thought she should have felt fear when they took her into the room and attached the apparatus, but was mildly surprised that she did not. The only fear was experienced when she first realized the little beings around the "truck" were not human. This faded completely when she entered the craft, and was amused at their child like qualities. She appeared to be quite comfortable in the presence of this strange looking being she was describing so calmly. She studied the creatures with a scientific type of objectivity.

D: By skull like, do you mean the skin appears very tight?

B: Very tight. There must be some covering, I suppose. Okay, now, his eyes are very, very big. They're bigger in proportion to his face than the little grayish ones' eyes are.

D: *Are they the same color?*

B: No. Theirs were more of a blue black, or black with kind of a deep blue tinge. His are more of a dark brown, almost black, but toward the brown. And they're a different shape. They're more like a vertical rectangle, except they have curved corners. They are not sideways across the face like ours are. They're more up and down.

That was a surprise, as I was trying to mentally visualize the creature she was describing.

B: They're longer lengthwise, up and down, vertical, than they are wide. And they're slightly wider at the top end than at the bottom end, but they cover a lot of his face. So mostly what you see when you look at him are these eyes. I'm trying to think in terms of inches. (Pause) The eyes themselves might be about three and a half to four inches tall, and maybe about three inches wide.

D: *Those are large eyes. Are the rest of his features similar to the little ones?*

B: Well, the whole face shape is different. The little ones have much more of a larger, rounded top of their head and temples. And then they taper down to a very small chin. But his face shape is bigger at the top part, and it does taper down. I keep wanting to say it's more like a horse shaped face, if you were to look at a horse's head, head on. But he doesn't have a nose like a horse, or a mouth like that. I'm just talking about the shape.

D: *More elongated. Is the mouth or nose similar to the little ones?*

B: No, because, again I want to think about a horse. The whole face comes out a little in the middle and lower structure, but there's no delineation of a nose. I'm really having trouble even finding where the mouth is. Let me see. (Pause) Yes, there's a mouth. It might be the equivalent of down by the chin, or maybe even under the chin, because I don't see it going across the face like I did with the little ones. He's very different.

D: *What about his hands? Can you see those?*

B: No, I can't. I can see a very long, thin neck, which is pure white too. And I can see shoulders.

D: Any clothes?

B: He's completely white. And I think he has some sort of white clothing on, that sort of falls from the very thin shoulders. I'm trying to see now. (Pause) Right up at the base of his neck - it looks like a circular opening, but without a collar. Where we usually would wear jewelry, a choker or something. But I can definitely say he has very, very narrow shoulders, a very, very thin torso, and thin arms. And yet I don't see a delineation of that. It's appears like a gown or something a little looser. It doesn't seem to be form fitting like with the little gray guys.

D: All right. Do you think he can answer questions now?

B: Yeah, I think so.

D: Tell him we're very curious. We want to know many things.

B: We're very curious, and I've thought about you a lot. I'd also like to say that every time I've thought of you, I've felt really okay about it. In fact, if anything, I feel quite honored. I've never had any fear or bad feelings about you, or the other little ones. And I want to thank you too, because I've never had any fear in driving since then, by myself or late at night, or anything. He's just looking at me with these eyes. It's so interesting about the eyes of all of these beings. Because I don't see a pupil or anything different *in* the eyes, and yet they seem to be very alive and responsive. They seem to move, but I really can't figure out how they move. And they don't have eyelids that blink, but they seem to have expressiveness on them. And I can't quite figure out how that is. But there it is.

D: Let's ask him. How are his eyes different from ours?

B: He's saying they have the ability to see into things more than our eyes do. They see beneath the surface.

D: Literally?

B: Like they see into me. They penetrate into the interior of me.

D: You mean like an x ray?

B: Yeah, like an x ray. He can see the physiognomy, but - more important to them - they can see the thoughts, and the feelings. They don't always understand the feelings, but they can see what's going on in us as individuals. That's what I meant by they can see below the surface. And it's very curious to them that our eyes are *so small.* (I laughed.) Of course, it's curious to us that their eyes are so big.

D: And our eyes can't see on more than one level.

B: No, no. Their eyes can see beneath the surface of many things too, and they have a much broader range of vision than we do. Like for instance, looking down on that stretch of freeway. They see the whole length, as far as they need to see. Or shall we say "width," depending on how they're looking at it.

D: You mean as he looks at the freeway from the craft where he is, he can see the entire length.

B: (The change was abrupt.) I'd like to speak for myself now.

D: Okay, go ahead. It might be easier that way.

B: We see the whole area. We see everything that's right here in the ship. And we see what's right down there below us. And we see the whole territory. We see up and down the freeway, and to both sides of the freeway. We see way out in the ocean, and way inland. And we see way north up along the coastline, and way down. Just all at once.

D: You mean simultaneously?

B: Right. We don't have to shift our eyes like human beings do. We see a very broad spectrum. And not only that, but we see within everything that's in that field of vision. We see each person that's in any vehicle in that whole area, or even in boats that are out in the ocean. And we see everybody who's in any house. See into every building, every house. See beyond the hills that Bonnie was looking at when she was driving along. We see our craft over there. We see four other houses all spread out on different roads. We see all the rough hills. We see the city of Ventura. We see the city of Santa Barbara and Montecito, Carpinteria.

These large eyes reminded me of insects. We have no way of really knowing how large an area an insect can see, because we are unable to enter its mind. Is it similar? Do an insect's large eyes take in more information than we know?

D: Wouldn't it get confusing to take in so much information at one time?

B: No, no. I think it would be for human beings.

D: (Chuckle) Yes. I'm thinking from the human aspect.

B: No. This is what we always do. What I'm talking about right now is the three-dimensional physical Earth reality. But there's more that we see as well. We see other dimensions.

D: Do the little beings ...?

B: Are you asking if the little beings can do that too?

D: Yes, do their eyes function the same way?

B: They don't see in quite as broad a swatch, but they definitely see *in*. Like they're over there right now looking at Bonnie. And I'm looking at the back of their heads. (This switch in perspective definitely showed that Bonnie was no longer communicating. The being was speaking from his viewpoint.) And they see everything going on in terms of her thoughts and her feelings and her whole history. And how her physiological functions work. They're seeing how her eyes work. Her eyes are open. They see how her brain works. How all the little connecting tubes work. All the little glands and nodes and textures. They see the nasal passages and the little hairs in there. And the fluids and the sinuses.

D: Is that why they're observing her so closely?

B: Yes. They're just having a wonderful time. (I laughed.) She knows that they're very curious.

D: But she doesn't know they can see all that.

B: She has no idea what they can see. They can see the ear canals, and how the hearing is working. And they can see the wax in the ear. They see the saliva and the sinus fluids. Oh, yes, there's an awful lot to see.

D: Why don't you have coverings to protect your eyes the way we do?

B: We do have coverings. They're built in. It's almost like you might call it: a membrane.

The description earlier sounded like an insect, but this reminded me somewhat of a reptile's eyes.

D: This protects the actual eye?

B: Yes, yes. It has sort of a gloss to it. It's a self-renewable membrane. We don't need to close eyes the way human beings need to close eyes. Human beings have a different system entirely. They have a lot of moisture right on the surface of the actual eye. And that moisture attracts things like dust. But our membrane covering, which is a natural part of us, does not have the kind of surface that attracts dust particles and other bits. We have a way with this membrane of sloughing off anything that would want to stick to the eye.

D: *I have also been told that you can know the intentions of people by observing them. That there's no way to fool you.*

B: Yes. This is part of what we see. I think human beings might tend to think of it in terms that "we see to the true motivations." We see to what they would call the "soul." We see the essence, as well as all the extra overlay, all the conditioning, to the essence. Human beings are most amazing to us, because they have so many conditionings, and teachings, and theories, and beliefs, that are applied as one goes through life. Applied on top of the pure essence that is born as a human being. And by the time the person even reaches reasonable adulthood, that pure essence might be totally, completely covered over with teachings and beliefs and indoctrinations. So that it's hard for the person to even have any sense that he is really a pure soul essence. And all he can know is all these layers of teaching and belief and doctrine and so forth, that have been applied over that essence as it has come into a lifetime.

D: *I have been told that one of the reasons they will work with me and probably with Bonnie, is because you know our true motivation. Is that correct?*

B: When you say "they," whom are you referring to?

D: *You, whom we call "extraterrestrials." The people that speak through the subjects we work with.*

B: Well, we do know that your motivation is very good. It's for helping and bringing forth the truth.

D: *Because I was told that we couldn't hide our motives. That you knew our intent better than we did.*

B: Yes. And not only that, but you and Bonnie are very committed to bringing out information from deep within the person. Whether it's to look into a former lifetime, or bring back information from centuries ago, as you do yourself. Or whether it's to go back early into this lifetime and find things that are helpful for the person to know. Or go into other past lives for the causes of current difficulties. Or whether it's to go into experiences that people have with beings like us. But the motivation from you and Bonnie and others doing the work like you, is that you're trying to bring forth the other layers and other dimensions of what has happened. You're trying to get to the truth. Trying to get to the true source. And it's very laborious the way you have to do it. We can do it almost instantly. But nevertheless, we give you a lot of credit, because you do - and maybe you've never thought about it this way before - but you do a lot of what we do. That is, to look deeply inside and see what is in there. See more of the pure essence, and the overlays that have been applied in past lives and in the current lifetime to the pure essence.

D: It's just harder for us to do. It takes more time.

B: Yes. It's not so much you looking into the person, although you do have people you call "psychics," who have more of that ability. But you and Bonnie, in particular, do help the person get into this state of consciousness, so the person can let these memories come up through all the layers of the overlay.

D: Well, Bonnie had some questions she wanted me to ask you. (Yes) *You said they were taking information from her mind about the cases she has worked on and the people she has helped.* (Yes) *And you were putting this into - what? - like a computer? Is that a good example?*

B: We do this with our minds, yes. That could be a simile, but we do not put it into a machine.

D: I have to use human terms that I understand.

B: Yes, yes. It would be similar in the sense that in the structure of our minds we have what you would call a "computer" type of apparatus. So we use this information ourselves.

D: She wanted to know what you were going to do with the information you copied from her mind.

B: We have connections with many, many other beings. Of our type, and also of other types who are very interested in Earth and Earth people. Sometimes we telepathically share this. We send it out with our minds. It's like projecting thought out.

D: Then anyone who wants to can receive it?

B: Yes. To those other beings who are interested in this type of thing. For there are many, many beings interested in Earth people. Some of them have more of a sense of what you might call "conscience." *Conscience!* And want to know how human beings are being affected by our visits. There are other beings interested in Earth people, who, however, do not *care* how the Earth people are being affected by their interactions and their visits. It's like a broadcast system, except that we're not using wires and some of the apparatus you use on the Earth. It's more what you would call "immediate" or "telepathic." We have amongst us a different strata, a different medium, of communication. And it does not have to rely on physical apparatus. If we wanted to make that a bit more understandable, it's as if there is - I'm trying to put this in terms that you can understand as an Earth person.

D: *That's always the hard part.*

B: Yes, because we operate so differently. It's as if there's an invisible meshwork or netting multi-dimensionally, that is in all directions. I keep trying to remember that you tend to think in physical terms mostly. And if you could picture looking upward from where you are on the Earth, and imagining there is a completely three dimensional meshing or netting. Not two dimensional like stretched across something, but all dimensions going in all directions. It is similar to your picturing of that, in the sense that wherever one of us is in the middle of this all-encompassing multidimensional meshwork - I'm trying to think of something that would be a simile or an analogy to what you would know. Okay, let's look at an electric light bulb, without a shade on it. When that light is turned on, on Earth, if unimpeded by a shade or a wall or anything, that light would shine out equally in all directions. So it is with this netting and meshing of communication, of thought. Almost like thought waves that, from the sender, like myself, radiate out equally in all directions. All around and both below. So that anyone in that frequency, who has this capacity, can pick up these same thought waves. And those who are interested will pick it up, or those who are not interested do not pay attention.

D: *Because the ones who are interested are looking for it.*

B: Yes. It's like it's all shining out there. It would be as if you have a computer in your office, and the Internet and World Wide Web, which is absolutely *teeming* with incredible amounts of information. And some people come into their offices, turn on their computer, access the Internet, and get a lot of information from it. But there are many things on the Internet they don't even access at all. They are simply not interested. So they don't, as you would say, "click" on that bit of information. There are also some people who come into their office, and never turn on their computer at all. And some people don't even have a computer. So it's the same with all of us.

D: *That makes sense to me.*

B: In our dimension there are some that are going to be interested, and some are not.

D: *Okay. Well, she was wondering, do you live on your craft? Or do you return from time to time to where you originally came from?*

B: Where we are right now is a very large craft. And it's quite high above the Earth. Earth people don't tend to see it. Only occasionally is there a person who *does see* one of our very large craft, and reports it. But again, because we have this vision, and we can see *into* everyone in our very broad spectrum of vision, when we detect someone has seen us, we usually do a cloaking, so they won't see us. Or we may remove ourselves from that area. We still feel Earth people are not ready, in any kind of large numbers, to really be faced with the reality of us and being in such large craft. So many of us do live - I live - on this one. And my little friends here, they live on this one.

D: *Do you have a place that is like a home?*

B: Yes, but that's very far away. And it's much, much more expedient for us to stay on this craft. Now what any one human Earth person sees when they come - like Bonnie has come, to be with us right now - is a *very* small portion of this whole facility. We have living quarters, and work quarters. This is one of our little workrooms right here. She's only seen two parts of this very vast complex. And that's fine. Maybe there will be some other occasion when we can show her more, if she'd like. If she wants. But to be expedient here, we wanted to do what we needed to do in a relatively short period of time. So we just brought her and the car into the bay of the ship. And then we escorted her into this little room. And we'll escort her back out to the car, and back on down again.

D: *But she's curious about where you come from. Is it any place we could identify with our star maps or constellations?*

B: We're definitely within what can be seen on Earth star maps. But we in particular, don't have one of those names more known to Earth. We know that people talk about Sirius and Lyra and Pleiades and Antares, Andromeda galaxy, and various places. We don't have a name that Earth people will recognize. In fact, we don't even use a name for ourselves at all.

D: *That's what I thought. I have heard that before.*

B: It's all done by energy and vibration. That is, when we travel back there - which we don't do very often - it is an effort and a long way. We can hone in and find it, but not the way airplane pilots do on Earth. And our recognition is more in a sense of a vibratory frequency, rather than control tower people.

D: *Of course, I'm speaking again in human terms, but you don't have a family you might miss and want to see?*

B: Many of us have families right here on this very large craft. So we do see them.

D: *So they travel with you.*

B: They can go back too. Not everybody has a family here, but many of us do. My family is here.

D: *Which brings me to the question of procreation. (Chuckle) I'm curious about that.*

B: Well, it's different for different types of beings.

D: *What about your type?*

B: From the Earth person point of view, we're more, in a general sense, like an insectoid type. We don't think of ourselves that way, but we know many Earth people do. So we have more of an egg situation. We do not have the kind of copulation we are aware of that human beings have. In fact, human Earth people are very curious to us. That they can get into such a state of excitement when procreation happens the way it does directly between a male and a female. But in our case, our females generate and lay eggs, and we fertilize those eggs. And they're already out of the body of the female. So it's very different. We don't get together with our females the way people on Earth do.

Insects are born with race memory preprogrammed through their DNA. They do not need to be taught or trained by their parents. So I think they are this type of creature.

In other cases in this book the beings sound more insectoid than humanoid. They said their offspring are born knowing many things. The parents do not bond with the young because they develop quickly into adults and need little training.

D: What about the little gray beings? Are they the same way, or do they procreate in another way? Or do they need to procreate?

B: There are many different kinds of little gray beings. I think Earth people tend to lump them all in one category. And really there are many variations.

D: I have found that is true in my work. There are different types.

B: I have to think about this for a minute, because I also work with some other types. These particular types of little beings that are around Bonnie right now do not procreate the way human beings do. They do not have penises and vaginas.

D: They're not sexual creatures?

B: No, they do not have sexual intercourse as human beings do in order to have pleasure or in order to procreate. With these little ones it is more of a laboratory procedure, of taking cells from these beings and mixing them. There are very subtle differences between male and female in these little gray ones. You do not see the differences bodily from the outside between male and female, like you do with Earth people. It's more of a genetic structure difference. So we take samples from them. Usually we take it from their protected tender places. It would be akin to what you would call taking a skin "scraping," skin cellular samples. So one of the popular places to take that scraping is from under the arms of the male.

D: Like the armpit?

B: The armpit, yes. That's a very protected area. And sometimes we can ....

D: I must interrupt you a moment. I have to tend to my little black box. You understand, don't you?

B: I see what you're doing.

I took the tape out and put another one in the recorder.

D: We don't have the ability to remember everything that is said. We need a machine to capture the words.

B: Oh, yes, and that's what I was going to say. That we have, oh, rather like a patient tolerance for all of you on Earth who are so sincerely interested, as you are, and want to record and remember and be able to replay. And so it would be almost like you as an accomplished adult human looking at a child, and realizing they might have to add numbers by counting on their fingers, for instance, for a while. You are like that to us, but we do not mean that condescendingly. It's almost like a loving amusement slightly and a tolerance and acceptance. It's perfectly all right.

D: *(Chuckle) But we're doing the same thing, because we're trying to pass the information. And we want to do it in the most accurate way we can. We don't want to rely on our memories.*

B: Yes, I appreciate that very much. So back to the reproduction. Sometimes we might take these samples - we call it the "genetic material" - from the surface of the skin. I'm talking about these little gray type beings. And sometimes we take the sample from between the legs. Not because there are genital apertures there, openings, but because that too, being between the legs, is a place that's not open to all the air and dirt or pollutants or anything. It's more enclosed or protected. We have a room right here on our ship where we do that reproducing process. We take the scrapings from the males, and again, they are not enormously different from the females, but just enough. And we take it from the females, and mix them together. We have very *strict* pristine laboratory conditions. And we - I suppose you would use the word "breed," or you have fish hatcheries, don't you? *(Yes)* And other kinds of facilities on Earth where you breed and gestate certain cultures, certain lifeforms. And we have the same. Except that we will *breed* the male substance and the female substance, the genetic substance, in controlled liquid situations, until we feel that lifeform is ready to come out of the fluid and live as a regular being.

D: *But this means this type of being cannot reproduce without the laboratory.*

B: That's right.

D: *It sounds similar to some of the cases we've heard where some aliens have taken samplings from humans.*

B: Yes, yes. Although in some cases - as I'm sure you are aware, and I know Bonnie is - they intermix the genetic material between the human male or human female with another species, and create a hybrid being. And different groups do it in slightly different ways, but sometimes that's done in a very, very similar way to what I've been describing. And sometimes with certain groups, they will, well, the equivalent of what you would call "fertilize" the ovary, the eggs from the human woman. And then implant them back into the womb of the human woman for two, two and a half or so months of gestation. Maybe three at the most. And then will remove that being or that fetus, and place it in our particular protected environment again for the rest of the gestation period.

D: *What is the purpose of mixing the genetics of humans with other types of beings?*

B: Our group, *my* group, does not do that directly. But I certainly am aware that some of the other groups do. And just like with so many aspects of these interactions between other beings and human beings, there are many different groups doing many different agendas. And so there are groups coming to the Earth to take these genetic materials and mix them with their own, in order to perpetuate their own species, because they do feel they are in grave danger. In fact, some of those species do not even have their own home planet to live on any longer, and they are living on craft. And some of them send emissaries to the Earth to get the genetic material to keep their own species going. Some of the species have found the method that I was talking to you about, about taking the scrapings, the genetic material from under the arms or between the legs, for instance. Some species found that worked for quite a while, but is no longer viable. And they need *other* genetic material different from their own. After having done the interbreeding for such a *vast* amount of time, they're needing other genetic material from other species. And they're choosing humans.

D: *Because it wasn't working anymore?*

B: Yes, it wasn't working. Not enough of the offspring were surviving. One thing I don't know if you're aware of, is that some of the species doing that work with human Earth people, have also tried doing it with other species whom you would call "extraterrestrial." Other species that do not live on Earth. And so there is, actually, even at this time, a very large range of experiments and experiences going on between some of these species who are doing this reproductive work, and, not only Earth people, but other beings from other locations in the universe as well. All in a great attempt - in fact, you would even use the word "desperate" - attempt to perpetuate their species. Wherever life is found, whether it's in the millions of species on Earth, or the many, many different types in existence elsewhere, it seems to be a basic common feature of life that each species wants to perpetuate its own. And, as you know from your animal kingdom et cetera, on the Earth, that species will do what they have to do to survive. So this is part of that outreach to survive for some of them. Now there are other agendas as well. There are species who feel they want to create a new species that can *understand* Earth people, by being part Earth human species, and the other species that genetically are being mixed for these offspring. These offspring will then be able to understand *both* species: The human Earth species and the other species, and be a more direct go between. That is very needed. And that's a very big program. So there's the survival program, and there's the go between or the ambassador program. Some of us refer to that as the friendly ambassador program.

D: *The problem is that some humans feel this is a violation, because they feel they have not been consulted.*

B: Yes. What they don't realize, and I do appreciate this, is that they are giving agreement. But so often it's not on a level that people recognize in their full conscious waking life.

D: *I understand that, because I've heard this before, but it's the ordinary person that doesn't understand it. Bonnie wanted to know, how do you choose the people you work with? Is there a selection process?*

B: We do it in various ways. And other groups do it in still different ways. So it's hard to come up with a simplistic answer.

D: *These are all very complex questions.*

B: Yes, and very good questions, for you to understand more of what you want to know. Some of us work more on that soul essence level that I referred to earlier. We can see through to the soul, the essence, beyond all the layers of overlay and conditioning of the Earth person. Those of us who tend to really look for that, tend to work with the person when the person is simply - although I shouldn't use the word "simply," because it's all there really is - a soul level, a soul essence, before the person has even incarnated into this lifetime. We work with that soul essence before coming into this lifetime. And we have a wonderful telepathic rapport with the person, and with the helpers of the person. We tend to call those "guides," spirit guides, and refer to the same as "helpers." We talk with the person. This is all telepathic, but often they have a sense of seeing us in that state of being. We explain what we're doing, and ask if they would cooperate with us in that lifetime they're about to go to. We only work with those individual souls who say, yes, they will and they agree. Now just as with all the other things a person decides in that soul essence experience before coming into an *Earth* life, they usually do not remember when they're living that life. It's one of the differences between Earth people and some of the other species, like ourselves, for instance. But because we are closer to the essence of who we are and can see into each other in the essence, and can be seen that way by each other, we have much more clarity about our purpose than many, many Earth people do. However, some Earth people do have that sense.

D: I understand, because I've heard this from other people I've worked with. But it's the average person that can't quite grasp it.

B: That's probably true for Earth people.

D: We are under time constraints here, because I don't allow my subjects to stay in this state too long. I'm very protective of the person. We only have a few more questions I would like to ask.

B: I think Bonnie's doing fine. She's done a lot of regression work.

D: She was wanting to know about herself. Has she ever been taken by any other groups besides yours, that may not have a high purpose? Has she ever been taken by any other kind of groups that were not positive?

B: I'm not aware of that. I don't think so. The reason we were attracted to her is because we have been keeping an eye on many Earth people, and on our experiencers. We are aware that she had been doing a lot of hypnotic regression work, and that she had been very, very interested in this. She had been talking publicly to many individuals about these experiences. You see, I think most people on Earth don't realize how much so many of us know about them, because we have this increased amount of sight, breadth, depth, longevity of sight and knowingness. We know *infinitely* more about Earth people than Earth people know about us, and keep our eye on certain people.

D: Well, one of her other questions was, do you also take similar information from other regression therapists?

B: Yes, yes, sometimes we do. And we do it in various ways. We're trying to get a broad picture here of how we and the other groups are affecting human beings. From our point of view we would like to improve on how we interact with human beings, and personally, for our group, we do not want to cause distress, harm, fear, and trauma. We are aware that many Earth people, who do experience these things, become very distressed and very traumatized, and negatively affected.

D: *But as a human being that's very normal.*

B: Yes. So we would like to have all of this done in a much more well received way. We would like to have the Earth people benefit from knowing us, and having contact with us. We definitely feel that we benefit from having contact with them. However, I must hasten to say that in broadcasting what we find, for instance from Bonnie, there is the opportunity for less altruistic groups from space to use this information in a more self-serving way, from your point of view. It's terribly important that human beings come to realize there are other beings coming to the Earth and interacting with people, who are very self-serving and uncaring about the effects on people. But there are many groups that are very caring about humans, about the whole of humanity, and what humanity is experiencing in terms of negativity in their warlike nature. We're terribly concerned about their greed, their selfishness, and about what humanity is doing to the beautiful, living being that the Earth is. So there are many of us who have great concern, and would like to help as much as possible. But we know there is *enormous* prejudice on the Earth even about our existence.

D: *Yes, and many think it's totally negative. But I've never believed that.*

B: Yes. And many don't even believe that any of us exist at all.

D: *That's true also.*

B: Which is perfectly ludicrous. So we're really up against a lot. There are some of us who would like very much to have good equal negotiations and contacts with people. And there are a few human beings here and there who would like that as well. But it's very hard, for those of us who feel that way, to adequately get together with the Earth people who feel that way too. So this experience right now is very prized, because we are very decently and openly talking with you as an Earth person. And you are very receptive. And it's all going very well.

D: *But I've done this before. That's probably why.*

B: Yes, and Bonnie's very comfortable with this as well.

D: *So we're not the normal ....*

B: Very definitely not the normal Earth people in this regard.

D: *Can I ask you, have you ever taken information from me? Not you particularly, but some of your other groups?*

B: Yes, I believe some of our other kind have. I personally have not. I did not personally meet you until the last time we had this sort of experience with Bonnie. But I believe there are others who have, because you do know a tremendous amount about this. You will continue to work with people, and we value you very much for that work.

D: *I always told them I didn't want to see them. I thought I could be more objective that way.*

B: Yes. Well, we try to honor that sort of thing. Just as we tried that night with Bonnie to do this in a way that would not freak her out, as she might say.

D: *And not disrupt.*

B: No. We disrupted her enough so she would have to change her windshield, and then wonder about the experience. But we didn't harm her in any way.

D: *That's very important. At least the information she's getting now will be very valuable to her in her work also.*

B: Yes. And I do want to say too that we are aware she recently had a very, very distressing event, again on the road, in her car, the same car. And we want you to know we had nothing to do with causing that event, that accident. But we were aware after it happened, particularly when she was lying there on the road, in her mind calling out to anyone who could be aware and anyone who could help. We're very proud of her for even thinking of us, and other dimensional beings who know of her. She asked for healing help, and I want her to know we're doing what we can to speed up her healing. And she's doing very well. She's going to be coming through this very, very well.

Before the session began Bonnie told me about a serious auto accident she had been involved in only a few weeks before. Her car was demolished, and the people in the other cars [more than one car was involved] were seriously hurt. Her injuries were mostly to her back, and it was still causing her discomfort. When we began the session she was wondering whether it would cause distraction and maybe prevent her from going under. She positioned pillows around and under her back so she would be more comfortable. Of course, I knew that the relaxation of deep trance would relax the muscles and give her relief, rather than distracting her.

D: That's very good. I know she appreciates your help very much. And it's very kind of you to do that, and to have concern over her.
B: Yes. Well, we have concern because we have concern anyway, but also she's important to us and we want her to be all right.
D: I know she will thank you for your help. All right. I think on our end we are running out of time. We always have that time factor.
B: I understand. That's very strong on Earth.
D: So I'm going to ask that you leave us now. And I would like to speak to you again at another time.
B: Yes, that's fine. We appreciate this opportunity as well. And thank you. We look forward to the next opportunity.
D: So I ask that you recede and go back to your work where you live on your craft. And I'm asking all the consciousness and personality of Bonnie to once again return to this body.

I then oriented Bonnie and brought her forward to full consciousness.

When she awakened she remembered only snatches of the session. She said her back felt much better and was not bothering her like it was when she first arrived. We knew it was because of the deep relaxation she had just experienced.

Both Bonnie and I knew we would continue to work together because the entity was more than willing to share information with us. But that, as they say, is another story, another book. I am only including the portions here that I think pertain to the subject matter of this book. And to illustrate again how my work has proceeded gradually over twelve years from the simple to the complex. I have now opened the doors and the information will continue to flow forth. I only hope mankind will be open and adjust their minds to include these advanced ideas and concepts and integrate them into their reality. Such will the world of the future be composed of. The free thinkers, those with open minds who can truly accept and understand other realities and other dimensions. Those who have the ability to throw off the fetters that keep them chained to our three-dimensional way of thinking.

CHAPTER 15
THE CONCLUSION

The material in this book has been sitting dormant for over ten years waiting until the time was right to present it to the public. The aliens said I would not be allowed to write some of it until I had the entire picture. They did not want it given out until there was a full understanding on my part. As I prepared the material I could see my viewpoint in the beginning of my research, and how naive it was compared to the way I look at it now. I could see how I was being spoon fed bits and pieces of information, and only given more as I could comprehend and digest it. This is the way I wanted to write this book, to take the reader gently by the hand and lead him down the path of the unknown, stopping along the way to give him time to smell the roses, and for the information to sink in before moving on to the next step. My research has led me from the simple to the complex, and I know there is much more ahead of me. When I began in 1986 I would have been overwhelmed by the theories I am receiving now. And if I was overwhelmed I would have thrown my hands in the air and proclaimed that this was better suited for physicists and scientists to comprehend and try to explain. In other words, I would have given up because the entire subject was too complex. But apparently they understood my curiosity and desire to learn and understand mysteries, and I was only given what I could handle at the time. Even when it became complicated they gently tried to demonstrate with analogies and simple explanations (as simple as they could make it). Their patience with me has been phenomenal, and they never became aggravated. They were as anxious to get the information out as I was to write about it.

When I first began working with MUFON the hard-core investigators ridiculed the information I was receiving about using the power of the mind to propel spacecraft. They insisted the answer had to be in developing some type of fuel in order to travel to the nearest star. There was also the belief that the astronauts would have to be placed in suspended animation, because the trip would take so long. At the time they could not open their minds to alternative possibilities. Now in the summer of 1998 an announcement was made that could change that way of thinking forever. A group of scientists in Japan have proved the theory will work. They have invented a machine that harnesses the power of thought. They said scientists have known for a long time that thought is energy. That certainly was no revelation in my work, because I have been lecturing about that very concept for years. In the news program the scientists demonstrated the machine, which was placed on the head. It looked somewhat similar to virtual reality machines. Amazingly, by thinking the person could turn lights on and off, start and stop machines, and turn on an alarm to signal for help. It was demonstrated how each type of thought created a different frequency, and this was amplified and used to control things in the room. It did not take strong concentration. The simple thought was enough to power the mechanisms. They said the first uses of this machine will be for the handicapped, but I can see much broader potential in the future. Another startling discovery: it did not matter what language the person spoke, the machine interpreted the thought, not the spoken word. They said, "The thought's the thing." The Japanese have now shown a way around the language barrier, which is exactly the method the aliens use. I can see that it would only be a small step from controlling lights and alarms to controlling a car or a spacecraft with the mind. Scientists all over the world are also working on creating a way to propel an object faster than the speed of light. This was once considered an impossibility based on Einstein's theories. What was at one time considered science fiction has now entered the realm of science fact. Maybe we will look at the other claims made by the aliens as being logically possible.

As I was preparing the final draft of this book a special edition of Discover Magazine came out in May 1998. It was devoted to the subject of cloning and the duplication of human beings. It could not have happened at a better time (if anything is ever a coincidence), because it caused some of the passages in the book to fall into place. At this time the Scottish scientists had successfully cloned the sheep Dolly, and our scientists followed by announcing the cloning of calves and rhesus monkeys. The world, and especially politicians, were going crazy debating the ethics of cloning humans. They were trying to draft laws that could curtail this, or at least regulate it. It was like closing the barn door after the horses have escaped. Several laboratories in America and elsewhere have already announced they are working on the experiment, and expect to announce the first successful human clone within two years. They said, "If it can be done, it will be done." This is the way scientific curiosity works. If science is presented with a challenge, it will take it up regardless of the consequences. Hundreds of people are lining up to be the first candidates. The scientists said the cloning of a human would be much easier than the cloning of a sheep.

In the magazine article it was reported that scientists in the 1930s first showed that cloning was possible. Then the research was dropped until the 1970s when frogs were successfully cloned. Then no more was reported until the recent developments with mammals. Do people really think that no one was working on this for 40 years? Do they really think that once the scientists made the first breakthrough in the 1930s that the research was dropped? I believe that research was continued in secret because they were afraid of the very outcry that is occurring now. They knew people would be debating the moral issues of attempting to "play God" etc. My work has convinced me that the government especially has been conducting experiments for many years, and have perfected the techniques that are now being announced. They are just now dropping a few crumbs, releasing bits and pieces of information to prepare an astounded world to accept what was long ago accomplished. After all, they said the successful human clone would appear no different than any other human, and there could be many living among us. The same, of course, goes for alien clones and hybrids. Quote from the article: "People will tell her (the clone), 'You look just like your mother.' But no one will know, at least not until the kid is 16 and decides to sell her story to the tabloids."

Many people (especially in the religious field) think that a clone would be some type of mindless robot. Nothing could be further from the truth. Scientists have been perfecting techniques of fertilization outside the human body for many years, and hundreds of perfectly normal children have resulted that cannot be distinguished from any other "normally conceived" child. We all are clones resulting from a mixture of our mother and father's genes. An exact clone would be the result of only one person's genes.

In "normal" conception the mother's egg must be impregnated by the father's sperm, whether within the body or in a petrie dish in a laboratory. In cloning the sperm is not needed, but the egg is activated by other means (chemical or electrical). When the egg first begins to develop it is a mass of cells that are absolutely identical. Within several days the cells reach a point where they begin to differentiate. Some of the cells will become bone, some will become certain organs, some will become skin, etc. Something deep within the cell triggers this response and tells the cell what part of the human body it will become. Thus the scientists can work with the cells before they differentiate, before they instinctively know what their role is to be, and produce a clone. But the developing embryo must be inserted into a woman's body to grow to term.

All of this sounds very familiar to the alien information I have been receiving for over ten years. The sperm and ova samples, the scraping of cells from different parts of the body. The reinsertion of embryos into the human body, and the taking of the embryos when they estimate they have reached term. One important difference is that the aliens also have developed methods of incubating the developing fetus outside of the human body. In *Legacy From the Stars* the cells were taken from the fluid in the human eye, and the child developed in artificial wombs in laboratory conditions onboard laboratory craft. There have been many examples in my books of people seeing alien scientists working with cells in dishes in laboratories.

Our scientists say that any cell of an adult body can be used because it contains the DNA to create a duplicate copy. But they claim they have not yet developed a way to trigger the development because an adult cell has already been differentiated. In other words, it has already been told the role it is to play in the body, whereas a new cell has not. But they claim it can be done, so it will be done.

The article said that no clone would be an exact duplicate anyway, except physically. Even if you could obtain cells from Einstein or Shakespeare, for example, and create a clone, would it possess the same genius of the original? How much is determined by genes and how much is determined by environment and the culture in which the person is raised? A person being cloned would be forever separated from the original by at least a generation. The duplicate would be raised and influenced by entirely different social, cultural and environmental conditions than the original. They also said they do not know how much influence the mother has over the developing child while it is in utero. This is exactly what the aliens said about Janice. They said there were two decidedly different types of individuals that could be produced. One that was cloned from the mother's genetic material would be an *exact* duplicate. One that was carried within the womb would be influenced by what the mother experienced as she went about her daily life, and this would create a different type of individual.

One very crucial point has not been brought up as to why the clone would not be an exact duplicate of the donor, except physically. We are *not* a body. We *have* a body. The real essence of the human being is the eternal soul or spirit. The body cannot have life until that soul enters the body. No matter how much science concentrates on developing the body, it will remain a lifeless shell until the soul activates it. That soul brings with it its own karmic lessons and its own objectives for the new life it is embarking upon. This has to create a different person than the donor, because they are two individual souls. Even the aliens recognize this. In *Legacy From the Stars* the people who were living in a future world beneath the Earth had lost the ability to reproduce. They recreated an exact copy of the body in a sarcophagus type container, but they knew it would remain lifeless unless the soul made the decision to enter. In that book I discussed how we have all inhabited alien bodies at some time in our long life cycles, because our souls or spirits have been around forever, and will continue to be around forever, constantly entering new and different bodies to learn lessons of every conceivable type. Earth is a young planet when you consider the age of the cosmos, so we have had many adventures in different forms before deciding to experience the lessons of emotions and limitations that Earth offers. The aliens know we all have an eternal soul, and that we came originally from the Source (their name for God). This is why in that book I said, "They are us, and we are them. We are all one."

One reason I believe that the government has already perfected these techniques is because of the reports from people who have been in underground secret bases. They have seen, what they described as "strange monsters," being developed. This would suggest that they have perfected cloning, and have been working on the combining of genetic material from humans and other species. Such work could only be performed away from the light of day, in secret. The aliens said they have worked with government scientists, and have tried to give advice, because they had already perfected the techniques. But the government had gone on their way ignoring the advice, and were trying to perfect what was already perfected. The aliens knew the scientists would be making mistakes, but they decided to let them find out on their own. The aliens also said they have conducted such experimentation of combining different species, but for different reasons. It was not totally out of curiosity, but to produce species that would be suitable and able to function on other planets in other solar systems. What was considered monstrous and repugnant to us would be totally acceptable in another environment. Thus there are many things dealing with the government and extraterrestrials that will never be revealed to the public.

The aliens said another planet was being prepared for humans to inhabit in case of the probability that we destroy this Earth. It is very similar and some of the genetic duplicates they have produced are already being taken there. They said human life must not be allowed to perish. Life is too fragile, and too precious. So our human species is being preserved in this way. These are things that the average UFO abductee does not have any comprehension of. Their genes are very valuable and are being used to preserve life, both here and on other planets in other galaxies. They may unknowingly be supplying the answer to the survival of the human race.

I believe there will come a day, it may not be in my lifetime, but I think it will come nevertheless, when the blinders will be removed and scientists will consider these radical ideas as possibilities. Once they think that something is possible, their minds will then be free to explore and travel down unknown and strange pathways. This is the way new discoveries are made, by those willing to attempt the untried and to explain the impossible. When that day comes we will find that there is much, much more than the physical reality which is available to only our five senses. We will find that there are other planes of existence, other dimensions, other universes, existing side by side with this one. We will discover that travel between these is not only possible, it is desirable. We will find that these are not simply crazy theories, but that they are rooted in fact. Once we have removed the blinders that impede our progress, and escape the limitations imposed by linear thinking, we will find it is true that we are only limited by our imaginations. Then we will be able to loose the fetters chaining us to Earth and to join our brothers, our ancestors, and coexist among the stars. It has been said that space is the final frontier, but other dimensions and parallel universes (coexisting alongside our own world) could be the next challenge. First we need to understand them so they can be explored.

Thus I will continue to search and ask questions, and I will add my material to the growing mass of evidence.

THE ODYSSEY CONTINUES.

About the Author

Dolores Cannon, a regressive hypnotherapist and psychic researcher who records "Lost" knowledge, was born in 1931 in St. Louis, Missouri. She was educated and lived in Missouri until her marriage in 1951 to a career Navy man. She spent the next 20 years traveling all over the world as a typical Navy wife and raising her family.

In 1968 she had her first exposure to reincarnation via regressive hypnosis when her husband, an amateur hypnotist, stumbled across a past life while working with a woman who had a weight problem. At that time the "past life" subject was unorthodox and very few people were experimenting in the field. It sparked her interest, but had to be put aside as the demands of family life took precedence.

In 1970 her husband was discharged as a disabled veteran, and they retired to the hills of Arkansas. She then started her writing career and began selling her articles to various magazines and newspapers. When her children began lives of their own, her interest in regressive hypnosis and reincarnation was reawakened. She studied the various hypnosis methods and thus developed her own unique technique which enabled her to gain the most efficient release of information from her subjects. Since 1979 she has regressed and cataloged information gained from hundreds of volunteers. In 1986 she expanded her investigations into the UFO field. She has done on-site studies of suspected UFO landings, and has investigated the Crop Circles in England. The majority of her work in this field has been the accumulation of evidence from suspected abductees through hypnosis.

Her published books include: Conversations with Nostradamus Volumes I,II,III - Jesus and the Essenes - They Walked with Jesus - Between Death and Life - A soul Remembers Hiroshima - Keepers of the Garden - Legacy from the Stars - The Legend of Starcrash.

Jesus and the Essenes & They Walked with Jesus have been published by Gateway Books in England. Several of her books are now available in different languages.

Dolores has four children and fourteen grandchildren who keep her solidly balanced between the "real" world of her family and the "unseen" world of her work.

If you wish to correspond with Dolores about her work, you may write to her at the following address. (Please enclose a self-addressed stamped envelope for her reply.) You may also correspond through our Web Site.

Dolores Cannon
c/o Ozark Mountain Publishing, Inc.
P.O. Box 754
Huntsville, AR 72740

WWW.OZARKMT.COM

Other Books by Ozark Mountain Publishing, Inc.

Dolores Cannon
A Soul Remembers Hiroshima
Between Death and Life
Conversations with Nostradamus,
    Volume I, II, III
The Convoluted Universe -Book One,
    Two, Three, Four, Five
The Custodians
Five Lives Remembered
Horns of the Goddess
Jesus and the Essenes
Keepers of the Garden
Legacy from the Stars
The Legend of Starcrash
The Search for Hidden Sacred
    Knowledge
They Walked with Jesus
The Three Waves of Volunteers and the
    New Earth
A Very Special Friend
Aron Abrahamsen
Holiday in Heaven
James Ream Adams
Little Steps
Justine Alessi & M. E. McMillan
Rebirth of the Oracle
Kathryn Andries
Time: The Second Secret
Will Alexander
Call Me Jonah
Cat Baldwin
Divine Gifts of Healing
The Forgiveness Workshop
Penny Barron
The Oracle of UR
P.E. Berg & Amanda Hemmingsen
The Birthmark Scar
Dan Bird
Finding Your Way in the Spiritual Age
Waking Up in the Spiritual Age
Julia Cannon
Soul Speak – The Language of Your
    Body
Jack Cauley
Journey for Life
Ronald Chapman
Seeing True
Jack Churchward
Lifting the Veil on the Lost
    Continent of Mu

The Stone Tablets of Mu
Carolyn Greer Daly
Opening to Fullness of Spirit
Patrick De Haan
The Alien Handbook
Paulinne Delcour-Min
Divine Fire
Holly Ice
Spiritual Gold
Anthony DeNino
The Power of Giving and Gratitude
Joanne DiMaggio
Edgar Cayce and the Unfulfilled
    Destiny of Thomas Jefferson
    Reborn
Paul Fisher
Like a River to the Sea
Anita Holmes
Twidders
Aaron Hoopes
Reconnecting to the Earth
Edin Huskovic
God is a Woman
Patricia Irvine
In Light and In Shade
Kevin Killen
Ghosts and Me
Susan Linville
Blessings from Agnes
Donna Lynn
From Fear to Love
Curt Melliger
Heaven Here on Earth
Where the Weeds Grow
Henry Michaelson
And Jesus Said – A Conversation
Andy Myers
Not Your Average Angel Book
Holly Nadler
The Hobo Diaries
Guy Needler
The Anne Dialogues
Avoiding Karma
Beyond the Source – Book 1, Book 2
The Curators
The History of God
The OM
The Origin Speaks

For more information about any of the above titles, soon to be released titles,
or other items in our catalog, write, phone or visit our website:
PO Box 754, Huntsville, AR 72740|479-738-2348/800-935-0045|www.ozarkmt.com

Other Books by Ozark Mountain Publishing, Inc.

Psycho Spiritual Healing
James Nussbaumer
And Then I Knew My Abundance
Each of You
Living Your Dram, Not Someone Else's
The Master of Everything
Mastering Your Own Spiritual Freedom
Sherry O'Brian
Peaks and Valley's
Gabrielle Orr
Akashic Records: One True Love
Let Miracles Happen
Nikki Pattillo
Children of the Stars
A Golden Compass
Victoria Pendragon
Being In A Body
Sleep Magic
The Sleeping Phoenix
Alexander Quinn
Starseeds What's It All About
Debra Rayburn
Let's Get Natural with Herbs
Charmian Redwood
A New Earth Rising
Coming Home to Lemuria
Richard Rowe
Exploring the Divine Library
Imagining the Unimaginable
Garnet Schulhauser
Dance of Eternal Rapture
Dance of Heavenly Bliss
Dancing Forever with Spirit
Dancing on a Stamp
Dancing with Angels in Heaven
Annie Stillwater Gray
The Dawn Book
Education of a Guardian Angel
Joys of a Guardian Angel
Work of a Guardian Angel
Manuella Stoerzer
Headless Chicken

Blair Styra
Don't Change the Channel
Who Catharted
Natalie Sudman
Application of Impossible Things
L.R. Sumpter
Judy's Story
The Old is New
We Are the Creators
Artur Tradevosyan
Croton
Croton II
Jim Thomas
Tales from the Trance
Jolene and Jason Tierney
A Quest of Transcendence
Paul Travers
Dancing with the Mountains
Nicholas Vesey
Living the Life-Force
Dennis Wheatley/ Maria Wheatley
The Essential Dowsing Guide
Maria Wheatley
Druidic Soul Star Astrology
Sherry Wilde
The Forgotten Promise
Lyn Willmott
A Small Book of Comfort
Beyond all Boundaries Book 1
Beyond all Boundaries Book 2
Beyond all Boundaries Book 3
D. Arthur Wilson
You Selfish Bastard
Stuart Wilson & Joanna Prentis
Atlantis and the New Consciousness
Beyond Limitations
The Essenes -Children of the Light
The Magdalene Version
Power of the Magdalene
Sally Wolf
Life of a Military Psychologist

For more information about any of the above titles, soon to be released titles,
or other items in our catalog, write, phone or visit our website:
PO Box 754, Huntsville, AR 72740|479-738-2348/800-935-0045|www.ozarkmt.com